The European Union and the United States

THE EUROPEAN UNION SERIES

Series Editors: Simon Bulmer, Neill Nugent, Frank Schimmelfennig

The European Union series provides an authoritative library on the European Union, ranging from general introductory texts to definitive assessments of key institutions and actors, issues, policies and policy processes, and the role of member states. Books in the series are written by leading scholars in their fields and reflect the most up-to-date research and debate. Particular attention is paid to accessibility and clear presentation for a wide audience of students, practitioners and interested general readers. The series editors are **Simon Bulmer**, Professor of European Politics at the University of Sheffield, UK; **Neill Nugent**, Emeritus Professor of Politics at Manchester Metropolitan University, UK; and **Frank Schimmelfennig**, Professor of European Politics at ETH Zurich, Center for Comparative and International Studies, Switzerland. Previous co-editors of the series were **Vincent Wright** and **William E. Paterson**.

General textbooks

Published

Laurie Buonanno and Neill Nugent Policies and **Policy Processes of the European Union (2nd edn)**

Desmond Dinan **Encyclopedia of the European Union** [Rights: Europe only]

Desmond Dinan **Europe Recast: A History of the European Union (2nd edn)** [Rights: Europe only]

Desmond Dinan **Ever Closer Union: An Introduction to European Integration (4th edn)** [Rights: Europe only]

Simon Hix and Bjørn Høyland **The Political System of the European Union (4th edn)**

Dirk Leuffen, Berthold Rittberger and Frank Schimmelfennig **Differentiated Integration**

Paul Magnette **What Is the European Union? Nature and Prospects**

John McCormick **Understanding the European Union: A Concise Introduction (8th edn)**

Brent F. Nelsen and Alexander Stubb **The European Union: Readings on the Theory and Practice of European Integration (4th edn)** [Rights: Europe only]

Neill Nugent (ed.) **European Union Enlargement**

Neill Nugent **The Government and Politics of the European Union (8th edn)**

John Peterson and Elizabeth Bomberg **Decision- Making in the European Union**

Ben Rosamond **Theories of European Integration**

Mette Eilstrup Sangiovanni (ed.) **Debates on European Integration: A Reader**

Sabine Saurugger **Theoretical Approaches to European Integration**

Ingeborg Tömmel **The European Union: What It Is and How It Works**

Esther Versluis, Mendeltje van Keulen and Paul Stephenson **Analyzing**

the European Union Policy Process

Hubert Zimmermann and Andreas Dür (eds) **Key Controversies in European Integration (3rd edn)**

Micheal Smith, Terrence Guay and Jost Mogernstern Pomorski **The European Union and the United States: Competition, Convergence and Crisis in the Global Arena**

The major institutions and actors

Published

Renaud Dehousse **The European Court of Justice**

Justin Greenwood **Interest Representation in the European Union (4rd edn)**

Fiona Hayes-Renshaw and Helen Wallace **The Council of Ministers (2nd edn)**

Simon Hix and Christopher Lord **Political Parties in the European Union**

David Judge and David Earnshaw **The European Parliament (2nd edn)**

Neill Nugent and Mark Rhinard **The European Commission (2nd edn)**

Ariadna Ripoll Servent **The European Parliament**

Sabine Saurugger and Fabien Terpan **The Court of Justice of the European Union and the Politics of Law**

Anne Stevens with Handley Stevens **Brussels Bureaucrats? The Administration of the European Union**

Wolfgang Wessels **The European Council**

The main areas of policy

Published

Karen Anderson **Social Policy in the European Union**

Michael Baun and Dan Marek **Cohesion Policy in the European Union**

Michelle Cini and Lee McGowan **Competition Policy in the European Union (2nd edn)**

Tom Delreux and Sander Happaerts **Environmental Policy and Politics in the European Union**

Wyn Grant **The Common Agricultural Policy**

Sieglinde Gstöhl and Dirk de Bievre **The Trade Policy of the European Union**

Martin Holland and Mathew Doidge **Development Policy of the European Union**

Jolyon Howorth **Security and Defence Policy in the European Union (2nd edn)**

Johanna Kantola **Gender and the European Union**

Stephan Keukeleire and Tom Delreux **The Foreign Policy of the European Union (3rd edn)**

Maren Kreutler, Johannes Pollak and Samuel Schubert **Energy Policy in the European Union**

Brigid Laffan **The Finances of the European Union**

Malcolm Levitt and Christopher Lord **The Political Economy of Monetary Union**

Janne Haaland Matláry **Energy Policy in the European Union**

John McCormick **Environmental Policy in the European Union**

John Peterson and Margaret Sharp **Technology Policy in the European Union**

Handley Stevens **Transport Policy in the European Union**

The member states and the Union

Published

Simon Bulmer and William E. Paterson **Germany and the European Union**

Carlos Closa and Paul Heywood **Spain and the European Union**

Andrew Geddes **Britain and the European Union**

Alain Guyomarch, Howard Machin and Ella Ritchie **France in the European Union**

Brigid Laffan and Jane O'Mahoney **Ireland and the European Union**

Issues

Published

Senem Aydın-Düzgit and Nathalie Tocci **Turkey and the European Union**

Derek Beach **The Dynamics of European Integration: Why and When EU Institutions Matter**

Thomas Christiansen, Emil Kirchner and Uwe Wissenbach **The European Union and China Thomas**

Christiansen and Christine Reh **Constitutionalizing the European Union**

Desmond Dinan, Neill Nugent and William E. Paterson (eds) **The European Union in Crisis**

Tuomas Forsberg and Hiski Haukkala **The European Union and Russia**

Andrew Geddes, Leiza Brumat, and Leila Hadj Abdou **Migration and Mobility in the European Union (2nd edn)**

Sieglinde Gstöhl and Simon Schunz (eds) **The External Action of the European Union**

Robert Ladrech **Europeanization and National Politics**

Cécile Leconte **Understanding Euroscepticism**

Steven McGuire and Michael Smith **The European Union and the United States Wyn Rees The US–EU Security Relationship**

Mark Rhinard, Neill Nugent and William Paterson **Crises and Challenges for the European Union**

Magnus Ryner and Alan Cafruny **The European Union and Global Capitalism**

Doug Webber **European Disintegration?**

Richard Youngs **The European Union and Global Politics**

The European Union and the United States

Competition, Convergence and Crisis in the Global Arena

Michael Smith,
Terrence R. Guay and
Jost Morgenstern-Pomorski

BLOOMSBURY ACADEMIC
LONDON • NEW YORK • OXFORD • NEW DELHI • SYDNEY

BLOOMSBURY ACADEMIC
Bloomsbury Publishing Plc
50 Bedford Square, London, WC1B 3DP, UK
1385 Broadway, New York, NY 10018, USA
29 Earlsfort Terrace, Dublin 2, Ireland

BLOOMSBURY, BLOOMSBURY ACADEMIC and the Diana logo
are trademarks of Bloomsbury Publishing Plc

First published in Great Britain 2008

This edition published 2025

A catalogue record for this book is available from the British Library.

Library of Congress Cataloging-in-Publication Data

Names: Smith, Michael, 1947 April 10- author. | Guay, Terrence R., author. | Morgenstern-Pomorski, Jost-Henrik, author.
Title: The European Union and the United States : competition, convergence and crisis in the global arena / Michael Smith, Terrence R. Guay and Jost Morgenstern-Pomorski.
Description: 2nd edition. | London ; New York, NY : Bloomsbury Academic, 2024. | Series: The European Union series | First edition entered under: Steven McGuire. | Includes bibliographical references and index. |
Summary: "This new edition of The European Union and the United States provides an interdisciplinary approach to transatlantic relations and their global contexts. Revised to account for major challenges like Brexit and climate change, it touches on all key facets of EU-US relations in the 21st century, including the political systems of each side, the architecture of the relationship and distinct policy areas such as trade and security. Incorporating speeches, policy documents and key quotations, this new edition is suited to undergraduate and postgraduate students of European integration and external action, US foreign policy, and politics of the West"-- Provided by publisher.
Identifiers: LCCN 2024014575 (print) | LCCN 2024014576 (ebook) | ISBN 9781350414273 (hardback) | ISBN 9781350414280 (paperback) | ISBN 9781350414266 (epub) | ISBN 9781350414259 (ebook)
Subjects: LCSH: European Union--United States.
Classification: LCC HC240.25.U5 M34 2024 (print) | LCC HC240.25.U5 (ebook) | DDC 337.1/420973--dc23/eng/20240612
LC record available at https://lccn.loc.gov/2024014575
LC ebook record available at https://lccn.loc.gov/2024014576

HB: 978-1-3504-1427-3
PB: 978-1-3504-1428-0
ePDF: 978-1-3504-1425-9
Series: The European Union Series

Typeset by Deanta Global Publishing Services, Chennai, India

To find out more about our authors and books visit www.bloomsbury.com and sign up for our newsletters.

Contents

Detailed contents

List of illustrations

Figures

Tables

Boxes

List of abbreviations

ACP	African, Caribbean and Pacific states
AIIB	Asian Infrastructure Investment Bank
APEC	Asia-Pacific Economic Cooperation
ASEAN	Association of Southeast Asian Nations
ASEM	Asia–Europe Meeting
BASIC	Brazil, South Africa, India and China grouping
BITs	bilateral investment treaties
BRI	Belt and Road Initiative
BRICS	Brazil, Russia, India, China and South Africa grouping
CAFTA	Central America Free Trade Agreement
CAI	Comprehensive Agreement on Investment
CAP	Common Agricultural Policy
CCP	Common Commercial Policy
CEECs	Central and East European Countries
CFIUS	Committee on Foreign Investment in the United States
CFSP	Common Foreign and Security Policy
CJEU	Court of Justice of the European Union
CNOOC	China National Offshore Oil Company
COP	Conference of Parties (in global environmental negotiations)
COREPER	Committee of Permanent Representatives
CPTPP	Comprehensive and Progressive Agreement for Trans-Pacific Partnership
CRS	Congressional Research Service
CSCE	Commission on Security and Cooperation in Europe
CUSFTA	Canada–United States Free Trade Agreement
ECB	European Central Bank
ECJ	European Court of Justice
ECSC	European Coal and Steel Community
EDC	European Defence Community
EEC	European Economic Community
EMS	European Monetary System
EMU	Economic and Monetary Union

EP	European Parliament
EPA	Environmental Protection Agency
EPC	European Political Cooperation
ERM	Exchange Rate Mechanism
ERP	European Recovery Plan
ESDP	European Security and Defence Policy
ESS	European Security Strategy
FDI	foreign direct investment
FIRRMA	Foreign Investment Risk Review Modernization Act
FSC	Foreign Sales Corporation
GAAP	Generally Agreed Accounting Principles
GATT	General Agreement on Tariffs and Trade
GDP	gross domestic product
G-7	Group of Seven industrial nations
G-8	Group of Eight (G-7 plus Russia)
G-20	Group of Twenty leading economies (including the EU and African Union)
IAS	International Accounting Standards
IASB	International Accounting Standards Board
ICBC	Industrial and Commercial Bank of China
ICN	International Competition Network
ICPAC	International Competition Policy Advisory Committee
IFRS	International Financial Reporting Standards
IMF	International Monetary Fund
IOSCO	International Organization of Securities Commissions
IP	intellectual property
IRA	Inflation Reduction Act
ISDS	Investor-State Dispute Settlement
ISMs	Investment Screening Mechanisms
IT	information technology
ITO	International Trade Organization
JCPOA	Joint Comprehensive Plan of Action
M&As	mergers and acquisitions
MCR	Merger Control Regulation
MEP	Member of the European Parliament
Mercosur	Common Market of the South
MFN	most-favoured nation
MNC	Multinational Corporation
MTF	Merger Task Force

NAFTA	North American Free Trade Agreement
NATO	North Atlantic Treaty Organization
NGO	Non-Governmental Organization
NOAA	National Oceanic and Atmospheric Administration
NTA	New Transatlantic Agenda
NTM	New Transatlantic Marketplace
OECD	Organisation for Economic Co-operation and Development
OEEC	Organization for European Economic Cooperation
OPEC	Organization of Petroleum Exporting Countries
OSCE	Organization for Security and Cooperation in Europe
PTA	preferential trade agreement
RTA	regional trade agreement
SAARC	South Asian Association for Regional Cooperation
SEA	Single European Act
SCOTUS	Supreme Court of the United States
SGP	Stability and Growth Pact
SMEs	small and medium enterprises
SMP	Single Market Programme
TABC	Transatlantic Business Council
TABD	Transatlantic Business Dialogue
TACIS	Technical Aid to the Commonwealth of Independent States
TAD	Transatlantic Declaration
TPP	Trans-Pacific Partnership
TRIMs	Trade-Related Investment Measures
TTC	Trade and Technology Council (EU-US)
TTIP	Transatlantic Trade and Investment Partnership
UN	United Nations
UNCTAD	United Nations Conference on Trade and Development
USMCA	United States, Mexico and Canada Trade Agreement
USSR	Union of Soviet Socialist Republics
USTR	United States Trade Representative
VAT	value-added tax
WEU	Western European Union
WHO	World Health Organization
WTO	World Trade Organization

Acknowledgements

This book is a successor to a volume originally published in 2008 by Palgrave Macmillan, and authored by Steven McGuire and Michael Smith (*The European and the United States: Competition and Convergence in the Global Arena*). Since then, a very large amount of water has flowed under the bridge, to such an extent that the current book has been extensively re-written and re-structured. It also has lost an author (Steve McGuire is now Pro-Vice Chancellor at the University of East Anglia, and understandably has other preoccupations), and gained two in Terrence Guay and Jost Morgenstern-Pomorski. A significant amount of material contributed by Steve McGuire to the original volume has been retained, and we are extremely grateful that he has allowed this material to be re-used.

This successor volume was initially mooted in 2017 with the original authors, but in 2019 the current authors committed to producing it. Since then, the nature of transatlantic relations, and of international relations in general, has been subject to arguably the most profound changes since the end of the Cold War in the early 1990s. Throughout the last five years, we have been provided with admirable support and patience, first of all by a series of editors at Palgrave Macmillan, and then by the ever-helpful and ever-forgiving team at Bloomsbury, especially Milly Weaver and Tallulah Griffith. Without their patience and forbearance, even five years might not have been enough; we will forever be in their debt. We also wish to express our appreciation to six anonymous reviewers, whose comments were both timely and constructive, and to participants at several international conferences at which we presented some of our ideas. As always, all errors, misinterpretations and omissions in the text are the responsibility of the authors.

Introduction

Significance and challenges

The relationship between the European Union (EU) and the United States of America (US) is simultaneously highly significant and immensely challenging, both as the subject of academic analysis and as a subject of policymaking in both the EU and the United States. It is significant because the EU and the United States are two of the most weighty actors in the world arena, and because they are highly engaged in each other's economic and political processes. What happens between the EU and the United States matters, both to those directly involved and to those within the broader world arena by whom the effects of EU–US interactions are felt. The relationship is challenging because in addition to being highly significant, it is complex and dynamic: EU–US relations take place and have their effects in a multiplicity of issue areas and 'sub-arenas' within the world arena, and the openness of the transatlantic relationship means that changes in the world arena will in turn have important repercussions for EU–US relations.

No clearer evidence of this set of challenges could be found than the events of the past decade. In terms of security, the challenge of conflict in the Middle East, in Eastern Europe and potentially in the Indo-Pacific region has become a major preoccupation of policymakers on both sides of the Atlantic. In terms of political economy, the fall-out of the financial crisis that began in 2008 is still being absorbed in the 2020s, but has been supplemented by concerns about the economic impact of climate change, the demand for energy security in a world where oil and gas are increasingly seen as political weapons and the continuing politicization of trade policy. In terms of global organizations and global governance, the challenge of competing models represented most strikingly by the G-20 of the world's largest economies and the BRICS (Brazil, Russia, India, China, South Africa) grouping has increasingly permeated all of the regions in the global arena. Meanwhile, the United States has been through a tumultuous period in domestic politics, centring on the confrontation between a Republican Party increasingly dominated by the populist influence of Donald Trump and a Democratic Party dedicated to the preservation of liberal institutions.

At the same time, the EU has endured financial crisis, the defection of the UK through the process labelled 'Brexit' and the growth of 'illiberal democracy' in a number of member states, led by Hungary and Poland, but now including Italy, Sweden and potentially Spain. Most notably, the Russian invasion of Ukraine in February 2022 crystallized many if not all of the trends referred to earlier, by challenging both the EU and the United States in areas of security, political economy and domestic policymaking. Set against this turbulent context, this book is an attempt to expose the complexities of the relationship and its impact on the world arena, to subject it to analysis and to evaluate its past, its present and its possible futures. Each of the issues noted here will be addressed at many points in the text, in relation to specific areas of the EU–US relationship, and the conclusion to the text will return to them as part of its overall evaluation of the Euro-American system.

Relations between the EU and the United States are rooted in a history, and have been affected by the development of international politics and the international political economy over a long period, from the 1950s to the early years of the 21st century. So one of the first tasks of any book on the subject is to establish this history and the major trends or turning-points within it. A second task is to explore the 'analytical history' of the relationship, and to look at what successive waves of scholarship and commentary have to say about the nature of the relationship, its dynamics and its impact. A third task is to assess the changing domestic and broader international settings for EU–US relations, and thus the changing place of the relationship in broader processes of politics and political economy. Only if these three contexts – of historical development, analytical awareness and political/economic change – are established can effective appraisal of the current nature of the relationship take place.

A fourth and consequential task is to explore the detailed development of the relationship in respect of the international political economy. The establishment of the European Economic Community in 1957 through the Treaty of Rome, and the ways in which this contributed to an emerging 'adversarial partnership' between the EEC and the United States during the 1960s and beyond, are central to an understanding of the contemporary world economy, and to the analysis of key trends within it. The EU and the United States come into contact – or collision – in a multitude of economic domains, and the continuing development of the world economy in its turn shapes the ways in which the EU and the United States relate to each other. Thus, EU–US relations have been and are central to the development of world trade, monetary relations, technological innovation and the management of commercial organizations such as large firms through competition and related policies. Both actors have left their 'imprint' on the operations of a variety of international organizations and regimes, and have played a central role in the development of key current international issues such as those surrounding climate change and energy security.

The existing structure of the global economy and security system thus owes much to European and American conceptions about the exercise of political power. But the EU and the United States are not alone; they are joined on the world stage by an increasing number of strong competitors and potential partners, from Japan to Russia to China, India and Brazil. They are also involved in a growing range of interregional relationships extending to all continents, which will help to shape the international political economy of the future. The international economy thus presents us with a paradox. Though the Euro-American relationship was central to the construction and operation of the global economy over the past decades, the conditions it created have allowed other states to emerge as successful economies and, as a consequence, political competitors. The increasing reach of this 'constitutionalized' or rules-based international economy was a feature of the post-Cold-War decade, yet as more and more states integrate into this system, policymaking becomes more complex and the potential for crises more widespread. Europe and America cannot dominate economic policy matters as they did even a scant 20 years ago, and the scope and scale of challenges to them has accelerated as the 21st century has unfolded, epitomized by the global financial crises and subsequent conflicts in the global political economy after 2008.

A fifth task, particularly pressing in recent years, is to investigate the relationship between the EU, the United States and world order in the political and security domains. European integration was at its origins a matter of security, with the aim of stabilizing Western Europe and of forestalling any possibility of renewed war between the European powers. For much of its life, it developed within the 'western security community' led by the United States in opposition to the Soviet Union and its allies. Thus, from the outset, the links between European integration and the United States were highly political and linked to the preservation of western security. With the end of the Cold War in the early 1990s, the security context was given an entirely new complexion, and one in which the EU was both motivated and encouraged to find new security roles. Once it did this, the EU was bound to come into potential competition and conflict with the United States, and the result has been a series of more or less successful 'experiments' in the development of EU–US security relations. With the impact of transnational terrorism, and the 'securitization' of new areas of international life such as those relating to energy and the environment in the late 20th and early 21st centuries, both the EU and the United States faced new challenges in defining their mutual relationships and responding to the opportunities presented by a changing world order. But, since the turn of the millennium, a series of conflicts and crises centring on key states and regions, beginning in the Balkans and the Persian Gulf, extending to the Caucasus and Central Asia and then to the EU's 'neighbourhood' in Central and Eastern Europe, has created geopolitical challenges with both novel and traditional features, culminating in the Russian invasion of Ukraine during 2022 and the subsequent war.

How have the EU and the United States developed their respective policies in these areas of close mutual engagement? Once developed, how have those policies created competition and sometimes open conflict between the EU and the United States, while at the same time leading to areas of close cooperation? What are the implications of the EU–US 'adversarial partnership' for the rest of the world, and how might this partnership impact the future development of its members and the rest of the world arena? As noted earlier, these are not purely academic questions; they concern policymakers not only in the EU and the United States but also in a host of other countries and in a wide range of non-governmental bodies, from giant corporations to environmental, humanitarian and other pressure groups. The purpose of this book is to sharpen these questions and to provide the means to work towards at least some of the answers to them.

The nature of the book

The book takes as its key theme the interplay between competition and convergence in an age of economic, political and security crises, basing this on the fact that in every aspect of their relationship the EU and the United States are increasingly part of an integrated policy space, but that within this space they are in often intense competition (sometimes formulated as 'competitive interdependence' or 'competitive cooperation'). Not only this, but as already indicated, the EU–US relationship has had to absorb or respond to a range of economic, political and security challenges often expressed in terms of crisis, both within and around it. Though Europe and the United States share common understandings about many issues, how they conceptualize – and operationalize – solutions and how they respond to challenges can be quite different. Increasingly also, EU–US relations have close connections with broader issues of world order and global governance, and with the relations between key regions in the world arena. The book deploys a range of approaches to analyse and evaluate both the changing nature of the relationship and specific areas of policy formation. It draws on the rich tradition of scholarship in EU–US relations, but also looks at work from broader areas of international relations, comparative politics and political economy as a way of exploring the role of national political forces, firms, non-governmental bodies and other stakeholders in the relationship. The volume also uses primary data from a variety of sources. We aim to explore the arguments and to reach conclusions not by using one single analytical perspective, but rather by deploying the appropriate methods of analysis to deal with specific areas of policymaking and interaction.

Chapter 1 deals with the historical evolution of the relationship, using an approach centred on key points of change or transformation to point out important areas of continuity and discontinuity, and deploying a range of historical evidence such as documents and speeches to illustrate specific phases of change and development. This chapter thus establishes the growth of the 'competition and convergence' which are central to the relationship and provides the historical context which is vital to an appreciation of current and possible future trends. Chapter 2 deals with the range of frameworks available for analysis of the relationship and aims to identify the key concerns for analysis and the key approaches that can be utilized. It argues that EU–US relations can be seen as a kind of 'mixed actor system' in which political and economic interactions take place at a number of interconnected levels, and in which the roles of institutions both within and between the key participants have considerable importance. Chapter 3 focuses on the impact and implications of domestic political arrangements in both the EU and the United States, in order to tease out the ways in which institutions, political forces and the broader social and cultural contexts help to shape their relations. Chapters 1–3 as a whole provide the historical, conceptual and analytical background to the rest of the book.

Chapters 4 to 10 deal with specific areas of policy formation and interaction, starting with the longest-established areas in EU–US relations, and thus with issues of political economy. Chapters 4 to 6 deal with key aspects of the political economy of EU–US relations, working from trade and monetary relations through to investment and competition. Chapters 7 to 10 deal with issues not only of political economy but also of diplomacy and security, moving from the place of power and security in EU–US relations (Chapter 7), through the issue of security and order in the 'new Europe' (Chapter 8) and the engagement of both the EU and the United States as regional powers in forms of interregional diplomacy (Chapter 9) to issues of world order and global governance (Chapter 10). This sequence reflects the empirical reality of EU–US relations, in which as the post-Cold-War era has unfolded the political and security dimension has become more and more salient and challenging. Chapters 4 to 10 as a whole thus provide a detailed study of the key elements in EU–US relations and also in their links to the rest of the world arena.

The intention in all of these chapters is to identify key areas of development, dispute and convergence and to explore the ways these issues have been managed. Thus these chapters are constructed to a common template: they deal first with policy issues and policy development in the EU and the United States, then with issues of competition, convergence and crisis and then with mechanisms of management. The rationale for this structure is simple: it is impossible to discuss the relations between the EU and the United States unless we are aware of the key ways each of the parties constructs its policies and its roles within the world arena. Each chapter ends with an overall evaluation and a discussion of present and future policy developments cast explicitly in terms of competition, convergence and crisis. The thematic structure of the chapters means that each of Chapters 4–10 contains a number of case studies and illustrations: thus for example there is no single chapter on EU–US–China relations, or on EU–US relations in terms of environmental politics, but these are examined in a number of chapters and can be explored by using the overall index to the book.

Finally, Chapter 11 takes the foundations established in Chapters 1–3 and uses them to inform a comparative evaluation of the present and future Euro-American system centred around the EU and the United States. It also reassesses the utility of the analytical frameworks deployed in Chapter 2, and the perspectives from comparative politics explored in Chapter 3. The overall conclusion to the book is that the tensions and sometimes open conflicts within the Euro-American system will not be easily resolved, but that the increasing economic and institutional integration, and the continuing political dialogue, that characterize the system will not allow for an easy 'divorce' or a pattern of 'separate development'; indeed, recent developments in international political economy and security may have driven a deepening of EU–US cooperation alongside the persistence of competition and contestation. The EU and the United States have got well under each other's skin, and this will continue to be the source of both competition and convergence in a changing world arena.

Chapter 1

European integration, transatlantic relations and the United States since 1945

Introduction

The system of relations that has grown up between the European integration project and the United States is dense and complex, and it is one of long standing. Central to the argument in this book is the growth and development of this system of relations, and its impact not only on its members but also on the world as a whole. For much of its life, the system has dominated the global economy and has played a key part in the management of global diplomatic and security issues. It is thus vital to understand the structure and functioning of the system, its central rules and assumptions, and the ways it has changed and developed since its origins in the late 1940s. This is the focus of the first two chapters in the book.

In a way, as Alfred Grosser has argued, there is no 'year zero' in relations between the United States and Europe (Grosser 1980). The influence of the 'old continent' was central in the establishment and growth of the United States, and increasingly from the late 19th century onwards, the United States came more and more to play a central part in the European arena. From the beginning of the 20th century, American investment and economic influence were important to the management of the European economies; nowhere was this more clear than in the aftermath of the First World War, when the capacity of the United States to contribute to the recovery of Europe, and its willingness or unwillingness to make such a contribution, played a central role in the development of the interwar order. During the 1930s, the American economy and its troubles after the 'great crash' of 1929 fed directly into the increasing instability of Europe, and the uncertainties of US diplomacy in the age of isolationism played a major role in the onset of the Second World War. The fates of the United States and

Europe were deeply intertwined even before the great catalytic drama of the war in Europe and beyond (Grosser 1980: Chapter 1; Lundestad 2005: Chapter 1).

This said, detailed analysis of the ways in which the relationship between European integration and the United States was established and evolved should start in the aftermath of the second global conflict. It was at this point that US involvement became structural and in some ways organic, and the growth of European integration itself became a central pillar of the emerging relationship. This chapter sets out to map the historical evolution of the relationship since the end of the Second World War and to identify the key forces contributing to the process of historical change. Chapter 2 will look more closely at the underlying structures and functioning of the 'Euro-American system' and at the issues and institutions around which it has centred.

The first part of this chapter examines the foundations on which the relationship between European integration and the United States was constructed in the first decade after the Second World War. In the second part, the focus is on the growth of partnership and rivalry between an integrating Europe and the United States. The third, fourth and fifth parts of the chapter focus respectively on processes of change, transformation and crisis: first, the changes that took place within EC–US relations during the 1970s and early 1980s, second, the dramatic changes that surrounded the relationship in the late 1980s and 1990s, and finally the crises that have beset the relationship in the early 21st century. The key questions underlying all of this are simple: how much of what was established during the 1950s and 1960s still survives, how substantial has the transformation of the relationship been, and how fundamental are the crises that have surrounded the relationship in the 21st century?

Foundations: 1945–58

At the most general level, it could be said that the end of the Second World War saw the collapse of Europe and the dominance of the United States. At one time or another, almost all of the European states had been defeated during the war, while even those that had emerged victorious and never been occupied, such as Britain, were exhausted. The European economy had in many respects ceased to exist, because of the divisions and dislocations created by war, while European society was racked by tensions and insecurities. These insecurities emerged partly out of the challenge to governmental legitimacy in almost every European country, but also out of the perceived challenge from communism represented most clearly by the Soviet Union and the presence of the Red Army in the heart of Europe. At the same time, the United States had ended the war in a position of unprecedented strength: its economy had boomed, its military might (bolstered by possession of the 'ultimate weapon' in the shape of the atom bomb) was unchallenged, and American ideas of democracy and progress seemed to be the wave of the future.

This situation was not of course unproblematic. For European governments, particularly those of the western half of the continent, the challenge was not simply one of re-establishing economic and political stability; it was also one of recreating or adapting the European model of statehood in a context where the nature of statehood itself was in question. For their Eastern and Central European counterparts, the challenge was one of resisting or adapting to the fact of Soviet dominance. For the Americans, the challenge was that of coming to terms with international predominance and resolving the clash between isolationism and internationalism – a clash that ran through the heart of US political life, and does to this day. It was out of this complex and unstable mix of political, economic and security problems that the initial 'bargain' between the US and European governments emerged (Grosser 1980: Chapter 1; DePorte 1986; Ellwood 1992; Lundestad 1998: Chapters 1–2; Lundestad 2005: Chapter 1; Sloan 2016: Chapters 1–3).

Between 1945 and 1950, the elements of what later came to be seen as a grand strategic bargain between the United States and Western Europe were put in place. The initial driving forces were a combination of insecurity, the search for governmental legitimacy and the search for a formula to maintain and express US engagement with the international system. For Europeans, the need to counter the Soviet threat and to keep the United States committed to European stability rapidly became a central fact of diplomatic life. The Roosevelt administration in Washington had proclaimed near the end of the war that they would aim to withdraw all US forces from Europe within two years, a prospect that fuelled European fears of instability and Soviet opportunism. As a result, a series of European leaders, led by Winston Churchill, the British prime minister, expressed their concern about the prospects of instability and threat in the event of a US withdrawal, and this concern itself became part of an extensive debate in Washington about the future of US foreign policy. The working out of this debate thus became crucial to the future of Europe itself, especially after the replacement of Roosevelt by Vice-President Harry Truman in 1945 (Hoffmann and Maier 1984; DePorte 1986; Hogan 1987).

The intersection of European fears and US domestic debate led to a process of incremental commitment between 1945 and 1949 that culminated in the North Atlantic Treaty of April 1949. Before that military 'bargain', however, the key thrust of US commitment had been economic and diplomatic. In 1947, the 'Truman

Doctrine' had set out the basis for US commitment to the defence of democracy on a global level, but especially in postwar Europe. This was followed in mid-1947 by the initial moves in what came to be known as the Marshall Plan: in June of that year, General George Marshall, the US secretary of state, made a speech at Harvard University in which he set out the terms for continued US economic assistance to Europe (see extract in Box 1.1). His premise was that if Europe was allowed to continue in economic chaos, this would sharpen the political and security threats of communism, and would increase the power of domestic Communist parties in countries such as France or Italy. The speech represented a key element in the emerging transatlantic 'bargain' – not least because of the terms on which the aid was to be given. These included the establishment or strengthening of 'free institutions' and free markets and, significantly, the construction of a cooperative plan through which the Europeans themselves were to specify the nature and the allocation of the aid itself (DePorte 1986; Hogan 1987; Gann and Duignan 1998; Lundestad 1998, 2005; Sloan 2016: chapter 2).

Box 1.1 The Marshall Plan speech (extracts)

It is evident . . . that, before the United States Government can proceed much further in its efforts to alleviate the situation and help start the European world on its way to recovery, there must be some agreement among the countries of Europe as to the requirements of the situation and the part those countries themselves will take in order to give proper effect to whatever action might be undertaken by this Government. It would be neither fitting nor efficacious for our Government to undertake to draw up unilaterally a program designed to place Europe on its feet economically. This is the business of the Europeans. The initiative, I think, must come from Europe. The role of this country should consist of friendly aid in the drafting of a European program and of later support of such a program so far as it may be practical for us to do so. The program should be a joint one, agreed to by a number, if not all, of European nations.

Source: Secretary of State George C. Marshall, Address at the Commencement Exercises of Harvard University, Cambridge, Massachusetts, 5 June 1947.

The Marshall Plan thus can be seen as a keystone of three processes. First, by restricting the aid to 'free' countries, it contributed strongly to the division of Europe that became solidified in the Cold War. Although some Central and Eastern European governments displayed initial interest in the plan, they were brought rapidly into line by the Soviets, and a political-economic division of Europe was accentuated. At the same time, Communist parties that had aspired to power or in some cases achieved it in some Western European countries were marginalized through a combination of economic restructuring and associated political realignment. Finally, the requirement that European countries should cooperate to respond to the plan (soon labelled the European Recovery Programme or ERP) can be seen as setting in motion processes that proved fundamental to the European integration process. The plan was to be delivered via the ERP and an associated organization, the Organization for European Economic Cooperation (OEEC), and it is plausible to see this as the breeding-ground for what became the European Coal and Steel Community (ECSC), the first institution of European economic integration. In the background, the establishment of the institutional framework that came to be known as the Bretton Woods system, encompassing the International Monetary Fund (IMF), the World Bank and the General Agreement on Tariffs and Trade (GATT), created a set of multilateral rules that were to be crucial in shaping the development of the European economies and of European integration (Mee 1984; Milward 1984; Hogan 1987).

It can be argued that by 1949, with the signing of the North Atlantic Treaty between the United States, Canada and 14 European countries, the key elements of the 'transatlantic bargain' were in place. The ERP (and in broader terms, the Bretton Woods system) expressed the political/economic end of the spectrum, while the North Atlantic Treaty represented the guarantee of continuing US involvement with the security of the continent – and both together had the effect of constructing the boundary between the 'free world' and the Communist bloc that became the centrepiece of the Cold War. The ERP also seemed to have contributed to (if not actually having inspired) the proposal made by Monnet and Schuman of France in May 1950 for the ECSC, in which France and Germany would form the core of a new kind of economic and (by implication) political integration centred on the key strategic industries of coal and steel. But this process was not without its tensions and divisions. In the first place, the 'new Europe' gradually emerging from the chaos of the postwar period was not a comprehensive Europe: the division between the original six members of the ECSC (France, Germany, Italy and the Benelux (Belgium, Netherlands and Luxembourg) countries) and those who were left or chose to remain outside set up a new division within the western half of the continent. Most obviously, Britain, the largest single recipient of Marshall Aid, had declined with almost no hesitation the opportunity to join the ECSC (Grosser 1980: Chapter 3). Second, the process of US commitment to the security of Europe had exposed significant divisions between European governments, particularly between those such as France that saw Europe as a potentially independent 'third force' and those such as Britain that saw the North Atlantic Treaty as a vital strand in the new Atlantic partnership. Finally, in the United States, the debate about the nature and extent of US international engagement had served to sharpen the fear of Communism and to set in motion the domestic forces of McCarthyism, which led to a strongly anti-Communist atmosphere. This was only sharpened further by the onset of the Korean War in 1950, which seemed to demonstrate the worldwide threat from the Soviet Union and its allies, including China.

During the 1950s, these coexisting trends towards transatlantic cooperation and tension were perpetuated by a series of events in both Europe and the United States. From the European perspective, the period between the establishment of the ECSC in 1950 and the signing of the Treaty of Rome in 1957 – the latter establishing the European Economic Community and the European Atomic Energy Community – was one of progress and setbacks. The ECSC prospered, partly as a result of natural economic recovery but also as a result of a lowering of barriers and the achievement of economies of scale, and by the mid-1950s this was leading to calls for a decisive extension of the European integration process. But at the same time, attempts to further European integration in the fields of diplomacy and defence were unsuccessful. In 1952, the French had proposed a plan for a European Defence Community (EDC), in which there would be substantial integration of military units and military command structures; this was in part a response to American calls for the rearmament of West Germany, and in part a perpetuation of the idea that Europe could be a 'third force' in world politics (Fursdon 1980; DePorte 1986; Winand 1993: Chapters 2–3; Lundestad 1998: Chapter 5; Lundestad 2005: Chapter 3; Sloan 2016: Chapter 3). By 1954, the project lay in ruins, ironically in large part because of its rejection by the French National Assembly, but also because of the abstention of the British and perceptions of a clash with the North Atlantic Treaty Organization (NATO), which had been constructed on the foundations of the North Atlantic Treaty and which now encompassed 16 European countries. This defeat had two significant implications for the relationship between the United States and European integration. First, it meant that for the foreseeable future collective European defence would be conducted through NATO (of which West Germany became a member through joining the Western European Union (WEU) in 1955). Second, it meant that the European integration project would remain overwhelmingly 'civilian' in character, whatever the attempts by countries such as France to move it in the direction of diplomatic or security coordination.

This was the foundation for the 'relaunching' of European integration in 1955–7 through the negotiations for what became the Treaty of Rome. Because of the defeat of the EDC, the EEC was to be 'civilian' and to be based on a massive extension of economic coordination between the original six member states of the ECSC. Although other countries such as Britain were by this time much more interested in – or worried by – the European project, the prospect of supranational influence over national economic policies was still enough to make them hesitate, thus contributing to the continuing dominance of France and Germany within the project (Lundestad 2005: Chapters 2–3). For the Americans, as might have been expected, the extension of European integration was a two-edged process. On the one hand, it consolidated the economic and social stability of Western Europe, and thus contributed to the stabilization of the continent as a whole (DePorte 1986), so many US policymakers were strongly in favour not only of the EEC but also of British membership (Camps 1960; Winand 1993: Chapter 5). On the other hand, those Americans who looked at the aims of the EEC and discerned a threat to US economic interests in areas such as agriculture were less enthusiastic; the fact that one of the first common policies to be adopted by the EEC was the Common Agricultural Policy (CAP) was to have a shaping – and sharpening – effect on transatlantic relations throughout the 1960s (Krause 1968; Beloff 1976). The ECSC had already attracted the suspicion and in some cases the outright hostility of American steel interests, who saw it as an unfair cartel designed to exclude them from the European market (Diebold 1959), and the EEC looked like a much wider and more dangerous threat.

By the late 1950s, therefore, the tone of relations between the United States and the European integration project was in important respects set. In 1958, the major European currencies achieved convertibility into each other and into the US dollar: this was a key indicator of their continuing recovery and consolidation, and of their full participation in the Bretton Woods system of international economic institutions, including the International Monetary Fund, the World Bank and the General Agreement on Tariffs and Trade. The rules established by those institutions constituted important parts of the foundations for transatlantic relations, but those relations were also surrounded by ambiguities and uncertainties about their future course.

Partnership and rivalry: 1958–71

We have seen that the relationship between European integration and the United States as it had developed by the end of the 1950s contained important coexisting but often conflicting elements of cooperation and competition. The European project on one level was a vital component of the consolidation of the 'west' in the Cold War, contributing to stability and to the growth of what Marshall had called 'free institutions'. At another level, it was a source of concern to American economic interests and a focus of aspirations for a European 'third force' that could express a particular identity in the world arena. During the 1960s, these tensions were to multiply, partly for reasons inherent in the European project, partly for reasons reflecting US positions and priorities and partly because of wider changes in the international system. Ironically, it may seem, the period between 1958 and the beginning of the 1970s was littered with proclamations of 'Atlantic partnership' at the same time as it gave increasing evidence of Atlantic rivalry (Diebold 1960; Cleveland 1966; Pfaltzgraff 1969; Calleo 1970; Diebold 1972; Calleo and Rowland 1973; Winand 1993: Chapters 6–12; Lundestad 1998: Chapter 6; Lundestad 2005: Chapter 4; Sloan 2016: chapter 4; Larres 2022: chapters 1–2).

From the point of view of European integration, this period was one of consolidation but also of internal tensions and often open conflicts. A number of common policies were initiated, among them two that were to be central to transatlantic relations, the Common Commercial Policy (CCP) and the CAP. Institutional development and consolidation were apparent, especially in the role of the European Commission which became established as a key generator of initiatives on the road to greater integration. At the same time, the economies of EEC member states continued to flourish, led by the West-German economy and the 'economic miracle' it represented. But there were also strong trends in the direction of internal conflict and fragmentation (Camps 1967; Grosser 1980). In the early 1960s, the French tried to set in motion the development of a 'European foreign policy', but this was limited and not supported by key 'Atlanticist' member states; in 1969 there was a further initiative in this direction with the beginnings of what became European Political Cooperation (EPC), but the basis remained strongly intergovernmental and diplomatic rather than integrationist and security-related. During the mid-1960s, the implementation of further integrationist measures in agriculture and the development of the 'common market' for goods created sharp perceptions of gains and losses for major member states and in the case of France led to its declaration of an 'empty chair' policy between 1965 and 1966, in which it refused to participate in key meetings. As a result, the 'Luxembourg Compromise' of 1966 signalled a retreat from full-blooded integration to a situation in which vital national interests could form the basis for an effective veto of legislation within the EEC. Alongside all of this, the prospect of the EEC's first enlargement continued throughout the 1960s. In 1963, French president Charles de Gaulle had effectively vetoed the first application for membership by Britain (thus also excluding Denmark, Ireland and Norway who had also applied). This veto was repeated in 1967, but by 1970 the installation of a pro-integrationist government in Britain combined with the fall of de Gaulle to produce an agreement on British membership.

The turbulence of developments in European integration during the 1960s was paralleled by problems within American politics and foreign policy. The rich promise of the John F. Kennedy administration (1961–63) was eroded by the president's assassination, by domestic tensions over such issues as civil rights, by increasing US entanglement in Vietnam and by the continuing threat of Soviet nuclear capability, which led to a major intensification of the arms race. This latter process was reflected in US relations with Europe, leading to the 'nuclearization' of NATO and to the growth of domestic anti-nuclear protest movements. But the tribulations of US administrations were not simply political: the US economy proved sluggish and in some respects uncompetitive, and was increasingly distorted by the focus on military spending and military commitments (Calleo and Rowland 1973). By the end of the 1960s, the Nixon administrations (1969–74) had begun to unwind some of these issues, not without considerable suspicion or difficulty. They had begun the process of 'détente' with the Soviet Union, focusing especially on the control of nuclear weapons, had initiated a broader diplomacy designed to respond to the needs of what they saw as a potentially multipolar world, engaging the Chinese and the Japanese as well as the Soviets and the Europeans, and had begun a reassessment of US economic commitments in the light of the generally poor performance of the economy (Larres 2022: chapter 2).

The intersection of these trends in Europe and the United States created a series of tensions throughout the 1960s. Even before the Kennedy administration had been installed, President de Gaulle had called for a greater degree of power-sharing in NATO, and had begun to present the EEC as the basis for a new challenge to US dominance (Calleo 1970; Harrison 1982). When in July 1962 President Kennedy made a speech in which he outlined a 'declaration of interdependence' between the United States and a 'uniting Europe' (see Box 1.2), this was greeted in some quarters as a visionary response to the new realities of world politics and in others as an attempt to perpetuate US hegemony over a resurgent Europe in particular (Winand 1993: Chapter 9; Sloan 2016: 51–6). Thus it is not surprising that the rhetoric of 'Atlantic partnership' and 'Atlantic community' that arose after Kennedy's speech was accompanied by major efforts to counter it through a discourse of European independence and difference. But not all Europeans were united in this respect: de Gaulle's strident anti-Atlanticism (see Box 1.2), reflected in his veto of British membership in the

EEC, and in French withdrawal from the NATO integrated military command in 1966, was balanced not only by British Atlanticism, but also by that of such countries as the Netherlands, Italy and Germany within the EEC itself (Cromwell 1969; Grosser 1980; Harrison 1982; DePorte 1986). Even such Atlanticist countries were perturbed by the increasing US commitment in Vietnam and by the evidence of US–Soviet diplomacy in the context of 'détente', so the overall picture was a complex one, which could not be reduced to a simple EEC–US partnership or rivalry.

Box 1.2 Kennedy and de Gaulle

The nations of Western Europe, long divided by feuds far more bitter than any which existed among the 13 colonies, are joining together, seeking, as our forefathers sought, to find freedom in diversity and in unity, strength. The United States looks on this vast new enterprise with hope and admiration. We do not regard a strong and united Europe as a rival but as a partner. To aid its progress has been the basic object of our foreign policy for 17 years. We believe that a united Europe will be capable of playing a greater role in the common defense, of responding more generously to the needs of poorer nations, of joining with the United States and others in lowering trade barriers, resolving problems of commerce, commodities, and currency, and developing coordinated policies in all economic, political, and diplomatic areas. We see in such a Europe a partner with whom we can deal on a basis of full equality in all the great and burdensome tasks of building and defending a community of free nations.

. . . I will say here and now, on this Day of Independence, that the United States will be ready for a 'Declaration of Interdependence', that we will be prepared to discuss with a united Europe the ways and means of forming a concrete Atlantic partnership, a mutually beneficial partnership between the new union now emerging in Europe and the old American Union founded here 175 years ago.

Source: President John F. Kennedy, Address on the Goal of an Atlantic Partnership, Philadelphia, 4 July 1962.

[the entry of Great Britain and others] will completely change the whole of the actions, the agreements, the compensation, the rules which have already been established between the Six. . . . Then it will be another Common Market whose construction ought to be envisaged. . . . Further, this community, increasing in such fashion, would see itself faced with problems of economic relations with all kinds of other States, and first with the United States. It is to be foreseen that the cohesion of its members, who would be very numerous

> and diverse, would not endure for long, and that ultimately it would appear as a colossal Atlantic community under American dependence and direction, and which would quickly have absorbed the community of Europe.
>
> Source: President Charles de Gaulle, Press Conference, Paris, 14 January 1963.

Alongside this diplomatic complexity, the political economy of EEC–US relations was no less significant. One of the most obvious manifestations of this significance was the growth of all forms of exchange between the United States and the EEC during the early 1960s: trade, investment and travel all experienced a major increase and it is difficult to avoid the conclusion that this was caused by the establishment of a large market among the six EEC member states (Cooper 1968; Diebold 1972). It is also important to note that at this time Britain accounted for much more in all of these areas than the whole of the EEC combined. By the beginning of the 1960s, there was also evidence of the Europeans' increasing capacity to engage collectively with the Americans within the world arena. Most obviously, the Dillon Round of trade negotiations within the GATT during 1961 had seen the EEC adopting a collective position. More dramatically, the Kennedy Round of 1963–6, proclaimed by the president as part of his 'declaration of interdependence', saw the creation of a substantive EEC trade diplomacy, which enabled the Europeans to resist US pressure on a number of fronts, particularly agricultural trade (Calleo and Rowland 1973). This set of developments is perhaps best cast in terms of the capacity to resist, rather than the capacity to initiate and lead, but it did signify a distinct set of new directions in international trade diplomacy. There were also the beginnings of European capacity to construct new interregional relationships: the most obvious of these were to be found in the framework of the Yaoundé Conventions, which constructed relationships with a set of mainly French ex-colonies in Africa.

Despite this evidence that the EEC was gradually acquiring the ability to exercise collective weight in the context of transatlantic relations and the broader world economy, the 1960s did not provide conclusive evidence of the emergence either of a true transatlantic partnership or of transatlantic rivalry. If anything, they provided evidence that any form of cooperation in the international political economy was hard work, that it would be characterized by disputes as much as by progress and that it remained fragmented in the continuing absence of Britain and other significant European states from the EEC. By the end of the 1960s, it was clear that this 'gap' was likely to be filled in the near future, but by that time also it was clear that the world economy as a whole was in a state of turbulence and potential chaos. The impact of the war in Vietnam and of conflict in the Middle East, the uncertainties of US–Soviet 'détente' and the unevenness of economic performance in the major western economies created a breeding-ground for uncertainty and instability (Calleo and Rowland 1973; Hanrieder 1974; Shonfield and Oliver1976; Hanrieder 1982). As a result, the Bretton Woods system of financial institutions, and the rules relating to fixed exchange rates and domestic economic adjustment, were increasingly under pressure. It was apparent that both in the diplomatic and in the economic sphere the 1970s would be challenging to say the least, and that the challenge to the assumptions behind EEC–US relations would be potentially momentous.

The pressures of change: 1971–85

On 15 August 1971 in a television broadcast to the American people President Nixon proclaimed what came to be known as his 'New Economic Policy'. At around the same time, in a number of speeches and papers, the administration also enunciated what became known as the 'Nixon Doctrine' relating to its foreign policy and diplomatic commitments, especially to allies. It is no exaggeration to say that these two sets of developments shaped the course of EEC–US relations for at least a decade, and that when combined with developments within the EEC itself and in the broader world arena they created a series of significant changes within the transatlantic relationship (Kaiser 1973; Czempiel and Rustow 1976; Kaiser and Schwartz 1977; M. Smith 1978). Indeed, Klaus Larres has argued that these events and trends signalled the end of US 'benign hegemony', reflecting a new range of uncertainties and tensions in ECUS relations (Larres 2022). During the early 1980s, the relationship was given an additional and severe testing by the policies of the Reagan administration and by the beginnings of a new phase of European integration itself.

Nixon's August 1971 speech (see Box 1.3) encapsulated what rapidly became known as the 'Nixon Shock'. As we have already noted, the US economy had been giving cause for concern for some time, with low growth accompanied by rising unemployment, declining competitiveness and a balance of payments deficit. For some in the US administration, this set of conditions was linked closely to the burden the United States had been carrying as leader of the 'free world' for the past 25 years, and there was a move to declare America an 'ordinary country' in economic affairs, prepared to defend its own interests against all comers (Rosecrance 1976). There is no doubt, as already noted, that the economic problems faced by the United States also related to the burden of the Vietnam War, which had created inflationary pressures as well as distorting the balance of the US federal budget. The combination of rising welfare spending with rising external expenditure on foreign and security policy was a potent one (and one that would be seen again in the 1980s). The administration's response, as expressed through the 'Nixon Shock', was to inject a dose of economic nationalism. The dollar was detached from its previous fixed price against gold, resulting in its decline against other leading currencies (thereby making US products cheaper for consumers in other countries), while measures were taken to control imports and to boost the competitiveness of US industry. While this might be seen as a logical and rational response to economic difficulties, in the circumstances of the early 1970s it was an explosive set of measures (Calleo and Rowland 1973; Calleo 1981). The administration justified it at least in part by the need for allies to take up the burden of defending democracy, thereby continuing what had been a growing chorus of complaint against the Europeans' unwillingness to either adjust their currencies against the dollar or take up more of the burden of defence spending. But the measures can also be seen – as they were at the time – as an attack on cherished principles of the Bretton Woods system. The effective devaluation of the dollar meant that the United States was asking its allies to pay the price for the loss of US competitiveness, while the imposition of an import surcharge went against one of the central principles of the GATT (Larres 2022: chapters 4–5).

Box 1.3 The 'Nixon Shock'

I have directed secretary [of the Treasury John] Connally to suspend temporarily the convertibility of the dollar into gold or other reserve assets, except in amounts and conditions determined to be in the interest of monetary stability and in the best interests of the United States. . . . To our friends abroad . . . I give this assurance: The United States has always been, and will continue to be, a forwardlooking and trustworthy trading partner. In full cooperation with the International Monetary Fund and those who trade with us, we will press for the necessary reforms to set up an urgently needed new international monetary system. Stability and equal treatment is in everybody's best interest. I am determined that the American dollar must never again be a hostage in the hands of international speculators. . . . As a temporary measure, I am today imposing an additional tax of 10 per cent on goods imported into the United States. . . . At the end of World War II the economies of the major industrial nations of Europe and Asia were shattered. . . . Today, largely with our help, they have regained their vitality. They have become our strong competitors, and we welcome their success. But now that other nations are economically strong,

> the time has come for them to bear their fair share of the burden of defending freedom around the world. The time has come for exchange rates to be set straight and for the major nations to compete as equals. There is no longer any need for the United States to compete with one hand tied behind her back.
>
> Source: Address by President Nixon on the Challenge of Peace, 15 August 1971.

Alongside this set of economic measures, the administration continued its exhortations to its allies – the Nixon Doctrine (Hoffmann 1968; Hanrieder 1974; Hoffman 1978); essentially this consisted of the demand that the allies (whether in Europe or elsewhere) should take up more of the burden of their own defence and stand on their own two feet. As applied to the conflict in Vietnam, this was a means by which the United States would eventually disengage and leave the South Vietnamese to fend for themselves. As applied in Europe, it sharpened the pressure on those European allies (now almost all members of the EEC) that had in American eyes grown richer under the protective umbrella provided by the United States. But the problem was that these demands were coming from an administration which was progressively weakened internally by the Watergate scandal, in which it became entangled after the 1972 presidential election. This erosion of internal legitimacy for the administration, along with the doubts long harboured by Europeans about US involvement in conflicts outside the NATO area, combined to create a new scepticism among EEC member states when it came to US leadership in all of its forms.

By the time Britain along with Denmark and Ireland entered the EEC in January 1973, there was thus a good deal of turbulence in transatlantic economic relations and more broadly in the western alliance. Although in other circumstances this might have seemed like an opportunity for the enlarged Community to assert itself on the world stage, in fact it militated strongly against that kind of initiative. The conditions that had fostered economic progress and the deepening of European integration during the 1960s had actually been short-lived; financial instability, fears of protectionism in world trade and the increasing politicization of economic disputes were to become a key theme of the next 15 years in transatlantic relations, and thus part of the world with which the Community had to cope (Warnecke 1972; Tsoukalis 1986).

The year 1973 was in fact symptomatic of the problems. In April, US secretary of state Henry Kissinger delivered a speech in New York proclaiming this to be the 'year of Europe' and calling for a new transatlantic bargain to express the new balance of influence between the United States and its European partners (see Box 1.4). This speech, delivered in the United States and not discussed with the Europeans before its delivery, served as a catalyst for European resentment of the Americans' leadership, and among other results prompted the formulation of a 'declaration on European identity' by the Community – a declaration that focused strongly on the need for partnership rather than domination in the relationship with the United States (see Box 1.4). By the end of 1973, the October War in the Middle East between Israel and its Arab neighbours had created a double twist to the tension: on the one hand, it fulfilled many Europeans' fears of US domination and risk-taking through the declaration of a nuclear alert by Washington over the heads of the allies, while on the other hand it precipitated a 400 per cent rise in the price of crude oil, creating an energy crisis and stretching the domestic economic management capacities of European countries to breaking point (Kaiser 1973; Kaiser 1974; Vernon 1973; Lieber 1979; Chase and Ravenal 1976; M. Smith 1978).

The European Community, already absorbing the impact of its new member states and the longer-term effects of the crises of the late 1960s, was ill fitted to respond dynamically to this set of simultaneous crises. Grand plans for the creation of economic and monetary union by 1980, and for the establishment of a European political union, were undermined both by external developments and by the new internal complexities arising especially from British entry into the Community. A period of 'Eurosclerosis' set in, in which it appeared impossible to take significant new initiatives and in which member state governments were unwilling to contemplate the costs of further integration. Indeed, they spent much of their time focusing on the costs of such integration as already existed, with conflicts over the CAP and over the Community budget lasting through the 1970s. There were, however, at least some signs of a more hopeful kind, and some of these were visible in transatlantic relations. Not for the last time, concerns about relations with the United States were accompanied by some moves towards greater international coordination among member states. In the 1970s it was the growth of EPC that promoted greater coordination of diplomacy among member states, albeit on an explicitly intergovernmental basis. Such coordination was apparent in the Community's activities in the Conference on Security and Cooperation in Europe (CSCE, also known as the Helsinki Process) during the mid-1970s, and was also evident increasingly in the growth of a 'European' diplomacy towards conflict in the Middle East during the late 1970s (Allen and Wallace 1977; Allen and Smith 1982; Allen and Pijpers 1984).

Box 1.4 The 'Year of Europe'

The problems in transatlantic relationships are real. They have arisen in part because during the fifties and sixties the Atlantic community organized itself in different ways in the many different dimensions of its common enterprise. In economic relations, the European community has increasingly stressed its regional personality; the United States, at the same time, must act as part of, and be responsible for, a wider trade and monetary system. We must reconcile these two perspectives. In our collective defense, we are still organized on the principle of unity and integration, but in radically different strategic conditions. The full implications of this change have yet to be faced. Diplomacy is the subject of frequent consultation, but is essentially being conducted by traditional nation states. The United States has global interests and responsibilities. Our European allies have regional interests. These are not necessarily in conflict, but in the new era neither are they automatically identical. In short, we deal with each other regionally and even competitively in economic matters, on an integrated basis in defense, and as national states in diplomacy. When the various collective institutions were rudimentary, the potential inconsistency in their modes of operation was not a problem. But after a generation of evolution and with the new weight and strength of our allies, the various parts of the construction are not always in harmony and sometimes obstruct each other.

Source: Secretary of State Henry A. Kissinger, Address to the Associated Press Annual Luncheon, New York, 23 April 1973 – 'The Year of Europe'.

The Europe of the Nine is aware that, as it unites, it takes on new international obligations. European integration is not directed against anyone, nor is it inspired by a desire for power. On the contrary, the Nine are convinced that their union will benefit the whole international community since it will constitute an element of equilibrium and a basis for cooperation with all countries, whatever their size, culture or social system. The Nine intend to play an active role in world affairs and thus to contribute in accordance with the purposes and principles of the United Nations Charter, to insuring that international relations have a more just basis, that prosperity is more equitably shared, and that the security of each country is more effectively guaranteed. In pursuit of these objectives the Nine should progressively define common positions in the sphere of foreign policy. . . . The close ties between the United States and the Europe of the Nine – who share values and aspirations based on a common heritage – are mutually beneficial and must be preserved; these ties do not conflict with the determination of the Nine to establish themselves as a distinct and original entity. The Nine intend to maintain their constructive dialogue and to develop their cooperation with the United States on the basis of equality and in a spirit of friendship.

Source: Communiqué of European Community Summit Meeting, Copenhagen, 15 December 1973, Annex II: 'Declaration on Europe's Identity'.

The 1970s were thus not an entirely barren period in EC–US relations, although throughout they were fraught with difficulties. Although the Nixon administration, succeeded by the Ford administration (1974–77) after the resignation of the president in 1974, did little to bind the wounds created by the events of the early 1970s, the Carter administration (1976–80) was less confrontational and more inclined to seek consensus. By the nature of things, given the economic difficulties faced by the United States, the type of international policy coordination favoured by Washington was based on others (now including Japan as well as the Europeans) taking up more of the burden and taking responsibility for world economic growth (Keohane 1979). At the same time, protectionist demands grew in the United States itself, especially from industries such as steel or shipbuilding that were feeling the heat of new competition from both Europe and Asia. Resentment over US attempts to get others to adjust was thus persistent, and towards the end of the 1970s it was reinforced by further concerns in the Community about US diplomacy outside the Atlantic area. In particular, European concerns focused on the onset of new tensions with the Soviet Union in Africa, and on the escalation of tensions in the Persian Gulf after the Iranian revolution of 1978–79. By 1980, when the Soviet Union undertook its invasion of Afghanistan and was immediately subjected to sanctions by the Americans, a 'new Cold War' was proclaimed, a concept with which many European governments found themselves distinctly uncomfortable (Kolodziej 1980–81; Freedman 1982, 1983; Allen and Smith 1989).

One of the key problems in EC–US relations during the 1970s was that of US leadership. The assumption that America would (and should) lead in all areas of western international life was challenged in a number of dimensions simultaneously. Economically, it was put in doubt by the fragility of the US economy and by the attempt to get others to pay the costs of US economic decline. Politically, it was thrown into question by the internal turmoil surrounding Watergate and by the frailty of successive US administrations in the wake of Vietnam. In terms of security and defence, it was shaken by the 'Vietnam syndrome', which created doubts about the effectiveness of the use of force, and by the growth of new tensions leading to the 'new Cold War'. For the EC, the issue expressed itself most forcibly in the economic dimension, with the growth of disputes and the threat of protectionism, but the Community was not immune from the impact of the broader diplomatic and military controversies. Indeed, a key development of the time was the increased linkage between economic issues and political or security matters, and this was bound to make the management of relations with the United States more challenging for the Community and its member states.

Given these general conditions, the election of Ronald Reagan as US president in 1980 gave an additional twist to already significant tensions.

Reagan was committed to the reassertion of US primacy, both globally and in transatlantic relations, and his administration proved troubling for the Community in many ways. Firstly, the practice of what became known as 'Reaganomics' threatened the kind of international economic instability that the Community found profoundly uncomfortable. A series of measures including substantial tax cuts and spending increases, both in welfare and in defence, had the effect of spreading financial instability worldwide, and especially across the Atlantic. The West-German chancellor of the time, Helmut Schmidt, once famously accused Reagan of creating the highest interest rates since the death of Christ, as the Americans tried to square the circle of massive tax cuts and spending increases. The US dollar gyrated erratically on the international exchanges, undervalued and overvalued in quick succession as the administration tried to use interest rates to control the money supply. Unilateral US attempts to cure their financial problems intersected with continuing difficulties within the EC over the budget and agriculture to perpetuate 'Eurosclerosis' and to exaggerate economic divergence among the member states. Only in 1985 did some measure of international financial coordination reappear, with the Plaza Agreement on coordination of monetary policies (Oye, Lieber, and Rothchild 1983; Tsoukalis 1986; Woolcock and van der Ven 1986; Oye, Lieber, and Rothchild 1987; Patel and Weisbrode 2013: chapter 7).

By the mid-1980s, therefore, the economic scene resembled a war zone, with instability and fluctuations a central theme of policymaking. Within the EC, however, there had been some progress in the face of considerable difficulties. The European Monetary System, set up in the final year of the Carter administration, had created a level of monetary coordination among its members that provided some insulation from the wilder gyrations of the dollar (Ludlow 1982; Patel and Weisbrode 2013: chapter 11). In 1984, at the Fontainebleau summit, Community leaders had at least partly resolved the issue of agricultural financing and the Community budget (including the creation of arrangements for Britain that moderated its contribution to the budget for the foreseeable future). They had also begun to move forward on reforms to improve decision-making within the Community and to make possible the completion of what had become known as the 'Single Market' (Pelkmans and Winters 1988; Sandholtz and Zysman 1989). One central theme of these reforms was the need to make the Community competitive in a world economy where both the United States and Japan constituted formidable rivals.

The policy impact of Reaganism, however, was not felt only in economic matters. Indeed, for the citizens of the Community in the early 1980s, the preoccupation was not so much the economic and financial impact of Reaganite policies as the perception of danger created by US diplomacy and defence policy. Reagan's election had reflected the demand from Americans that the United States be made strong again, after the uncertainties of the 1970s, and the administration set out to deliver on this promise with massive increases in defence spending as well as a much more assertive and muscular diplomacy. This was aimed primarily against the Soviet Union but inevitably had an immediate impact on European perceptions and policy options. As the rhetoric of US policy was ratcheted up during the early 1980s, and European governments were faced with demands that they accept new deployments of nuclear weapons on their territory, popular disquiet grew. At the same time, US responses to Soviet actions in Central and Eastern Europe, including the imposition of martial law in Poland during 1981, placed additional pressures on European governments to go along with diplomatic and economic sanctions, in circumstances where they almost instinctively would have preferred to negotiate and look for ways out that did not damage the existing European order (Allen and Smith 1989). One of the results of this pressure was an increasing tendency in the Community to explore the possibility of new forms of European foreign policy cooperation, both within the 'civilian' realm of European Political Cooperation and within the distinctly more sensitive area of European security and defence cooperation (Treverton 1985; Joffe 1987; Patel and Weisbrode 2013; chapter 11).

From change to transformation: 1985–2000

Up to the mid-1980s, it is persuasive to talk about transatlantic relations in terms of continuity and evolution. Many aspects of the relationship were recognizably the same in the 1980s as in the 1950s, although in a number of important respects the world had changed around them and there had been a clear impact of political and economic change both in the EEC and in the US. A number of the key issues encountered within the system had remained relatively constant since the 1950s: the problems of leadership and followership, the question of burden-sharing in its broadest context, the role of institutions and the questions raised about them (Sloan 2016: chapter 5). This part of the chapter is based on the perception that between the mid-1980s and the beginning of the new millennium the changes in and around the transatlantic relationship amounted not to a further stage in evolution but to a radical transformation whose implications have not yet been fully realized. The previous section drew attention to the ways in which during the early 1980s the combination of Reaganism in the United States and slow but steady resolution of some key issues in the EEC had created a new momentum and arguably a redefinition of US attitudes towards the Community and Western European attitudes towards the United States. In the United States, the globalism of many policies pursued under the Reagan administration from 1980 to 1984 had created a new awareness that American interests encompassed the Pacific as well as the Atlantic, and that the Europeans were less reliable than they might have been as underwriters of an assertive US posture on economic, political and security issues (see Box 1.5). In the EC, the very assertiveness of US policies combined with a consciousness of new developments in European economic and security policies to foster a sense of difference and of divergence.

This means that although 1989 and the fall of the Berlin Wall is often seen as a crucial turning-point in transatlantic relations, it can equally be argued that the turn had been in progress since 1985 at least. From the EC point of view, there were three key ingredients in this process. First, there was the resolution of key institutional and budgetary issues in the Fontainebleau agreement of 1984, rapidly followed by the Single European Act (SEA) of 1985 and in particular by the inception of the Single Market Programme (SMP) in 1986. The latter was a five-year plan to radically reduce the barriers to a single European market, with the anticipated effect of substantially enhancing the competitiveness of community industries and enabling the EC to stand on equal terms with the United States and Japan in a changing world economy (Hufbauer 1990: Chapter 1; Schwok 1991: Part II; Smith and Woolcock 1993: Chapter 3; Hocking and Smith 1997: Chapters 1–2; Patel and Weisborde 2013: chapter 12). As such, it had not only an economic but also a profoundly political set of implications, relating to institutions and regulation in the world economy and to the effective use of market power by the Community to enhance its world role. The SEA underpinned this set of aims by making what appeared to be relatively small institutional changes such as the widespread use of qualified majority voting in the Community legislative process; these changes actually had a major cumulative effect on the capacity of the EC to make decisions in vital areas of political economy (Keohane and Hoffmann 1993). At the same time, the Community completed a new phase of enlargement with the entry of Spain and Portugal in 1986 to follow that of Greece in 1981. One result of all these developments was a distinct wave of confidence in the EC and its institutions during the late 1980s, part of which spilt over into the aspiration for new measures, specifically Economic and Monetary Union (EMU) and further development of foreign and security policy cooperation.

Box 1.5 Lawrence Eagleburger on the transatlantic relationship, 1984

I have often discussed with European friends the different requirements for a nation with global responsibilities to those with more regional concerns. The use of the word global is not meant in any arrogant fashion. Nor is it to deny the interests that several European nations retain in areas of the world beyond their continent. But the sheer scope of American interests engages us in a different set of perspectives and imperatives. I am persuaded that despite periodic inconsistencies (mainly on our part) and even more frequent crises of policy disagreement (emanating frequently from the European side) members of the alliance can still forge a strong consensus on most issues of importance . . . [but] . . . now may well be the appropriate moment for all of us – Europeans and Americans – to take a new look at where we should be going together and how we should get there . . . The two pillars of a 'smarter' relationship, in my opinion, are: increasing respect for the differences in our alliance; and a more coordinated approach – across the board – to all political, economic and security issues with our European allies.

Source: Under Secretary of State for Political Affairs Lawrence Eagleburger, speech to the National Newspaper Association, Washington, DC, 7 March 1984.

Set against the 'ring of confidence' that began to surround the EC in the late 1980s, US policies and institutions presented a complex and unstable picture. The massive expenditures and the economic fluctuations of the early 1980s created an equally large 'hangover' in the late 1980s, symbolized best by so-called 'Black Monday' in October 1987, when US stock markets nosedived and created worldwide uncertainty about the economic future. The Reagan years had created a very large 'double deficit' in the US economy, affecting both the balance of payments and the federal budget, and it was not entirely fanciful to see the United States as being kept afloat by the willingness of the Japanese and the European to buy US government bonds. Although as noted previously there was a return to elements of monetary policy coordination from 1985 onwards, first with the Plaza accords and then in 1987 with the Louvre agreement, the picture remained one of considerable volatility and risk. Diplomacy and defence policy under 'Reagan II' from 1985 onwards were also a source of uncertainty: continued confrontation with the USSR was accompanied by the initiation of the so-called 'Star Wars' (or Strategic Defence Initiative – SDI) programme of space defence from 1985 onwards, but in 1986 there began a process of

US–Soviet rapprochement which created the possibility of substantial nuclear disarmament. Mikhail Gorbachev, the new Soviet leader, proved open to new and often radical initiatives, but this was not always a source of reassurance for the Europeans, many of whom feared US–Soviet friendship (and a possible reduction in Washington's commitment to regional security) as much as they did confrontation between the superpowers. By the late 1980s, therefore, it appeared that issues of trust and risk in EC–US relations pervaded both the economic and the diplomatic/security spheres (Allen and Smith 1989).

It was against this backdrop that in 1989 the Berlin Wall was first breached and then destroyed, with fundamental implications for the continued existence of the Soviet bloc and the Soviet Union itself. At one level, this is of course best seen as a profound event in superpower diplomacy and security policy: the confrontation between the USSR and the United States, which had been heightened by Reaganite policies, had resulted in the collapse of the Soviet sphere, politically, militarily and economically. As such, it was bound to have immediate effects on the relationship between the United States and its key allies in Europe. But it is clear that the events of 1989–91 were also profoundly European in their origins and impact. The collapse of the Soviet bloc, the end of the Soviet Union and the unification of Germany did not see the Americans as mere bystanders, but they did give a new focus to the diplomatic and political evolution of the 'new Europe' which was distinct simply from the superpower game (Allen and Smith 1991–92; Keohane and Hoffmann 1993; Story 1993; Smith and Woolcock 1993: Chapter 1; Laffan, O'Donnell, and Smith 2000: chapter 3). Another dimension of the events is also central to the story in this chapter: the end of the Cold War was as much an economic process as it was a political or military one, since it entailed the destruction and then the reconstruction of what had been a divided world economy, allied to the need to rebuild a pan-European economy as the basis for political stabilization. Because of this, the EC was thrust almost immediately to the centre of the process and remained there throughout the 1990s. This much was recognized as early as December 1989 by US secretary of state James Baker who in a speech delivered in Berlin called upon the EC to play its full role in the stabilization of the new Europe through welcoming membership applications from newly liberated countries of Central and Eastern Europe (see Box 1.6). The Community was in many respects unable to live up to the expectations of rapid and comprehensive expansion, but the incorporation of East Germany was followed by a broad-ranging aid programme for the Central and East European countries (CEECs). While this did not initially come with the promise of membership, by 1993 a process had begun which led in 2004 to the entry of eight new CEEC member states along with Cyprus and Malta, to be followed in 2007 by Bulgaria and Romania, and in 2013 by Croatia.

Box 1.6 James Baker on the role of the European Community after the Cold War

As Europe changes, the instruments for western cooperation have got to adapt. Working together, it is up to us to design and generally to put into place what I refer to as a new architecture for this new era. . . . The future development of the European Community will also play a central role in shaping the new Europe. . . . As Europe moves toward its goal of a common internal market, and as its institutions for political and security cooperation evolve, the link between the United States and the European Community will become even more important. We want our transatlantic cooperation to keep pace with European integration and with institutional reform. To this end, we suggest that the United States and the European Community work together to achieve, whether it is in treaty or some other form, a significantly strengthened set of institutional and consultative links. . . . We propose that our discussions about this idea proceed in parallel with Europe's efforts to achieve by 1992 a common internal market, so that plans for US–EC interaction would evolve along with changes in the Community. The United States also encourages the European Community to continue to expand cooperation with the nations of the east. The promotion of political and economic reform in the east is a natural vocation for the European Community. . . . We see no conflict between the process of European integration and an expansion of cooperation between the European Community and its neighbors to the east and west. Indeed, we believe that the attraction of the European Community for the countries of the east depends most on its continued vitality. And the vitality of the Economic Community depends in turn on its continued commitment to the goal of a united Europe envisaged by its founders – free, democratic and closely linked to its North American partners.

Source: Secretary of State James A. Baker III, Address to the Berlin Press Club, 12 December 1989.

The Community was thus earmarked both in the United States and in Europe itself for a major role in what became known as the 'new world order' (Laffan, O'Donnell, and Smith 2000: chapter 8). Its institutional, financial and political capacity to play such a role was tested to the limit throughout the 1990s and had a fundamental impact both on its internal make-up and on its international role. Beginning with the Maastricht Treaty of 1991 and proceeding through the Amsterdam Treaty of 1997 and the Nice Treaty of 2000 to the unratified

Constitutional Treaty of 2004, the European Union (as it became with the implementation of Maastricht in 1993) was continuously faced with the challenge of redefining and 'reinventing' itself in the face of a rapidly changing world arena.

Part of this challenge was inextricably bound up with EU–US relations: the EU was seen by many Americans as playing a major supporting role in the redefinition of US foreign policy and its attempts to cope with the disappearance of its superpower rival, as well as forming the basis for a much expanded economic partnership and rivalry. This perception was widely but not completely shared in the EU itself, and fed into the key debates about the EU's appropriate world role that came to characterize much of the 1990s and beyond (Forster and Wallace 2000; Niblett and Wallace 2001; K. Smith 2003; Hill and Smith 2005; Bretherton and Vogler 2006). These debates in turn were greatly sharpened by events both in the European 'neighbourhood' and in the wider world during the early and mid-1990s. The Gulf War of 1990–1 and the series of conflicts in the former Yugoslavia that erupted in 1991 ran alongside and were intertwined with the institutional changes in the EU that established a Common Foreign and Security Policy (CFSP) and then, in the late 1990s, the European Security and Defence Policy (ESDP, later the Common Security and Defence Policy, or CSDP) as a consequence of the St. Malo Declaration of 1998 by France and the UK (see Box 1.7 for the elements of the agreement and the US Secretary of State's response). But they also accompanied the progress of most EU member states towards Economic and Monetary Union, and the attempts by the Union as a whole to wrestle with the economic adjustments necessitated by simultaneous processes of enlargement and domestic economic management in a globalizing world.

Box 1.7 The St. Malo Declaration and the 'three Ds'

The St Malo Declaration (extracts)

The European Union needs to be in a position to play its full role on the international stage. . . . This includes the responsibility of the European Council to decide on the progressive framing of a common defence policy in the framework of CFSP. The Council must be able to take decisions on an intergovernmental basis, covering the whole range of activity set out [in the Maastricht Treaty].

To this end, the Union must have the capacity for autonomous action, backed up by credible military forces, the means to decide to use them, and a readiness to do so, in order to respond to international crises.

Madeleine Albright's warning to the EU on the 'three Ds' in 1998

Our . . . task is working together to develop a European Security and Defense Identity, or ESDI, within the Alliance [NATO], which the United States has strongly endorsed. We enthusiastically support any measures that enhance European capabilities. The United States welcomes a more capable European partner, with modern, flexible military forces capable of putting out fires in Europe's own backyard and working with us through the Alliance to defend our common interests. The key to a successful initiative is to focus on practical military capabilities. Any initiative must avoid pre-empting Alliance decision-making by de-linking ESDI from NATO, avoid duplicating existing efforts, and avoid discrimination against non-EU members.

(Albright 1998; Madeleine Albright was US Secretary of State)

It is basic to an analysis of what happened in EU–US relations during the 1990s to understand that economics, diplomacy and security issues were mutually entangled and highly demanding, and to be aware of the ways in which these issues engaged both the external policies and the internal politics of the EU and the United States (Haftendorn and Tuschhoff 1993). At the same time as the 'adversarial partners' were immersed in processes of self-definition and adjustment to new realities, they were also locked together in a number of much more wide-ranging global processes. Among these were the negotiations within the GATT for a new global trade agreement that led in 1993 to the conclusion of the Uruguay Round and the subsequent establishment of the World Trade Organization (WTO), to be followed by a series of key sectoral trade negotiations and then in the late 1990s by renewed demands for a new global negotiating round. At the same time, the approach of EMU and the introduction of the euro as the new single currency for 11 EU member states fed into the wider need for international monetary management in a turbulent world, where global conflicts and global currencies were often closely linked. In all of these processes, the EU and the United States were inevitably at centre-stage and were equally inevitably assailed by a mass of domestic and external demands. Whereas in the economic field, it might plausibly be claimed that the EU and the United States were engaged on equal terms in key global management processes, this was not the picture in global diplomacy and security policy, despite the progress made in the EU towards foreign and defence policy coordination during the late 1990s (Featherstone and Ginsberg 1996; Peterson 1996b; M. Smith 1998; Howorth 2003; Smith and Steffenson 2005; see also Chapter 9).

Around these shifting EU–US relations, there grew up during the 1990s a network of institutional arrangements that for some achieved the status of 'transatlantic governance' (Philippart and Winand 2001; Pollack and Shaffer 2001; Petersmann and Pollack 2003; Steffenson 2005: chapters 1, 2). In 1990, the EC, its member states and the United States signed the Transatlantic Declaration (TAD) which set out in very general terms the needs for intensified consultation and cooperation. In December 1995, the EU and the United States signed the New Transatlantic Agenda (NTA), which set out in more detail the mechanisms of cooperation and specified a wide range of areas for 'joint action', including the creation of a New Transatlantic Marketplace (NTM). Alongside the NTA, a series of transatlantic dialogues were created, for business, for legislators, for trades unions and for others in specific sectors such as environmental cooperation. And in 1998, the EU and the United States concluded a more focused agreement for a Transatlantic Economic Partnership (TEP), designed to create concrete mechanisms for mutual recognition and other policy initiatives. By the end of the 1990s, therefore, there had been created a wide-ranging set of institutions and mechanisms for communication and consultation, especially in economic and social policy matters, that seemed to set the framework for new processes of cooperation across the Atlantic, and a consolidation of the transformations undergone since the late 1980s. These were transformations not simply of the overall context but also of the transatlantic partners, and particularly of the EU, which had acquired more of the institutions and resources that would potentially enable it to assert its interests against those of the United States. The next period of transatlantic relations would put this judgement to the test in no uncertain manner.

Transatlantic crises in the 21st century

The frameworks described earlier – and the very foundations of EU–US cooperation – came under intense and sustained pressure in the early years of the new millennium. While there had been tensions and disputes during the 1990s, in areas as diverse as conflict in the former Yugoslavia, global environmental policies and global currency management, these seemed to have been largely contained. After the election of George W. Bush as US president in November 2000, tensions were ratcheted up by a series of policy initiatives from Washington that seemed to express a new unilateralism and a willingness to disregard existing international commitments in the cause of US national security (Peterson and Pollack 2003; Gordon and Shapiro 2004; M. Smith 2004; Andrews 2005; M. Smith 2005a). These initiatives were such as to link together the economic, the diplomatic and the security aspects of international policies, and as such they directly attacked some central assumptions of EU–US relations, at a time when the EU was preoccupied with the implementation of EMU, the continuing attempt to reform the European institutions and the wide-ranging challenge of enlargement. They were greatly intensified in the aftermath of the terrorist attacks which Islamists associated with the Al-Qaeda network carried out on the US on 11 September 2001, and by the subsequent US declaration of a global 'war on terror'. The attack on Iraq in spring 2003 led to divisions within the EU between what the US Secretary of Defense, Donald Rumsfeld, described as 'old' and 'new' Europe, but also led to an initiative by France, Germany and others (effectively, Rumsfeld's 'old Europe') to establish an enhanced 'European Security and Defence Union' (see Box 1.8). For some commentators, the US position and European responses expressed a radical new challenge to the foundations of the transatlantic system and presaged its possible dissolution (Lieven 2002, Lindstrom 2003; Peterson 2004a, 2005; Pond 2004). Alongside the military and security challenges this posed to EU–US relations, there went a series of tensions and recriminations in new or newly-politicized policy areas such as those of human rights and the environment, and an intensification of disputes and differences in global trade and development policies. At the same time, however, there was an expansion of EU–US cooperation in areas of 'soft security' relating to the challenge of terrorism, although this in itself generated frictions about the exchange of information and the extent to which the EU could assert its interests, and a continuation of day-to-day economic cooperation (alongside continuing disputes) in the context of a wide range of bilateral and multilateral institutions (Petersmann and Pollack 2003; Dannreuther and Peterson 2006; Rees 2006, 2009). Thus although during the later years of the George W. Bush presidency, after his re-election in November 2004, it was possible to discern a new flexibility and willingness to cooperate in US policies, there is no doubt that during the previous five years the EU–US 'partnership' had been shaken to its core (Zaborowski 2006a).

Box 1.8 The Iraq War and EU–US relations

Donald Rumsfeld on 'old' and 'new' Europe in 2003

Q: Sir, a question about the mood among European allies. . . . If you look at, for example, France and Germany . . . it seems that a lot of Europeans rather give the benefit of the doubt to Saddam Hussein than President George Bush. These are US allies. What do you make of that?

A: What do I say? Well, there isn't anyone alive who wouldn't prefer unanimity. I mean, you just always would like everyone to stand up and say, Way to go! That's the right [thing] to do, United States. . . . Now, you're thinking of Europe as Germany and France. I don't. I think that's old Europe. If you look at the entire NATO Europe today, the center of gravity is shifting to the east. And there are a lot of new members. . . . They're not with France and Germany on this, they're with the United States.

(Donald Rumsfeld, US Secretary of Defense, Press Briefing at the Foreign Press Club, Washington DC, 23rd January 2003)

Proposals by some EU members for a common operational headquarters

We propose to our partners the creation of a nucleus collective capability for planning and conducting operations for the European Union . . . . Open to every member state of the European Union expressing that wish, it would have to establish liaison arrangements with its national counterparts. In order to maintain a close link with NATO, it would also have to establish liaison arrangements with SHAPE [Supreme Headquarters Allied Powers Europe] . . . in this spirit, and until such a capability will have been created by the European Union, interested states will establish a nucleus of a collective capability which, instead of national means, they would make available to the EU for operational planning and command of EU-led operations without recourse to NATO assets and capabilities.

[Meeting of the Heads of State and Government of Germany, France, Luxembourg and Belgium on European Defence, Brussels, 29 April 2003]

In part, this shaking of the foundations intersected with important changes in the nature of the European project, which were to re-shape transatlantic relations over the longer term – and which were also linked to tensions and crises within the EU itself. From the late 1990s, there had been discussion of a potential 'leap forward' in the organization and powers of the Union, and this continued in the early years of the new millennium with the development of a Constitutional Treaty. This promised to make the EU a more comprehensive actor both in internal and in external affairs – the latter especially by installing major features of a 'real' foreign policy, such as a diplomatic service and enhanced defence cooperation alongside the existing powers in the organization of the European economy and the conduct of international economic policies (Hill 1998; M. Smith 2006). The creation of the European Central Bank and the inauguration of the euro as an international currency at the turn of the century also contributed to the feeling that the EU was entering a new phase. Added to this, the enlargement of the Union with ten new member states in 2004, a further two in 2007 and the most recent in 2013, predominantly from Central and Eastern Europe, seemed to promise a new weight for the Union.

But this was in part deceptive: the Constitutional Treaty failed in the teeth of opposition in a number of popular votes, the euro's introduction created new stresses on international monetary cooperation, and the absorption of 13 new member states created new institutional and policymaking complexities. The negotiation and implementation of the Lisbon Treaty, which entered into force in 2009, created new tools of EU external action, especially the European External Action Service (EEAS) headed by the High Representative for Foreign Affairs and Security Policy, who was also a Vice-President of the European Commission (thus abbreviated as the HRVP), and the hope was that this would give the Union a new international 'voice', despite the continuing reservations of major member states such as the UK (Hill and Smith 2005; Keukeleire and Delreux 2014).

The challenging nature of US foreign policy, as epitomized by the George W. Bush administration, equally reflected longer-term processes of change, particularly the challenges to US predominance in the global arena from emerging (or re-emerging) powers such as China and Russia (Leffler and Legro 2008; Cox and Stokes 2018: Part 5). While the Bush administration's response had been to try and re-assert American predominance especially in the area of 'hard security', many of the new challenges were in areas such as trade and finance, in which the US position was rather less dominant. The successor administrations to the Bush administration reflected very different responses to this situation. On the one hand, the Obama administrations (2009–17) seemed ready to accept the changing nature and distribution of power, and to work in a cooperative way to address the problems of a changing world order (while retaining a sense of US leadership) – a position based on the use of 'smart power' which chimed with the policy preferences not only of the EU but of most Europeans, and cast the EU as an 'essential partner' (Gordon 2010; Nye 2012). The administration led by Donald Trump (2017–21) had a very different approach to the world, with a central position based on 'America First' and the reassertion of US predominance through the weaponization of economic strength and the use of economic sanctions rather than through diplomacy and cooperation. Not only this, but the Trump administration set out to challenge the nature of the EU as a means of organizing Europe, and potentially to undermine the European project in general (M. Smith 2018a). While it is possible to overstate the seemingly radical changes introduced by the Trump administration, it is clear that the atmosphere of EU–US relations was subject to significant and sometimes wild fluctuations between 2005 and 2020, and that this reflected not only internal changes in the EU and the United States but also broader global trends (M. Smith 2018b).

One of the key catalysts for these fluctuations was the global financial and economic crisis from 2008 onwards, which threatened to overwhelm the capacity of governments and central banks to maintain international and domestic order. In the years immediately prior to the onset of the crisis, there had been signs of new EU–US cooperation in political economy. In 2007, the move to a Transatlantic Economic Partnership gathered pace, with the establishment of the Transatlantic Economic Council (TEC) and agreement on new areas of collaboration. But the economic crisis, which originated in the US sub-prime mortgage market and was quickly transmitted across the western world, meant a sudden and urgent concentration on domestic economic affairs, which thus created new obstacles to international cooperation. Tensions between the United States, which favoured radical measures to stave off the effects of the crisis, and the EU, which reacted in a relatively conservative way focused on financial stability, were inevitable. The creation and use of the Group of Twenty (G-20) representing the 20 largest economies went some way to supporting international cooperation, but with strictly limited powers. For the EU, the problems were compounded by the fault-lines in the eurozone, which led to a crisis in a number of the weaker economies (especially the Greek economy, but also the Portuguese and Irish) and which created conflicts that seemingly threatened the very existence of the euro. At the transatlantic level, the desire for more cooperation led to negotiations from 2013 onwards aimed at a Transatlantic Trade and Investment Partnership (TTIP), which proved difficult not only at the EU–US level but also within EU member states, with intense opposition in Germany and other countries as well as opposition in the US Congress (Morin et al.2015; De Ville and Siles-Brugge 2016; see Chapter 5).

While the global economic crisis preoccupied policymakers on both sides of the Atlantic, a series of geopolitical crises demanded attention in the area of 'hard security', and more broadly in the search for world order in the post-Cold War world. In some ways, this was the post-post-Cold-War world – in other words, a series of challenges to international order that reflected the long-term unwinding of processes set in train during the 1990s. Successive crises in Moldova, Georgia and the Caucasus – areas between the EU's 'neighbourhood' and the revived geopolitical ambitions of Russia under President Vladimir Putin – revealed both the unwillingness of the Americans to become directly involved and the limitations of the EU's new foreign policy instruments. The Europeans' development of a formal European Neighbourhood Policy (ENP) from 2009 onwards was driven by the desire for stability and order in Europe but also was based predominantly on 'civilian' instruments without the possibility of military action (see Chapter 8).

The constraints on such a policy were starkly revealed again in the crisis that emerged in Ukraine after 2013 – a crisis that did lead to military conflict as well as the annexation of Crimea by Russia, but in which the EU was largely powerless – and the United States unwilling – to intervene. In the so-called 'southern neighbourhood' of the EU – the Middle East and North Africa (MENA) – the emergence of domestic rebellions from 2011 onwards in the so-called 'Arab Spring' led to full-scale internal wars with external interventions, for example in Libya (by the British and the French with the United States in the background) and in Syria (by a wide range of external forces including Russia, Turkey, Iran, the United States, the UK and others). Although the EU was inevitably deeply engaged in these crises, its involvement was diplomatic and economic, rather than geopolitical and coercive, and its interactions with the United States were inevitably limited.

Within the EU, the challenges of the period 2010–15 led to a searching debate about the nature, purposes and organization of 'European foreign policy'. As noted earlier, the Lisbon Treaty had created a new system of EU diplomacy, centred on the EEAS and the HRVP. The aim of building a 'joined-up' foreign policy with strengthened institutional foundations came up against the challenges – economic, political and security – outlined earlier – and the outcomes were often patchy. As a result, in 2015–16, there was a sustained effort to produce a new focus for the Union's external action, which culminated in the production in June 2016 of a Global Strategy (European Union 2016; see also Tocci 2017 and Chapter 7). Among the key principles of this strategy was 'strategic autonomy' – an aim which had obvious implications for relations with the United States, and which was focused further by the proliferation of challenges faced by the Union both in its neighbourhood and beyond.

By the time Donald Trump (2017–21) was elected to the US presidency in November 2016, there was thus a long history of transatlantic crises in the post-post-Cold-War world, accompanied by significant changes in the Union's capacity for 'joined-up' external action. These trends reflected not only the shifting power structure of the world arena but also the changing positions and internal politics of the EU and the United States themselves. Both in the EU and in the United States, there was in some ways a crisis of legitimacy in which the established institutions had revealed their limitations, and this was linked to a broader crisis of international order, in which the existing institutions and rules were challenged on a number of fronts and by a number of 'rising powers' (M. Smith 2018b). The Trump administration promised – or threatened – to disrupt even the remaining elements of transatlantic and international order. In political economy, it pursued trade wars and economic sanctions against target regimes (notably China but also the EU). In security, it confronted the Chinese, the North Koreans, the Iranians and others with military threats if they did not modify their behaviour. In political ideology, it preached a kind of 'transnational nationalism' in which every country was on its own and in which populist forces in Europe and elsewhere were implicitly or explicitly supported in their challenges to the established order.

Not surprisingly, the EU was in the line of fire as a representative of a commitment to multilateral institutions and to an international order based on rules and norms rather than on national power. Whereas the Obama administration had been at pains to restate its commitment to the European project despite short-term turbulence, the Trump administration did not hesitate to describe the EU as a 'foe' and as an obsolete form of international cooperation (see Box 1.10). Major negotiations with the EU were suspended (for example, the TTIP although that had been in trouble before Trump's election), sanctions were imposed on EU steel and aluminium producers among others, major international agreements were denounced (for example the Joint Comprehensive Plan of Action on Iran's potential nuclear weapons, and the Paris Accords on climate change, both reached in 2015 and subject to US withdrawal from 2020). Trump as a candidate and then as president was also quick to support the UK's drive to withdraw from the EU after its referendum in June 2016 – not least because it could be seen as a means of undermining the European project more generally.

Box 1.9 President Trump on relations with European allies, and EU responses

Our allies are not paying their fair share, and I've been talking about this recently a lot. Our allies must contribute toward their financial, political, and human costs, have to do it, of our tremendous security burden. But many of them are simply not doing so.

They look at the United States as weak and forgiving and feel no obligation to honor their agreements with us. In NATO, for instance, only 4 of 28 other member countries besides America, are spending the minimum required 2 per cent of GDP on defense. We have spent trillions of dollars over time on planes, missiles, ships, equipment, building up our military to provide a strong defense for Europe and Asia.

The countries we are defending must pay for the cost of this defense, and if not, the U.S. must be prepared to let these countries defend themselves. We have no choice.

Donald Trump, foreign policy speech 27 April 2016 – https://www.nytimes.com/2016/04/28/us/politics/transcript-trump-foreign-policy.html (accessed 16th November 2020)

Donald Tusk, president of the European Council, May 2018

Besides traditional challenges such as the rise of China, or the aggressive stance of Russia, we are witnessing today a new phenomenon: the capricious assertiveness of the American administration. Looking at the latest decisions of President Trump someone could even think: with friends like that who needs enemies. But, frankly speaking, Europe should be grateful to President Trump. Because thanks to him we have got rid of all illusions. He has made us realise that if you need a helping hand, you will find one at the end of your arm. Europe must do everything in its power to protect, in spite of today's mood, the transatlantic bond. But at the same time we must be prepared for those scenarios, where we will have to act on our own.

(Remarks by President Tusk ahead of the EU-Western Balkans Summit. European Council, 16 May 2018)

By 2020, it was not at all fanciful to describe EU–US relations as being in crisis, on a number of key dimensions. In political economy, the resonances of the global financial crisis, added to the Trump administration's determination to use its economic strength as a weapon and to the broader state of flux in the global economy, had created a toxic atmosphere. In security, the limitations of EU action in its 'neighbourhood' (including in dealing with the refugee and migration crises arising from conflicts in the MENA region) and the United States' increasing attention to the Indo-Pacific region as a focus of conflict had fed into a wider geopolitical crisis and into the undermining of a series of international agreements on subjects such as nuclear proliferation and arms control more generally. The increasing salience of populist groupings in the EU, often at least tacitly supported by the United States, had created a crisis of legitimacy at the national and the European level, which intersected with the populism and 'America First' policies of the Trump administration. In many respects this was a 'perfect storm' of intersecting crises, throwing into question the established structures of transatlantic cooperation, and creating new (or newly prominent) questions about leadership, followership and cooperation in the world arena. The presidential election of November 2020 brought at least a temporary end to 'Trumpism' as US government policy, and replaced him with Joe Biden, whose presidency was hailed as a return to the politics of EU–US partnership and the consolidation of cooperation, but the key issue was whether the transatlantic partners were capable of restoring a deep partnership.

Any prospects of a new EU–US partnership under the Biden administration were subject to an increasingly volatile and threatening global arena, in which new elements of geopolitics and geo-economics took a central role. In addition to the challenges of the COVID-19 pandemic, the continuing challenge of global heating and environmental emergency, and the challenges posed by a resurgent China that attracted a large part of US geostrategic attention, the onset of war in Ukraine after the Russian invasion of February 2022 constituted a fundamental challenge to the idea that European order could be consolidated through negotiation and economic integration. It plunged the EU into a world where increasingly it had to consider 'hard-edged' security policies at the same time as it faced major economic challenges because of the effect of the war on global energy and food supplies. Subsequent chapters in this book will focus on more specific elements of this situation, building on the historical context supplied here, and also on the possibilities for management of the multiple crises that have characterized the post-Trump era.

Overview and conclusion

This chapter has set out to provide a broad understanding of the historical forces and current pressures that have shaped the relationship between European integration and the United States. A number of key phases have been used as the means of organizing what is a complex and often strongly debated historical process, leading to the following overall conclusions:

- First, the 'foundation' period between 1945 and the late 1950s put in place many policies, institutions and practices of which the traces can still be seen, and raised questions about the operation of the transatlantic relationship that remain key to its development.
- Second, during the 1960s a series of tensions emerged within transatlantic relations as the European Communities grew and as the focus of power and interests within the system was contested from a variety of sources.

- Third, between 1971 and the mid-1980s there was a continued process of change, in which relationships were intensified but also conflicted, and during which the impact of external forces from the world arena became more apparent.
- Fourth, between 1985 and 2000, the coming together of radical international changes with intensified change in the European integration process and significant fluctuations in US policy created a process of substantial transformation, which was unfinished yet profoundly important both for the EU and for the United States.
- Finally, between 2000 and 2023, a series of crises both in transatlantic relations and in the broader global arena combined to create continuing turbulence in EU–US relations. These crises were partly domestic, partly regional (especially in the EU's 'neighbourhood') and partly global, especially in relation to the global political economy and new forms of regional conflict.

It is important to remember that many of the tensions and pressures that came to a head after 2000 had been fermenting since the end of the Cold War and the radical changes of the early 1990s. In turn, many of the issues on which attention focused in the 1990s and 2000s can be seen as radically intensified versions of issues that had been characteristic of transatlantic relations since the early days, and which give rise to the central themes of this book: competition, convergence and crisis. Much of the rest of this book is dedicated to the systematic exploration of the ways in which these pressures and tensions have been defined, analysed, managed and – in some cases – mismanaged, but this chapter has attempted to set out the broad historical sweep of the evolution of transatlantic relations as the backdrop against which this exploration can be set. In the next chapter, we will look successively at the components, the structure and the functioning of what can be conceptualized as the 'Euro-American system', as a means of further setting the scene for detailed policy analysis.

Chapter 2

Analysing the Euro-American system

Introduction

Chapter 1 provided an account of the evolution of the relationship between European integration and the United States since the end of the Second World War. The emphasis was on processes of historical continuity and change, and on the ways the relationships between the United States and the European integration process have been surrounded by other forces of broad continuity and change in the world arena. In this chapter, the focus shifts: the key concern here is to identify the primary components of the Euro-American system, to show how they work together and the ways in which they produce issues for policy and policymakers, and to show how analysts have approached the problem of explaining such a complex set of relations. In providing this more analytical focus, the chapter will make use of the 'historical' information from Chapter 1, and also of further case-study material.

In conducting this analysis, the chapter makes the assumption that there is a Euro-American system which has persisted over three-quarters of a century, which has a discernible size and scope and which has generated characteristic patterns of behaviour (for related approaches, see Czempiel and Rustow 1976; Peterson 1996b; Philippart and Winand 2001). This does not mean that such an approach rules out change: rather, it means that it is possible to locate changes that take place as part of the system, and also to understand in a more precise way the impact of particular processes of change within and beyond the system. For analytical purposes the chapter conceives of the Euro-American system as the patterns of relations that have grown up and persisted between the societies of the North Atlantic area since 1945, and sets out to identify the key participants, processes and outcomes of activity within this changing system. European integration has been a central component of the system, and thus it is a key aim to show the ways in which the significance and impact of this component has altered over time. But European integration, although central, is only one major component of the system, and this is key to assessing the current relationship between the EU and the United States. The argument will be that in the current period the 'EU–US system' has become largely but not completely identical with the Euro-American system and that this has important policy consequences.

The first part of the chapter deals with the key components of the Euro-American system: the actors and their interests, the key sub-systems within the system and the key levels of interaction between the participants. The chapter looks at the range and diversity of participants, at the ways they are arranged in markets, hierarchies and networks, and the several levels within which 'Euro-American politics' take place. It argues that the politics of EU–US relations are carried out within an increasingly interconnected and multi-level policy space, within which national governments are still of major importance, but within which they have long since been joined by a variety of other actors in a 'mixed actor system'.

In the second part of the chapter, the focus is more on the dynamics of the system and the ways they can be characterized for the purposes of analysis. The argument focuses first on the policy processes that characterize the system, both within the European Union and within the United States. It moves on to look at the ways in which distinctive policy processes at the transatlantic level have emerged and been consolidated during the past 20 years and more, and at the ways in which they have reflected the end of the Cold War and the post-Cold-War period (as introduced in Chapter 1). The chapter then goes on to explore the characteristic institutions and processes of governance that have emerged between the EU and the United States, arguing that there is strong evidence of a process of 'transatlantic governance' in a growing number of policy areas. Finally this part of the chapter focuses on how change in a set of overlapping and often interlocking policy arenas has characterized the Euro-American system, and especially EU–US relations.

Both parts of this discussion will form the background to subsequent chapters dealing with policymaking in the EU and the United States and with key policy areas in EU–US relations, and will be taken up explicitly in the conclusions (Chapter 11).

Components of the Euro-American system

Actors and interests

At one level, the Euro-American system is an example of a key phenomenon in classical and contemporary international relations: a system of states. As noted in Chapter 1, at the end of the Second World War the United States, Canada and a number of Western European countries came together to form and then consolidate the 'Atlantic alliance' centred initially on the North Atlantic Treaty Organization (NATO). These states – winners and losers in the war – came together for classical reasons: partly because of the dominant influence of one country (the United States) and partly because of an external threat (from the Soviet Union). In doing so, they did not sacrifice their external sovereignty, since they had entered an alliance of sovereign states with the aim explicitly of preserving their independence and national security. Since the 1940s, this system of states centred on NATO has expanded dramatically – first with the acceptance of former enemy states and those who had initially remained outside the alliance (for example, West Germany, Greece, Turkey, Spain and Portugal) and then, after the end of the Cold War, with the entry into the system of countries which had formerly been part either of the Soviet bloc or of the Soviet Union itself, along with two Mediterranean countries. From an initial membership of 12 countries, by 2020 NATO had expanded to 29, and in 2022, proposals for the entry of Sweden and Finland were made as a result of Russia's invasion of Ukraine. Both these latter proposals were initially opposed by Turkey, but Finland entered in 2023 after Turkish objections were removed, and Sweden in 2024. In these terms the boundaries and membership of the system have expanded to encompass almost all of the 'Euro-Atlantic area'. In a similar way, the diversity of the system has also increased, to include members with varied national histories, levels of economic and social development and geopolitical sensitivities.

Alongside this expansion and diversification of the 'Euro-American state system' however has gone another trend: the growth of new forms of institution and alignment which have challenged the idea that Euro-American relations are solely about the relations between states. Mention has already been made of NATO, which is distinctive among alliances for its longevity and for the level of joint planning and commitment that it demands from its member states. A number of other international organizations, such as the Organization for Economic Co-operation and Development (OECD) and the Organization for Security and Cooperation in Europe (OSCE), have been established as means of expanding cooperation between states within the system, although both the OECD and the OSCE contain 'outsiders'; in the case of OECD, these include other developed countries such as Japan, Australia and South Korea, and in the case of the OSCE, crucially, they have included Russia and a number of other ex-Soviet states. But the key development in this area has been the establishment first of the European Economic Community and its accompanying European institutions (Euratom and the Coal and Steel Community), and then of the amalgamated

European Community and in 1993 the European Union. These organizations are special because they go beyond the normal level of commitments among members of an alliance or an international organization such as the OECD: the member states of the EU and its predecessor organizations have formally yielded a portion of their sovereignty and national independence to the larger organization, giving it the power to represent them on the international stage in a number of key policy areas. As noted in Chapter 1, by the beginning of the 21st century these policy areas included trade and broader commercial policy, monetary relations (for more than half of the EU member states), key aspects of regulatory policy such as competition policy and environmental policy, and some areas (much debated) of foreign, security and defence policy. To put it simply, this is why this book is about EU–US relations: the expansion of European integration, and its impact on a growing number of policy areas, means that the EU has become a central pillar of the Euro-American system. Indeed, as will be argued later, by the 2020s the 'EU–US system' had become almost identical with the Euro-American system in a number of important areas of politics and policy.

This is not the end of the story, though. The Euro-American system can be conceived of as a state system, or as a system of EU–US relations with a mix of intergovernmental and supranational participation, but it is also a system in which there is a strong and flourishing element of private relations between a range of non-governmental actors (Pollack and Shaffer 2001; Smith 2001a). From the beginning of the European integration process, there has been a notable involvement of private investors, producers and others with essentially commercial interests in the development of the Euro-American system. As noted in Chapter 1, the deepening of this largely private form of participation was strongly stimulated by the Marshall Plan and by the establishment of the EEC in the late 1950s, and has responded to successive waves of 'deepening' within the EC and then the EU during the past 50 years. In a very concrete sense, the engagement of multinational corporations in European integration has been vital to the progress achieved by the European project throughout its life. In addition, there has grown up a wide range of transatlantic bodies with cultural, humanitarian and other purposes, which have been said at times to constitute the building-blocks of a kind of 'Atlantic community' going far beyond the simple interactions of states and their governments.

The diversity of participants in the Euro-American system has therefore grown continuously during its existence – and so quite naturally has the diversity of their interests. One way of characterizing this – and one highly significant for later parts of this chapter – is in terms of the types of political aims espoused and pursued by this diverse range of participants. At the level of 'high politics', the

Euro-American system encompasses a wide range of interests in national and international security, and in the survival and prosperity of its member states. At the same time, there has been a continuing development of interests in what is often termed 'low politics': the social, economic and cultural concerns that exist among member states but also among the wide range of non-state actors present in the system. Finally, there has been intense development of what can be termed 'sectoral politics', with political actions and preferences centred on specific areas of activity that often carry high stakes and the potential for significant costs and/or benefits to both states and non-state groupings. For the EU and the United States, it is clear that interests and activities encompass all of these dimensions, and that one of the key elements in their relationship is the pursuit of coexisting and often competing aims at each of the three levels – high, low and sectoral. As the EU has expanded and extended its policy activities, it has also become clear that the balance of attention and interests between the EU, its member states and the United States has shifted, in complex and challenging ways.

Markets, hierarchies and networks

Given that the range of participants and interests within the Euro-American system has developed and diversified over its lifespan, it is important to analyse the ways those participants and interests are distributed and arranged within the system. It has already been noted that the impact of European integration on the system has been profound, and that the end of the Cold War has had extensive political and economic consequences, but here the aim is to say more about the types of sub-systems that exist within the system, and how they relate to each other.

One key type of sub-system is *markets*. Indeed, it could be argued that for a large part of its existence, the Euro-American system as it relates to EU–US relations has largely been about markets, their extension and deepening and their regulation. In the immediate post-1945 period, the need to recover the European market, both as a source of political and social stability and as a source of demand, was a key element in many US policies. Likewise, the foundation of the European Coal and Steel Community and then the EEC during the 1950s was explicitly about the need to instil economic recovery and to do it by re-establishing strong and developing markets in Western Europe. Here, as elsewhere, the establishment of markets and their regulation was always linked closely to political and security objectives in the context of the Cold War. As the European integration project prospered and deepened during the 1970s and 1980s, it also became apparent that competition between different types of market economies and regulatory structures could emerge within the Euro-American system. By the early 1990s, there was widespread discussion of the frictions between the so-called 'Anglo-Saxon' model of free market, deregulated economies and the 'social market system' said to be characteristic of continental European economies within the EC, with its higher levels of social provision and its pursuit of social solidarity (Albert 1992; see also Smith and Woolcock 1993: Chapter 3). This social market model, sometimes called 'Rhineland capitalism', was also seen to be characteristic of many EC policy initiatives and activities, a fact that was linked to tensions between different groups of EU member states. By the end of the 1990s, this tension had eased, in the eyes of some observers because the 'neo-liberal' model espoused by the United States and the British had prevailed and was now being pursued through the EU itself (Cafruny and Ryner 2003: Part 1), but it had not altogether disappeared. The neo-liberal model itself was closely linked to ideas of globalization, which emphasized the spread of transnational market structures underpinned by new forms of communication and production; and in its turn, this set of ideas and practices has been implicated in the crises of the past two decades, especially the global financial and economic crises that became apparent in 2008. In its turn, this allowed space for proponents of state capitalism to tout the attractiveness of their economic model (Bremmer 2009).

Accordingly, the Euro-American system is in part a market system, engaging those with economic interests to pursue and linking the regulatory and social systems of those involved on both sides of the Atlantic. At the same time, however, it is possible to see the system as embodying a different type of relations: those of *hierarchy*. The most obvious place to look for such relations is between the member states of the system, where there is often a profound gap between the resources and interests of those at the top of the hierarchy and those at the bottom. As noted in Chapter 1, this imbalance has been evident throughout the post-1945 period, especially in areas to do with 'high politics' and security. The military dominance of the United States (and of US–Soviet relations) during the Cold War had deep and long-lasting effects on the ability and inclination of Western European governments to assume the burden of their own defence, either individually or collectively, and this in turn has echoes today in the limitations of European foreign and defence policies, despite significant developments at the EU level (see Chapters 7 and 8 especially). The end of the Cold War and the collapse of the USSR served only to accentuate this divide: the idea of the United States as the 'only superpower' had a profound effect both on US policies and on the collective responses of EU member states, within the EU itself, within NATO and at the national level. In the early years of the 21st century, the ways in which US policymakers tried to come to terms with their changing position in the global hierarchy were at the core of tensions and sometimes open conflicts with a more assertive European Union.

But the impact of hierarchy does not end with security and defence. In the political economy of the Euro-American system, the key role of the US dollar as the predominant medium of exchange was cemented into the Bretton Woods system of post-1945 multilateral institutions and found its expression in a wide range of areas of commercial and industrial activity (Foot, MacFarlane and Mastanduno 2003). The freeing up of trade within the North Atlantic area, the later impact of globalization and the general intensification of patterns of international exchange and production were all affected by the background of US predominance and what has been termed 'structural power'. The development of the European integration project has gradually modified this picture, most obviously in the area of trade relations (see Chapter 4) and to important degrees in the realms of monetary relations and investment, innovation and competition policy (see Chapters 5–6). The result has been a series of frictions as the foundations of the system have adjusted to the new reality. Last but not least, the impact of hierarchy has been experienced within a range of social and cultural areas, as the impact of US popular culture and related phenomena has intensified. As will be seen later in the chapter, this has not been a uniform or even impact, and areas of resistance have not been unknown within the EU, but it is important to note the pervasive and continuing impact of hierarchy within the Euro-American system. As noted in Chapter 1, the global hierarchy has been complicated by the emergence of new 'powers' especially in the area of political economy, most obviously exemplified in the rise of China and the so-called BRICS grouping (Brazil, Russia, India, China and South Africa) and emerging markets more generally. China has moved from being a regional trading and security power to becoming a challenger to the United States in a number of spheres as well as a central focus of the EU's external relations. As noted in Chapter 1, the result of this power shift has been a set of increasingly severe frictions (Alcaro, Peterson, and Greco 2016).

Finally in this section, it is necessary to highlight the importance alongside markets and hierarchy of *networks*. As already noted, the Euro-American system has experienced intensive development of private patterns of commercial exchange, and this has generated a wide-ranging set of commercial networks spanning the Atlantic. While one key component of these is clearly the multinational corporation, with its networks of internal trade, investment and production, this is not the only commercial networking that can be seen within the system. Transatlantic alliances of companies, through licensing arrangements or strategic partnerships fortified by cross-investment, have been a key part of the commercial developments within the system, to such an extent that it is sometimes difficult to say with certainty what is a 'European' or an 'American' company or product. This tendency has been underlined by the rise of companies based on the internet, such as Google, Amazon and Facebook, and the difficulties associated with their regulation.

Alongside these private commercial arrangements, there has also grown up a set of networks sponsored by governmental authorities on both sides of the Atlantic, engaging business, non-governmental organizations and regulatory bodies in the oversight and monitoring of developments within their areas of concern. A number of these grew up around EU–US partnership agreements reached in the 1990s, such as the New Transatlantic Agenda or the Transatlantic Economic Partnership (see Chapter 1 and later in this chapter), and they well represent the desire of many organizations to establish networks of communication and influence in the Euro-American system (Cowles 1996; Peterson 1996b; Cowles 2001a; Pollack and Shaffer 2001; Steffenson 2005). A third type of network is rather less public and accessible: the range of contacts between the United States and individual EU member states' policymakers in areas of security and intelligence cooperation. While there was some extension of this to the EU–US level in the wake of the terrorist attacks on the United States in September 2001, and there is increasing collaboration on intelligence between the United States and overall EU bodies in the field, there is clearly a strong legacy of past 'special relationships' between the United States and countries such as the UK, which was evident in such episodes as the Iraq conflict from 2003 onwards and has influenced developments such as the AUKUS grouping that have emerged since the UK left the EU. Alongside these three types of 'official' networks, there exists a fourth built upon the activities of a wide range of non-governmental organizations: many of these emanate from civil society, and they include humanitarian, media, educational and cultural bodies focused on cross-national communication and influence. While these bodies are often centred on efforts to influence governmental bodies, they can also be subversive of the 'official' networks through their activities at the transnational and global level as well as the transatlantic level.

What does the proliferation of relations based on markets, hierarchies and networks in the Euro-American system indicate about the nature of the system itself? One conclusion that can be drawn at this stage is that there are several different 'maps' of the system, depending on the precise focus of any mapping process. These maps overlap: sometimes they come into collision with each other, sometimes they reinforce each other and often they can also be manipulated for political or other purposes by key participants within the system. But they also mean that it is impossible to generalize about 'who runs the system', since in each of the many overlapping and conflicting or complementary areas there are different distributions of power, resources and leverage. As we shall see in later chapters, this has major implications for policymaking and for the management of relations.

Multi-level politics in a 'mixed actor' system

The expansion and diversification of the actors in the system, their coexisting and often competing interests, and the ways in which they enter into markets, hierarchies and networks, imply a Euro-American system in which politics can take place at several different but interconnected levels, with direct and significant consequences for policymaking and policy implementation. Mark Pollack and Greg Shaffer (2001; see also Steffenson 2005) have identified three levels of action and interaction, which they relate to the demand for and supply of transatlantic governance mechanisms: intergovernmental, transgovernmental and transnational. A brief exploration of these three levels can help to complete the picture of the key components in the Euro-American system.

First, as is clear from much of the preceding discussion, the Euro-American system embodies a strong element of *intergovernmental relations* between the member states of an admittedly expanding and diverse system. This process of intergovernmental relations can include certain activities of the EU itself, particularly those conducted in such areas as trade and commercial relations, where the EU has powers similar to those of national governments. It is important, however, to remember that EU policies are themselves often the product of intergovernmental processes at the European level, with member states negotiating and exerting influence to determine the shape of EC policies. In other areas of EU activity, there is even more of an intergovernmental tinge, since when it comes (for example) to the EU's foreign, security and defence policies, member states have retained a great deal of the initiative, albeit within an increasingly 'Europeanized' or 'Brusselized' policy process (Hill 1995; Keukeleire and Delreux 2014; Hill, Smith, and Vanhoonacker 2023). Alongside the activities of the EU or its component parts, there is still a very important intergovernmental dimension to many areas of transatlantic convergence or competition, particularly those dealing with issues of security or defence – where NATO often enters into the picture – or those dealing with matters such as the regulation of investment, where the Lisbon Treaty extended the reach of EU policies but there remains a good deal of variation between national regimes.

Second, despite what has just been said about the persistence of intergovernmentalism both at the European and at the transatlantic level, there has also been strong growth of *transgovernmental relations* within the Euro-American system. These are relations between officials and departments within national governments (sometimes including elements of subnational or regional governments as well), which come to constitute semi-permanent networks and which shape the behaviour of their members both at the transatlantic (or EU) level and at the level of their national governments. To put it simply, the increasing intensification of contacts between officials of national governments in areas as diverse as agriculture, environmental policy, policing policy and defence has created a set of transgovernmental networks in which the participants do not always act predictably as agents of their national governments. They can develop – and feed back into national policy – distinctive perspectives and policy prescriptions specific to their sector of policy, and they can thus 'Europeanize' or 'Atlanticize' the responses of their national authorities. This transgovernmental image subverts the apparent tidiness of an intergovernmental image where national governments are united and act as one on all areas of national concern. The intensification of transgovernmental contacts, when added to the expansion and diversification of the Euro-American system, becomes an essential component of policymaking and what some have termed 'transatlantic governance' (Pollack and Shaffer 2001: Steffenson 2005; M. Smith 2011a).

Finally, the Euro-American system has seen a growth and intensification of *transnational relations* – that is to say, of relations that spill across national boundaries and often ignore the influence of national authorities. As noted earlier, the most frequently used term to describe such relations is that of the network, implying the development of a spider's web of relations that develop largely independent of national influences as a response to problems that are essentially transnational or global in nature. In terms of the earlier discussion, such networks can often be seen as essentially subversive, although some of them are actually closely linked to the interests and activities of national governments or EU institutions. They can generate perceptions of interest and values that are more rooted in the overall stability and development of the Euro-American system than in the national preferences of governments or even in the preferences of EU institutions. As such, they raise issues of regulation for national and European authorities, and within the transatlantic arena these problems have become both time-consuming and often fraught with difficulties.

In addition to the three levels of relations emphasized by Pollack and Shaffer, though, it is necessary here to introduce a fourth category: *multilateral relations*. By this is meant the range of interactions between actors within the Euro-American system in other contexts, often those of a global scope. Although it is clear that a huge range of relevant interactions are essentially contained within the system, there are those that inevitably spill over onto the global stage (M. Smith 2005b, 2018a). Perhaps the longest established of the settings within which such European-American interactions take place is that of the WTO and its predecessor the GATT. Chapter 1 described the process whereby since the late 1950s there has been continuing and intensifying contact between the EU and the US in this set of institutions, and it is clear that over more than 70 years this has generated its own distinctive momentum and set of constraints. But this is only one of many global and/or multilateral settings in which the Euro-American system is implanted; many of these are economic, but a growing number are cultural, social, humanitarian, environmental and now security-related. The expansion of the collective action undertaken by the EU is clearly part of this story, but it is also clear that the expansion of the multilateral institutions themselves and of the rules they generate has been a key shift in the context within which EU–US relations occur. By the same token, the challenges posed to the multilateral system by the Trump administration between 2017 and 2021, and by the development of competing multilateralisms in a world of new 'great powers', became a defining part of the context for EU–US relations as the 21st century wore on (Peterson, Alcaro, and Tocci 2016; M. Smith 2018a, 2021; see also Chapter 10).

It is apparent from the discussion so far in this chapter that the Euro-American system is complex and multidimensional. This complexity and multidimensionality reflect the ways in which over a period of at least 80 years, successive layers of activity and interaction have been laid down within and around the system. As noted in Chapter 1, this can be seen in essentially historical terms, but here the aim has been to identify the key components of the system in a more analytical fashion. Figure 2.1 summarizes what has been argued so far, and from this the complexity is readily apparent. It seems clear that the Euro-American system complies with what Oran Young once described as a 'mixed actor system', within which a multiplicity of actors interact with no necessary or permanent assumption about hierarchy or the use of power resources (Young 1972). Up to now, though, the emphasis has been on the components of the system at the most general level. The chapter now turns to what might be termed the dynamics of the system, in terms of policy processes and policy outcomes.

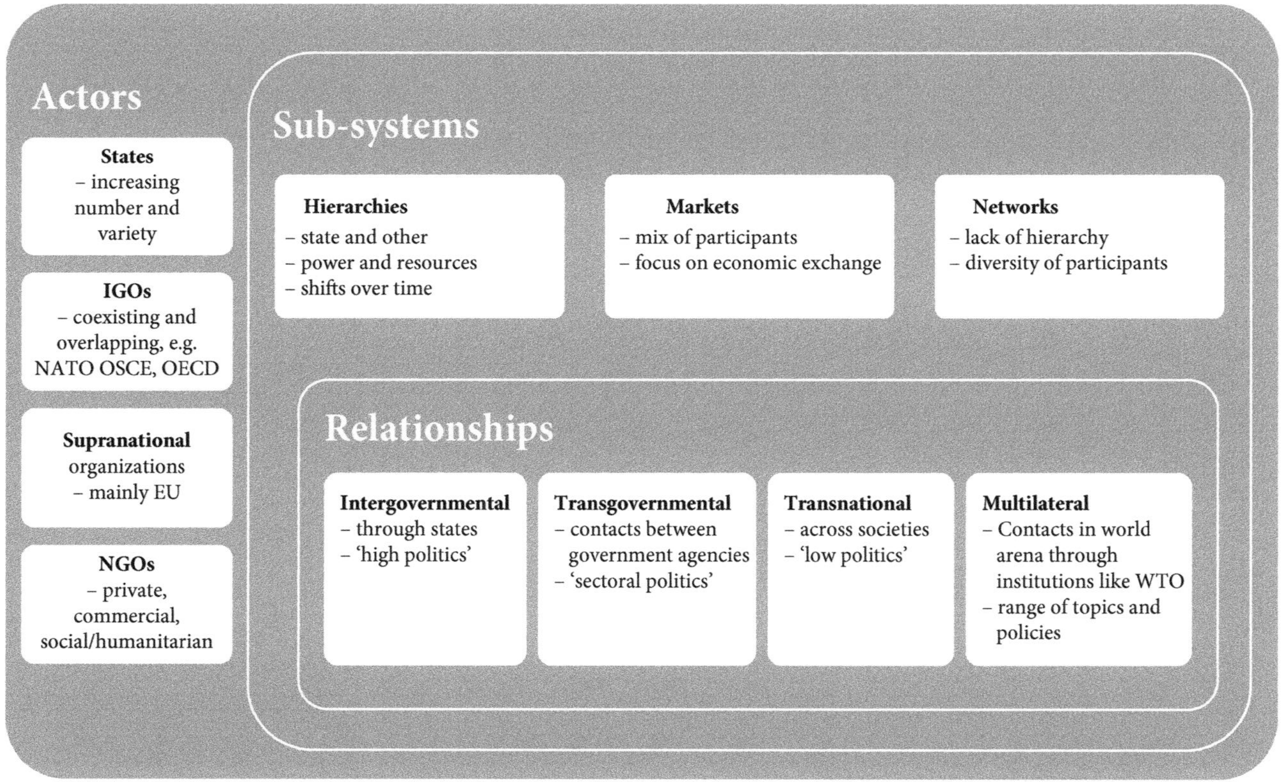

Figure 2.1 Key components of the Euro-American system.

Processes, institutions and policies

Policy processes

When considering the dynamics of the Euro-American system and within it those of EU–US relations, it is clearly important to explore the mechanisms and processes of policymaking that characterize the system. For the purposes of the analysis here, it is possible to discern two key levels of policymaking: first, the processes that occur within the EU on the one hand and the United States on the other, and second, the processes that occur at transatlantic level and which relate both to EU–US relations strictly defined and to the broader policymaking framework of the Euro-American system broadly defined. The latter distinction is important, since as has already been pointed out on a number of occasions, the EU–US system of relations is not wholly identical to the broader system of transatlantic interactions, and this has significant impacts on the policymaking process in a number of key areas. This two-level approach to the analysis of EU–US policy issues – focusing on EU policies, then on US policies and then on their interaction – will be a key organizing theme for Chapters 3–10 of this book.

The EU's 'US policy'

As early as the mid-1970s it was apparent that if the European Community developed a foreign policy, the first target of such a policy would have to be the United States (M. Smith 1978). The position of the United States as the 'significant other' of the European integration process was by then already well established, reflecting the forces at work during the Cold War and within the international political economy from the late 1950s onwards (see Chapter 1). However, it is rather easier to identify the United States as the prime target than it is to develop a coherent and coordinated 'European' policy towards Washington. From the outset, the European Communities and then the EU have had to take account of the United States in the field of political economy, both as a key external force facing European trade and related policies, and as a key – if not *the* key – shaping force in the broader global economy. The earliest 'European' policy targeted on the United States was thus almost inevitably the Common Commercial Policy, together with the EEC's activities in the multilateral trade institutions, primarily the GATT. This remains, in the context of the WTO, perhaps the EU's most concentrated and coherent 'US policy'. It is also clear, however, that many of the 'internal' policies of the EU have an inescapable American dimension. If the policy discussion is about agriculture, competition policy, research and development or the regulation of 'big tech' firms, the Americans are often not only the key external point of reference but also to some extent an 'insider' group through the activities of US companies and broader commercial groupings. This tendency is as evident in the more recent politics of the euro or in areas of external action such as development policy or environmental policy as it has been in more long-established policy areas, where the European voice is more concerted and audible. Thus the dollar has always been a key point of reference not only for external European monetary policies but also for internal policymaking and implementation, since it affects the policy environment in a pervasive way. At the same time, the US position on development issues, or on climate change and its economic and social impact, has inevitably been a key consideration for policymakers in Brussels.

If one moves away from the political economy, it is clear that the United States is equally if not more significant in the development of EU policies in the diplomatic and security fields. The diplomatic coordination that lies at the heart of the CFSP and is expressed since the Lisbon Treaty by the EEAS and the HRVP is strongly conditioned by the positions of the United States, not only because they affect the environment within which CFSP emerges and European diplomacy is conducted but also because they strongly shape the policies of key EU member states (Vanhoonacker, 2001; M. Smith 2011a). The existence of 'special relationships', of which the most celebrated or imagined is that between the United States and the UK, is thus a key element of transatlantic politics. The achievement of diplomatic coordination and consistency has always been an issue for the EU, and the United States has the potential both to promote it and to erode it – often both at the same time. The end of the Cold War and the United States's position as the 'only superpower' thus fundamentally re-shaped the possibilities for European diplomatic coordination, and this has been further underlined by the policies of successive US administrations (see Chapters 1 and 7). The more recent elaboration of a European security and defence policy has of course made the issues even sharper (Howorth 2005, 2007, 2014, 2017). Is the EU through collective action in defence likely to mount a challenge or present an alternative to US positions, or is it more likely to be disrupted by the Washington policy process? Here it is clear not only that the EU–US relationship is one between two politically influential actors, but also that in some ways they are part of each other's policy processes (more of this and its implications later).

Above all, it is clear from both historical experience and contemporary policy issues that for the EU, the development of a 'US policy' is both uniquely necessary and uniquely challenging. It is uniquely necessary because the United States as the 'most significant other' of European integration and as a global power is there in all areas of EU policymaking. This means that the United States is not only a material factor in policy formation but also a key shaping force in the development of a 'European identity' within the world arena. The development of a 'US policy' is uniquely challenging because it demands internal coordination within the EU, between and across European institutions and between the European and the national levels on a continuous basis across all areas of policy development. As students of the EU in general and of 'European foreign policy' in particular have pointed out (K. Smith 2003; Bretherton and Vogler 2006; Hill and Smith 2005, 2023; Keukeleire and Delreux 2022), these challenges of consistency, coordination and balance across different levels and sectors of policymaking are a key aspect of the European integration process in general. In respect of the United States, the challenge is underlined and sharpened on a daily basis as well as on the more strategic level of policymaking. At the same time, as generations of foreign-policymakers have discovered, the shifting policymaking balance between institutions in Washington, complicated by the different levels of government in the US federal system and by the fluctuating effects of US domestic politics, makes the formation of a 'US policy' by the EU and its member states a complex and demanding process at other levels (see for example Smith and Woolcock 1993; Winand 1993; M. Smith 2006a; Smith and Steffenson 2023).

The United States' 'EU policy'

In many ways, the problems for the United States in dealing with the EU are a mirror image of those for the EU in dealing with Washington – with some crucial differences. The EU presents a policymaking challenge because of its internal complexity, the shifting nature and continuous evolution of its institutional and policy frameworks, and because it is a factor in most if not all of the key areas in which US policy is made. So policymakers in Washington as in Brussels and European capitals have to confront the problems of making policy towards a 'moving target' and one in which significant policy developments can be prompted by influences coming from a number of levels within the system. We have seen in Chapter 1 that the development of a consistent set of policies towards European integration has always been a challenge for US administrations, since although they have been broadly consistent in their support for the European project (with the exception of the Trump administration, perhaps), they have found all sorts of reasons to be concerned about it at anything but the broad strategic level. In the late 1950s and 1960s, this concern was predominantly focused on political economy, with the emergence of trade disputes and the complexity of adjustment to the postwar 'new Europe' (Krause 1968; Diebold 1960). Even at the level of political economy, though, the Americans have found that the policymaking calculus is formidably complicated. Nothing demonstrates this more clearly than US responses to the Single Market Programme of the late 1980s and early 1990s, which had to reconcile the interests of almost every department and agency in the US administration, and which required negotiations not only at the EU–US level but also at subnational and global multilateral levels (Calingaert 1996; Hocking and Smith 1997; Hufbauer 1990). The challenge of achieving policy consistency across the full range of EU–US relations in political economy remains, and if anything has become more complex with the introduction of the euro and the continuing extension of EU policy competence in areas such as competition policy and investment policy during the past few years (see Chapters 4 to 6).

Since the late 1980s, the United States has also had to address the issues arising from the concrete development of European policies in the diplomatic, security and defence spheres. While the emergence of European Political Cooperation during the 1970s and 1980s caused momentary concern for US policymakers, it could largely be viewed as 'procedure as a substitute for policy' (Allen and Wallace 1977) with little concrete or immediate effect. The development of CFSP in the early 1990s, and the later emergence of CSDP as a security and defence arm for the EU, was more challenging, coinciding as it did with the removal of the 'Cold War overlay' in security relations between the United States and Europe as a whole. If a European foreign and defence policy was to become a reality, it had to raise important questions about US leadership, the role of NATO and the capacity of Washington to define the foreign policy consensus in the Atlantic area (M. Smith 1992; Smith and Woolcock 1993). This posed a challenge to some key assumptions in US foreign policy that had been present in the Cold War and that had been given additional force by the disappearance of the Soviet Union.

The challenge was also one to institutions and policymaking processes at the more restricted level, since it raised in a new and more concentrated form the question 'Who speaks for Europe?' first raised for the Americans during the 1970s (Allen 1998). Washington had to adjust to a situation in which on an increasing number of diplomatic and even defence issues the first point of call was not key national capitals or NATO headquarters, but the European institutions. Even if they were not the first port of call, these institutions increasingly framed the national policies of growing numbers of European states and also their positions within NATO (a trend only accentuated by the enlargement of the EU to 28 members in the early 2000s, alongside the enlargement of NATO itself). But the reality of 'European foreign and defence policy' was characterized even after the turn of the millennium by an often wide and always fluctuating 'capability-expectations gap' which meant that US policies had to cope with the mismatch of rhetoric and reality (Hill 1998; Howorth 2005, 2014: chapter 4). A tendency to revert to 'special relationships' with key partners within the EU is both understandable and could often be seen as desirable in US policy terms (M. Smith 2011a) – a situation made more explicit by the departure of the UK from the EU after the referendum of 2016, since London claimed a wide-ranging 'special relationship' with Washington.

The framing of a coherent and consistent 'EU policy' by the United States is thus challenging in many of the same ways as the framing of a 'US policy' by the European Union. As in the case of the EU's 'US policy', there is a continuing and often pressing need for American administrations to recognize and respond to important pressures from within the EU's multi-level policymaking process, and a continuing difficulty in taking into account the multiple sources of policymaking. A key area of difference, though, is that the United States possesses a full federal government that can mobilize the resources of US society over the full range of external action – a claim that the EU is in no position to make or to fulfil despite recent developments. This means that the policymaking relationship between the EU and the United States is a mismatch, exhibiting a gap in resources and capacity to mobilize them that can never (and perhaps should never) be bridged. The consequences of this gap will be explored in many of the chapters that follow, and especially in Chapter 3.

Policymaking at the transatlantic level

Given the complexities and unevenness in EU and US policymaking processes, it might be expected that little in the way of coherent policymaking would take place at the transatlantic level itself. As will be seen shortly, despite the development of a range of institutional frameworks for the better conduct of transatlantic (and particularly EU–US) relations, it remains the case that there is no consistent mechanism for the coordination of policies at a comprehensive level between the EU and the United States. The open and fluctuating nature of many of the relationships that make up the Euro-American system makes it inevitable that no single centre of authoritative decision-making can be contemplated. But this does not mean that there are no mechanisms for the management of policies within the system. In this section, we explore three possible such mechanisms: transatlantic governance, hard and soft balancing and crisis management.

We have already noted that the growth of institutions and interactions within the Euro-American system since the 1960s has created conditions in which mechanisms of governance are both necessary and possible (Pollack and Shaffer 2001; Steffenson 2005). On the basis of mutual benefit, or the limitation of mutual damage, highly interdependent entities such as the EU and the United States can develop both formal and informal means of regulating common problems and achieving policy convergence. Indeed, John Pinder argued as far back as the early 1980s that the mismatch between intensifying transatlantic issue interdependence and the lack of policy interdependence was so striking that ways of dealing with it would have to be found if there was not to be a damaging outcome for all concerned (Pinder 1983). Recognition of this problem, at least in the area of political economy, has led to continuous efforts on the part of both the United States and the EU to increase mutual communication and sensitivity, short of creating any authoritative transatlantic body. Policy convergence and adaptation has taken place in a number of sectors, such as competition policy or environmental policy, but without curtailing the independence of either party in a formal way and without ruling out the possibility of significant divergence (Pollack and Shaffer 2001; Peterson and Pollack 2003; see also Chapters 4 to 6). In this way, a degree of transatlantic governance has been achieved, including the development of limited formal institutions (see later). It has to be remembered also, as noted earlier, that this transatlantic level of governance is embedded in many respects in broader structures of global governance, which also produce convergence (and the recognition of common interests) between the two sides of the Atlantic (Alcaro, Peterson, and Greco 2016). In the area of security and defence policy, there have also emerged, over a very long period, the structure and habits of 'security governance' at the transatlantic level, but as noted earlier these are often more fragile and the challenges to them more severe than those of governance in the political economy (Mahnke, Rees, and Thompson2004). Quite apart from these variations, the policies of the Trump administration after 2016, with its explicit rejection of many aspects of global governance, threw into doubt the possibility of transatlantic governance in many areas (see also Chapter 10).

Alongside mechanisms of governance, it is also possible to discern a second type of transatlantic policymaking mechanism: balancing. Implicit in much of what has been said both in Chapter 1 and in this chapter is that there has been a long-term shift in the transatlantic balance: first, in the area of political economy and then – and less profoundly, perhaps, thus far – in diplomacy, security and defence. In this process, European integration has played a major role, since it has created at least the possibility of sustained collective action by EU member states. Indeed, one way of viewing the entire integration process is as a means of producing 'political economies of scale' in the international arena, and thus making the combined weight of the EU and its member states more effective, not least in relation to the United States (Ginsberg 1989); the most recent expression of this underlying tendency was the EU's Global Strategy of 2016, with its emphasis on the benefits of 'joined-up policymaking' and the use of resources at the EU level, followed in 2022 by the publication of a 'strategic compass' with a programme for investment in new resources for foreign policy action (see Chapter 7). If this balancing process is viewed as what has been termed 'hard balancing', based on material power and particularly on military capabilities, then the Europeans despite the EU have no really effective means of countering the United States as long as Washington pursues a consistent and united course. But if the process is seen as one of 'soft balancing' in which negotiation, policy coordination and the use of 'soft power' are more characteristic, then it is clear that the Europeans have more to say for themselves (Pape 2005; McCormick 2007; see also Posen 2006). Their experience of policy coordination and their enforced reliance on negotiation and persuasion rather than on imposition or coercion might be seen as giving them a comparative advantage not only in transatlantic relations but also in the broader global arena.

A final mechanism that can be identified in policymaking within the Euro-American system is that of crisis management. As noted in Chapter 1, the system has been characterized by periodic internal crises, in which the possibility of a 'transatlantic divorce' or a 'transatlantic rift' has been discussed, and yet the system has persisted. Partly this may reflect the impact of enduring common interests and the need for governance mechanisms to handle both policy convergence and policy competition. Partly also it may reflect the impact of balancing strategies as outlined earlier, and the growing impact of the EU on those strategies at the transatlantic level. But the process may also reflect the growth of mechanisms of crisis management, in which the members of the Euro-American system have developed conventions or habits of adjustment and the management of risk, thus avoiding fundamental breakdown of the system. As was seen in Chapter 1, the Euro-American system has generated crises on a regular basis: in the 1960s with the disputes over 'Atlantic Community', in the 1970s with the impact of the 'Nixon Shock' and conflict in the Middle East, in the 1980s with Reaganism and greater European assertiveness, in the 1990s with the series of adjustments needed after the end of the Cold War, in the early years of the new millennium with the impact of the 'war on terror' and the invasion of Iraq, in more recent times with the financial crisis, crises in the EU's neighbourhood and the determined unilateralism of the Trump administration. Yet the system has persisted, not only through recognition of the risks inherent in its breakdown but also because certain conventions of crisis management have been developed and have themselves persisted (M. Smith 2005d; see also Abelson and Brooks 2022). In this process, the development of European integration has played a significant part, particularly since the end of the Cold War, since it has enabled the Europeans to concert their positions and provided an increasingly authoritative interlocutor for Washington at a continental level. This is not to say that there have not been crises within the EU, often precisely because of the attempt to coordinate a position *vis-à-vis* the United States (see Chapters 7–10 especially), but it does mean that the EU provides a means of crisis management at the European level in diplomatic terms, which then in its turn facilitates the operation of the mechanisms at the transatlantic level. Later chapters will explore this possibility more fully.

Institutional development

This chapter has touched often on the nature and impact of institutions within the Euro-American system. It is clear that there are many such institutions, covering a growing range of interactions within the system, and that they can be both formal and informal in nature (see also Frelleson 2001; Gardner 2001). The general proposition to be explored in this section is that the Euro-American system has become increasingly institutionalized, and that this process of institutionalization has contributed to the working of the system in the early years of the 21st century. Along with this central proposition, the argument is that the specifically EU–US institutions within the system have become the predominant ones, and that other competing institutions have been reduced to a supporting role, albeit often a highly significant one. To explore these general propositions, the chapter focuses on three key issue areas in the system: economic, diplomatic and security/defence.

In the economic sphere, as has been noted already, the EU–US relationship is both heavily institutionalized in itself and part of a broader framework of institutions for global regulation and governance. The institutionalization of EU–US relations has been especially intensive and progressive since the end of the Cold War, prior to which there were few formal mechanisms for the management of EC–US relations *per se*. During the 1980s, mechanisms of coordination centred not so much around EC–US relations as around the multilateral system represented especially by the GATT and the International Monetary Fund, and around the Group of Seven (G-7) of major industrial countries. During the 1990s, however, mechanisms for bringing together policymakers in the EU and the United States, and formal institutional agreements, multiplied (Peterson 1996b; Pollack and Shaffer 2001; Steffenson 2005). First, there was the 1990 Transatlantic Declaration, whose purpose was as much diplomatic as economic: it set out the broad framework for EC–US cooperation based on annual summits, the development of sectoral working groups and the exchange of information about a range of international concerns (Schwok 1991; Peterson 1996b). Second, in 1995 came the New Transatlantic Agenda (NTA) and accompanying Action Plan. While based on the same presumptions as the TAD, the NTA went further in specifying concrete areas for joint action and in setting up monitoring mechanisms, specifically the so-called Senior Level Group of EU and US officials (for details see Pollack and Shaffer 2001: Chapter 1; Steffenson 2005: Chapters 2–3). Tellingly, whereas the TAD was an agreement between the United States and 'The European Community and its Member States', the NTA was concluded between the United States and the EU. One of the key elements of the NTA was the project for a New Transatlantic Marketplace, in which barriers to trade and exchange would be reduced if not eliminated. While this was not achieved in the short term, it was followed up by the Transatlantic Economic Partnership agreement of 1998, which made much more specific commitments to such processes as mutual recognition of product standards. In 2005, a major review of the NTA concluded that yet more needed to be done in order to reduce barriers to Transatlantic Economic Partnership, but this represented a further step in the evolution of these institutions rather than a revolutionary break (European Commission 2005, ; Pollack 2005). As a result of this review, a new commitment to the Transatlantic Economic Partnership was undertaken, buttressed by the creation of the Transatlantic Economic Council; this led eventually to the unsuccessful but extensive negotiations for a Transatlantic Trade and Investment Partnership between 2013 and 2016, and in 2021 to the establishment of the EU-US Trade and Technology Council (TTC) (to be discussed in Chapters 4 and 6).

Alongside the formal large-scale agreements on economic issues went transatlantic efforts to build up non-governmental networks in the economic domain. Most notable among these was the Transatlantic Business Dialogue, which was established at the same time as the NTA and which persisted for nearly 20 years with fluctuating levels of activity and impact, before merging in 2013 with the European-American Business Council (Cowles 2001a, 2001b; see also Chapter 4). Other dialogues were established on legislative issues, in environmental and consumer affairs and in labour issues, again with variable success. These initiatives were important in a diplomatic sense as well as the practical sense, but in a way they only scratched the surface of other institutional links that have intensified within the transatlantic political economy. Most obviously, the vast range of economic and commercial groupings that have profited from the intensification of transatlantic interdependence constitute a major institutional network at the private level that has profound implications for the management of the Euro-American system. Trade associations and similar groupings on both sides of the Atlantic spend a lot of their time trying to influence policies as they emerge both in Brussels and in Washington, and by so doing they contribute to the flows of information and ideas that are key to the development of the system more broadly (see for example Cowles 1996). They shape the need for 'early-warning mechanisms' on trade disputes, or on competition policy issues, and they support the use of such mechanisms both by the EU and by Washington, thus constituting a major point of resistance to fundamental splits in the transatlantic political economy.

The Euro-American system has also witnessed a major growth of institutions for diplomatic coordination. Perhaps most obviously, the commitment to annual EU–US summit meetings engaging the key officials on both sides of the Atlantic has seen the emergence of new expectations and habits of consultation, although these have at times been interrupted, for example by the Trump administration. The NTA itself, as noted earlier, has had an impact on broader diplomatic issues as well as on the management of the transatlantic political economy. Consultation between the EU and the United States in international institutions such as the United Nations has grown in intensity, assisted by the strengthening of coordination between EU member states in such multilateral contexts (Laatikainen and K. Smith 2006). Within the EU, the institutional changes that have produced the EEAS and the HRVP, as well as the establishment of special representatives for particular areas of conflict, have provided a more secure basis for transatlantic policy coordination.

But there are severe limits to this coordination, primarily because of the persistence of strong national diplomatic relations between EU member states and the United States. In other words, here we can see an area of institutional competition, in which on many issues there are choices to be made about which channels are most useful and most secure for the pursuit of national or European policies – EU–US, US–member states or both. The aftermath of '9/11' itself produced an intensification of diplomatic coordination, accompanied by the growth of new links in areas such as intelligence and policing (Rees and Aldrich 2005; Dannreuther and Peterson 2006; Rees 2006, 2009). But here again the intensification of activity at the EU–US level was accompanied by parallel and sometimes conflicting developments at the bilateral level between EU member states and the United States. While it is quite appropriate to point to an intensification of EU–US diplomatic institutions, both formal and informal, it is not possible to see these as the consistently predominant mode of institutional coordination on transatlantic diplomatic concerns. Indeed, both the Obama administration and the Trump administration displayed a certain amount of scorn for such coordination mechanisms as the annual summit meetings (M. Smith 2011a, 2021).

In security and defence policy, inevitably, the institutionalization of EU–US coordination is most recent and most challenged. The growth of CSDP in the late 1990s and early 2000s created concerns in the United States that there might ensue the 'three Ds': decoupling, duplication and discrimination (Albright 1998; see Chapter 1). From the US point of view (and from that of a number of EU member states, most notably the UK), the danger was that a new institutional competitor might be created for NATO, an organization whose continued existence was under question in the aftermath of the Cold War. Despite the fact that in all EU treaties it has been explicit that CSDP would not undermine NATO, the concern has not been banished. Indeed, the promotion of 'strategic autonomy' in the context of the EU's Global Strategy after 2016 raised it in a new and more directly challenging way (see Chapters 7 and 8), while the Trump administration openly discussed a reduction of the US commitment to NATO if the Europeans did not raise their contributions. During the 1990s and early 2000s such frictions were muted by the development of arrangements for the sharing of NATO assets under the so-called 'Berlin Plus' agreements, and by the way in which a division of labour grew up around successive NATO and EU peacekeeping operations in the Balkans and elsewhere (Howorth 2005, 2007, 2014; Webber 2007: see also Chapters 7 and 8). While these issues will be dealt with more fully later, the point here is that in areas of security and defence policy, the institutional development of the Euro-American system has not been based on the centrality of the EU–US relationship. As compared with the political economy of the system, there is a higher degree of institutional competition and overlap, with greater uncertainty about the ways in which institutions interlock on specific policy issues.

The impact of change

The discussion in Chapter 1, with its 'historical' focus, dealt inevitably with processes of change, in both the long and the medium term, within the Euro-American system. The purpose here is not to repeat that discussion, but to point out in more analytical terms what has been the impact of change on the system and on the ways it operates. The discussion centres on differential patterns of change in three key areas of Euro-American relations; incidentally, and importantly, it also uncovers important variations in the impact of the European Union and of EU–US relations in the three areas.

The first area – or arena – of change is the political economy. Since the establishment of the EEC in the 1950s, this has been an area of persistent and perhaps fundamental change. The range of actors involved in this area has multiplied, its scope has expanded, and the boundaries of the policy arena have shifted, sometimes in dramatic ways. Not only this, but here is an area in which the establishment and development of the EU has had profound consequences: first for policymaking both in Europe and in the United States and second for the ways the policy area is managed. The 'balance of power' in this area has shifted inexorably towards the collective EU position, though it has not of course created a position of EU dominance. Rather, it has created a twofold process: on the one side of policy convergence under the pressure of interdependence and common concerns, and on the other of competition between public and private actors for influence and advantage. This has in turn led to the elaboration of institutional arrangements both in the EU and in the United States and at the transatlantic level with the aim of managing and profiting from this process of 'competitive cooperation' (M. Smith 1998), such that the density of transatlantic institutions and of 'transatlantic governance' is intense and highly significant in terms of the global political economy. The result is a situation of intense but still uneven interdependence, in which the EU and the United States operate as 'adversarial partners' at both the transatlantic and the global level. While this remains the case, it has been profoundly modified by the changes taking place in the global political economy as a whole, with the impact of 'rising powers' led by China, the growth of globalized production structures and the impact of information and communication technologies.

In the second arena – that of diplomacy – the picture is more mixed. This is an area in which initial analysis shows the United States still to be in a leading position and able to take the initiative both at the transatlantic level and – more tellingly – at the global one. The range of participants here is more restricted than in the political economy, and more of those that do participate are governmental in the broad sense. A crucial element in this arena is the relative underdevelopment until the end of the 1990s of the EU's diplomatic apparatus, and the continuing influence in EU positions of strongly held and independently pursued national policies. The boundaries of this area have been expanded greatly with EU enlargement and the new fluidity following the end of the Cold War, but this has in many cases produced new uncertainties about EU collective action and its consolidation. Institutions to manage this area have been developed, but they are still subject to fluctuations in salience and effectiveness and to the possibility of defection by those with 'special relationships' of various kinds within the system. Here, the EU is not alone on the diplomatic or the transatlantic stage, but there has been a significant move towards policies of 'soft balancing' by EU member states in respect of the United States, facilitated by the development of the EU's diplomatic machinery and practices. The establishment of the EEAS and the HRVP as key EU diplomatic actors has underlined such tendencies, especially when combined with the limited diplomatic resources of many of the EU's new (post-2004) member states and their consequent preference to take advantage of the 'political economies of scale' afforded by the new EU system of diplomacy.

The third area – security and defence – shows a balance skewed even more firmly in favour of the United States – and in favour of institutional mechanisms that are not necessarily associated with EU–US relations. There is a long history in this area of institutional arrangements that have been deliberately kept separate from European integration processes, specifically NATO. The participants here are almost entirely governmental, and the mechanisms for their coordination or competition are almost exclusively intergovernmental in nature – even within the EU, where CSDP remains largely intergovernmental in character, at least for the time being (Mahnke, Rees, and Thompson2004; Howorth 2007, 2014, 2017; Webber 2007). The impact of '9/11' and the 'war on terror' changed this position at the margins, but not fundamentally – and as Chapter 1 has noted, more recent crises have not led to a transformation of the EU's capacities in the 'hard-security' field.

For EU–US relations, this means that the advantage held by the United States in terms of 'hard power' and its capacity to mobilize it remains a trump card, although the EU has begun to infringe on this predominance in certain tightly specified areas of activity. Given the institutional competition between the EU and other bodies within Europe itself, and the predominance of American 'hard power', it might be suggested that this is an area that for the foreseeable future will remain contested and uncertain for the Europeans themselves, let alone for the Euro-American system in general. As in the area of political economy, however, such a conclusion has to be seen in the context of change at the global level, with the rise of new regional and potentially global powers such as China, and the reassertion of Russian geopolitical aims in Eastern Europe, the Middle East and Central Asia (see Chapters 7–9).

Figure 2.2 attempts to summarize the arguments about processes within the Euro-American system that have been advanced in this section of the chapter, by bringing together the four elements outlined earlier: policymaking in the EU and the United States, transatlantic policymaking, institutional development and change. Many of the chapters that follow will pursue the general arguments raised here. The important conclusion at this stage is that the development of EU–US

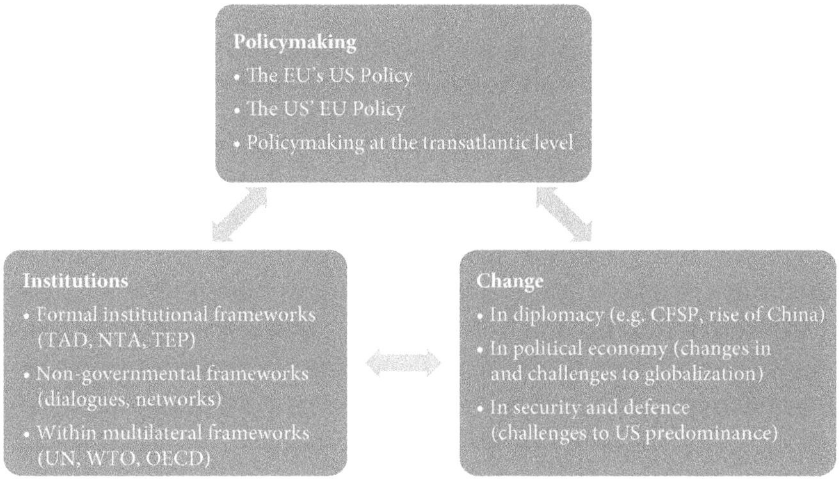

Figure 2.2 Processes, institutions and policies in the 'Euro-American system'.

relations within the context of the Euro-American system is essentially uneven and in some areas strongly contested. This differential picture of development and contestation is fundamental to the evolution of the boundaries, scope and rules of the system, to the institutions operating within it and to the political patterns produced within it.

Overview and conclusion

This chapter has set out to deal with the Euro-American system in an analytical manner, in contrast to the 'historical' narrative presented in Chapter 1. The two chapters are of course complementary, and this chapter has made use of many of the examples noted in Chapter 1. The chapter has dealt with:

- The key components of the Euro-American system and how they relate to each other. In doing so, it has uncovered a system of mixed participation in which strong elements of state and governmental power coexist with the development of transgovernmental and transnational relations in a 'mixed actor' system.
- The dynamics of the Euro-American system and their implications for policies and institutions within the system. This exploration has revealed many dimensions of the competition, convergence and crisis that lie at the heart of this book, and that create key issues of policy formulation and management.
- The challenge of policymaking in both the EU and the United States in the context of the Euro-American system, creating issues of coordination,

institutionalization and the response to change. The EU's 'US policy' and the United States' 'EU policy' are wide-ranging, complex and difficult to manage, especially in the context of change at the global and the transatlantic level.

The overall conclusion from the chapter is that the Euro-American system demonstrates many of the key characteristics of a 'mixed actor system', in which there are coexisting and often competing tendencies towards competition and convergence, and in which the study of different policy areas produces different impressions of the key institutions and processes of change within the system. EU–US relations have become a central if not a predominant part of the system, and this means that the study of EU–US relations must form a predominant part of our understanding of the system as a whole, bringing together elements of power (including structural power, domination and dependence), interdependence and integration, and cooperation. But EU–US relations are not yet identical with the system itself (and they correspond rather less after events such as the UK's departure from the EU), and this is an important consideration in the analysis of policy areas relating to defence and security in particular. The following chapters take this starting point as given, and will go on to explore in detail a range of issues within the Euro-American system with the aim of testing and illustrating these broad conclusions. Chapter 3 begins this analysis by focusing on politics and policymaking in the EU and the United States.

Chapter 3

Institutions and policymaking in the EU and the United States

Introduction

Comparing the United States and the European Union is not unlike comparing apples with oranges and creates some challenges for the casual observer. But just as comparing different types of fruit will yield at least some relevant results –contrary to what the idiom suggests – comparing different types of systems of governance will also offer instructive insights into how these systems operate. These insights will also allow for a better understanding of why these systems interact in the way they do in the Euro-American system of transatlantic relations that was introduced in Chapter 2. The distinct nature of the two sides requires the flexibility to think of them in different terms yet understand how they operate at various times in similar ways. This chapter will investigate the European governance system, linking the EU to the national political systems that it consists of, and highlight some characteristics that set them apart. It will then look at the institutional outline of the system of government in the United States and at some of its peculiarities in terms of institutions and politics as well as social values and public policy. Finally, the chapter will reflect on what the benefits of a comparative approach are and how they help us understand the interaction of these two systems, which is often characterized by both cooperative and competitive dynamics.

An understanding of the political structures and dynamics of interaction is important in a wide range of policy areas analysed in this volume, for example to determine the various roles of executive, legislature and judiciary in finding common ground in a trade agreement, visa rules or sanctions. These structures interact in cooperative ways, but can also act to create competitors, for example in agricultural and industrial subsidies on both sides of the Atlantic. Close collaboration in crisis, as demonstrated by the European Commission and the Biden administration in their coordinated responses to the Russian war of aggression against Ukraine, highlights specific roles actors can play in critical situations.

The European Union – a supranational system of governance and policymaking

In the study of the EU, the statement that the EU 'is not a state' is almost a truism: it is repeated frequently to remind the analyst that despite looking in some respects very much like a state, the EU differs fundamentally from other actors in the international system. Nevertheless, it is a good starting point for attempting to compare this system of governance. The EU has no army. No EU police would be knocking on your door if you were engaged in criminal activity. However, the EU does many things related to these core activities of any state. The EU has facilitated structures in which the police forces of its member states exchange information about criminal activity and cooperate in the training of police officers. It also facilitates the cooperation of the armed forces of its member states, albeit to a much lesser degree. At the same time, the EU makes laws that apply throughout all its members and are integrated in structures of judicial review that ensure the more uniform application of these laws. This seems more state-like than the generic term 'system of governance' appears to suggest. For this reason, the EU has been called a quasi-federation by some scholars, while others have used the term 'treaty federalism' for this system of inter-state cooperation (Hueglin 2013: p. 194). Comparing the EU thus means understanding the structures of governance at the EU level in Brussels, but also the inter-state relations of its members.

The EU executive

The EU as a governance structure rests on an intricate foundation of legal, economic and political relations between its independent member states (Nugent 2017). As the UK has demonstrated in 2020, a member state may leave the EU, even if it is a politically and economically difficult process. In comparison with the United States and its constitution, it is clear that American federalism is much less reversible, and no serious attempts to reverse it have taken place in the last century. Nevertheless, the EU treaties are not without political force. Member states frequently are found in breach of their obligations and are fined for it (European Commission 2012, 2019). The treaties set up an institutional system that is partly recognizable in the context of comparative politics: there is a parliament, the European Parliament (EP), with powers comparable to other legislative bodies. There is an executive, the European Commission, that manages the spending, proposes draft legislation and implements legislation. But the EU also has the European Council and the Council of the European Union, two bodies consisting of representatives of the member states, which directly participate in the making of policies in all areas of the EU's activity. As alluded to earlier, the EU has a high court, the Court of Justice of the European Union, which decides fundamental disputes on EU legislation and its applicability. The EU also has an independent central bank, the European Central Bank, much like all modern states with their own currency. The interaction of these institutions, a term with a specific legal meaning in the EU treaties, is at the heart of the multi-level governance process underpinning European integration (Hooghe and Marks 2001, Nugent 2017).

As summarized earlier, the EU's institutional structure is centred around a core of three institutions that interact to produce legal rules and other policy decisions: the European Parliament, the European Commission and the Council of the European Union.

The European Parliament

The EP is elected directly by citizens across all member states based on national lists and parties. Once the currently 720 members of the EP, or MEPs, take up their seats, most of them will belong to one of the political groups that capture the variety of political orientations across the continent. The largest groups are a consortium of Christian Democratic parties, the European People's Party and a group of Progressives and Social Democrats, known as the S&D group. But there are five other groups representing centrist liberal parties, a group of nativist-populist challenger parties, green and left-wing, as well as a growing group of right-wing conservative parties. This complexity of political groups may be confusing at first but reflects many of the national parliaments in European democracies, which are mostly also elected based on proportional representation. Like these national consensus system parliaments, the EP operates through collaboration in a committee system that involves a wide range of political groups in the decision-making process. Nevertheless, most decisions are taken through the collaboration of the two largest political groups plus additional support on varying issues (Hix, Noury, and Roland 2007, Hösli 1997, Mühlböck 2019, Ripoll Servent 2017). The powers of the EP, traditionally much weaker and advisory compared to national parliaments, have expanded considerably since its first direct election in 1979 (Ripoll Servent 2017). The powers the EP has in each policy area are generally determined by the treaties. They now encompass a wide set of legislative powers on, for example, the EU's budget and the regulation of the EU internal market. Its powers are still considerably weaker than national parliaments in not only issues of foreign and security policy and domestic security but also social issues such as pensions and health care. In general, policy issues that touch upon national preferences of social organization and national security remain less influenced by the EU's competences. This is reflected in the remit of the EP: it gives the parliament an equal say as 'co-legislator' on the internal market, environmental policies, agriculture and consumer protection, to name a few. Nevertheless, the EP is also a normal political arena, where the trend of populist challenger parties at the member state level is mirrored in the EP's composition and voting behaviour (Hix, Noury, and Roland 2018).

The European Commission

On the executive side of the European Union, there is at first sight a more easily comparable institution: the European Commission, the EU's core administrative structure (Bauer and Trondal 2015: p. 83). The Commission's roles are in a lot of ways the 'everyday' management of European integration. These roles derive from its right to initiate legislative proposals, its role in monitoring and if need be enforcing the rules that are in place, as well as managing the funds the EU spends. Its organization resembles the ministerial structures of the member states, being structured in policy-focused units with a senior administrative lead and, at the top, a politically experienced and appointed figure not unlike a minister, the commissioner. The European Commission operates in many ways like a government cabinet. The president of the Commission leads its meetings and has more general responsibilities. There are more senior 'ministers', the so-called vice-presidents with coordinating functions. And then there are regular commissioners with responsibility for a specific policy field like trade or agriculture. An unusual aspect of the Commission is that despite their role requiring independence from the member states, each commissioner comes from senior political roles in the member states. Jointly, acting as the College of Commissioners and with collective responsibility, they are meant to lead the EU's administration in an independent manner. This expectation is often illustrated with a phrase from the treaty, which designates the Commission as the 'Guardian of the Treaties', that is, the body upholding European law and acting in the interest of the Union as a whole. Nevertheless, commissioners informally also represent their member state in the deliberations of the Commission. This highlights the middle ground the Commission treads between independence as an executive body and its role as an agent of the member states (Pollack 1997; Wonka 2007). In addition to these competing demands, commissioners will also be of different party-political affiliations, having been elected to office by large majorities in the EP after nomination by the national governments. In day-to-day business, the commissioners are politically responsible for their departments and the work they carry out: drafting legislative proposals, reviewing and evaluating policy, managing (i.e. spending and controlling) EU budget funds, reviewing member states activities and gathering information, briefing on specific issues of the day and many other activities that are an international version of the routine tasks of ministerial structures throughout the world. The complexity of international trade and security policies also means that they are usually inter-departmental questions within the institutions, requiring a balance between trade and environmental, or security and industrial policy questions, to name a few. In Chapter 4, the regulatory approach of the Commission is highlighted in trade relations with the United States and the rest of the world.

The Council of the EU

The EU's legislative triangle would not be complete without the Council of the European Union. The Council embodies the greatest difference to national political systems. It gathers representatives of the member state governments, from ministerial level downward in the political-administrative hierarchy. The Council's main role derives from its position as co-legislator with the EP, and in some policy areas as a dominant legislative actor, as well as being responsible for the EU's international agreements (see Chapter 4 for its role in trade). It is involved in the full range of European policies and is the core driver of negotiations: the Council isn't as much a permanent institution like a government cabinet, but acts as a permanent meeting and negotiating space for the member states of the EU in interaction with the other EU institutions. It is jointly with the EP responsible for agreeing the Union's annual budget. Despite its executive nature, in the sense that representatives in the Council always belong to the executives of the member states, many of its tasks resemble a chamber of a bicameral parliament (Mühlböck 2019). It is the Council that agrees the majority of European legislation together with the EP in an intricate legislative procedure. In foreign and security policy but also in some aspects of competition law and internal market exemptions, the Council can still be seen as dominant vis-à-vis the EP, illustrating the limits of using traditional categories of comparative politics to analyse European Union institutions. The Council is also a type of executive body when its decisions relate to the member states' governments themselves. Its internal structure is an interesting expression of the negotiated nature of European governance – various thematic meetings of ministers take place on a regular basis. The most central bodies in this structure are the meeting of EU ambassadors of the member states and their deputies, the Committee of Permanent Representatives (or COREPER). In this meeting of senior ambassadors, the many lines of negotiation are combined and managed. The ambassadors and their deputies continuously attempt to develop solutions arising out of discussions above them at ministerial level and below them at administrative levels. It is also here that many cross-issue linkages can develop and be used to find negotiated agreements through log-rolling or other processes. Not all issues can be resolved, however, and some are specifically reserved to be discussed at the political level by ministers in order to find agreement. It also falls to the ambassadors' meeting or their deputies to negotiate with the EP as part of the legislative process. In order to find agreement between the variety of national interests represented in the Council and the EP's political groups, this process is formalized in the so-called conciliation parts of the EU's ordinary legislative procedure.

The three institutions discussed earlier interact jointly to produce EU legislation in nearly all areas of EU regulatory activity, even if their roles occasionally vary depending on the subject area. The best example here is the role of the EP in trade agreements, which are negotiated by the European Commission with a negotiating mandate from the Council. The EP joins the process through a vote of approval/disapproval rather than at earlier stages like in other internal market matters.

The European Council

On top of the triangle of legislative activity sits another, arguably the most important institution of the European Union, the European Council. Just like in the Council of the EU it is the representatives of member states meeting here, but at the highest political level. Each member state is represented by the head of state or government depending on each state's constitutional structure, for example, the French president as a head of state or the German chancellor as a head of government. The European Council deals with the most political and arguably important matters in European governance, such as the seven-year multiannual budget framework, which sets out the spending limits and allocation across policy areas. The treaty also tasks it with providing the 'necessary impetus for [the Union's] development' as well as defining 'the general political directions and priorities thereof' (Art. 15, Treaty of the European Union). Driven by the increasing importance of the executives in policymaking and the many crises facing Europeans, the European Council has become more involved in everyday EU decision-making than the treaty's general language suggests (Puetter 2012, 2014). The European Council meetings are prepared and chaired by its president, chosen by the heads of state or government for a term of two-and-a-half years.

As already hinted at earlier, one of the elements tying the EU together in regulatory terms is the role of the Court of Justice of the European Union, which is the highest judicial body of the EU and reviews the application of EU rules by EU institutions and the member states. Through a system called 'preliminary reference' national courts can ask the ECJ for interpretation of European rules in specific cases that develop into a set of precedents that matter greatly for the uniform interpretation of law across the Union. It also promotes a close and frequent interaction between national and European courts and has been seen as a core driving force of European integration (Alter 2008, Kelemen and Schmidt 2011). Over time, ECJ decisions have strongly promoted the integration of European markets into a more coherent environment for business and citizens.

Other relevant structures of European governance

Another institution playing a central role in the deep economic integration of a core group of member states is the European Central Bank (ECB) and its role within the European system of central banks. While a strengthening of its institutional remit was visible beforehand, the financial crisis of 2009 accelerated the centrality of the ECB in European policy responses to crises (Verdun 2020; Schimmelfennig 2018: p. 979–80, see also Chapter 5). Early signs in the response to the economic effects of the public health emergency caused by the COVID-19 virus suggested that member states were ready to add additional borrowing by the European Commission into the arsenal of expansive economic policy to respond to the economic consequences of the pandemic (European Commission 2021a). The ECB's independence remains high, despite being continually negotiated through its accountability mechanisms (Heldt and Müller 2021).

The diplomatic system of the European Union is another set of actors of relevance to the Euro-American system (Smith, Keukeleire and Vanhoonacker 2016). The EU's 'foreign policy chief' is the High Representative of the Union for Foreign Affairs and Security Policy who is also one of several vice-presidents of the European Commission. The HR/VP, as the role is commonly abbreviated, is also the chair of the Foreign Affairs Council of the Council of the EU, that is, the role links the executive arm of the Commission with the member state negotiations in the Council. The High Representative is supported by the European External Action Service (EEAS). The EU's diplomatic service was set up through a merger of different services in Brussels and maintains a network of delegations across the globe (Morgenstern-Pomorski 2018). The EEAS is a key actor in the EU's Common Foreign and Security Policy as well as the EU's Common Security and Defence Policy. How these institutions impact the foreign and security policy of the EU is illustrated in more detail in Chapter 7.

While thinking about the institutional arrangements at the EU level, it is easy to forget the centrality of member states' structures and domestic politics for the functioning of European policy processes. In order to grasp this national level of the multi-level politics of European integration, a brief look at the member states and their politics is necessary. With 27 individual countries as members, diversity in the European Union is to be expected and makes generalizations about European political systems rather difficult. There are a number of features, however, that at least a majority of European Union member states share. Most EU member states have consensus democracy features in some of their institutional structures (see Table 3.1), such as constitutional courts with powers of review and proportional electoral systems that lead to governments formed by coalitions of two or more parties. Some of the most common examples of these types of democratic features are found in EU member states such as Austria, Belgium and Germany. This is not to overstress the dominance of these power-sharing institutions and proportional representation at elections. A member state like France not only has a semi-presidential system of governance but also uses a two-round plurality election rather than other more proportional institutional arrangements (Blais and Loewen 2009: p. 357). Many member states' governments however tend to come from coalition-based governments, and even those that do not have positions that are domestically negotiated before they enter into negotiations with other governments and supranational institutions at the EU level.

The domestic politics of the EU and its member states – separate, but connected

While European citizens still voice their support for European integration with 46 per cent in favour, and trust in the EU was at a 10-year high in 2021 (European Commission 2021), the public spheres of the member states have become more similar in the contestation of European integration. Populist radical parties on the left and even more so on the right have appeared, and some have established

Table 3.1 Overview of Three European Political Systems

	France	Germany	Czech Republic
Executive characteristics	Directly elected president with strong executive powers and prime minister elected by parliament	Ceremonial federal president as head of state and federal chancellor elected by parliamentary coalitions as chief executive.	Directly elected president and prime minister elected by parliament
	Centralized system with regional governance	Federal system with strong state governance	Centralized system of governance
Legislative characteristics	Bicameral national legislature – lower house (National Assembly) directly elected in single member plurality districts, upper house (Senate) elected indirectly by electors	Strong bicameral system with upper chamber (Bundesrat) representing state governments, proportional representation in lower house (Bundestag) elections, but mixed system between district and state party lists	Bicameral system – lower chamber (Chamber of Deputies) elected every four years , upper chamber (Senate) one-third elected every six years
Judiciary	Limited judicial review	Strong judicial review	Strong judicial review
Support for EU	Medium	High/Medium	Medium

themselves in European political systems (Bernhard and Kriesi 2021)). European integration has become a more and more contested question in the member states' politics driven by right- and left-wing populist fringes of the electorate (van Bohemen et al. 2019: 371–2). In an extreme form of contestation, Hungary's Viktor Orbán has used European funds to establish a stranglehold on the state institutions, and Hungary has consequently become the first European member state that is no longer considered a democracy (Freedom House 2020) and has been classed as only 'partly free' by Freedom House (2023). Due to the nature of the EU as a creation of the member states, the EU struggles to act against members that do not fulfil its own rule of law requirements (Kelemen 2020).

European elections, that is, elections in all the member states to determine the make-up of the EP, are second order elections. A lower number of voters participate in these elections compared to other elections, and they are more likely to express preferences for a wide variety of parties as there is no European government to form as in national elections. In national elections, European policies only occasionally come to the forefront of political debate, even though in the long term, European crises appear to be major issues of contention in the national public spheres as well. And while Euroscepticism is a minority position, it is engrained at both national and European level in terms of parties and positions (Treib 2020: p. 11). This institutionalized contestation of the very nature of EU governance is a fluctuating, yet relevant characteristic of EU politics.

An important criticism towards policymaking at the European level has been the lack of Europe-wide public debates on important policy choices and the fact that Europe retains many national public spheres that dominate the process of opinion and policymaking (Trenz 2008: p. 9). As major international crises and developments impact the majority of member states, even if often in asymmetric ways, the European debate is not as disjointed as in the past. But substantive debates on the same issues in national public spheres also mean political decisions are seen purely as outcomes of negotiation between member state leaders (de Wilde 2019: p. 1028). Nevertheless, as more competence to set policy shifts to the European Union, more media and public attention has developed throughout the member states (Statham 2010: p. 285–86). This increase in awareness of the EU as a political entity is relevant also for the assessment of the level of democracy and public participation in European decisions, another major focus of criticism levelled at the EU institutions.

One event that highlights the flashpoints of democratic and legitimacy challenges faced by the EU has been Brexit. The UK's decision to leave the European Union with only limited remaining legal ties has had a significant impact on the EU as well as the UK as a formerly long-standing member of the club. It also highlighted the many different objectives of EU membership that European countries have held; some have seen the EU as a counterbalance to US dominance. After a popular advisory referendum, the UK government gave notice of withdrawal to the European Union (Prime Minister's Office 2017) and has since been in continuous negotiations to ensure an orderly framework of withdrawal and future collaboration. Without going into the minute details of the process at the domestic level in the UK and the back and forth of negotiations, 'Brexit' has highlighted that, while politically reversible, the cost of exit from the European Union remains high (Bulmer and Quaglia 2018). In order to maintain trading relationships and stay integrated into European supply chains, regulatory equivalence has had to be guaranteed and demonstrated. This contradicted the UK government's motivation of regaining regulatory power and flexibility that had been transferred to the EU earlier. The UK political and administrative system has undertaken efforts to balance out these competing objectives, but nevertheless the arrangement between the UK and the EU is a clear break from any form of membership or deep association. Key issues arising from Brexit concern the rights of citizens that have so far enjoyed freedom of movement across the EU, which has been ended. Access to each other's markets in goods and services has become more limited, and the question of border control between Northern Ireland as a part of the UK and the Republic of Ireland, an EU member state, was only partially solved. The exit of the UK from the EU also had significant transatlantic consequences, as with the UK a country with strong links to the United States in security policy and defence has left the EU's decision-making processes. The effects of this are difficult to assess in detail at this time but are likely to be noticeable as one avenue of collaboration and exchange is closed.

European public policies – redistribution, regulation and more

Since the policymaking powers of the EU stem from its beginning in specific economic spheres, this is reflected in the policies it controls. The EU's powers are particularly pronounced in trade and in regulatory policies, that is, policies that have an effect on the EU's internal market (Meunier and Nicolaïdis 2019, Kelemen 2011). Health care, social protection and taxes as well as public order measures such as gun control all remain within the powers of the individual member state. Nevertheless, the EU does make rules on cooperation within these fields; for example Europeans travelling to another EU country can make use of the public health care system via a European health insurance card. In the overall field of health care, however, this is a minor adaptation of what remain in fact national systems (Brooks and Geyer 2020).

One area in which the EU is engaged in what can be considered redistributive policies is agriculture. For a long time, agriculture spending has been a significant element of spending in the EU's budget. In the 2021 EU budget, the Common Agricultural Policy (CAP), as it is known officially, consumed roughly one-third of all spending. Agricultural subsidies and health and safety rules in food are frequent flashpoints for EU–US trade as both actors engage in a managed competition (Sbragia 2010, Skogstad 2002, Baylis et al. 2008). While a large item, the CAP is only one of a set of redistributive policies of the EU. Another set of spending lines are to be found in the Regional and Cohesion policy. These funds are more explicitly targeted at reducing the economic disparities that exist across the EU, even though there are also still funds going to regions that have 90 per cent of the average EU gross domestic product. Regional and Cohesion policies are therefore not only aimed at supporting poorer regions over others but rather are widespread funding measures that reach all the EU's regions to varying degrees. Over the course of the new budgeting period from 2021 to 2027, the EU has allocated 392 bn EUR to Cohesion policy (European Commission 2021b).

Beyond spending policies, the EU legislates in areas that relate to economic activity across its member states' borders. The economic area that is made up of the EU member states' economies is referred to as the 'internal market', or sometimes 'single market'. To enable the smooth functioning of this economic area, the EU regulates in a vast array of sectors, such as pharmaceutical and chemical products, machinery and motor vehicles but also financial services. One of the core functions of the European Commission discussed earlier is to ensure that member states abide by the rules of the internal market, and the Commission frequently challenges member states that fall short in the implementation of common rules through infringement proceedings.

The United States of America – the federal example

The core defining feature of the United States (US) from a comparative perspective with the European Union is that the United States is a state based on a constitutional document that sets up a republican form of democratic government. All parts of the state derive their authority from the US Constitution, which itself was dedicated in the name of 'We, the people', and derive legitimacy directly or indirectly from elections. Without going deeper into political theory, the United States is therefore a fully formed federal state, made up by the union of component states and the people that live in it. And while the framers behind the system of government looked to other federations across the globe for their inspiration, the US federation has since become a, if not the, major focus of understanding multi-level systems of governance elsewhere. Using approaches from political science such as comparative politics and federalism is fitting and applied practice for both the United States but also the EU and some of its members. The United States, however, displays a particular mix of characteristics that sets it apart from the European Union as a governance structure. In the following sections, we will look at some of the defining characteristics of the US political system: its specific institutional structure and its strong separation of powers at the central level, as well as the division of powers between the federal government and the governments of the individual states that make up the United States and have a larger role in the regulation of society than is commonly assumed.

The structure of US government

The US Constitution sets up a system of governance that splits the execution of governing tasks into three separate branches: an executive branch in the office of the president, a legislative branch in the form of a bicameral Congress, and the judiciary with the United States Supreme Court at its pinnacle. With this division, the United States represents one of the clearest examples of a separation of powers regime available to students of political science. Like all separation of powers regimes, however, the separation is not (and is not meant to be) perfect. The three branches interact to produce policy and legislation, and indeed also often interact to stop each other from producing policy (Tsebelis 2000). This interaction is often referred to as a system of 'checks and balances' introduced into the US system of government to avoid any one of the three branches dominating over the others. While for many academics this approach is the key to ensuring stability in the system, it often represents a frustrating element to political observers, and citizens, keen on decisions and a clearer categorization of responsibilities and lines of accountability. This is especially the case in the United States where two competing clusters of comparative political analysis developed by Lijphart (2012) coincide: on the one hand there are many characteristics that are majoritarian, that is, following the will of the simple plurality of voters – for example in the election of representatives. On the other hand, there are characteristics that show a streak of consensus democracy, that is, a system where larger majorities are needed, and coalition building is an important feature of politics. Consensus democracy is a category developed to describe political systems that balance majority decisions with strong minority rights' protection and can be applied to some European states (see earlier). These features interact with the Euro-American system of governance in uneven ways, depending on which policy area and category of relationships is the focus of attention.

Congress – a powerful bicameral legislature

Congress is the name given to the institutions of the legislative branch of the United States, including the House of Representatives and the Senate. The US legislative branch shows signs of strong bicameralism according to Lijphart (2012). The two chambers are elected on slightly different bases of legitimacy and maintain different sets of powers, even if collaboration is needed for many political decisions. The upper house, the US Senate, is a chamber designed to be a more deliberative body and sees a slower pace of change of electoral fortunes with a third of its seats up for election every two years (Senate.gov 2021). The 100 senators serve terms of 6 years. Senators represent the state in its entirety for their term, and generally incumbents stay in office for extended periods. Until 1913, senators were elected by the states, showing that traditionally they had a separate basis of legitimacy as representatives of states within federal decision-making. The lower house of the US legislature, the House of Representatives, is bound in much more frequent election cycles in 435 districts across the country every 2 years and a clear majoritarian organization (Cushman 2006). The districts that form the basis of the House elections are based on population and are therefore frequently adjusted in line with census data to account for population movement, making it a more dynamic and responsive system of representation in comparison to many European cases. The House of Representatives and its specific powers make it a driving force of legislative proposals in the US political system and therefore also of the policies that maintain the regulatory and funding elements of transatlantic links.

The two houses need to work together to agree on legislation although both are sovereign to their own intricate and historically layered rules of procedure and internal organization as well as other decisions taken independently of each other. The Senate, for example, approves international treaties negotiated by the executive (for more details on the process see Chapter 4), and its approval is also required for many of the most senior government appointments for posts in the executive. Both treaty-making and senior appointments, for example in the Defense or State departments, have a clear and direct impact on the transatlantic agenda even if they serve in the first instance a domestic purpose. The House, among other powers, has the right to initiate revenue bills, or taxation, an essential power for government income and therefore its ability to act. For the passage of legislative proposals, Senate approval is required. This is essentially the core nature of a bicameral legislature: both houses in principle need to approve legislation for it to be passed. As both houses are unlikely to have the exact same ideas about what a specific law should contain, a mechanism of negotiation between both houses allows for negotiation to identify what law can find approval in both houses. Should both houses pass legislation, the system of 'checks and balances' means that after the president signs it, the executive branch is tasked with implementing legislation through its departments and agencies. In this abstract description of political processes, at nearly every step, interests, regulation and outcomes that impact the transatlantic relation can occur, making a detailed understanding of current trends in Washington, DC, a major task for European nations' diplomatic services (as noted in Chapter 2).

Box 3.1 The Inflation Reduction Act and the international effects of domestic policies

In 2022, the US Congress passed a significant piece of legislation that addressed a number of domestic issues: health care, energy and adaptation to climate change, as well as tax provisions including tax enforcement. The legislation contains funding for climate change policies, such as lowering carbon emissions in a wide range of economic sectors and support for clean energy sources. It was described as the largest investment in climate change adaptation to date (Bistline, Mehrote, and Wolfram 2023) but includes a vast array of provisions beyond it. In health care, the legislation provides for price negotiation in government-run health care as well as inflation caps on prices of medicine and is likely to result in significant savings for consumers as well as the federal budget. The IRA also aims at raising revenue through a minimum corporate tax and funding to enhance tax collection capacities in the US government (McKinsey 2022). Additional funding becomes available if companies follow specific labour practices, such as apprenticeships (Bistline, Mehrote, and Wolfram . 2023), illustrating the wider reach of the legislation beyond inflation. The origins of the legislation were in the Biden administration's 'Build Back Better' agenda on domestic reform, which had run into opposition in Congress. It was enacted after protracted negotiations in the House and the Senate including negotiations between supportive and critical members of the Democratic Party. It was passed with votes along partisan lines in both chambers; in the Senate Vice-President Harris cast a tie-breaking vote in favour.

While most of the policy provisions were seen favourably in Europe, there was criticism of specific aspects of the legislation (Jurkovic 2023). European politicians criticized 'Buy American' provisions and proceeded to relax state aid rules on green energy out of concern that companies might invest instead in the United States (EP 2022). The EP's report also highlights a direct EU–US comparison can be misleading as, for example subsidies for electric cars are decided at the member state level and therefore do not appear in EU figures. There are also a number of conditions under which EU companies may benefit from the provisions in the United States, making the picture more complex than a simple subsidy competition. In an article on the transatlantic effects of the energy provisions, Crawford argues: 'The Biden administration's geopolitical internationalism is at odds with its geo-economic nationalism. The fact remains, however, that Europe is unlikely to be severely affected by the IRA' (Crawford 2023).

The dynamics of the US parliament are, however, driven not only by institutional structure but also by party politics. The United States is a clear example of a two-party system, and dominance of one party over another in each of the chambers has important effects for the ability to set policy. Even though parties other than the Democratic and Republican parties exist, and office holders also appear as Independents, the competitive dynamics between the parties are an essential feature of the operation of US democracy. While the parties are considerably less strictly structured in terms of manifesto and organization compared to many European counterparts, party cohesion is still a relevant factor of parliamentary voting behaviour also in the United States (Curry and Lee 2020: 7–10). Nevertheless, despite increasing cohesion of parties and polarization in Congress, bipartisan support is still an essential element of most successful lawmaking (Curry and Lee 2019: 59). This also implies that members are still more able and likely than most of their European counterparts to defy party lines.

The US executive – a limitless presidency?

When studying the executive in the US political system, the US presidency is understandably the focus of attention, even if the notion of the executive is much wider than the office of the president. Its powerful international political role captures the attention of observers around the globe and makes it of key importance for European allies. US presidential elections are followed closely in a way that no other domestic political contest is broadcast. One of the reasons is that the office's powers have expanded considerably alongside the role of the United States in global politics since the First World War. The president's role as top military decision-maker alone guarantees worldwide attention. Security policy decisions by the office holder have a large impact on other countries, even if the decisions are not to do with enemies but allies. In this 'high politics' with direct impact on the Euro-American system, reallocations of troops within Europe, for example, are highly important political decisions for the strategic policy of a number of European countries. But beyond these headlines, the president's role is important in the management of the different parts of the US executive and more often than not goes unreported. A vast number of managerial governmental positions depend on the nomination by the presidency and subsequent approval of the US Senate. Somewhat more attention is paid to the nomination process when it concerns the federal judiciary, even though its impact on the transatlantic agenda is less immediate. This ability to influence the day-to-day management of the executive through nominees has become a hotly contested issue even beyond the core executive departments and now concerns many governmental agencies that are built on specific (scientific) expertise but are run by political appointees like the National Oceanic and Atmospheric Administration or the Environmental Protection Agency. But also, away from individuals, the presidential role in relation to managing specialized administrative actors is ever increasing (Workman 2015). This is particularly visible in areas of regulation where scientific insights meet politicization, such as environmental protection. Many of these executive agencies deal with matters of the low politics of the Euro-American space, with impact on the regulation of production, trade, immigration and travel to name a few.

The judiciary and its increasing politicization

As a third power in the governance system of the United States, the court system at the federal level plays an essential role in the political system. The Supreme Court of the United States (SCOTUS) at its apex has shaped and continues to shape the outcomes of the system on a vast array of matters, including immigration, health care, workers' rights and gun ownership regulation to only mention a few salient issues in the domestic politics of the United States. As the US Constitution is a rigid written framework of governance that is not easily changed or challenged, the interpretation of these basic rules alongside the issue of who gets to choose the judges who interpret constitutional rules have become a focal point of political competition. The Supreme Court consists of a chief justice and eight associate justices, nominated by the president and approved by the Senate. While focusing on the domestic role of the court in this chapter, it is important to bear in mind that the effects of domestic legal and political power frequently reach beyond the domestic intent of the constitutional design in both the United States and the EU. The Supreme Court is also a focal point for partisan conflict over institutional rules that has continued to grow as established mechanisms of nomination and appointment are contested. This is seen for example in the debate around nominations to the court in the final year of a presidential term. Under what conditions the Senate is to give 'advice and consent' to a presidential nominee for the Supreme Court has become part of an exercise of political power by the majority. The Supreme Court is not the exclusive focus of this competition, as inferior federal courts also play an important role in the US policymaking process. US district courts, US courts of appeals and other tribunals are the larger part of the system of dispute resolution. In addition to the federal judiciary, there is the state-level judiciary of Supreme Courts and lower courts, as well as specialized courts that deal with aspects of the law. As state judiciaries are based on state constitutions, there is more variety as to structural design, institutional rules and practice.

The judicial reach of the Supreme Court is wide-ranging in the constitutional structure, with the court acting as the court of last resort in cases coming through the federal judicial system and state judicial systems as well as questions of individual rights. Because of the wide range of issues put to the SCOTUS for consideration, its decisions also indirectly shape the government and private actions with an impact on the EU–US system. As a matter of fact, scholars have already begun speaking of and analysing aspects of this system as a 'transatlantic community of law' (Fahey and Curtin 2014). Fahey and Curtin highlight the incorporation of legal arguments by the US Supreme Court into European jurisprudence, and regular meetings of both courts' members as easily visible examples of this connection, but only the beginning of 'transatlantic judicial communication' between the top judicial bodies (2014: p. ix–xi, Mak 2014). In the collection, some authors argue against the general understanding that transatlantic legal relations are generally light and irrelevant (Fahey and Curtin 2014: p. 2). In any event, these links certainly reflect at the very least a network of contacts and exchanges in the Euro-American system with an impact on public policy in both (see Chapter 2).

While politicization of the nomination and appointment of justices and societal reactions to rulings of the Supreme Court are not new developments, these dynamics have increased in relevance over the past decade. The refusal to allow a regular nomination process to then-president Obama and the subsequent nomination of conservative justices to the court during the Trump administration has resulted in a significant shift of the court's political position. The new majority has overturned a long-standing legal position on abortion, Roe v. Wade. The 2022 decision in Dobbs v. Jackson Women's Health Organization resulted in an end to the federal and therefore nationwide right to abortion. It has triggered a varied legal and political reaction, including changes to state constitutions to restrict as well as safeguard that right. It has also brought the issue back as a factor in current elections. Changing the status quo in a highly politicized part of the law that affects women will have long-term consequences for the way the court is viewed in society. It will also highlight the diversity of social rules prevalent in the United States as states respond to the changes in federal law by adopting local rules.

Federalism and American multi-level governance

One core recurring feature of the US system of government discussed in this chapter is the multi-level nature of political structures and how the constituent units play a formative role in American politics. US federalism is a complex arrangement of rights, powers and cooperation across levels of governance that have evolved in very specific historic conditions and retained some unusual features that impact US policymaking (Weissert 2011). Most observers from outside the United States are by now aware of the federal element in choosing the chief executive, that is, the electoral college and the locally determined, and therefore diverse, electoral rules of the various states. There is also a federal element to the implementation of a vast array of public policies making the division of powers across levels of government a central area of arguments about public policy as illustrated in Chapter 2 for the United States' 'EU policy'. It also ensures that, in terms of regulation, funding and the actual implementation of policies, levels of government are forced to cooperate, driving conflict in a variety of arenas (Konisky and Nolette 2022). This dynamic has nevertheless also led to a deep entrenchment of intergovernmental relations within the United States (Hueglin and Fenna 2015: p. 57). Even the legislature is an expression of federalism, although the most obvious link to the states was reformed with the 17th Amendment, which removed the state legislatures' power to elect senators and replaced it with direct elections by the people. The fully institutionalized judiciary of the states and their interaction with the federal court system may be less scrutinized from a European perspective but are nonetheless core for the enforcement of rules across the United States and matter for example for EU investors who need to manage relations with a state and local government. Across three branches of government, federalism plays a role in the way rules are made, by whom they are made and how they are interpreted and implemented. There is also the question of enforcement, which also requires cooperation between departments and agencies of the federal government and the states' executives. This complexity needs to be navigated as part of the Euro-American system by governmental as well as non-governmental actors.

Domestic politics of the United States

After looking at the institutional set up of the domestic political system of the United States, it is essential to also reflect on the politics that drive the institutional structure and the values behind political action at the individual and collective level. The domestic politics of the United States have seen long-term trends of polarization and significantly differ on a number of socio-political and economic issues when compared to European domestic spheres. In order to get an insight into this dynamic, it is useful to look at the views of the citizens of public institutions and the system of governance first and then look at some of the salient issues that drive political stances in the population in a second step.

The public trust in the federal government 'to do the right thing' in the most general terms has been declining to a low level since the early 2000s and remains stagnant at this low level (Pew Research Centre 2020: p. 6). Naturally, this general tendency does not mean Americans are entirely without trust in their government, or that they don't see a role for it. On the contrary, when asked where the federal government 'should play a major role', the answers of safety from terrorism, responding to natural disasters, ensuring food and medicine safety and managing the immigration system score very highly (Pew Research Centre 2020: p. 9). Even other, more politicized issues such as strengthening the economy and protecting the environment still receive three-quarters of support by respondents (ibid. p. 9). This mixed picture when it comes to trust in government is further complicated by the differences of views across party lines. Scope and performance assessment of government is divided along partisan lines in a clear fashion: Democrats and Republicans differ by 33 points in their average assessments of government performance. The partisan differences are clearest on issues such as the social safety net, environmentalism and labour unions. The smallest differences exist on matters of political engagement, government responsiveness and optimism about the future (Pew Research Center 2012). The movement towards greater partisan divides has continued since (Pew Research Center 2017).

There are also notable partisan differences on foreign policy, which is of particular relevance to the transatlantic system investigated here (Smeltz et al. 2015, Gries 2020). Supporters of the Democratic Party are more likely to be concerned with improving relations with allies, with 70 per cent listing it as a top priority as opposed to 44 per cent of supporters of the Republican Party. Republicans are considerably more likely to consider military superiority as the top issue for US foreign policy (Pew Research Center 2018). There is also a partisan distinction in threat perception. Whereas Democrats were more likely in 2018 to argue for limiting Russia's power as a priority, Republicans identified Iran as the country that needed to be contained. Republicans were also more likely to support getting allies to assume more of the cost of maintaining the global order (Pew Research Center 2018). On a number of issues, partisan differences however are entirely negligible, for example there was widespread agreement on the containment of North Korea as well as preventing the spread of weapons of mass destruction. There has also been a growing cross-party consensus on the challenge posed by China in both economic and political terms, which has made itself felt in transatlantic relations across successive US administrations. Nevertheless, partisan affiliation and support matter for the identification of foreign policy priorities, even as other factors and current events will sway positions as well.

An American way of public policy?

This system of government with its unique features and comparatively long history among constitutional democratic government combined with specific views of the public on policy also produces specific outcomes that set it apart from other countries. The policy areas discussed here are thus not a random selection but were rather chosen to illuminate the areas where the United States departs from what could be considered typical. More specifically these policies set the United States apart from European counterparts, and some of them have a direct impact on the competition and convergence (or lack thereof) between the two systems. The policy areas in which the United States diverges most noticeably are tax policy, employment protection, health care, gun ownership and regulation, as well as the penal system (Taylor et al. 2014). On both social policy issues, employment protection and health care, the United States is an economically liberal outlier. The limited role of legal protection against firing employees and related rules such as collective bargaining in the American labour market is, however, a feature shared with other countries with an Anglo-Saxon legal system (Venn in Taylor et al. 2014: p. 340). This clustering of policy approaches to regulation has been studied from the perspective of political economy in the varieties of capitalism debate and more specifically for social policy in the study of welfare regimes (Schröder 2019). While the clusters put forward in the literature are not perfectly precise descriptions of reality, they highlight that typically social policy features occur together. In the US case, this means that its flexible labour markets and the limited role of unemployment insurance coincide with a more limited scope for state involvement in health care and pensions. The US government does pursue policies in all of these fields, and some of the social policy programmes have high rates of approval among the population. A similar observation extends into the field of health policy, where the United States has a system based on private insurance and market dynamics in line with this liberal market economy model. Health care spending in the United States as a percentage of GDP has been higher than European countries' spending by a significant margin. At the same time, the amount of this spending that comes out of the public purse is lower than in most European countries (OECD 2020b).

Another example of a divergence in public policy is tax policy. If compared to other high-income countries, for example the members of the Organisation for

Economic Co-operation and Development (OECD), the US tax share of GDP at 24.3 per cent in 2018 was well below the average of 33.7 per cent in the OECD as a whole (OECD Tax Policy Centre 2018). In line with the market economy model discussed earlier, a larger share of US taxes is based on income, and it relies much less heavily on taxes on goods and services. The share of goods and services taxes is only 18 per cent for the United States compared with an OECD average of 32 per cent. This is largely because there is no national value-added tax (VAT) system in the United States. All other members of the OECD apply a general consumption tax of this nature. This tax model clearly advantages the consumption of goods and services as part of the economic model and removes at least direct and national tax collection for a significant part of economic activity. If added to the fact that corporate tax rates remain low, a low-tax regime gives the US economy an advantage over EU economies that drives competition over company settlement, tariffs and more. At the same time, both systems have collaborated to a degree through the OECD and G7 in the push for a global minimum corporate tax rate that has taken effect in 2024.

One of the more obvious divergent policy approaches that is non-economic in its nature is gun control. Due to historic constitutional protection, a high level of interest group activity and high level of politicization, gun control in the United States is extraordinarily limited compared to other high-income countries and specifically European states. This divergence is nothing new, but what makes it an interesting domestic policy area to observe is that the gap between the United States and other countries appears to be growing. New Zealand has experienced cases of gun violence to which the country responded with strict gun control legislation at the central state level (Council on Foreign Relations 2022), which includes registration, the banning of specific types of weapons for civilian ownership and other approaches. In the EU, all member states have some of these elements in place. The UK, a former member of the EU, is widely known to have police who are not generally armed. US gun policy is, however, reflective of social views and practice. A large section of US society owns a gun or lives in a household with gun ownership, even if almost half of Americans agree that gun violence is a problem in the United States (Pew Research Centre 2021). And while there is some agreement on for example background checks and mental health exclusion across social and political groups, views diverge widely by partisan affiliation on a national database of gun ownership and a ban on assault weapons as well as the sale of high-capacity ammunition (Pew Research Centre 2021). These different views ensure that gun control will remain a highly controversial US domestic policy for the future.

Recent issues in transatlantic politics

The core issue of transatlantic cooperation in recent years has been the joint response to Russia's full-scale invasion of Ukraine in 2022 (see also Chapter 8). This security crisis in Europe has triggered into action common threat perception and cooperation at new levels of intensity for the post-1989 era. European security has been a core pillar in joint Euro-American security interests. The coordinated response by the United States, the UK and the EU and other countries through sets of sanctions as well as an increasing amount of military assistance as the war continued had not been expected at the level of consistency it delivered. In an overview of the response by the Congressional Research Service in early 2023, EU–US cooperation was summarized:

> The United States and the EU have cooperated closely in responding to Russia's aggression against Ukraine. Many sanctions are identical or substantively similar. The two partners have worked together on enforcing sanctions, suspending Russia's preferential trade treatment under WTO rules and formulating the G7 price cap on Russian oil exports. (CRS Insight 2023)

Despite this positive assessment, the report warns that pressure on EU energy supplies and economic difficulties may still create problems for the convergence on this threat. In many ways, despite the difficulty, the EU has achieved considerable unity in supporting Ukraine, and the threat perception has resulted in a range of domestic EU responses that are likely to have a significant impact on the EU's foreign and security policies in the coming decade. At the level of markets, it has also renewed EU member state investment in US advanced military equipment, as part of a modernization strategy, in which older systems are passed on to Ukraine as military support. While a rational response to the crisis, it is likely to drive political pressures to support domestic national suppliers as well.

Challenging and restoring the transatlantic status quo? From the Trump to the Biden administration

The election of Donald Trump to the presidency in 2016 sent shockwaves across European member states, as policies announced by Trump challenged the status quo in transatlantic relations. From cancelling US participation in the Paris climate agreement (BBC 2016) to his outspoken support for Brexit (CNN 2016) to throwing doubt on NATO's role in Europe (Reuters 2016), Trump's policy ideas were directed at core elements of how the EU and US cooperated with each other. During his presidency, European leaders tried in varying ways to maintain a stable relationship and to blunt some of the effects of the policies referred to earlier. Even EU institutions and their leadership attempted to adapt to Trump's style by stressing the nature of the 'deal' that the EU and the United States had struck, in this instance on transatlantic trade (Deutsche Welle 2017). Since we have seen earlier that the EU contains within it a wide range of actors with a wide range of preferences, it is perhaps unsurprising that not all European governments were critics of Trump and his administration. The right-wing populist governments of Hungary and Poland embraced the Trump administration and some of its rhetoric to advance their own objectives. In the Polish case, this included negotiating with Trump on the establishment of 'Fort Trump', a US military base in Poland (Ministry of National Defence 2018). In the case of Hungary, links to Trump and his supporters in the US political system continued past Trump's attempt to overturn the election of Biden with conferences in Hungary dedicated to radical conservative themes and dominated by US speakers.

In 2021, the inauguration of Joe Biden as president almost immediately resulted in at least a declaratory rebalancing in transatlantic relations. European governments were competing for a new approach to the new US administration: the German foreign minister Heiko Maas spoke of a 'Transatlantic New Deal' shortly before the US elections using the imagery of historic US domestic reform (Maas 2020). French president Emmanuel Macron stressed a new start with the administration to further 'results-oriented multilateralism' but without sacrificing European sovereignty in the process (Walla 2021). At the same time, some European outliers who more closely aligned with Biden's predecessor delayed their official congratulations to Biden's election for an unusually long time, mirroring the politicization of the US election results also in Europe. Early decisions of the Biden administration have gone some way towards signalling a rebalancing of the 'status quo ante', for example the decision to increase troop levels in Germany to balance the reduction in troops pursued by the Trump administration. Increased military cooperation with Poland has nonetheless been maintained and expanded on by the Biden administration (The White House 2021). Biden has also engaged in a renewed call for cooperation among democracies around the globe through a 'Summit for Democracy'. In addition to the regular meeting of leaders of democratic nations across the world, the initiative also included spending priorities on technology for democracy, independent media, anti-corruption and supporting free elections as well as human rights promotion (The White House 2023b). Both the Biden administration's policies and the Russian war of aggression on Ukraine have led transatlantic relations to a familiar state of alliance, but some of the domestic dynamics that challenge cooperation remain.

Table 3.2 Comparing the EU and US Systems

	European Union	United States
Political system	Treaty-based supranational organization	Constitutional republic
Executive	Dispersed executive (European Commission, Council of the EU and national administrations)	Presidential system with two four-year terms
Legislature	EP and Council of the EU as co-legislators	Strong bicameralism
Judiciary	Court of Justice of the EU with limited judicial review – national systems of justice	Supreme Court with strong judicial review
Core 'federal' competences	Trade, competition and internal market, agriculture, regional development	Defence, foreign policy, trade, regulatory oversight
Core competences of constituent units	Defence, police, education, social policies	Police, regulation, some social policies
Party system	Multi-party system	Two-party system
Interest representation	Leaning pluralist with some level of corporatism common at the member state level	Pluralist
Economic approach	Social market economy, but trend to liberalization	Market economy with limited safety net

Overview and conclusion

Over the past decades, scholarship comparing the EU and the United States has expanded in scope. In addition to works that directly address the two entities and compare them on the basis of their political systems (e.g. Fabbrini 2005; Kelemen 2004; Kreppel 2012; Nicolaidis 2001; Menon and Schain 2006), the direct comparison of specific elements has proliferated as well (Tortola 2014). Tortola argues that this trend is likely to continue, specifically because of the relevance of these two large actors (Tortola 2014: p. 1352). But beyond the importance the EU and the United States have in international politics in general, they are bound to be relevant material for those studying their continued and evolving interactions in the Euro-American system of transatlantic relations that has been laid out in Chapters 1 and 2 of this volume.

An understanding of these two political systems summarized in Table 3.2 illustrates why the United States is still a necessary ally for the Europeans and why the EU is still important to the United States irrespective of domestic political constellations.

- Every starting point for a meaningful comparison needs to include the acknowledgement that the EU and the United States are not the same type of entity. Nevertheless, understood as two systems of governance in the Euro-American system, some relevant comparative insight can be gained from looking at the way they set and implement rules and what political forces drive this process.

- The EU is a supranational entity based on an international treaty, which has acquired particularly strong powers in market regulation and trade. It has much less power on defence and social issues, which are mainly reserved to the member states. The EU member states tend to favour an expansive welfare state that in relative terms exceeds the US safety net. Their economies are more structured according to a coordinated market economy model.
- The United States is a full federation with a rigid constitution and an executive that is especially strong in the field of security. The United States is not only set apart from its European counterparts by its specific constitutional structure, but also the nature and substance of politics. The varieties of capitalism literature identifies the United States as a core example of a liberal market economy. The United States differs from European economies on tax policy as well as social spending such as healthcare.
- Despite these differences, some dynamics are similar across these systems. A systemic perspective shows that the EU in some ways resembles the United States, for example when it comes to interest representation, which is more pluralist at the EU level than the EU member states' systems. Like the United States, the EU needs its different 'branches' to interact to make broad international (trade) agreements, but it also needs the approval of its component states. The EU and the United States share similarities in regulatory practice as well due to the interaction between different levels of government (regulatory federalism).

These differences and areas of convergence link with points that were made in Chapter 2 about the challenge for the EU of its 'US policy' and for the United States of its 'EU policy', and thus provide us with a broader view of the ways in which the Euro-American system can respond to specific policy challenges and opportunities. At many points in the following chapters, they will assist in the analysis of interactions between the EU and the United States in areas of international political economy, security and diplomacy.

Chapter 4

Trade

Introduction

This chapter is the first in this book to deal with a specific policy area and with the trends and issues that have occurred within it. Whereas Chapters 1 and 2 have covered broad trends and the changing nature of the relations between European integration and the United States (US), and Chapter 3 examined the domestic influences on policymaking from a comparative perspective, here the focus is much more on the particular characteristics of the policy area and of European Union (EU) and US policies, on the ways in which they have generated tendencies towards competition or convergence and on the ways in which the relationships have been managed. The chapter thus draws upon Chapters 1 and 2 for broad background and Chapter 3 on sub-state forces, but focuses strongly on recent and current policy developments and their implications. It begins by describing the rapidly changing patterns of global trade, explains the rise and fall of multilateralism in this issue area, explores some of the main features of Euro-American trade and EU–US trade policies and then moves on to deal with some of the issues of management that have emerged within the relationship in recent years.

Changing patterns of global trade

Though the growth of China, India and other developing states has eroded the dominance of the Euro-American partnership in international trade, the United States and the EU remain key markets and players in the conduct of international commercial relations. Indeed, the economic weight of the EU in trade terms makes it a central player in the conduct of international trade negotiations. The United States remains central as the world's largest national economy, with a gross domestic product (GDP) of $28.0 trillion in 2024 (IMF 2024), followed by the EU ($19.4 trillion) and China ($18.6 trillion). The EU is the world's largest trading entity, with strong trade positions across merchandise (goods) and services trade (see Table 4.1). The EU's merchandise trade (excluding intra-EU trade) was worth $5.9 trillion in 2022, slightly behind China's $6.3 trillion, but ahead of the United States' $5.4 trillion (WTO 2023: table A.7, p. 61). Germany is the world's third-largest exporter of goods (including intra- and extra-EU exports), worth $1.7 trillion in 2022, based on high demand for capital goods from developing and developed countries. The EU is the world's largest trader in services. Its $2.6 trillion total in services imports and exports is 65 per cent more than the United States, and three times more than China's services trade.

In effect, international trade is dominated by two countries (China and the United States) and the EU, which together accounted for 41 per cent of global exports and 43 per cent of global imports in 2022. The addition of China to what had essentially been a trade duopoly from the end of the Second World War to the early years of the 21st century has complicated and politicized trade in fundamentally new ways, as will be discussed later.

While the EU and United States are two of the three major traders in the global economy, their relative influence has declined over the past two decades. In 2000, an EU comprised of 15 countries exported 17.3 per cent of all global exports, while the US share was 15.7 per cent (see Table 4.2). By 2022, the EU's share (consisting of now 27 member countries, but no longer including the UK) dropped to 13.2 per cent, while the United States fell to 10.1 per cent. The aggregate amount of EU and US trade did, in fact, increase over that time period, but not as quickly as the exports of emerging markets like Brazil, South Africa, India and China (the so-called BASIC countries) and other countries in Asia, Africa and Latin America. China's share of global exports increased from 5.0 per cent in 2000 to 17.6 per cent in 2022. In light of the rising economic prominence of emerging market countries, the EU's trade patterns are also changing (see Table 4.3). Between 2005 and 2022, China's share of EU trade increased from 9.3 percent to 15.4 per cent. EU trade with India, South Korea and Turkey also increased in percentage terms, while the importance of EU trade with Japan and Norway declined. The share of trade with the United States fell by 2.8 percentage points. A similar trend has transpired in US trade, with Canada and Japan seeing a relatively large decline in percentage terms, while China, India, Vietnam and others have seemingly replaced their share (see Table 4.4). From 2015 to 2018, China was the biggest trading partner of the United States. The country fell to third in 2019 due to the tariff war (see later), returned to the top spot in 2020 and again fell to third from 2021 through 2023.

Table 4.1 Merchandise Goods and Services Trade, Selected Countries (2022, $US billion)

	Goods exports	Goods imports	Total goods trade	Services exports	Services imports	Total services trade	Total goods plus services trade
Extra-EU*	2 704	3 155	5 859	1 377	1 223	2 600	8 459
China	3 594	2 716	6 310	422	461	883	7 193
United States	2 065	3 376	5 441	900	671	1 571	7 012
Germany	1 655	1 571	3 226	406	458	864	4 090
Netherlands	966	899	1 865	270	264	534	2 399
UK	529	824	1 353	492	313	805	2 158
France	618	818	1 436	336	286	622	2 058
Japan	747	897	1 644	163	207	370	2 014
India	453	723	1 176	309	249	558	1 734
S. Korea	684	731	1 415	132	135	267	1 682
Italy	657	689	1 346	123	133	256	1 602
Belgium	633	621	1 254	137	144	281	1 535
Mexico	578	626	1 204	36	46	82	1 286
Spain	418	493	912	167	87	254	1 166
Ireland	214	146	360	355	373	728	1 088
Switzerland	402	356	758	146	157	303	1 061
Poland	361	381	742	95	57	152	894
Brazil	334	292	626	39	78	117	743
Austria	212	232	444	80	74	154	598
Sweden	198	202	400	94	98	192	592
Czech Republic	241	236	477	34	30	64	541
World Total	24,905	25,621		7,043	6,509		

Source: World Trade Organization (WTO). (2023), *World Statistical Review 2023*, Geneva: WTO, Tables A6, A7, A8, A9. Available online: https://www.wto.org/english/res_e/booksp_e/wtsr_2023_e.pdf (accessed 9 October 2023).

*Assumes EU is one unit. Exports and imports between EU member states not counted.

Table 4.2 Share of Global Exports, 2000, 2010, 2022

	2000 (%)	2010 (%)	2022 (%)
China	5.0	13.3	17.6
EU*	17.3	15.1	13.2
US	15.7	10.8	10.1
Japan	9.6	6.5	3.7
South Korea	3.5	3.9	3.3
Mexico	3.3	2.5	2.8
UK	4.5	2.7	2.6
Russia	2.1	3.4	2.6
India	0.9	1.9	2.2
Brazil	1.1	1.7	1.6
South Africa	0.6	0.7	0.6
Indonesia, Malaysia, Thailand, Vietnam	4.9	5.2	6.4

Sources: World Trade Organization (WTO). (2001a), *International Trade Statistics 2001*, Tables I.5, I.6. Available online: https://www.wto.org/english/res_e/statis_e/its2001_e/stats2001_e.pdf (accessed 9 October 2023);

World Trade Organization (WTO). (2011), *International Trade Statistics 2011*, Tables I.8, I.9. Available online: https://www.wto.org/english/res_e/statis_e/its2011_e/its2011_e.pdf (accessed 9 October 2023).

World Trade Organization (WTO). (2023), *World Statistical Review 2023*, Geneva: WTO, Table A7. Available online: https://www.wto.org/english/res_e/booksp_e/wtsr_2023_e.pdf (accessed 9 October 2023);

*EU had 15 member states in 2000 and 27 in 2010 and 2020.

Table 4.3 EU Top Ten Trade Partners, 2005 and 2022

	Goods trade 2005 (billion €)	Percentage of all EU trade	Goods trade 2022 (billion €)	Percentage of all EU trade
1. United States	414.3	18.4	868.1	15.6
2. China	209.8	9.3	856.8	15.4
3.UK*	N/A	N/A	545.3	9.8
4. Switzerland	148.3	6.6	333.4	6.0
5. Russia	165.5	6.9	258.5	4.6
6. Norway	100.8	4.5	227.7	4.1
7. Turkey	75.4	3.3	198.3	3.6
8. Japan	116.9	5.2	141.5	2.5
9. South Korea	53.6	2.4	132.1	2.4
10. India	40.0	1.8	115.3	2.1
Total Extra-EU Trade	2,250.8	100	5,575.2	100

Sources: European Commission. (2023a). *Overview of Top Trading Partners*, 10 July. Available online: https://circabc.europa.eu/ui/group/50a0487d-086a-4a75-a1ff-92bdd2ec2c4b/library/09539941-7d09-4e97-84ae-a5cd21f53283/details (accessed 1 November 2023); European Commission. (2006). *External and Intra-European Trade: Statistical Yearbook*. Available online: http://aei.pitt.edu/67458/1/1958%2D2005.pdf (accessed 1 November 2023).

*UK was a member of the EU in 2005.

Table 4.4 US Top Ten Trade Partners and EU, 2005 and 2023

	Goods trade 2005 (billion $)	**Percentage of all US trade**	**Goods trade 2023 (billion $)**	**Percentage of all US trade**
European Union	494.8	19.2	943.9	18.5
1. Mexico	290.2	11.3	798.8	15.7
2. Canada	499.2	19.4	774.3	15.2
3. China	285.3	11.1	575.0	11.3
4. Germany	119.0	4.6	236.4	4.6
4. Japan	193.5	7.5	223.5	4.4
6. South Korea	71.4	2.8	181.1	3.5
7. UK	89.7	3.5	127.5	2.7
8. Taiwan	56.9	2.2	114.1	2.5
9. Vietnam	Not top 10 partner		124.3	2.4
10. India	Not top 10 partner		123.9	2.4

United States Census Bureau. (2024a), *Foreign Trade: Top Trading Partners* – December 2023. https://www.census.gov/foreign-trade/statistics/highlights/top/top2312yr.html#total (accessed 5 July 2024).

United States Census Bureau. (2021), *Foreign Trade: Top Trading Partners*. Available online: https://www.census.gov/foreign-trade/statistics/highlights/top/index.html (accessed 5 July 2024).

United States Census Bureau. 2021b), *Trade in Goods with European Union*. Available online: https://www.census.gov/foreign-trade/balance/c0003.html (accessed 5 July 2024).

The rise and fall of multilateralism

Among all economic issue areas within the Euro-American system, arguably trade relations have the greatest political salience. This is partly because of the intrinsic importance of the area but that is not the entire explanation. In contrast to relations in antitrust or monetary policy, trade relations have become the most clearly 'politicized', with a large number of stakeholders and a significant public profile. Whereas monetary – and even more so, antitrust – sectors remain the domain of experts and policymakers, the development of trade policy is notable for the significant and deep involvement of firms and, at least in the EU, the active participation of non-governmental organizations (NGOs). Starting with the founding of the General Agreement on Tariffs and Trade (GATT) in 1947, the United States and the EU participated in an international trade system characterized by the expansion of trade, which grew more quickly than GDP. The GATT process of negotiated, reciprocal trade liberalization worked very well for over four decades and succeeded in dramatically lowering tariffs in the developed world. The World Trade Organization (WTO), GATT's successor as of 1995, now has membership of 164 countries. This institutionalization of liberalized trade owes much to the leadership of Washington and Brussels and is reflective of what the two powers are able to achieve working together.

Yet, it could be argued that the mid-1990s was the apex of a liberalized trade regime, as several factors have undermined this system in subsequent years. First, the addition of new countries to the bargaining table with interests that have diverged from the United States and EU has made it exceedingly difficult to achieve a consensus on which tariffs and trade barriers to tackle. Tariffs on manufactured goods are relatively low, so business interests in the United States and Europe have lobbied their governments to prioritize liberalization in services, such as finance, retail and transportation. But for many of the WTO's emerging market members, these are sectors that are highly politicized, subsidized and protected, and their companies and workers are not keen to see more efficient multinational corporations (MNCs) invade their turf. In turn, these countries have sought to use these industries as bargaining chips in trade negotiations as they pursue their interests, such as opening agricultural markets in richer countries, which requires Washington, Brussels and Tokyo to reduce subsidies, tariffs, quotas and other protections for their farmers. Add in concerns about state capitalism, intellectual property rights protections and dispute settlement processes for foreign investors, and the WTO has effectively ground to a halt given the difficulties in reaching broad-based agreements based on the consensus of the entire membership rather than a majority of votes.

As a result, countries have opted for regional or bilateral trade deals. This has the advantage of making consensus easier to reach (Guay 2019). Negotiations with a handful of countries are less complex than those within the WTO. According to the WTO, the number of regional trade agreements (RTAs) has skyrocketed.1 There were 52 RTAs in force in 1995. By 2024, there were 369. The EU is a partner in 46 RTAs with countries around the world – more than any other entity. The United States is a member of 14 RTAs, including the United States Mexico Canada Trade Agreement (USMCA), formerly known as the North American Free Trade Agreement (NAFTA), as well as bilateral deals with Australia, Chile and Israel, among others. Regional and bilateral trade agreements provide the EU and United States with more leverage, since they can allow or deny access to their large markets, which smaller countries are very dependent upon for exports (see also Chapter 9 for a discussion in the context of regionalism).

A third factor that has undermined multilateralism in trade is the move towards more protectionism. This occurred to some extent after the 2007–8 financial crisis, but accelerated with the election of US president Donald Trump in 2016,

---

[1]http://rtais.wto.org/UI/charts.aspx

though it must be emphasized that other countries including China, India and Brazil have in recent years exercised protectionist and unilateral actions of their own, too. A March 2016 Pew Research Center poll showed that 67 per cent of Trump supporters thought free trade agreements to be a bad thing for the United States, and even 53 pe rcent of Republican and Republican-leaning voters (a group that has been more closely associated with free trade than Democratic voters for almost 50 years) agreed (Stokes 2016). The Trump administration imposed tariffs on over $360 billion of Chinese goods over four rounds in 2018 and 2019, claiming they were in response to unfair trade practices and intellectual property theft (BBC 2020). In 2018, the United States imposed a 25 per cent tariff on imported steel and a 10 per cent tariff on aluminium, affecting companies in the EU and six other countries. In an effort to reduce transatlantic trade tensions and gain EU support on other global issues, the Biden administration replaced these tariffs with a quota system in 2022 (see Box. 4.1).

Box 4.1 President Donald Trump and European 'foes'

US president Donald Trump (2017–21) was noted for advancing an anti-multilateralist foreign policy agenda, that included scepticism of international organizations like the EU, WTO, United Nations and World Health Organization, among others. In a 2018 interview following a NATO summit meeting, Trump made the following remarks:

> Well, I think we have a lot of foes. I think the European Union is a foe, what they do to us in trade. Now, you wouldn't think of the European Union, but they're a foe. Russia's a foe in certain respects. China's a foe economically, certainly they're a foe. But that doesn't mean they're bad. It doesn't mean anything. It means that they're competitors. . . . The EU is very difficult. . . . In a trade sense, they've really taken advantage of us. (BBC 2018)

It is difficult to envision a prior US president using the word 'foe' to describe the EU. The Joe Biden administration strived to reverse this characterization of the US–EU relationship, as discussed elsewhere in this book.

Source: BBC (2018), 'Donald Trump: European Union Is a Foe on Trade', 15 July. Available online: https://www.bbc.com/news/world-us-canada-44837311 (accessed 9 October 2023).

To put all of this into perspective, eight GATT trade rounds were started, negotiated and concluded between 1947 and 1994, with each one chipping away at tariffs and various international trade barriers. Since then, only one trade round (the Doha Round in 2001) was started, but it has languished ever since. This is not really the fault of the transition from the GATT to the WTO, although there are important differences between the two, namely the authorization of countries that 'win' trade disputes as determined by the organization's judicial processes to levy counter-tariffs equivalent to their economic losses in the 'losing' country. Rather, the decline of US and EU influence in the global economy, as well as a growing ambivalence towards multilateralism, are the main culprits. An additional issue is that the renewal of a security dimension to trade issues (and more directly investment ones, see Chapter 6) is weakening political support for multilateral liberalization. Global supply chains, for example, are under intense scrutiny in the post-COVID-19 era, as governments in Europe and the United States have come to realize that much of the world's medical, health and personal protection equipment is manufactured in Asia, making it difficult to meet their domestic health security needs (Farrell and Newman 2021).

These three challenges to multilateralism in trade share common roots. The first may be described as the return to multipolarity; the rise of China, India, Brazil and other developing countries to economic prominence is challenging long-held assumptions about who, exactly, governs international trade. In the early years of the Euro-American system, American dominance was taken for granted; in the 1950s, the American economy accounted for half of total world output. However, the United States is increasingly challenged across a range of policy areas not just by the EU, but also by China and to a lesser extent India, Brazil and others. This political reality reflects important changes in the direction of trade in the international economy. The transatlantic relations literature traditionally began by noting how the EU–US relationship was the most important trading relationship in the world. This is rapidly changing. China now exports about 75 per cent more goods to EU countries than does the United States (€626 billion to €359 billion in 2022), though EU exports to the United States are more than twice those to China (€509 billion to €230 billion).2 However, for trade in services, the United States remains the EU's primary partner by far – €564 billion in 2021 as compared to €98 billion between the EU and China. China surpassed Canada in 2015 to become the top trade partner of the United States and held this position until 2019 when the Trump administration's tariffs bumped China to third (behind Mexico and Canada) before returning to the top trade partner spot in 2020. As the Euro-American economic relationship becomes one of several dense and

[2]https://policy.trade.ec.europa.eu/eu-trade-relationships-country-and-region/countries-and-regions_en

complex economic partnerships, its political salience vis-à-vis others becomes more problematic.

There is also a second and related root to the current features of the global trading system, and one that particularly affects EU–US relations. The multipolarity outlined earlier is linked increasingly to an important security element, where economic policy is developed and implemented with security considerations in mind. Members of Congress in Washington face increased calls for tougher stances on 'unfair' trade practices of other countries, with rationales for such calls being a complex mix of protectionist desires, preservation of manufacturing jobs and security concerns. These issues converge in the US manufacturing sector, which has declined from one-quarter of GDP in the 1960s to 18 per cent in recent years. Employment has also declined, although the amount attributable to international trade is hotly debated. Acemoglu et al. (2016) estimate 2.0–2.4 million job losses between 1999 and 2011 due to rising Chinese import competition, while Scott and Mokhiber (2020) argue that trade deficits with China cost 3.7 million jobs between 2001 (when China joined the WTO) and 2018. Other studies suggest that technology, automation and increased productivity have played a larger role than international trade in the decline of blue-collar manufacturing jobs (Chien and Morris 2017). US goods exports, for example, have more than doubled between 2000 ($785 billion) and 2022 ($2.1 trillion) even with fewer workers.3 But politically, it is easier to blame trade and foreign countries than scientists and engineers for the plight of many working-class families and the 'hollowing out' of the manufacturing sector.

At the same time, in the EU, the increasing salience of concerns with energy and environmental security also has strong repercussions for the shaping of external trade policies. Finally, the judicialization and increasing institutionalization of the global economy also presents challenges. The EU (like other actors) is increasingly constrained in the types of policies that can be effectively developed and implemented: this arises mainly from the increased importance of trade for both economies. The combination outlined here, of increased multipolarity in world trade, linked with growing politicization and judicialization, is a potent one. For the EU and the United States, it means that the days when trade could be dealt with in a relatively 'technical' way among experts are gone, and this has implications both for their trade-policymaking processes and for the management of their mutual trade relations.

[3] https://www.census.gov/foreign-trade/statistics/historical/gands.pdf

European Union trade policymaking and trends

As noted in Chapter 2, the EU is something of a 'moving target' for its policymaking partners, as its institutions develop and evolve and its member states' preferences shift in response to domestic and international pressures. The elaboration and consolidation of the Common Commercial Policy from the 1960s onwards has gone alongside a continual growth in the European Community's (and the EU's) role in the global trading system. The enlargement of the Community and then the Union has played an important part in this growth and has also given the EU a distinctive set of international trading relationships, reflecting the influence of its diverse membership and the members' historical links with different parts of the world. The articulation of common rules for the EU's internal market has made the Union even more important in international trade, as foreign firms see the creation of a generally affluent and growing common economic space (Young and Peterson 2006, 2014). The EU is now the largest trade partner of both the United States and China and is an attractive export market for firms around the world. This gives the EU considerable leverage in international negotiations and makes other states keenly interested in both EU commercial policy and the process by which the Union formulates its positions. This process is complex and highly institutionalized, and not surprisingly the academic literature on EU trade policy pays considerable attention to the internal constraints on the effective development of EU trade policy. Voting rules within the Council of Ministers matter decisively for international trade negotiations; the unanimity requirement makes it relatively easy for the EU to resist external pressures for change but also constrains its ability to offer policy changes (Meunier 2005). This internal division is a key element of the EU's trade power: 'The EU has been able to obtain more in international trade negotiations than it might have if all decisions had been made through strict majority voting and with lots of flexibility granted to European negotiators' (Meunier and Nicolaidis 2006: 909).

Another important internal feature with implications for international negotiations is the competence question: whether member states or the Commission (acting on behalf of the EU) have the legal authority to negotiate international trade agreements on behalf of the EU, particularly in the area of services trade, which was not a significant element of international commerce when the Treaty of Rome was signed. The competence issue seemed to have been settled with the Treaty of Nice, which extended the EU's competence into the areas of services and intellectual property (IP) (WTO 2004: viii). Leaving aside the legal issues, it is also true that the EU is a fractured polity, with many deep and longstanding institutional differences among member states.

Traditionally, this has been portrayed as a simple cleavage between the more free-trading northern members (Netherlands, Germany and former member UK) and the more protectionist southern states led by France. The addition of new members and the rise of new issues on the trade agenda have made this simple division a partial explanation at best for internal divisions over trade (Meunier and Nicolaidis 2023).

The focus on internal constraints helps us a great deal but can take us only so far. Much of the literature on EU trade is written as if the EU did not trade with anyone, so tight is the focus on internal processes and norms. This is perhaps an inevitable result of the focus on the EU as a regional integration process. Yet, it can be suggested that the EU is increasingly constrained internationally, and if one wants to understand the internal dynamics of (for example) state aid policy or agricultural policy in the EU, one needs to grasp how the international environment is influencing events. The WTO influences the EU in two ways: first, it fosters the adoption of certain modes of behaviour; and second, the dispute settlement understanding is sufficiently robust (at least until around 2020) to alter WTO member behaviour. The WTO caused 'broad institutional change' in the EU, as the norms and expectations of the multilateral institution diffused down to Brussels (Knodt 2004; see also Young and Peterson 2014: chapter 4). This argument, while situated in the multi-level governance tradition, owes much to regime theory, with its emphasis on actor expectations and the development of an enlightened self-interest among parties to a multistate cooperative arrangement. The important contribution of Knodt's work to the discussion here is that it moves the emphasis away from the WTO as arena to WTO as actor. For the EU and its trade policymaking, this constitutes a major shift in the global context.

In recent years, most major states have opted for some form of multi-track approach to trade negotiations that blends participation in the WTO with efforts to gain preferential access to one or more foreign markets through preferential trade agreements, thus the growth in RTAs. They have done so for two reasons. First, most states are frustrated by the increasingly complex and fruitless multilateral track at the WTO. Second, their firms have lobbied each government to negotiate preferential trade deals so as to neutralize the gains made by competing firms whose governments have already signed such agreements (Guay 2019; Manger 2005). The EU, by contrast, has always adopted a multi-track approach to commercial policy negotiations. This should not be surprising, as the Common Market itself is a preferential trade agreement, one that operates under article 24 of the GATT relating to plurilateral agreements negotiated among GATT (now WTO) members. In 2023, the EU had trade agreements in force with

78 countries around the world, and another 25 agreements in the process of being adopted or ratified.4

Regulation and EU trade policy

Where the EU does differ from other WTO members, not least the United States, is the degree to which it places international regulatory matters at the heart of its trade strategy (Young and Peterson 2014: chapters 6–7). Regulation as a trade issue differs from the 'classic' trade defence instruments such as anti-dumping and quotas; the latter are 'at-the-border' issues whereas regulation refers to how a product or service is developed and delivered. As such, regulatory issues push trade politics well behind national borders and make national laws and procedures topics for negotiation. The successive rounds of GATT negotiations effectively removed tariffs as barriers to entry, but the reduction of tariffs does not automatically make the market more contestable. As we explore further in Chapter 6, internal regulations can hamper effective market access for foreign firms. Thus, there is a logic to the extension of trade liberalization negotiations to the issue of regulation (McGuire 2004; De Bièvre 2006). The interesting question is why the EU has pursued this with so much more vigour than other parties. One line of explanation would locate the reason in the existence of the Commission itself; it should not surprise anyone that a supranational bureaucracy – which is exactly what the Commission is – develops a preference for regulation. The Commission thus saw an opportunity to turn the WTO 'into a regulatory agency in its own image' (Young 2004; Jones 2006; Sally 2004: 114). This process arguably reached its zenith in the early stages of the Doha Round negotiations, with the EU officials being the staunchest advocates of the inclusion of a range of regulatory areas (trade facilitation, competition policy, investor protection and government procurement). These 'Singapore issues', so called because they were first agreed as an agenda item at the WTO's Singapore meeting of trade ministers in 1996, presented a particular problem for developing states; all these issue areas are complex regulatory areas requiring significant legal and bureaucratic infrastructure. For these states, the EU's position represented an attempt to impose on them a model of governance suitable for an already affluent and stable polity. In the event, the Commission agreed to drop all but trade facilitation from its Doha negotiating stance. However, as noted earlier, the Doha trade round has made virtually no progress to date.

---

[4]https://policy.trade.ec.europa.eu/eu-trade-relationships-country-and-region/negotiations-and-agreements_en

Though it has largely failed through multilateral negotiations, the Commission showed no signs of retreating from an interest in regulatory issues and international trade. The EU remained keen to use regulatory standards for food and other products, both to protect EU consumers and, perhaps, to restrict access to the European market. Europe had been at the forefront of these new types of trade disputes thanks to its long-running battle with the United States (and latterly other countries, including Canada) in respect of the export of hormone-fed beef and genetically modified soybeans and other crops to Europe. However, Europe is hardly alone in using product standards in this way. Indeed, according to one study, the United States in the early 21st century had the largest number of notifications to the WTO of product standards that appeared stricter than prevailing international levels (Gallagher 2007). The EU has also pursued the regulatory agenda through its RTAs. It is now commonplace for the EU to include competition policy, investment protection and a raft of other issues in any negotiation with a prospective trade partner. Though these efforts can be resisted, the EU's emphasis on institution-building and on the cultivation of norms and values associated with democracy can be attractive to developing states, more so than the US approach that pays much less attention to the normative element of relations (Doctor 2007).

The changing nature of American trade policy

The United States has long been ambivalent about the international political economy but has nonetheless led developments that sought to develop an international regime to regulate trade. In 1945, the charter of the International Trade Organization (ITO) was drawn up as part of an American-led effort to create postwar economic institutions capable of avoiding the economic catastrophe that had in the view of many contributed to the slide towards war in 1939 (Wilkinson 2005). Though the ITO was effectively killed off by a threatened Senate veto in 1948, American presidents got around that setback and were instrumental in the creation of the GATT. Designed only as a stop-gap institution until the ITO was resurrected, GATT nevertheless overcame this handicap to become a remarkably successful organization. GATT worked effectively for many years thanks to its congruence with American trade interests and its organizational structure (Goldstein 2000; Lindeque and McGuire 2007). Much of the GATT's rules and regulations derived from American practice and custom. US rules on injury and anti-dumping (i.e. policies that retaliate against firms who export and sell products abroad for lower prices than they charge in their home market) were important influences on the eventual wording of the GATT equivalents

(Sen 2003). GATT thus enjoyed American support for many years: it helped deliver dramatic reductions in tariff levels and so catalysed increased global trade in the postwar period. However, by the time of the Kennedy Round in the early 1960s, increased import pressures started eroding what had been broad support for GATT. By the 1970s, American managers found it more convenient to blame the unfair practices of foreigners rather than look at their own companies' performance.

In addition, the perception grew that the American market was substantially more open than the markets of other countries and so was allowing foreign firms access without reciprocal US access to overseas markets (Shaffer 2003). Criticism began to focus on the Kennedy Round outcome on a trade policy process too dominated by professional diplomats and technical experts unused to the business world. Changes to the policymaking process included statutory requirements for private sector consultations, thus ensuring that business has a powerful role in the shaping of US trade policy. A complex network of private interests, agency officials at the office of the US trade representative (USTR), Congress and other government departments ensures that American trade policy is a contested process, as described in Chapter 3. However, successive reorganizations of agencies have strengthened the hand of USTR relative to other units of the executive. Originally designated as an agency under the president's office, USTR has gradually developed into a full 'member' of the executive branch alongside departments like Commerce and State. Congress urged this building up of USTR authority as part of its desire to make the protection of US trade interests more central to a president's economic policy. The more independence it gained, the more USTR found itself depending on private interests for political support.

The active support of the United States was key to the creation of the WTO during the Uruguay Round negotiations (1986–93). Nonetheless, American support for multilateralism has always been contested. The United States maintains a relatively open economy with comparatively few restrictions on foreign firms seeking to do business; subsidies to industry are not used extensively in normal economic times (although as will be discussed in Chapter 6, this may be changing); and foreign firms operate in a robust legal and regulatory environment. American leadership has at times been severely undermined by domestic political pressures and a suspicion that sovereignty was being surrendered to an international organization. Members of Congress' House of Representatives, facing election every two years, are especially sensitive to constituency pressures for trade protection. Elaborate legislative arrangements designed to facilitate trade negotiations in spite of this handicap include trade promotion authority, by presenting the Congress with a take-it-or-leave-it package, aiming to frustrate attempts to unpick agreements via concessions to constituency lobbies. American trade politics is thus characterized by both considerable protectionism and aggressive efforts to liberalize (Cohen etal. 2003). In the case of low-skill industrial sectors and agriculture, the Congress has turned to US trade remedies to offset increased international pressures. Where American firms are technologically advanced or represent service-based sectors, US policy has been to use multilateralism as a means of opening markets (Porter 2005).

American support for multilateralism was dealt a severe blow, however, with the failure of the WTO's Cancún trade ministers meeting in 2003. This meeting reflected not only the 'traditional' tensions between the EU and the United States over agriculture but also a new set of pressures from major emerging economies, including notably China, India and Brazil, and it made both the EU and the United States reassess their strategies. Competitive liberalization, based on bilateral and regional trade agreements, became the operative policy in the wake of this setback; it was seen both as a mechanism to retrieve something from the stalled liberalization process and also an opportunity for the United States to revitalize that process, since foreign states would worry that a full-scale move to regional trade by the United States would present unique dangers for market access (see Chapter 9 for further discussion in the context of regionalism). Robert Zoellick (the USTR at the time) outlined the essential characteristics of the new policy shortly after the Cancún meeting. Rather than wait for all WTO members to agree a new round of trade liberalization, the United States would work with 'can-do' states willing to liberalize on a bilateral basis. The danger with competitive liberalization is the asymmetry in power it represents. The United States used RTAs as an easy way to gain particularly good deals for American-based firms, since the partner state was almost always more dependent on access to the US market than the reverse (Feinberg 2003). The negotiations between the United States and the South African Customs Union, for example, were criticized for the extent to which areas like insurance and banking – areas of American competitive strength – were liberalized to a greater degree than other sectors (Whalley and Leith 2003). The Central American Free Trade Agreement (CAFTA) came in for similar criticism, namely that it did little to open US markets but did more to throw open developing country markets to American firms. This perception was hardly dispelled by the then-USTR Robert Allgeier, as he sold the benefits of the CAFTA during his 2005 testimony to Congress: 'The chief effect of CAFTA is not to further open our market, but rather to tear down barriers to our products and services in Central America and the Dominican Republic' (Allgeier 2005).

As with the EU, it is clear from this discussion that the US role in world trade is ambivalent and beset by a number of internal and external pressures. Neither the Obama administration, nor the Trump administration, made serious efforts to revive Doha negotiations, and the Biden administration was no different. Other than MNCs, there are few constituencies advocating for this. The complexity of internal trade policy-making, with Congress in a strong position to champion 'parochial' interests, and the cultural predisposition to resist attack on US sovereignty, have lent a distinctive flavour to US trade policies, and this has been given an additional twist by the recent tendency to look for bilateral or interregional trade agreements which are seen as better serving US interests than global rules and negotiations. Not surprisingly, the United States has been sensitive to these features and quick to respond to perceived challenges.

The Brussels–Washington axis

For decades, the transatlantic relationship was the foundation-stone of EU trade policy. In the wake of the Second World War, American determination not to repeat the errors of trade protectionism and economic strife that generated such disastrous consequences helped forge the postwar economic architecture of multilateral institutions and forums to govern international commercial relations. The GATT was the trade-related component, though because of American concerns the GATT did not become the true third pillar alongside the International Monetary Fund (IMF) and World Bank until the body attained full treaty status with the approval of the Uruguay Round agreements in 1994. From 1947 to 1994 it ran as a surprisingly effective agreement among contracting parties. Eventually, this arrangement had run its course and consensus grew that a more formal and robust organization, with 'teeth' to enforce trade dispute rulings, was required. The WTO subsumed the GATT and significantly expanded its remit beyond trade in goods; it now covers trade in services as well as the treatment of intellectual property.

From 1947 to 1957 European members of the GATT negotiated tariff concessions with other contracting parties as individual states. During the early years of GATT, the policy focus was firmly on tariff reductions but this changed over decades, in part because the evolution of European cooperation began to raise issues for American policymakers in respect of sectors like agriculture. The Kennedy Round of GATT negotiations (1964–7) was prompted by American concerns about the impact the formation of the Common Market – and particularly the Common Agricultural Policy (CAP) – would have on international trade (Meunier 2005). In language that prefigured debates decades later, American politicians voiced concern about the creation of a single European economy more or less the same size as that of the United States and the resultant need to ensure that this new creation – valuable though it was – nonetheless maintained a commitment to open markets and trade. Thus, virtually from the outset of the Community in 1957, American trade policy has been deeply informed by the perception that Europe is both a key market and home to internationally competitive firms.

In the subsequent decades the American-European trade relationship deepened, and two aspects stand out in this evolution. The first has been the emergence of the EU as a fully established negotiating partner with Washington; the second is the dramatic expansion of the trade agenda to encompass a growing variety of commercial activities. In respect of the former, the Commission assumed negotiations on behalf of all six members of the Common Market with the signing of the Treaty of Rome. Rather like competition policy, the development of a common external commercial policy was an absolute requirement for the construction of a viable and credible marketplace in Europe. But legal competence is no guarantee of negotiating effectiveness, and early EU negotiators' hands were weakened as national governments kept tight control over the GATT process. Member states did not wish to imperil their new European venture through reckless commitments at the multilateral level (Meunier 2005). Another reason, however, was the simple need for EU negotiators to develop the expertise required to be effective negotiators. This took time and even in the Tokyo Round negotiations (1973–9) some national governments doubted whether Brussels bureaucrats adequately understood the technical aspects of some negotiating areas (McGuire 1997). Over the years, though, the trade portfolio became one of the most prized and powerful within the European Commission. Leon Brittan (1993–9), Peter Mandelson (2004–8) and Karel De Gucht (2010–14) were particularly aggressive in pursuing EU trade interests both within the WTO and in RTAs.

As noted earlier, the evolution of American trade policy has been much less significant than Europe's since the 1950s, but two structural aspects of the US process deserve mention. First, the separation of powers in the US constitutional system means that the president is less able to make credible commitments on trade (or many other matters) than is a prime-ministerial counterpart in a parliament. Though Congress delegated negotiating authority to the president under the 1934 Reciprocal Trade Agreements Acts, its oversight is assured by the requirement that any trade agreement receive Congressional assent. In some respects then, Congress plays the same role of 'veto point' as individual member states do in the EU. Both European and American negotiators are adept at employing 'tied hands' negotiating strategies, or 'two-level games' (Putnam 1988), where the difficulty of gaining internal approval is used as a mechanism to force trade partners to make more concessions.

Traditionally, there has been a remarkable symmetry in the trade flows between the two partners, with the EU typically enjoying only a small, generally politically uncontentious trade surplus. This has changed, however, particularly under the Trump administration which viewed trade deficits with any partner as a sign of American weakness. In 2022, the EU's largest surplus in the trade of goods was with the United States to the tune of €151 billion – an amount that doubled since 2010. Aside from the value, the breadth of the trade is also remarkable; European and American firms sell virtually everything to one another and to consumers – everything from cars, appliances and designer goods to insurance and legal services. In a world of rapid but fairly recent globalization the transatlantic zone has been well integrated for decades, and the depth of this relationship is revealed in the extent to which European and American firms have ceased to be 'foreign' in each other's economies. Opel (a subsidiary of GM until it was sold to Groupe PSA in 2017) and Ford of Europe have sold cars for so long in Europe that their affiliation with their American parent causes not the slightest notice. The situation is similar for companies like Ahold Delhaize (which owns the supermarket chains Food Lion, Giant, Hannaford and Stop & Shop in the United States), the French hotel conglomerate Accor and many banks, household appliances and consumer goods retailers.

Competition is based on the high degree of intra-industry trade between Europe and America. This might explain the number of significant EU–US trade disputes, ranging from areas such as subsidies to government procurement policies to safeguard and anti-dumping policies. European and American firms compete with each other in most markets, and occasional trade disputes are to be expected. The major 'growth area' for disputes is not in traditional trade areas like anti-dumping, however, but in regulatory policies, such as technical standards, taxation and issues relating to human and animal health (Pollack 2003b; Young and Peterson 2006). As tariffs and other formal trade barriers are removed, how commercial exchange is regulated comes to be contested. Thus, Brussels and Washington have had disputes over the export of hormone-fed US beef and genetically modified crops and the tax treatment of US exports. Nonetheless, given the importance of trade across the Atlantic, European–American disputes tend to be large relative to cases involving other states. American-European trade conflict serves as an important legal and procedural guide for other WTO members (Petersmann 2003; Busch and Reinhardt 2006). The United States and the EU account for the bulk of the WTO's case-load:

in 2024, the EU was the complainant or respondent for 203 cases, which was second only to the United States with 282 cases.5 Many of these cases are between the United States and EU, and these bilateral disputes are an important element in trade conflict in that they offer guidance to other WTO members on developing trade law (Lindeque and McGuire 2007). In the terms used in Chapter 2, this would seem to be evidence of the growing interdependence and integration that has taken place within the transatlantic 'economic space': neither interdependence nor integration eliminates disputes, but each of them can generate ways of resolving or managing the inevitable disputes that do occur.

The areas where the EU and the United States agree are at least as important as the disputes. Though disagreements generate better headlines, it should not come as a surprise that two large advanced economies to a large extent have similar policy preferences. For example, both Brussels and Washington advocated the significant extension of IP rights during the Uruguay Round. Though the United States began the process of bringing IP issues under the aegis of the WTO (then GATT) in the Uruguay Round, the EU quickly grasped the potential significance; Europe was the home base of a vast number of firms rich in IP in sectors as varied as electronics and perfumes and these corporations were keen to protect their innovations from piracy (Capling, 2004). Enforcement of WTO IP provisions has remained a mainstay of EU–US summits. Financial services liberalization was another area where Brussels and Washington shared interests. The United States had pressed other GATT members for significant commitments on financial services but had withdrawn from the talks in frustration when faced with recalcitrant partners (Sell 2003). The EU, backed by support from national governments – particularly the UK – and business groups, restarted the talks in the absence of the United States and was crucial to brokering a solution acceptable to Washington. In both Europe and America there was a widespread desire for more robust, pro-market financial services regulation and governments' views in both were influenced by the financial services industry.

Managing the relationship

Trade relations illustrate a central theme in this book: that European–American relations are conducted through a dense network of stakeholders. It should not be assumed that power is held by states, or even coalitions of them, but

[5]https://www.wto.org/english/tratop_e/dispu_e/dispu_by_country_e.htm#complainant

is rather diffused among a wider variety of actors – most notably firms – but also international institutions and NGOs. 'Institutions, by providing a venue for the ongoing, systematic exchange of information and ideas, foster consensus formation' (Eichengreen and Ghironi 1998). The Transatlantic Business Dialogue (TABD) was one important firm-based actor, as is the American Chamber of Commerce in Brussels. In the 1990s, both these actors were important in the development of, among other items, mutual recognition treaties which helped facilitate trans-atlantic trade by allowing goods to be sold in either market so long as different product regulations in the EU and United States were functionally similar. The organization has also been important in the area of standards harmonization in the automobile sector, particularly with regard to curbing emissions (Shiroyama 2007). TABD's precise influence can be overstated; its influence waned noticeably in the late 2000s in the absence of strong corporate leadership. However, this hardly signals the diminishing role of business in trade policy. In 2013, TABD merged with the European–American Business Council (which lobbied in the United States on behalf of European companies) to form the Transatlantic Business Council (TABC). The TABC aims to influence both US and EU leaders by presenting a united front on trade and investment issues that are important to companies on both sides of the Atlantic. Additionally, both the United States and the EU have developed mechanisms to consult with business on various trade issues at all stages in the negotiations, as well as with disputes processes at the WTO. The trade relationship demonstrates that in the area of business-government relationships firms do have an important role to play in the provision of expertise and from time to time exert more influence than some observers are comfortable with. Firms can also be important in forcing an end to trade disputes, as it is they not governments that actually suffer financial and reputational effects from disputes (Busch and Reinhardt 2006).

Losing control – the move to multipolar trade

As noted earlier, the Doha Round talks were suspended in the summer of 2006 after negotiations broke down. As trade diplomats attempted to revive the round, both the United States and the EU faced considerable international pressures: the EU on agriculture and the United States on IP and anti-dumping. As with other policy areas, the transatlantic relationship, while very important, is no longer as central to the global trading system as it once was. The changing balance of power in multilateral trade bodies like the WTO can be understood in this way: some 85 members of the GATT launched the Uruguay Round in 1986, and in Seattle in 1999 some 130 national delegations participated. On the eve of the Doha meeting, the WTO could boast some 144 members and by the end of the meeting of trade ministers both China and Taiwan had been admitted as members. Strong though they are, both the United States and the EU participate in an organization where their influence has been diluted, both by an expanding membership and by procedures that do not favour large trading members. Unlike the IMF, for example, with its weighted voting, the WTO works on a one-member, one-vote system. To a much greater extent than in some other international organizations, both the United States and the EU must work diplomatically to get their preferences accepted: simply outvoting other members is not an option when unanimity is required.

The accession of China to the WTO in 2001 was of course absolutely key to this fracturing of the negotiating order. Nonetheless, China continues to feature prominently in EU and US trade policy, with some scholars identifying a shift in Brussels that integrates trade into discussions on strategic autonomy (Eliasson, Costa, and Garcia-Duran 2023). Both actors target Chinese products with anti-dumping duties and press Beijing to honour its commitments to cracking down on intellectual property violations. The tone of US-Chinese economic relations is increasingly shrill, with US politicians and political commentators calling for tougher action. The tone of EU-Chinese relations is noticeable for its lack of public interface, though many of the irritants are common. The US political system gives elected politicians in the Congress powerful incentives to speak out strongly on trade issues; this structural feature of American politics does not have an equivalent in Europe, where trade policy remains more technocratic and consultative, although Young and Peterson (2014) have pointed to increasing parochial influences on EU external trade policy in a number of areas. Two member states in particular have traditionally had a keen interest in open trade policies: the UK because of its trade surplus in services trade due to London's status as a global financial hub; and Germany, which is the world's third-largest exporter of goods (behind China and the United States), many of which find their way to the rising and increasingly affluent markets of Asia, China and Latin America. The departure of the UK from the EU will force Germany to rely on smaller economies like Denmark, Ireland and the Netherlands for trade liberalization support.

One area where the decline of the European–American axis can clearly be seen is agricultural trade. In this policy area, Brazil has become increasingly influential, as its diplomats seek to open markets in response to the growth of a powerful domestic food-processing lobby. At the same time, European policies for international trade in agriculture cannot be understood in isolation from the continuing conflicts within the EU over reform of the CAP. The EU has always had to deal with internal disagreement among member states; in agricultural trade it also has to cope with a heterogeneous group of developing states. It is not the case that all developing states support free trade in agriculture; some small states that enjoy preferential access to the EU, such as Mauritius, fear that their small producers will be wiped out in open competition. The United States, too, maintains many protectionist policies with respect to agricultural trade. To name but two cases, West African countries have expressed opposition to US policies that protect domestic sugar producers with price supports, quotas and tariffs. After winning a WTO case in 2009 against the United States over cotton subsidies to domestic farmers that were depressing prices in developing countries, Brazil began targeting pharmaceutical and cosmetics imports from the United States. In 2014, the two countries came to an agreement whereby the United States would pay Brazil $300 million, while continuing to subsidize American cotton farmers (Hufbauer 2014). It is also true that many developing states are net food importers, and free trade would result in their paying higher prices as the subsidies that currently keep many commodities below market prices would vanish.

A final contributing factor to the shift from multilateral trade through the WTO to regional agreements is the impact of the dispute resolution process. Many commentators argued that the key development of the Uruguay Round was the creation of a robust dispute settlement mechanism that succeeds in being at once effective at settling disputes without trampling on national sovereignty (Jones 2006). From one perspective, the aim of the dispute settlement body (DSB) was to tie down large trading members – particularly the United States – and make them subject to the same rules that bind other states. The system has been used regularly since its creation, with over 200 cases being decided (and many more settled by mutual agreement), and hundreds more in various stages of the adjudication process, though resource asymmetries among WTO members affect the fair working of the system. Consequently, developing states struggle to make truly effective use of the system.

Powerful members like the EU and United States have often been reluctant to abide by DSB decisions. For example, in 2004, a WTO panel ruled that key elements of the EU's sugar regime were inconsistent with obligations under the Uruguay Round's Agreement on Agriculture (WTO 2004). The domestic support price, at over three times the prevailing world price, had the effect of subsidizing exports. Moreover, the EU had vastly exceeded its allowable export level of subsidized sugar and was asked to withdraw the measure. The panel noted that developing states with preferential access to the European market could be adversely affected by this decision (ibid., p. 200) and so urged the Commission to take this into account when developing a new scheme. Consequently, the Commission issued a paper outlining the key changes, all of which meant the withdrawal of key subsidies to sugar producers.

In the United States, too, various WTO decisions have reinforced the traditional scepticism of American policymakers towards multilateral institutions such as the WTO. Controversial issues like the Foreign Sales Corporation (FSC) case illustrate these tensions: here, the EU referred a complaint about the workings of US domestic legislation, which gave privileges to MNCs operating abroad, to the WTO, and the organization found in favour of the EU, allowing them in principle to impose up to $4 billion a year of penalties on US firms. Few American legislators would have imagined that the WTO might have the ability to pass judgement on US tax law. A key element of selling the Uruguay Round agreement to US legislators in the early 1990s was that the new organization represented no threat to American sovereignty (Pigman 2004). Likewise, US anti-dumping laws have been a favourite target of other WTO members. The EU, as well as Japan, South Korea and other states, brought a series of cases to the WTO in respect of US anti-dumping policies (Lawton and McGuire 2005). In particular, the Byrd Amendment allowed petitioning US firms to keep money raised by the United States from successful anti-dumping investigations. The law outraged many trade partners, as it provided even greater incentives for US firms to file such cases. In a rare case of non-compliance, the United States refused to withdraw the Byrd Amendment, in spite of WTO panel rulings that it should do so; eventually, years of pressure led them grudgingly and gradually to withdraw it in 2005. However, the constant stream of anti-dumping cases has served to heighten the political salience of the issue, both within the United States and among trade partners. Moreover, as other states such as China and India make greater use of the anti-dumping instruments as well as the disputes process, the efficacy of anti-dumping for major traders like the United States (and the EU for that matter) has been called into question. There is considerable evidence that the overall use of anti-dumping is in gradual decline (Lawton and McGuire 2005; WTO 2006). Critically, losing WTO cases like these, where the bureaucracy of an international organization and its rules (even if mutually agreed upon by member states) seemingly supersedes US national sovereignty, is partly responsible for the rise of American opposition to similar international organizations that Donald Trump so effectively blamed for domestic problems. The Trump administration made consistent attempts to dilute the force of WTO judgements, most obviously by preventing appointments to the organization's Appellate Body; significantly, the EU was influential in efforts to counter this by developing new procedures (Hopewell 2021).

The WTO's legalistic nature is both a virtue and a vice. On the one hand, countries involved in trade disputes are given plenty of opportunities to present evidence and appeal decisions. However, one notable problem is the length of time it takes to resolve trade disputes. The Airbus–Boeing case is a somewhat extreme example in taking over 15 years to resolve (see Box 4.2). But sometimes a country will impose tariffs or other trade barriers simply to buy time for domestic companies to restructure or find other ways to regain competitiveness. By the time a WTO panel rules in favour of discriminated countries, which may take two to three years, the offending country may remove the tariffs, thereby avoiding any penalties. As of January 2024, the EU had 110 active cases where it claimed other countries were violating trade rules to the detriment of European companies in various stages of the WTO dispute process. The EU was a respondent in 93 cases. The United States had brought 124 cases against other nations, while responding to 158 cases (the most of any member) of unfair trade policies. China, by contrast, had initiated 23 cases and was a respondent in 49 instances. This is another reason for the decline of the WTO, namely that it is ill-equipped to deal with the economic development and industrial strategies of 21st-century economies. The 'state capitalism' model of development uses strategies of state ownership of banks and key companies and even industries, and government intervention and regulatory policies to protect home markets and minimize competition (Bremmer 2009).

Box 4.2 The Airbus–Boeing trade dispute

The Airbus–Boeing trade dispute has been the biggest challenge for the WTO and the multilateral trade system (Olienyk and Carbaugh 2011). Founded in the late 1960s, Airbus was the company that the governments of France, Germany, Spain and the UK pinned their hopes on to challenge US supremacy in the aerospace sector. The governments provided so-called 'launch aid' that consisted of funds offered at below-market interest rates to fund the research and development of new aircraft. By the early 1990s, Boeing realized it had a serious competitor to contend with. In 1992, governments in the United States and Europe agreed that launch aid for Airbus would be limited to 33 per cent of development costs, and indirect subsidies to Boeing were capped at 3 per cent of revenue. Boeing's subsidies were indirect insofar as the company was a major contractor for the Department of Defense and National Aeronautics and Space Administration (NASA), and the innovations and manufacturing processes the company learned for rockets, satellites and military planes would spillover to their commercial aircraft. By 2003, Airbus had surpassed Boeing in both deliveries and new orders of large aircraft (other companies like Canada's Bombardier and Brazil's Embraer dominated the market for smaller and less profitable aircraft). Attempts to resolve Boeing accusations that Airbus had violated the 1992 agreement failed, and so Washington filed a suit in the WTO in 2005. The EU filed its own claim that Boeing had violated the agreement, and also had collected direct subsidies from state and local governments in the United States. The dispute wound its way through the WTO dispute process for over 14 years until seemingly endless appeals were exhausted. Finally, in 2019, the WTO ruled that Airbus was still getting subsidies that harmed Boeing and gave the United States permission to impose tariffs worth up to $7.5 billion on imported European goods. The Trump administration imposed tariffs of 10 to 25 per cent on a wide range of goods intended to punish European countries where Airbus production is concentrated, mainly France, the UK, Germany and Spain. Some of the products included Scottish whisky, cashmere sweaters, wine, cheese and, of course, Airbus planes and aerospace products. In 2020, the WTO ruled on the EU's charge that Boeing receives unfair subsidies in the form of tax breaks from Washington state, authorizing the EU to impose about $4 billion in tariffs on US goods.

Finally, in June 2021, the United States and EU agreed to remove all tariffs related to the aerospace dispute for five years (BBC 2021). The United States and UK reach a similar agreement several months earlier. The primary impetus for the change was a shift by the Biden administration to enlist European cooperation to deal with China's state capitalist economic strategies. By putting the aerospace dispute behind them, at least for a few more years as both sides work to reduce the financial assistance that the WTO objected to, the United States and Europe may be trying to set new ground rules to shape the global competitive environment. In 2022, Airbus delivered far more planes to airlines than did Boeing (663 to 480), had more orders (820) than Boeing (774), which has suffered from the problematic 737 MAX planes, and had a much larger backlog of planes ordered but not yet built (7,239 to 5,430) (Oestergaard 2023). The COVID-19 pandemic had a devastating effect on airline travel, and both Boeing and Airbus were forced to make job cuts. However, the biggest challenge going forward is the rise of new competitors. Japan's Mitsubishi, Russia's United Aircraft Corporation and especially China's COMAC are eager to enter the market for large aircraft, rather than continue to cede this lucrative market to Airbus and Boeing indefinitely. This is particularly important given the medium-term projections for this market. Boeing predicts that between 2023 and 2042, global demand will require 42,595 more aircraft to be produced and delivered, with 40 per cent of these destined for Asia (Boeing 2023). The COVID-19 pandemic put a dent in these numbers. But by 2024, air travel numbers had largely recovered and global demand is likely to expand, especially where the global middle class is growing – namely in Asia. If other companies are going to enter this market, they will need government support as Airbus and Boeing received. If the United States and Europe cannot reach agreement on what a 'fair' amount of subsidy is, there is little to stop the Chinese government from using its deep pockets to pour considerable sums of money into this sector, given the high-skilled jobs, technological spillovers to other industries and huge export earnings that success would bring.

It is clear from this discussion that both the EU and the United States have been affected by the growth of the dispute settlement process and its increasing effectiveness. It is also clear that disputes specifically between the EU and the United States have been central to the 'testing' of the process. Some of these EU–US cases, such as the Foreign Sales Corporation dispute, have involved potentially huge penalties for one party or the other; for the FSC case, the penalties would have fallen on the United States, but in other cases, such as those involving the EU's banana regime, the Union has felt the weight of retaliation. There is a series of ongoing trade disputes between the two partners, but as noted earlier this is only to be expected in a highly interdependent and competitive relationship. On the other hand, while none of the disputes has led to the breakdown of EU–US relations, they have collectively contributed to the decline of the WTO. As noted in Chapter 2, the idea of 'competitive cooperation', in which the parties compete as much over how to cooperate as over substantive issues, may help in understanding this situation.

A post-multilateral era

Multilateralism in the form of additional WTO trade agreements is effectively dead. Two major trade initiatives underscore the challenges to the multilateral trade system and its revival. One is the Transatlantic Trade and Investment Partnership (TTIP). With the Doha Round going nowhere, and RTAs proliferating, it became quite obvious that the world's two biggest traders should forge a trade agreement with each other. Thus, TTIP negotiations began in 2013 on an ambitious agreement that would cover not just tariffs on goods, but also on enhancing market access in services and government procurement (European Commission 2016; see also Morin et al. 2015; De Ville and Siles-Brugge 2016). TTIP also would cut red tape as a result of regulatory cooperation in areas like food safety and animal and plant health, automobiles, pharmaceuticals, cosmetics and medical devices. It would harmonize rules in areas like sustainable development and to aid small and medium-sized enterprises (SMEs), IP and competition policy, as well as establish an investor-to-state dispute settlement system (ISDS) to resolve foreign investment-related legal challenges. In sum, TTIP would be the most encompassing trade, investment and regulatory agreement ever agreed. Hopes for a successful conclusion of an agreement were high. EU Trade Commissioner Cecilia Malmstrom viewed TTIP as a means to 'renew and confirm' the transatlantic relationship, while NATO Secretary-General Anders Fogh Rasmussen referred to TTIP as an 'Economic NATO' (Kundnani 2016).

But TTIP was in trouble even before the election of Trump. The issue garnered more attention in the general public in Europe than in the United States, and a range of interest groups there generated media attention and protests against the agreement (Eliasson and Garcia-Duran 2019). Concerns included European countries being forced to water down environmental, food safety and other regulations to 'lowest-common-denominator' US levels (e.g. removing EU restrictions on genetically modified foods and lowering consumer protection standards); privatization of national health care systems and other government-operated services to allow greater market access for US firms; and that TTIP was too business-friendly, especially in regards to ISDS, by prioritizing investor rights over government policies through the use of tribunals outside the traditional judicial systems. Although TTIP attracted less attention in the United States, the agreement was being negotiated at a time when Americans were becoming increasingly sceptical about the advantages of trade. A Pew Research Center survey showed that only 47 pe rcent of Americans believed that globalization over the past few years was a good thing for their country, as compared to 59 per cent in Germany (Poushter and Schumacher 2020). The Obama administration was finding it increasingly difficult to make the case that trade agreements were, on balance, good for the United States. In 2017, the Trump administration placed negotiations on hold, and two years later the EU accepted the reality of the end of TTIP with a Council decision that the negotiating directives 'must be considered obsolete and no longer relevant' (Council of the EU 2019). Since then, the United States and EU have agreed to negotiate a much narrower agreement focused on industrial goods, but to date little has been accomplished. This is partly due to the trade tensions that have arisen in other areas, as well as the indifference by both parties towards the urgency of a new trade deal given the distractions of an election year in the United States in 2020, the COVID-19 pandemic, the prioritization by the EU of a post-Brexit agreement with the UK, US preference to include trade in agricultural goods in the negotiations and a weakened constituency for free trade on both sides of the Atlantic. Since 2021, the Biden administration's interests focused on domestic considerations such as the pandemic and infrastructure building, and globally on tensions with China and wars in Ukraine and the Middle East. While Biden sought to improve political relations with Europe since the Trump era, a resurrection of TTIP or even more limited agreements with Europe have received virtually no consideration, although the establishment of the EU–US Trade and Technology Council in 2021 revived hopes for future convergence.

The Trans-Pacific Partnership (TPP) began as a trade agreement among four Pacific Rim countries. In 2008, the Bush administration announced that it would negotiate with the group. But it was the Obama administration that advanced the talks as the United States accelerated its foreign policy 'strategic pivot' from Europe to Asia (McBride and Chatzky 2019). The TPP had two main objectives. The economic goal was to reduce trade barriers among the United States and 11 countries: Australia, Brunei, Canada, Chile, Japan, Malaysia, Mexico, New Zealand, Peru, Singapore and Vietnam. These 12 countries at the time accounted for nearly 40 per cent of global GDP, making TPP the world's biggest free trade deal. In 2013, 44 per cent of US goods exports were shipped to TPP countries, as well as 42 per cent of agricultural goods exports and 27 per cent of services exports (USTR 2014). The second objective had a security dimension. China's economic growth and increasing importance in global trade and investment over the past few decades have given the country the resources and confidence to exert political and military influence in Asia. These efforts have startled many of China's neighbours, including Japan, Vietnam and Australia. TPP, while strengthening economic ties with the United States, also provides some degree of American security for these countries. It also signals to China that the United States is committed to countering attempts by Beijing to pressure countries in the region. For example, China became the biggest export market for Australia in 2007 and now accounts for almost one-third of its exports, as Chinese companies and consumers take in minerals, agricultural goods and wine, and tourists and students travel to Australia (Mao 2020). Beijing has used this dependence as leverage to support state-owned and other Chinese investors to make business and real estate acquisitions in Australia, to encourage Canberra to support Chinese initiatives like the Asian Infrastructure and Investment Bank and to influence Australian government policies (Tan 2020). The TPP intentionally excluded China, not just because of concerns about the country's commitment to market economy rules and norms, but also to cordon off to the extent possible real and perceived security threats. After 19 official rounds of negotiations, the text covering 30 chapters was signed in 2016. But like TTIP, TPP was destined to fail with the election of Trump, who disparaged both trade deals in his 2016 campaign. Inaugurated on a Friday, President Trump withdrew the US from TPP the following Monday, preventing its ratification by Congress. The remaining 11 countries in the TPP group agreed to the Comprehensive and Progressive Agreement for Trans-Pacific Partnership (CPTPP), which went into effect in 2018. As with TTIP, the Biden administration made little effort to forge new trade agreements with CPTPP or its member countries.

The major trade deal under the Trump administration was a revision of NAFTA, which the president had referred to as 'perhaps the worst trade deal ever made' (Kirby 2020). The United States Mexico Canada Agreement (USMCA) went into effect in July 2020. It strengthens labour provisions and raises the price of labour for some automobile production, with the expectation that companies will be less attracted to locating in Mexico with higher costs. USMCA gives US farmers greater access to the Canadian market, requires 75 per cent of an automobile be produced in these three countries to be eligible for zero tariffs (up from 62.5 per cent under NAFTA) and includes new provisions on intellectual property and digital trade. Canada and Mexico gain few advantages from the new agreement over NAFTA, but were effectively forced to negotiate USMCA after the Trump administration imposed tariffs on both countries and threatened more. With both countries highly dependent on trade with the United States, because of their geographic proximity and the interwoven supply chains throughout the three countries, Canada and Mexico had little choice but to negotiate with the United States and minimize the adverse impacts a new trade deal would have on their economies.

And there is Brexit. The UK has become a pivotal player (or perhaps a desperate pawn) in a three-way trade game between the EU, the United States and China. Since leaving the EU in January 2020, the UK has sought to negotiate trade deals with virtually every country in the world. Not doing so would lead to the default tariffs of the WTO, but those are higher than could be negotiated on a bilateral basis. For companies in the UK that both import raw materials and component parts and export finished goods, the higher WTO tariffs would raise input costs and final prices, thereby reducing their competitiveness vis-à-vis other firms operating in countries with trade deals. One significant complication from Brexit, however, is that the UK needs trade deals with the EU, the United States, China, and other important economies more desperately than these other countries need trade deals with the UK. This places the UK in a weak bargaining position (US Census Bureau 2021; House of Commons Library 2020). The transactional approach to foreign (economic) policy of the Trump administration was replaced under the Biden administration by an emphasis on keeping the border between the Republic of Ireland and Northern Ireland barrier free – a situation complicated by the 2021 trade deal between the EU and UK that effectively places a trade border in the Irish Sea between Northern Ireland and England, Scotland and Wales. With almost two-thirds of UK exports going to the EU or United States, expanding trade ties with countries in other world regions will take time. That leaves China as a likely partner, but currently neither the UK nor China are key trade partners of each other. Like the United States, China is a huge market and will be unwilling to grant important tariff and other market access concessions to the UK unless it gets valuable benefits in return. In the absence of a functioning WTO, the UK has little choice but to forge bilateral trade deals with dozens of countries.

The imposition of tariffs was the hallmark of the Trump administration's foreign economic policy. Their imposition was justified by a range of reasons (Brown and Kolb 2020). The first major tariffs came in January 2018 and targeted solar panels and washing machines, mainly from China and South Korea. In March 2018, tariffs of 25 per cent on steel and 10 per cent on aluminium were imposed on all trading partners under national security grounds. Ironically, most US imports of these metals originated from allied countries, including Canada, Mexico, South Korea and many in Europe. Canada and Mexico were exempted a year later, which was widely viewed as an attempt to pressure these countries to make concessions as part of a revised NAFTA. The EU responded with tariffs of its own on US goods, including steel, aluminium, food and some consumer goods. An additional round of steel and aluminium tariffs was imposed on all countries in January 2020. However, the primary target for tariffs was China. Long accused by Trump and, frankly, many US and foreign companies of IP violations and discriminatory practices that favour domestic firms, China faced the brunt of US tariffs imposed under the Trump administration. In summer 2018, tariffs ranging from 10 to 25 per cent were imposed on some $250 billion worth of Chinese goods, including computer and auto parts, consumer goods, machinery and electrical equipment. Eventually, tariffs on all of these goods were raised to 25 per cent. In 2018 alone, newly imposed tariffs covered $303.7 billion of goods, accounting for 12.6 per cent of all US imports. In addition to disrupting company supply chains and raising costs for US consumers, tariffs also adversely affected the fight in the United States against COVID-19 (Brown 2020). With tariffs imposed on most Chinese medical products, including at 25 per cent on CT systems, thermometers, patient monitors and disposable medical headwear, imports of these goods fell by $200 million between 2017 and 2019. Hospitals were forced to pay higher prices or spend valuable time finding new suppliers. While this 'tariff war' was happening, the United States was also subsidizing American farmers for lost exports in countries that had imposed counter-tariffs and filing challenges in the WTO, claiming counter-tariffs violated trade rules because US tariffs were imposed for national security reasons. In sum, tariffs and protectionism were the hallmark of the Trump administration's foreign economic policy. But the Biden administration, while removing most tariffs that Trump had applied on US allies, removed few of Trump's China tariffs, apparently viewing them as leverage as it seeks to influence China on other issues, such as Taiwan independence, China's reluctance to criticize Russia's invasion of Ukraine and other geopolitical and geo-economic matters.

Overview and conclusion

This chapter has reviewed key elements of the trade policy process in the EU and the United States and has linked these to their relationship, especially in the context of declining multilateralism. The key points in the argument have been:

- First, the EU–US trading relationship is both broad and deep; it is also underpinned by broadly similar conceptions about the role of markets and trade in promoting global economic growth and social development.
- Second, the extent of interdependence and integration between the EU and the United States in trade creates inevitable frictions and disputes, but the key to understanding these lies in the ways they are managed and 'contained'.
- Third, the global trading environment has changed dramatically over the past two decades. The demise of the Doha Round may signal the end of the time when WTO rounds – and thus the development of the trade negotiating framework – hinged on the ability of Brussels and Washington to hammer out a deal. Both the EU and the United States still operate as key actors, but must share the stage with China as an equal, and with developing countries seeking more influence at the multilateral level and pursuing different goals.
- Fourth, the EU and the United States are key participants in the management of trade disputes through the WTO, and their disputes often have major implications for the wider global trading system. At the same time, domestic interest groups are challenging the notion that international organizations like the WTO should have the ability to influence national trade policies and, indirectly, domestic legislation.
- Finally, both the EU and the United States are ambivalent about the future development of the global trading system. Both have been tempted to engage in bilateral or interregional trade agreements when determined to be more advantageous.

This set of judgements has considerable bearing on the key themes in this book, since it seems to demonstrate in a sharp form the coexistence of competition and convergence between the EU and the United States. It also demonstrates that the background against which the EU and the US conduct their relations is not static; rather, it is dynamic and often challenging, both to the partners individually and to the continuing dominance of their relationship.

Chapter 5

Money and the management of the global economy

Introduction

Although, as we have seen in Chapter 4, trade has formed the longest-standing and deepest area of interdependence between the EU and the United States, the transatlantic relationship in money and finance is rising in prominence. For political economists, international finance is a key, perhaps *the* key, driver of the international economy. The liberalization of financial markets, combined with technologies that enable virtually instantaneous trading, has allowed financial institutions to act globally. The power of investment banks, hedge funds, venture capitalists and other investors to influence, indeed in some respects reorder, national economies, seems almost limitless. Yet this view can understate the importance of political management of the sector. The chairperson of the Federal Reserve may earn vastly less than the managing partner of Goldman Sachs, but the former remains a powerful and influential figure in international finance, not least as they have access to the range of political actors and processes in the most important economy in the world. Moreover, as actors like China attain greater prominence in the international economy, their relative imperviousness to corporate interests underpins the importance of state-to-state relations for managing the world's money. Thus, while financial markets are indeed highly privatized, there remains an enduring management function at the political level, particularly among the big international economies: China, the United States, the EU and arguably the UK, given London's role as a global financial centre. In this regard, the EU has used its experience with the Single Market Programme, and the resultant leverage as one of the world's largest economies, to become increasingly active in the area of financial services legislation.

For most of the past 50 years, the US dollar was effectively a global currency: it remains the world's most popular reserve currency, and important goods and commodities, from oil to aircraft, are denominated in dollars. US dollars remain the principal reserve currency for the world's central banks, though the euro is gaining some ground. In 1999, when the euro began circulating, it accounted for 18 per cent of global foreign exchange reserves held by central banks. The US dollar comprised 71 per cent of reserves. The euro peaked at 28 per cent of reserves in 2009. By 2023, euro reserves had fallen back to 20 per cent, while the dollar dropped to 59 per cent. Other major currencies in 2023 were the Japanese yen (about 5.5 per cent), UK pound sterling (5 per cent) and Chinese yuan (about 2.5 per cent).1 The change in composition reflects, in part, relative shifts of the EU and United States in global trade as compared to emerging markets, and an interest in a number of central banks to diversify their holdings to include non-traditional currencies like Australian and Canadian dollars and, increasingly, the Chinese yuan (Arslanalp, Eichengreen, and Simpson-Bell 2022). Nonetheless, whatever other risks US firms might run when operating internationally, they are far less exposed to one risk that other firms take for granted: currency risk. Prior to the euro, other European currencies were important international currencies, most notably the German deutschmark. As such, this chapter will provide an overview of the important 'management' functions performed by monetary authorities across the Atlantic. Aside from day-to-day contact, more formal and important efforts occur from time to time. For example, in the 1980s, major European central banks joined Japan and the United States in managed intervention to realign the value of the US dollar. A similar effort was seen in September 2000, when central banks in Europe, Canada, Japan and the United States intervened to prop up the euro, which had steadily lost value against the dollar throughout 2000. The euro had eroded in value against the US dollar because America's strong economic performance at the time caused international investors to shift money out of Europe and into the United States, seeking better returns.

A key theme in this chapter is that the internal performance of the American and European economies has important implications for the international economy. As such, both actors are under immense international pressure to pursue responsible economic policies. However, what is good internationally may not be economically or politically wise internally. Moreover, this management function is made more complicated by the activities of Asian central banks and their economies. Years ago, it was possible for international monetary affairs to be governed by the Group of Seven (G-7) of Canada, France, Italy, Japan, Germany, the UK and the United States. But with the end of the Cold War and

---

[1]https://data.imf.org/?sk=e6a5f467-c14b-4aa8-9f6d-5a09ec4e62a4

the subsequent expansion of the global economy beyond the North Atlantic and East Asia region, the G-7's influence has declined. Exporters of oil (mainly in the Middle East) and goods (especially, but not only, China) have accumulated significant international reserves as part of their economic strategy and so their policy choices must be factored in. As with other economic issue areas, the Euro-American dominance of the system is slowly eroding. International finance is entering an age of multipolarity, similar to that seen in the trade arena. The removal of national controls on the flow of international capital has been a key catalyst for the growth of a truly borderless international financial system. Global finance has in turn provided the means by which new economic powers such as China facilitate economic development. These states now seek a place in the international governance structures commensurate with their new status (Ahearne and Eichengreen 2007).

The evolving role of the euro

In the quarter-century life of the euro – it has existed as a currency since 1999 with notes and coins circulating since 2002 – it has gone up and down wildly in terms of public and policymaker expectations as to its role in the European and international economies. However, it is important in this context to recall some of the background outlined in Chapter 1. Though monetary integration was considered as part of the negotiations for the Treaty of Rome, it was not at the forefront of states' collective vision of the Community. Rather, though it was appreciated that a common European currency would help in some respects, the Bretton Woods system seemed to obviate the need for greater European efforts in the area, since it established a broad framework for monetary discipline and stability. Moreover, with extensive welfare states to protect and nurture, member states were reluctant to accept the loss of fiscal and monetary control that would clearly flow from a common currency (Tsoukalis 2000). This thinking changed by the 1970s, as the Bretton Woods system crumbled. The realization that the United States was content to see a world of managed but floating major currencies sharpened the debate about how European states could best cope with currency movements and their attendant consequences. Although the preference for a single currency was a strong one, and the decline and collapse of Bretton Woods seemed to offer every incentive, robust plans for the currency did not survive either internal wrangling or the economic storms of the early 1970s, including the first OPEC oil crisis in 1973.

As the German economy grew to become Europe's largest, the process of monetary integration became essentially a system in the 1970s where some member state currencies were linked to the deutschmark in what was known as the 'snake'. The snake was essentially a pegged currency system where members agreed to assist each other in maintaining a given parity with the deutschmark. This initiative was fairly weak, in that countries dropped out altogether or merely opted for a looser peg when economic conditions like inflation or a decline in exports seemed to justify it.

Momentum for monetary union accelerated during the 1980s by building on Franco-German interests (Van Esch 2012). The European Monetary System (EMS) maintained many of the features of previous managed currency systems, particularly the use of fixed, but adjustable, parity rates. Throughout the decade, member states gradually joined in and by 1992 all the major European economies were in the managed exchange rate regime. The EMS, however, did not survive further international exchange rate turmoil in the early 1990s. The system still hinged on the willingness of Germany to take on the bulk of the adjustment costs of periodic intervention to defend a given parity. The system remained essentially a deutschmark peg. This would have been less of a problem had the EMS member states' economies continued their convergence. However, countries lacking the highly competitive productivity of Germany struggled to maintain their performance, and market expectations of greater divergence in economic performance became self-fulfilling. For example, a country experiencing sluggish economic growth might benefit from lower interest rates. But if that country's central bank lowered rates, its currency's value would fall outside the EMS bands. Even if the central bank did not lower interest rates, many investors in the currency markets would be betting the central bank would eventually do so. Central banks would exhaust their foreign exchange reserves by supporting their country's currency, and at some point give in, lower interest rates and reset their peg to the deutschmark. The lower exchange rate sometimes boosted a member state's exports in the short term, but raised the cost of imports, leading to higher inflation, reduced competitiveness and a repeat of the cycle. The hard work of enhancing economic competitiveness by tackling structural barriers, such as rigid labour and product markets and overburdensome regulations, was often resisted. As a result, German monetary authorities increasingly found themselves drawn into currency markets to defend the parities. By the mid-1990s, with Germany grappling with the economic and social effects of unification, the EMS passed quietly into history.

Instead of abandoning the idea of a monetary union, the EU doubled down on it. The development of the Single Market Programme was the catalyst, for once the notion of an integrated European market was conceded it became easier to press the political case for harmonized monetary relations through a common currency. The 1989 Delors Report provided the roadmap for Economic and Monetary Union (EMU), and the changed political environment of the 1990s, combined with widespread acceptance of greater economic liberalism, provided favourable circumstances. The currency, the euro, was launched in two stages. In Stage One, the currency remained merely a unit of account but was underpinned by greater capital movement liberalization among member states and the irrevocable fixing of exchange rates. In Stage Two, the new currency would circulate in member states and be overseen by the European Central Bank (ECB), whose central objective is price stability – not the promotion of economic growth (which in theory would be complementary) or achieving certain exchange rates relative to the dollar, British sterling or other currencies (which would be viewed as bending to political pressures to, for example, increase exports and reduce imports). In fact, the ECB aims to influence monetary policy mainly by setting interest rates at whatever level will stabilize inflation at about 2 per cent.

One consequence of this goal was to force structural change in European economies. Prior to EMU, governments and central banks that were influenced by political pressures often sought to devalue their currencies to stimulate economic growth via increased exports. Now, absent an ability to devalue the currency to maintain competitiveness, countries were forced to make changes in the structure of the economy. Regulations might need to be eased, infrastructure improved to attract investment and education and training programmes modified to enhance workers' skills. Productivity would have to improve once the monetary instrument was taken out of national hands. Because member states could no longer devalue their currencies to help their companies compete with German firms, some observers argue that Germany has been the main beneficiary of EMU (Krampf 2014).

A key component of EMU was the Stability and Growth Pact (SGP). To placate Germany, which was concerned that member states with a poor record of prudent fiscal and monetary policy could wreck EMU, agreement was reach by way of the SGP to discipline participants that exceeded pre-determined levels of government budget deficits and debt relative to GDP with fines. The SGP was viewed as an effective tool to keep profligate governments in line, since high levels of government debt could, among other downsides, result in bondholders demanding higher interest premiums, possible government debt defaults, the ECB entering unknown territory on how it should respond and even the expectation that other EMU participants would be required to provide bailouts. In effect, the SGP was the EU's way of adopting a monetary union without fiscal union, the latter being far more difficult given very different levels of government spending and taxation among its member states. Conceptually, there are good reasons for running a budget deficit in the short term, particularly during economic crises like the 2007–8 financial crisis and the COVID pandemic, and critics maintained that it was perverse to punish governments with sanctions during such times. The SGP makes it difficult to implement countercyclical fiscal policy (that is, increased government spending) in response to economic slowdowns. The pact does not simply impede deliberate countercyclical policies, but also automatic responses; government spending tends to rise automatically in a slow-growth environment as, for example, laid-off workers claim unemployment benefits and tax revenues fall (Baily and Kirkegaard 2004). In fact, the EU suspended application of the SGP in 2020 to permit member states to take aggressive financial steps to address the pandemic's economic and social impact (European Commission 2020a). A key issue internationally is whether the SGP impairs the ability of the EU to take on a leadership and managerial role in the international economy.

The euro's most serious challenge occurred in the wake of the 2007–8 financial crisis that originated in the United States. It became apparent that several member states were experiencing financial crises of their own. Irish banks, for example, had funded a property and construction boom for over a decade. When property prices began to collapse, many borrowers had loan balances that exceeded the value of their homes or commercial properties, resulting in numerous defaults and bankruptcies. To save the country's banks and signal to the foreign companies who had invested in the country that the economy was stable, the Irish government bailed them out, assuming many of the bad loans on their books. But the cost of those additional obligations placed a huge burden on the government's public finances. Spain and Portugal experienced similar problems, and Italy's public finances were strained as well.

But the biggest concern was Greece. For years, the government had spent lavishly, particularly on state employees and pensions, which some retirees could start collecting at the age of 55 for men and 50 for women for certain occupations. At the same time, the government was not collecting sufficient tax revenues, with tax evasion a common and serious problem. All of this came to a head when Athens was unable to pay back lenders, many domiciled in Europe, who held government bonds. Defaulting on its debt would be a blow to the euro and EMU. From the introduction of the euro in 1999 until the Greek crisis, yields (interest rates) on government debts for member state governments varied little, with investors assuming that EMU had largely eliminated government bond risk across countries. Another way of looking at it was that the German government's long history of fiscal discipline would somehow provide a level of security for the eurozone. But with the Greek crisis, investors realized that each eurozone member posed different risks and that the interest rates they demanded for holding government bonds should vary accordingly. The increased interest rates that investors were demanding to continue to buy and hold Greek debt became unsustainable. Athens turned to its fellow member states for help.

None of the possible options was attractive (Quaglia, Eastwood, and Holmes 2009). Bailing out Greece would set a bad precedent for other countries at that time (including Ireland, Spain, Portugal and Italy) and in the future, and would create resentment among citizens in other member states. Creating euro-dominated debt akin to US treasuries was rejected as a means to address this problem, future national crises and again during the COVID pandemic (Howarth and Quaglia 2021). Among the common criticisms presented by Europeans was why should they pay higher taxes to bail out Athens so that Greek citizens can retire ten years earlier than workers in some other member states? Negotiating with bondholders to receive a discounted price for the bonds they held also posed problems. Many Greek bonds (and other member state bonds) were held by a number of European banks, many in Germany. If those banks were forced to accept a reduced value for the bonds they were holding, might an EU-wide banking crisis ensue? Nobody was sure what the house of cards looked like because it was difficult for the ECB to get accurate information about the assets held by numerous European banks across multiple countries. The least bad option was for the EU and the International Monetary Fund (IMF) to jointly provide short-term financing to the Greek government. However, the support came with very strict conditions, including dramatic cuts in government spending on health care, education and the public sector and raising more tax revenues. The loan conditions resulted in major domestic and European political problems. Within Greece, extremist parties first on the left and then on the right came to power, in large part as a backlash against the conditions imposed by the EU and IMF. Many Greeks blamed German chancellor Angela Merkel for the harsh conditions imposed. Merkel and Germany were viewed as the rich neighbour that was unwilling to help during Greece's time of need. Within the EU, getting consensus among member states on the best course of action was fraught with political divisions over how much to help Greece or, in fact, to force the country out of the eurozone – an outcome that came close to becoming a reality (Schimmelfennig 2018; Posen 2005).

The Greek crisis presented much ammunition for critics of EMU and the euro (see for example Stiglitz 2016). The eurozone was comprised of countries with very different economies, not only in terms of size but also structure and degrees of diversification and international exposure, values on how much to tax and spend, political effectiveness in terms of managing public finances and transparency and political power within the EU. On the other hand, public support for the euro has increased across most eurozone countries since its introduction (Italy being the most notable exception), although support tends to rise and fall in particular countries based on macroeconomic conditions (e.g. inflation and unemployment levels) at the time (Roth et al. 2019).

Assessing EMU and the euro in the mid-2020s, it is clear that they have for the most part been a remarkable success (Howarth and Verdun 2020). Transaction costs (i.e. the fees paid to banks to exchange currencies) have been eliminated for trade among eurozone countries, and the euro is widely accepted in global trade and finance, though not as much as the dollar (as noted earlier). Economic policy coordination among member states has improved, as finance ministers and central bankers work together to minimize variations in macroeconomic policies, particularly with regard to fiscal policy. European companies have had mixed experiences, depending on how competitive they were within Europe and internationally. Despite a somewhat rocky start, the euro's exchange rate has become much steadier vis-à-vis the dollar. From an initial value of $1.16 in 1999 to an all-time low of $.84 later that year to an all-time high of $1.59 in 2008, the euro-dollar exchange rate has settled into a relatively stable range of about ten cents on either side of $1.12 since 2014 (Macrotrends 2023). This is a level of stability that most companies, large and small, and governments can work with.

The US economy: A tale of two deficits

As outlined in Chapter 1, during the formative years of the European Communities, the US dollar had provided a dominant currency against which others might be fixed. From an early stage, though, the dollar had begun to show signs of weakness, culminating in the 'Nixon Shock' of 1971, through which the US authorities effectively rewrote the rules of the Bretton Woods system. From the mid-1970s onwards, the system of fixed exchange rates gave way to floating or 'managed' exchange rates, and the dollar was notable for its relative instability. This meant that US interest rates also had to fluctuate in order to finance US investment and government expenditure, with consequent effects for the international monetary system. By the late 1980s, as member states began to plan for the euro, a certain amount of management had returned to the international arena, but the end of the Cold War and associated economic changes meant that once again there was pressure on both exchange rates and national economic policy management.

Beginning in the early 1990s, the US economy began to expand at a spectacular rate, well above European levels. Millions of jobs were created, and US firms enjoyed remarkable gains in productivity and their global presence. There was a vibrant debate in both academic and policymaking circles over the exact extent of this above-trend growth in productivity. For some, the information technology (IT) revolution had indeed lifted productivity throughout the economy, not least by increasing price transparency via auctions and allowing much tighter control of supply chains. Other analysts doubted this and pointed out that most of the observable productivity growth was contained within the IT sector (Gordon 2003).

The growth of the US economy in the 1990s had important implications for the transatlantic relationship. First, the explosion of consumer spending in the United States, buoyed by rising stock markets, saw an appreciation of the dollar as foreign direct investment poured into the United States as firms sought returns that could not be gained in the 'sclerotic' eurozone. The resulting slump in the value of the euro, as investors shifted assets from Europe to the United States, was not merely a symbolic blow to European pride; it also resulted in higher real interest rates in the eurozone as the ECB sought to attract money into the European economies. The concern was not merely perception; if Europe was not an attractive place to invest, it was only a matter of time before European multinationals would depart for locations around the world with better prospects.

George W. Bush came to the US presidency just as this economic miracle was running out. Though the expansion was coming to an end of its own accord, the catastrophe of 11 September 2001 also played its part. In the weeks after that event, US airlines went bankrupt, and manufacturers ran up huge losses as the enhanced security arrangements delayed shipments and added costs. Aside from terrorism, economic factors also played a role. The internet bubble burst amid concerns that these 'new economy' companies were hopelessly overvalued. Enron, WorldCom and Tyco were among the more prominent of a string of episodes of corporate fraud and misbehaviour. Buffeted by adverse economic and political conditions, the Federal Reserve cut interest rates aggressively, seeking to restart economic activity. This, in turn, made investors reconsider whether they wanted so much exposure to the American market.

President Bush provided his own solution to the recession of the mid-2000s: tax cuts. Politically controversial, Bush's tax cut package sought to reassure frightened investors with generous treatment of investment income. Economists argued that if an economic stimulus was needed, it ought to appear in the form of more broadly applicable tax cuts or even rebates, which are more likely to be spent. President Bush and the Republican-controlled Congress passed tax cuts with an estimated cumulative value of $2 trillion over the ten years from 2001 to 2010 (Leiserson and Rohaly 2006). The US budget deficit, which had disappeared under President Clinton, re-emerged and was heading towards $300 billion as the tax cuts, slower economic growth and increased US military commitments to deal with wars in Afghanistan and Iraq all took their toll on the country's fiscal health. See Figure 5.1 for recent trends in US government deficits and total debt.

The US budget and debt position deteriorated further in the aftermath of the 2007–8 financial crisis. Caused primarily by housing loans made in the sub-prime mortgage market, the crisis resulted in major banks including Bear Stearns and Lehman Brothers going bankrupt and the US government spending over $400 billion to buy toxic assets from banks to stabilize their balance sheets and support General Motors and Chrysler, since few people were buying new cars at the time. Spending on social supports like unemployment increased, while tax revenues dropped, the combined effect of which was to increase the budget deficit. In 2009, for the first time in US history (but not the last), the budget deficit exceeded $1 trillion ($1.5 trillion, to be precise).

The US government's financial situation worsened with the 2017 Tax Cuts and Jobs Act. President Donald Trump pressed for this $1.9 trillion tax cut, with much of the benefit going to corporations in the form of lower tax rates. Presented as

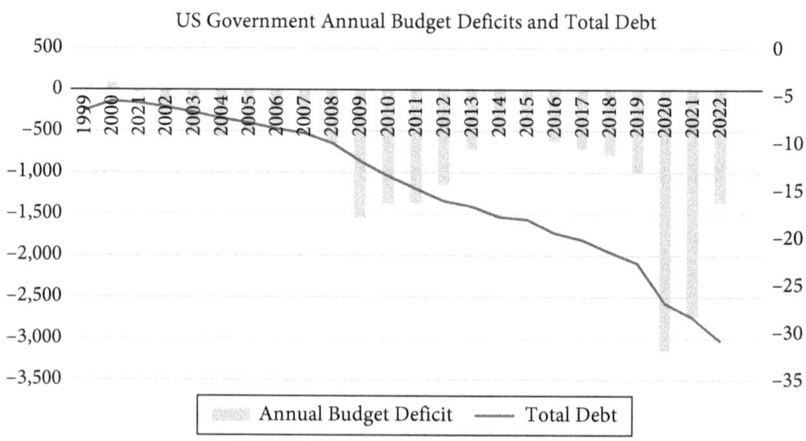

Figure 5.1 US federal government budget deficits, 1999–2022 (billions US $, left-side); US federal government total debt, 1999–2022 (trillions US $, right-side). Sources: US Congressional Budget Office (https://www.cbo.gov/data/budget-economic-data#2) (accessed 9 December 2023); The White House (2023) Historical Tables (https://www.whitehouse.gov/omb/budget/historical-tables/) (accessed 9 December 2023).

a means to promote investment and jobs in the United States, the Act produced little in the way of new investment and, instead, resulted in lower government tax revenues than would otherwise have been generated and gains mainly to wealthier Americans in the form of stock buybacks (Gale and Haldeman 2021). Most recently, the COVID pandemic pushed budget deficits higher further still, reaching $3.1 trillion in 2020, with the White House Office of Management and Budget predicting annual deficits of at least $1 trillion through 2028. With total government debt in 2024 exceeding $34 trillion, the United States is the most indebted country in the world, and one of the most indebted on a debt to GDP basis (about 150 per cent).

Budget deficits are not the only US financial problem. So, too, are current account deficits, caused primarily by America's persistent trade deficit (see Chapter 4). While the United States has a consistent trade surplus in services, given its strengths in areas like finance, consulting and entertainment, it has run a merchandise trade deficit for decades, owing to the high consumption rate of American consumers (almost 70 per cent of GDP) (see Figure 5.2). Current account deficits are financed by the willingness of foreign sources of capital to 'lend' the United States money in the form of the purchase of US debt securities (bonds) or assets. The United States has long confounded expectations about a correction in its current account: the widely expected depreciation has not seemed to happen. As long as the US economy performs well enough to attract capital, and the political system seems more stable than most other countries, the deficit can be financed. Moreover, exporting countries like China and Japan help with this process through the purchase of US treasury bonds (with holdings

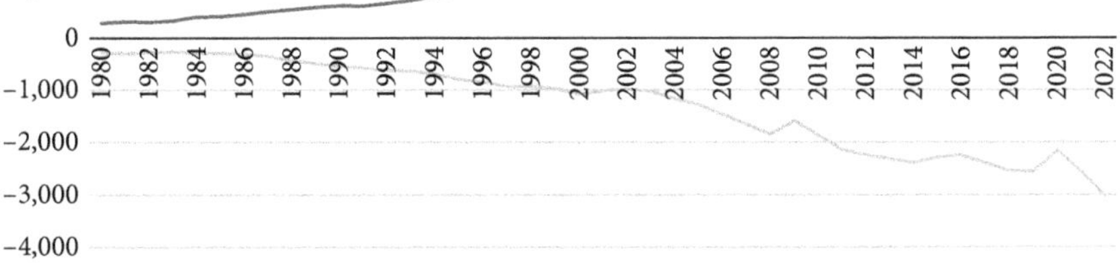

Figure 5.2 US exports and imports, 1980–2022 (billions US $). Source: US Census (2023), US Trade in Goods and Services – Balance of Payments (BoP) Basis (https://www.census.gov/foreign-trade/statistics/historical/gands.pdf) (accessed 9 December 2023).

of about $1 trillion each), thus keeping US interest rates and tax rates lower than they otherwise would be.

Competition and convergence in financial regulation

In much the same way that the dollar was the world's currency from the mid-20th century, so too American financial regulation was regarded as the *de facto* standard for a swathe of banking, insurance and related sectors. Even though many other states did not formally adopt, for example, American rules on accounting or corporate governance, firms with any stake in the US market would have to adopt those standards if they wished to tap the world's deepest, most liquid and most innovative capital markets. America's dominance of the world economy was reflected in its dominance of the regulatory agenda. This is changing, with European standards gaining international acceptance.

The EU has used the convergence dynamic of its Single Market Programme to set the regulatory agenda for a variety of operations in the financial services industry. The EU's efforts in financial services reflect a complex mix of internal politics and external events. In 2000, the EU embarked on the Lisbon Agenda, a ten-year plan that aimed to make the EU 'the most competitive and dynamic knowledge-based economy in the world capable of sustainable economic growth with more and better jobs and greater social cohesion' (Copeland and Papadimitriou 2012). Among other objectives, the Lisbon Agenda provided a rationale for the pursuit of wide-ranging harmonization and liberalization of financial services regulation within Europe. Experience of the single market for goods helped this process. Equally, however, American concerns about corporate governance in the wake of scandals manifested themselves as increased regulatory burdens and political risk for firms operating in the United States. This mix produced a situation in the early 2000s where Europe briefly appeared a more conducive environment. However, the Lisbon Agenda achieved few of its goals to boost European competitiveness and was followed in 2010 by another ten-year plan, Europe 2020, which was somewhat more successful, especially the development of the Digital Single Market.

In the wake of several financial scandals in the early 2000s, President George W. Bush signed the Sarbanes-Oxley Act. Among other actions, it set rules for corporate governance, auditor independence and financial disclosure, and led to the Securities and Exchange Commission's creation of the Public Company Accounting Oversight Board, a quasi-public entity that would oversee accounting practices. Likewise, after the 2007–8 financial crisis, the Barack Obama administration and Congress passed the Dodd-Frank Wall Street Reform and Consumer Protection Act in 2010. The legislation restricted some of the riskier activities of the biggest banks, increased government oversight of many of their activities and required banks to hold larger reserves to absorb losses associated with bad loans going forward. However, the Trump administration, with the aid of a Republican-controlled Congress, rolled back some of these regulations with the 2017 Financial Choice Act.

In the area of accounting standards, in 2005 the EU adopted a version of International Accounting Standards (IAS) from the London-based International Accounting Standards Board (IASB) for application to all member states. This use of the International Financial Reporting Standards (IFRS) obviated the need for firms to comply with two sets of accounting standards: their national system and the EU-level regime. The reverberations of this policy were seen around the world as other nations came to the view that, given the significance of the EU for their firms' operations, the *de facto* adoption of IASB regulations would simplify matters by reducing the need to prepare sets of accounts to two standards (Ashbaugh 2001). The United States, however, operates its own accounting system, the Generally Accepted Accounting Principles (GAAP), but, with more international firms (and their states) adopting IFRS, American policymakers and accounting experts opened discussions about how to harmonize IFRS and GAAP. In 2007, the US Securities and Exchange Commission allowed companies filing accounts in the United States to choose which standard they adopted (US SEC 2007). The cumulative effect of these developments was to galvanize international acceptance of IAS (Ding et al. 2007). Most countries now require IFRS for their own domestic companies, with some key exceptions. China requires domestic companies to use Chinese GAAP and does not allow IFRS, while Japan allows domestic companies to use IFRS, US GAAP and two different forms of domestic GAAP. Some scholars argue that a bit of competition between accounting standard setters, including GAAP and IFRS, is healthy to ensure that neither body becomes complacent in a rapidly changing global economy (Kothari, Ramanna, and Skinner 2010; Sunder 2011).

The UK's withdrawal from the EU, or Brexit, has impacted Europe's financial industry. Long one of the world's leading financial hubs, along with New York, London has faced tremendous pressure as a result of Brexit. Although the city remains the world leader in the provision of such financial products as cross-border bank lending, foreign exchange turnover and interest rate over-the-counter derivatives, its global market share in each of these dropped a few percentage points by 2022 from their pre-Brexit levels (TheCityUK 2023). Approximately 7,000 banking jobs left the UK as a result of Brexit, with many going to Amsterdam, Paris and Dublin. Although this is a small percentage of the 2.2 million banking jobs throughout the UK, it is significant that most EU countries are experiencing growth in this sector, with countries like Poland seeing a large growth in banking centre employment, particularly in back-office positions (Hall and Heneghan 2023). The fact that employment in financial services in the UK is stagnant at best, and several cities in the EU are picking up business from London, suggests that this sector will see more changes in the coming years.

Complexities and crises in the global economy

In an age of global finance, it has become commonplace for people to view international monetary affairs as an area of light regulation. This is partly because regulation has been relaxed compared with the late 20th century. During the early decades of the Euro-American system, monetary regulation sought to constrain the ability of states to engage in competitive devaluation or reckless monetary expansion – policies implicated in the economic collapse of the 1920s and 1930s. From the 1970s onwards, changes in the international monetary system created pressures for change at the national level as well.

In particular, capital controls, which constrain the flow of money from one state to another, were gradually removed during the 1970s in all major economies. Related to this, major currencies moved away from rigid fixed currencies towards managed float systems of economic governance. Technology also played a role: the explosion of private financial flows was made possible not merely by capital control removal, but also by the development of computerized trading systems and telecommunications infrastructures that facilitated this growth. New products were also developed, with many such as financial derivatives in response to regulatory changes.

As a result of these changes, it has become increasingly difficult for central bankers to manage exchange rates. The combined foreign exchange reserves of all of the world's central banks were about $12 trillion in 2023. Yet almost $8 trillion dollars are traded every day on foreign exchange markets. Interventions by central banks to, say, slow a decline in the value of their currency simply cannot match the amount of money available to investors who believe that economic and political fundamentals justify a decline. While in the past companies and banks were the traditional actors in the currency markets, which was natural given the need for different currencies to facilitate trade, today pension and hedge funds managers as well as speculators, who bet on exchange rate changes, and sovereign wealth funds help to dramatically increase daily volumes.

But any notion of international finance as a regulation-free zone is entirely illusory: private actors have an interest in a robust (that is not the same thing as heavy-handed) regime of cooperation. Both the United States and the EU thus play a key role in the governance of the international financial system. This management function is usually conceived of as the management of exchange rates as a policy tool to react to economic shocks and government policies. In 2007–8, both European and American central banks played the role of 'banker of last resort', pouring money into volatile markets that threatened to seize up as the crisis in the American housing market scared investors off all kinds of debt instruments.

The EU–US relationship here, as in other spheres, cannot be grasped by merely examining the interactions of top policymakers conducting economic summitry. Rather, high politics intersect regularly with daily meetings among private and public sector technical experts across a range of financial issues. However, a clear evolution in the relationship is the relative decline of political considerations as important variables in monetary relations. The relationship remains extremely important, yet is now more characterized by 'technical' interactions on exchange rates in support of macroeconomic stability. Arguably, the most 'politicized' monetary relationship the United States now has is with China, not the EU. The export-led growth strategy China has employed is underpinned by a dollar peg system created in 1994, with the yuan going from less than six to one US dollar to well over eight to one US dollar for over a decade, before settling into a range of about 6.3 to 7.3 per dollar from the mid-2010s to 2024. By keeping the exchange rate lower than what a freely floating currency might be valued at, Chinese exports are cheaper for foreign buyers, particularly those in the United States. This undercuts American firms in sectors like textiles and apparel, furniture and intermediate manufacturing, and increasingly higher technology products like solar panels and batteries for electric cars. As discussed in Chapter 4, this has been a major irritant in US–China relations and a key reason for President Donald Trump's imposition of tariffs on Chinese goods.

There are of course other reasons for worrying about the Chinese currency peg. China recycles its export earnings to buy US treasury bonds, and increasingly equities through state-controlled entities like sovereign wealth funds. In doing so, it accumulates US dollar balances that help keep the yuan peg, but the policy has two consequences, one domestic and the other foreign. When the Chinese government chooses to recycle export earnings, it penalizes the domestic economy. Firms have less money to invest in new plant and employees, while consumers have less money to spend on imports or themselves. It is not clear whether Chinese consumers will tire of waiting for export success to manifest itself in higher purchasing power for the masses, not just a lucky few. US and European firms with investments in China are, to a greater degree than Asian investors, concentrated in domestic sectors ('in China, for China') such as automobiles, restaurants and consumer goods (Lardy 2005). The trade surplus that China has with the United States (see Chapter 4) is not a direct result of investment by US companies in China who export back to the United States. In fact, 61 per cent of the $6.6 trillion total cumulative investment abroad by US companies is in Europe, with just $126 billion (2 per cent) in China (US BEA 2023: Table 6). Rather, China's trade surplus with the United States is largely driven by exports from Chinese-owned companies or other Asian companies manufacturing in China, including those subcontracting production for technology firms like Apple, Dell and HP. But foreign investors in China primarily to sell goods and services to Chinese customers are adversely affected by a government policy that depresses domestic demand. Export-led growth also starves the government of funds to invest in infrastructure and social programmes. The other consequence is foreign. China's willingness to buy US bonds and assets allows the United States to continue to live beyond its means, as noted earlier. China has held about $1 trillion of US government treasuries since the early 2010s (as has Japan), which was more significant when total US government debt was about $15 trillion in 2012 as compared to $34 trillion in 2024. Still, with all foreign investors including China holding about 25 per cent of US government debt, there are legitimate concerns about their appetite to continue to do so and the increased borrowing costs for the US treasury if global investors place their funds elsewhere.

Two events thus far in the 21st century have presented enormous challenges to US and European policymakers charged with managing the global economy: the financial crisis originating in 2007 and the COVID pandemic that began spreading around the world in early 2020. The financial crisis, often known as the 'Great Recession' because it was the most severe global recession since the Great Depression of the 1930s, originated in the United States with the explosion in prior years of sub-prime mortgages (i.e. loans to homeowners and other property owners of dubious creditworthiness). As housing and property prices began declining in 2007, borrowers and their lenders (a range of US and non-US banks) found that loan values exceeded property values. Investor and consumer confidence declined and the availability of lines of credit froze, forcing long-standing banks like Bear Stearns and Lehman Brothers to go bankrupt and others like Merrill Lynch to be acquired by other banks and financial institutions. Consumption of goods and services in the United States declined as unemployment rose to a high of 11 per cent, with these trends also spreading to Europe due to the deep transatlantic financial, investment and trade linkages.

The crisis affected developing countries by way of a collapse in commodity prices and less demand for imports in the United States and Europe. China was much less impacted, due to tight control over the country's banking system through regulations and state-owned banks, and a rise in domestic consumption. China's ability to advance through the economic turbulence faced by the United States and Europe emboldened Beijing to pursue its vision of a multipolar world through new international organizations (discussed later) and influenced many countries around the world to consider the merits of adopting China's state capitalism economic model (see Chapter 4), given the booms and busts associated with Western-style capitalism. But by 2023, China was experiencing a real estate bubble of its own with highly indebted developers, and it is not obvious that the country's state-owned banks, with 40 per cent of their total loans related to property, will weather the likely storm unscathed (Bradsher 2023).

The response by US and European governments was expansive and Keynesian with respect to fiscal and monetary policies (Hodson and Quaglia 2009). Governments spent heavily to support the unemployed, provide stimulus payments to consumers and bail out companies, including banks, insurance companies and automotive firms. The impact of unprecedented government non-war time spending between 2009 and 2012 greatly increased deficits and debt (see Figure 5.1). The US Federal Reserve, ECB and Bank of England implemented traditional policies like lower interest rates, and developed new instruments such as quantitative easing, which involves purchasing securities and Treasury bonds held by the public, thereby injecting cash into the economy to be used by consumers to make purchases and by banks to make new loans. The UK, where faith in markets and limited regulation most closely resembled the United States, was one of the most affected countries, with unheard of levels of government intervention in the economy, including the nationalization of Northern Rock, a building society (Hodson and Mabbett 2009). Within the EU, despite the presence of the ECB, banking was largely regulated by national authorities. Consequently, it was difficult to evaluate risk for the EU banking system as a whole, especially since banks in one country might have loans in and deposits from another member state (Begg 2009). Following this financial crisis, and in response to the Greek crisis described earlier, the Commission proposed more than 50 legislative and non-legislative measures, the most important of which were incorporated into the Banking Union (2014) and the Capital Markets Union (2015 and 2020), thereby transferring more oversight and regulation from the national to the EU level (Scheinert 2023; Smolenska 2021).

Less than a decade after this financial crisis, the world was struck by the coronavirus pandemic. Originating in China, then spreading to Europe, the United

States and eventually virtually everywhere in the world, the pandemic strangled global trade, travel, investment and shipping. Again, policymakers were forced to respond to a crisis that affected employment, economic growth and government finances, as well as public health. As with the previous crisis, fiscal and monetary tools were applied to alleviate the economic impact. The EU's response was a €2,364 billion spending plan consisting of €750 billion for a recovery effort (Next Generation EU), €540 billion in safety nets for workers, businesses and member states and €1,074 billion to fund digital and green transitions between 2021 and 2027 (European Council 2022). Member states injected additional sums from their own budgets. In the United States, the federal government budget deficit in 2020 was an unprecedented $3 trillion due to massive spending injections into the economy and lower tax revenues. On both sides of the Atlantic, inflation rates in 2021 and 2022 reached levels not seen in decades, due to supply chain constraints, a jump in consumer spending as people returned to pre-COVID purchasing behaviours, rising wages to lure workers back to jobs, government stimulus spending and rising commodity prices (particularly the impact of Russia's invasion of Ukraine on food and energy prices). The Federal Reserve, ECB and Bank of England went from cutting interest rates in 2020 when the pandemic struck, to rapidly raising rates in 2022 and 2023 as inflation became the greatest economic concern. Globally, developing countries' economies were especially hard hit by the pandemic, seeing global travel (including tourism), trade and investment fall precipitously in 2020 and 2021, not to mention the health impact due to the uneven introduction of vaccines. Unlike the financial crisis a decade earlier, which China weathered much better than the United States and Europe, the pandemic had a longer impact on that country. An important reason for that is Beijing's 'Zero COVID' policy and often draconian lockdowns of entire cities. This stifled economic growth and delayed the eventual contraction of the infection by many of the country's citizens. China's economy has struggled in the 2020s due to the pandemic, but also a burgeoning property bubble, President Xi Jinping's preference for state-led rather than private sector growth and geopolitical tensions, and no combination of fiscal and monetary policies is likely to reverse this.

Evolving management structures of the global economy

Managing these broad economic and financial changes has become increasingly difficult for Europe and the United States. With the US withdrawal from the Bretton Woods fixed exchange rate system, the Arab oil boycotts and stagflation creating a range of economic uncertainties in the 1970s, finance ministers from the United States, France, Japan, the UK and West Germany began meeting as the Group of 5, or G-5. Over the next few years, Italy and then Canada joined the group, creating the G-7, while the EU was represented at meetings but not an actual member. Until the end of the Cold War, these seven countries represented the major western economies. Regular meetings of their finance ministers and central bankers, and summit meetings for prime ministers and presidents, helped to address, indeed manage in some cases, what were essentially global macroeconomic issues that affected Europe, North America, Japan and a handful of other countries, with the 1985 Plaza Accord agreement to depreciate the US dollar perhaps its most noticeable achievement.

In 1997, Russia joined this grouping, thereby creating the G-8, not so much for the country's economic power, but as an incentive to undertake domestic economic and political reforms. However, Russia was suspended from the group in 2014 after its invasion of Crimea. In the 2020s, the G-7 is bordering on the edge of irrelevancy. The relative share of these seven countries' contribution to global GDP has dropped considerably over the past 50 years, from a high of nearly 70 per cent in 1987 to under 45 per cent in 2021 (*Economist* 2023). At the same time, the decisions they made in the past regarding currencies, interest rates and stimulating economic growth now impact (and are impacted by) many other countries that have no seat at the table. Consequently, alternative groups have formed that better reflect the global political economy.

One such group is the G-20. The G-20 formed in 1999 as a response to various financial crises during the latter half of that decade in Mexico, East Asia and Russia. However, it was the 2008 financial crisis that brought the G-20 to prominence as country leaders rather than finance ministers began attending annual summits, now hosted on a rotating basis. The G-20 was formed by 19 of the world's largest economies (including the United States, China, Germany, France, Italy and the UK) plus the EU, with the African Union added as a permanent member in 2023. The G-20 is far more representative of the present global political economy than the G-7. Each continent is represented, membership includes both economically developed and emerging market countries, and the combined members represent around 85 per cent of global GDP and 75 per cent of global trade (Munyati 2023). However, the G-20 has struggled to achieve any significant and tangible accomplishments (Berger, Cooper, and Grimm 2019). In large part, disagreements within the G-20 mirror those seen within the United Nations (UN), World Trade Organization (WTO) and other Bretton Woods institutions on virtually every issue area: finance, economics, trade, energy, environment and security. Global and regional rivals including the United States,

EU, China, Russia and India seek to influence other members in a forum where decisions are made by consensus (McBride, Siripurapu, and Berman 2023). Finally, the G-20 does not have its own bureaucracy, institutional mechanisms or finances to implement decisions or agreements, which are left to members to do as they please.

Another grouping that has received considerable attention is known as the BRICS. Initially a group comprised of Brazil, Russia, India and China that first met in 2009, the BRICS added South Africa the following year to complete the BRICS acronym. The five countries represent about 40 per cent of the global population and 30 per cent of world GDP, but population size and economic clout vary widely among them. Like the G-20, the BRICS seeks an alternative to Western-formed and led global structures and is absent any formal institutions, rules, policies or decision-making procedures. But unlike the G-20, BRICS membership excludes Western countries and aims to be a bridge between developing countries and the West. Over 40 countries have expressed interest in joining the group, driven by disenchantment with the global order over issues including the dominance of the US dollar in international finance, trade and investment flows, economic development and vaccine distribution during the COVID pandemic (Reuters 2023). In 2023, the BRICS invited six countries to join the group: Argentina, Egypt, Ethiopia, Iran, Saudi Arabia and United Arab Emirates.

However, the BRICS has struggled to achieve significant, tangible accomplishments. Part of the problem is that the divergent political systems of its members (Brazil, India and South Africa are democracies) can make cooperation difficult. Global economic influence varies, with China and India being larger trade and investment powers than the other three. Geopolitical interests also vary, with Brazil, India and South Africa more willing to stay engaged with the United States and Europe on global matters. As a result, China and Russia have failed to turn the BRICS into an anti-Western coalition (Mardell 2022). Additionally, all these challenges will be exacerbated with the addition of six new members and especially Iran, effective in 2024, and likely future expansions of the group. The BRICS founded the New Development Bank in 2014 as an alternative to the IMF and World Bank for developing countries seeking financial support. However, few loans have been disbursed, the bank is reliant on private capital to fund projects, there is a lack of transparency, local groups are not consulted about the impact of funded initiatives and projects often fail to support the bank's mission of financing sustainable development and infrastructure projects in the Global South (Millar 2023). On the other hand, Papa, Han and O'Donnell (2023) argue that, as an informal institution, the BRICS is inappropriately compared to other organizations. Instead, they recommend focusing on the convergence of member policies at the sub-BRICS level, for example on space policy. Despite the BRICS surviving well into its second decade, some modest accomplishments and a long list of aspirant members, neither the United States nor the EU have forged specific 'BRICS policies', but have instead focused on bolstering bilateral relations with individual members, particularly India.

A further challenge to the post Second World War global architecture is China's attempts to exert global economic and political influence. While China has sought to do so in traditional forums like the UN, WTO and IMF, Beijing has sought to put its own stamp on global financial and economic cooperation. One initiative was the creation of the Asian Infrastructure Investment Bank, or AIIB (Chin 2016). The AIIB's purpose is to help developing countries build infrastructure, on the belief that this is a precondition to attract investment and further economic development. The United States viewed the formation of the AIIB as a threat to its preferred international financial institutions like the IMF and World Bank, mainly because of perceived economic and political advantages for Beijing and Chinese companies, but was unsuccessful in preventing key allies, including Europe, Canada, Australia and South Korea, from joining the bank, which now has 109 members.

However, it is China's Belt and Road Initiative (BRI) that has received the greatest attention in the media, corporate boardrooms and government offices. Devised in 2013 by Chinese president Xi Jinping, the BRI aims to link China to Central Asia and Europe on an overland route akin to the Silk Road of medieval times (the 'belt'), as well as to southeast Asia and Africa on a maritime route (confusingly the 'road'). Much of the BRI consists of investment in infrastructure in member countries, such as ports, power plants, railways and telecommunications. Of the 151 countries that have signed up as BRI members in the hopes of receiving part of the $1 trillion that China has pledged to lend during the first decade of the plan, 17 are in the EU (mainly in the east). The BRI has been controversial for several reasons (McBride, Berman, and Chatzky 2023; Jie and Wallace 2021; Aoyama 2016). Funds provided by China to recipient countries often come with stipulations that a significant portion be spent on materials sourced from China or that Chinese companies do the work. Some critics argue that the BRI is a 'debt trap' in that some recipient countries find themselves unable to pay back funds lent for infrastructure development and are forced to renegotiate on terms much more favourable to Beijing. Finally, some see the BRI as a political tool for Beijing to curry favour with recipient countries, particularly when seeking support at the international level, including over disagreements with the United States, recognition of Taiwan, climate policy and human rights. Nonetheless, China has had little difficulty adding members to the BRI, even if funds offered to individual countries often fall short of actual projects. But some participants have become disillusioned with the BRI's proclaimed benefits. Italy joined BRI in 2019 but withdrew in 2023, partly because significant Chinese investment never materialized, Italian exports to China remained stagnant while Chinese imports increased and the Georgia Meloni government sought to more closely align the country's interests with the United States, NATO and an increasingly China-sceptic EU (Mazzocco and Palazzi 2023). Still, the significance of BRI is that it presents an alternative to the US and European approaches to a global financial architecture and inserts a wedge in transatlantic relations given that over half of EU member states are affiliated with BRI.

Overview and conclusion

International finance is at once one of the least-regulated economic sectors, and one of the most politicized. The United States and the EU have both benefited from the dramatic explosion of international capital mobility that has developed since the 1970s. However, both actors have a significant management function to play, not least because both the dollar and the euro are key international currencies for a range of financial and trade-related activities. Moreover, American and, latterly, European regulations for international finance have a profound effect on other states. European efforts to globalize EU standards in the financial world do present a challenge to the United States, yet EU efforts are liberalizing and as such very much reflect the Euro-American preference for open markets. The challenge, in other words, is one of process, not underlying philosophy. As with other policy areas, EU–US influence in shaping the structure of the international system is strong, yet both actors now confront increasingly influential players. China is the most obvious candidate here, as its dramatic economic growth and exchange rate policy have created both opportunities and tensions for Europe and America. In this chapter, we have outlined the key developments in monetary and macroeconomic relations between the EU and the United States. The following central points have emerged:

- First, because of their dominant positions in the international economy, the domestic monetary and fiscal policies of these actors assume international importance. Developments in the euro and the dollar since the end of the Cold War have given added weight to this point.

- Second, the bilateral relationship cannot be understood as comprising only the interactions of top economic policymakers. In this sphere, the private sector has a key role to play in broader issues of economic governance. For example, the accounting standards adopted by the EU, the IFRS, were developed by an international organization of accountancy professionals, the IASB. The vast resources held by banks, other financial institutions and private investors have significant influence on government policies, including the ultimate power of sending investment to or withdrawing money from any country in the world, including the United States and EU member states.
- Third, there has been a tension in the relationship between the demands of domestic economic management and those of international currency stability. In the case of the euro, this has a 'two-level' aspect, reflecting tensions between eurozone member state priorities and those of the ECB; in the case of the United States, there has been a continuing tension between the need for the United States to maintain a high level of domestic consumption and the resulting need to borrow large amounts of other people's money, contributing to significant federal budget and current account deficits.
- Fourth, both the EU and the United States have been affected by the rise of China, which has placed demands on their trade and investment policies, and which has demanded adjustment. The EU–US relationship is no longer as central as it was to the global economy, although it would be wise not to understate its continuing significance.

As with trade in Chapter 4, the EU and the United States display competition and convergence in global macroeconomic and financial matters. Competition remains a key component of this relationship as both aim to secure the economic benefits associated with a stable economic and financial environment based on self-interest and tools at their disposal, sometimes resembling a zero-sum game. Yet, global economic challenges, particularly from China and emerging economies, provide a strong justification for convergence to preserve a mostly free-market-oriented approach to global economic policy and to maintain the political influence that accompanies standard-setting and reserve currency status. We turn now to a related theme with economic and political dimensions – foreign investment and competition policy.

Chapter 6

Investment and competition policy

Introduction

Chapters 4 and 5 have dealt with two of the 'classic' issues of international political economy – trade and money. In each case, the development of policy and institutions in the European Union (EU) has come into contact – or collision – with policies and institutions in the United States. Thanks to the development both of trade and of the euro, the EU constitutes the United States' largest partner and/or rival (along with China) in the world arena, and not unexpectedly this has given rise to disputes and sometimes confrontations. At the same time, there have arisen practices of cooperation and areas of common interest, both within EU–US relations and between the two and the rest of the world. This chapter moves into a different area, one now especially prominent with the development of increased economic interpenetration and which involves the domestic regulatory structures of both the EU and the United States. The impact of processes of globalization, leading to the intensification of interconnectedness between societies, especially in the industrial world, creates new issues of management and of institutional development, and this is one of the key concerns here.

As seen in Chapter 4, the trade liberalization of the past several decades has allowed American and European firms considerable access to each other's markets and to those in third countries. The lowering of trade barriers, however, cannot necessarily achieve effective market contestability; it can still be the case that a market free of 'at-the-border' barriers can severely handicap foreign firms thanks to domestic regulations and practices. Dealing with these problems requires effective competition policy. An additional layer of complexity has arisen thanks to the vast increase in international investment flows, manifest among other ways in the increase in international mergers and acquisitions (M&A). This process has now made the international coordination of competition policies – and investment regulations where they exist – an object of European and American interest. However, unlike traditional trade barriers, investment and competition policies are deeply rooted in domestic political economy and national institutions which themselves embody decades – centuries even – of norms, traditions and practices. In many countries, investment and competition policy regulation is weak, and neither is a priority for poorer countries. This chapter will argue that the intricacies of the Europe–US–China relationship create a challenging dynamic that underscores the cooperative and competitive dimensions of transatlantic relations.

Investment and competition policy issues are also closely linked to innovation. In the not too distant past, much was made of the insecurity of the EU about its record of innovation relative to the United States. In the 1990s and 2000s, for example, critics asked where was Europe's equivalent to Microsoft, Apple or Amazon? What has changed on both sides of the Atlantic is an increasing scepticism about the social value of many recent innovations in the area of social media, artificial intelligence and the changing nature of employment relations. Europe's scrutiny of technology giants such as Alphabet (formerly Google) and Meta (formerly Facebook), as well as opposition in many European jurisdictions to Uber, used to be regarded as thinly veiled jealousy, but times have changed. Complaints about the gig economy, aggressive tax planning and privacy and security concerns have made EU scepticism seem more credible, yet underscore the different value systems on both sides of the Atlantic. Simultaneously, China has developed successful global technology rivals in the form of Alibaba, ByteDance and BYD using a combination of state capitalism (see Chapter 4) and ruthless domestic competition to challenge US and European companies globally.

This chapter will begin by examining foreign direct investment (FDI) flows and trends in the United States, the EU and other key countries, followed by the increasing use of screening mechanisms for inward FDI (especially by the United States and EU towards Chinese investment) and the effects of industrial policies on FDI flows and transatlantic relations. Next, this chapter will compare different approaches to US and European competition (antitrust) policies, focusing mainly on similarities and differences with respect to merger policy. Finally, the chapter will compare US and European approaches to internationalizing investment and antitrust policies.

Investment

Europe and America are the world's most important investors and bankers and as such occupy a key place in the international political economy. Of the $44 trillion of inward foreign direct investment (FDI) stocks in 2022, the EU's

27 member states were the recipients of $11.2 trillion (over 25 per cent of the total), while the UK accounted for $2.7 trillion, or 6 per cent of global FDI stocks (UNCTAD 2023). The United States was the destination for $10.5 trillion (almost 24 per cent), while mainland China hosted $3.8 trillion, with an additional $2.1 trillion in Hong Kong and $46 billion in Macao (totalling 13.5 per cent of global FDI stocks). Thus, the EU, UK, United States and greater China accounted for almost 70 per cent of inward investment in 2022 (see Table 6.1). What is particularly significant is that Europe and the United States have attracted FDI from around the world for decades due to the many factors that influence these flows, including political stability, quality work force, rule of law, good infrastructure and market opportunities. But FDI in China is a relatively recent phenomenon (UNCTAD 2006). In 2005, for example, a cumulative total of only $272 billion was invested in mainland China (with another $494 billion in Hong Kong). Thus, FDI stock increased a staggering 14-fold by 2022 in mainland China (and over 4-fold in Hong Kong). To some observers, this is the flip side of the role that China is increasingly playing in global trade, as was discussed in Chapter 4. Some critics argue that investment by multinational corporations (MNCs) in China, and emerging markets more broadly, comes at the expense of investment in Europe and the United States, and to the detriment of their workers and industrial base. President Donald Trump was one such critic, tweeting in 2019 that 'Our great American companies are hereby ordered to immediately start looking for an alternative to China, including bringing our companies HOME and making your products in the USA' (Rappeport and Bradsher 2020).

Although the number of country recipients of FDI is broadening, the sources of investment remain relatively small. MNCs headquartered in the EU, United States, and UK account for over 58 per cent of all FDI around the world (see Table 7.2). Add in MNCs from Japan, Canada, Switzerland and other advanced economies, and about three-quarters of all FDI is made by companies based in the world's richest countries. As will be discussed further later, China is quickly changing this cozy arrangement. As recently as 2010, mainland Chinese MNCs accounted for just $317 billion (1.6 per cent) of global outward investment. This increased to over $2.9 trillion (7.4 per cent of the global total) in 2022. Add $2.1 trillion of FDI made by Hong Kong-based investors, and the deep pockets and growing global ambitions of Chinese firms and the government in Beijing become evident.

Foreign investment provides numerous benefits to host countries. For example, the $4.0 trillion of investment by US companies in Europe (including Switzerland and the UK) was responsible for providing about 4.8 million jobs in 2021 (Hamilton and Quinlan 2023). Likewise, European companies had $3.2 trillion of FDI in the United States in 2021, employing five million Americans.

Table 6.1 Foreign Direct Investment Inward Stocks (2022)

	$ billion	**Global share (%)**
European Union (27)	11,170	25.2
United States	10,462	23.6
Mainland China	3,822	8.6
UK	2,699	6.1
Hong Kong	2,091	4.7
Singapore	2,368	5.4
Canada	1,440	3.3
Africa	1,053	2.4
Switzerland	1,037	2.3
Brazil	816	1.8
Australia	758	1.7
Mexico	649	1.5
India	511	1.2
Russia	379	0.9
All other countries	4,998	11.3
Global total	44,253	100

Source: United Nations Conference on Trade and Development (UNCTAD). (2023) *World Investment Report, Annex Table 01. FDI Inflows, by Region and Economy, 1990–2022*, 5 July (https://unctad.org/en/Pages/DIAE/World%20Investment%20Report/Annex-Tables.aspx).

Table 6.2 Foreign Direct Investment Outward Stocks (2022)

	$ billion	**Global share (%)**
European Union (27)	12,726	31.9
United States	8,048	20.2
Mainland China	2,932	7.4
UK	2,203	5.5
Hong Kong	2,055	5.2
Canada	2,033	5.1
Japan	1,949	4.9
Singapore	1,595	4.0
Switzerland	1,352	3.4
Brazil, India, Russia, South Africa	1,065	2.7
All other countries	3,895	9.8
Global total	39,853	100

Source: United Nations Conference on Trade and Development (UNCTAD). (2023) *World Investment Report, Annex Table 01. FDI Inflows, by Region and Economy, 1990–2022*, 5 July (https://unctad.org/en/Pages/DIAE/World%20Investment%20Report/Annex-Tables.aspx).

In some instances, acquisitions by foreign firms saved domestic firms from bankruptcy, thereby preserving jobs and sustaining communities. In other cases, they led to the development of industrial clusters, as when FDI by, say, BMW in South Carolina incentivized auto parts companies like tyre firms to follow suit in the same geographic area. The US auto company Chrysler, for example, declared bankruptcy in 2009 during the height of the financial crisis. Fiat initially acquired 20 per cent of Chrysler and, by early 2014, owned the entire company, thereby preserving thousands of jobs and a portion of the US auto industrial base while also giving the Italian company a foothold in the US market (Bertoldi et al. 2015).

Yet FDI is not without controversy. Sceptics are wary of the intentions of acquiring companies. This concern has intensified with the rise of acquisitions by Chinese firms (Guay and Smith 2023). As discussed in Chapter 4, China's state capitalism and particularly the activities of state-owned firms have inspired global worries that investments and acquisitions may be intended to acquire intellectual property and trade secrets or make inroads into key sectors. For example, Germany was concerned when the Chinese conglomerate Midea acquired the Bavarian robotics manufacturer Kuka in 2016 (Zhang 2018). Likewise, Virginia-based pork producer Smithfield's acquisition by the Chinese company WH Group (formerly Shuanghui) raised concerns about US food security (Thomas 2023). Similar concerns apply to China's Belt and Road Initiative (BRI) – a pseudo-Marshall Plan aimed to support investment and economic development across Asia, Africa and into Europe, as discussed in Chapter 5. Some critics argue that the main intention is to create an economic reliance on Chinese investment and financing that will leverage Beijing's political influence (Huang 2016). Other criticisms focus on the lack of reciprocity for foreign firms seeking to invest in China. China places 3rd (behind Indonesia and New Zealand) in the Organization for Economic Cooperation and Development (OECD) Foreign Direct Investment Regulatory Restrictiveness Index, while the United States is 13th and most EU member states are near the lower (less restrictive) end (OECD 2020).

European and US responses to the Chinese investment challenge are converging. The EU spent seven years negotiating the EU-China Comprehensive Agreement on Investment (CAI) in the hopes of opening the Chinese market to more investment opportunities for European companies and creating a more predictable regulatory environment. For China, the deal presented an opportunity to develop closer economic ties with Europe, given the increasingly frosty relationship with the United States under the Trump administration. Although a final agreement was reached in December 2020, its ratification was frozen by the European Parliament just five months later due to increasing concerns about domestic human rights violations, Beijing's crackdown on pro-democracy protests in Hong Kong, allegations of internment of Uyghurs in western China and a seemingly more aggressive Chinese foreign policy (McElwee 2023). Pressure from the Biden administration in early 2021 contributed to the collapse of the deal and ended attempts by the EU to resuscitate it (McElwee 2023).

At home, the United States and EU turned to investment screening mechanisms (ISMs) to evaluate the economic and security implication of Chinese FDI. In the United States, the Committee on Foreign Investment in the United States (CFIUS) dates to the 1950 Defense Procurement Act. CFIUS has evolved to become an inter-agency committee housed in the Department of the Treasury and includes representation from the Departments of Justice, Homeland Security, Energy, Defense, State, and Commerce and the Office of the US Trade Representative and Office of Science and Technology Policy. When a proposed merger or acquisition by a foreign entity of a US company raises potential national security issues, CFIUS determines whether the investment can go ahead, be subject to conditions or barred. Due to growing concerns about Chinese foreign investment, the Foreign Investment Risk Review Modernization Act of 2018 (FIRRMA) seeks to strengthen and modernize CFIUS to address modern security concerns more effectively. One new aspect includes investigating investments when the foreign entity does not have a controlling stake in the US company but may have indirect influence or access to assist in the diffusion of technologies to their home country. However, a section of the FIRRMA legislation that would have included an outbound screening component was removed after US industry opposition (Bauerle Danzman 2022).

For many years in the EU, member states had the right to vet foreign investment in their countries without any EU interference. But sentiment for change grew throughout the 2010s in light of an increasing number of foreign acquisitions, particularly Chinese companies buying all of, or large stakes in, Sweden's Volvo, Italy's Pirelli, Finland's Amer Sports and the German robotics maker Kuka, among others. In 2019, French president Emmanuel Macron claimed that 'China plays on our divisions. . . . The period of European naïveté is over' (Erlanger 2019a). That same year, the European Parliament voted overwhelmingly in favour of a proposal that empowers the European Commission to investigate foreign investments in critical sectors and give its opinion on whether they threaten European interests (European Commission 2020b; Reuters 2019). Supporters of the policy, which took effect in October 2020, argue the objective is to give further scrutiny to investments that are more political than economic in nature. Crucially, the Commission cannot block mergers and acquisitions. It can only give its opinion on whether vital infrastructure might be compromised, or valuable technologies could fall into foreign hands. The lack of an enforcement mechanism means the EU has a weaker vetting process than FIIRMA in the United States (Egan and Guay 2023). But national level ISMs have now been adopted in every member state, albeit with different degrees of screening (Meunier 2014).

US firms face less suspicion than Chinese companies in Europe, and vice versa. This is due to a much longer period of transatlantic investment, as well as the similar regulatory and business practices in Europe and the United States. Investment controversies do exist, but they assume different dimensions. One of the most contentious relates to tax. Accusations of MNCs avoiding tax in Europe are a major controversy because member states have been unwilling to agree a common corporate tax (Wasserfallen 2013). Ireland has used its 12.5 per cent corporate tax rate, one of Europe's lowest, to entice MNCs to set up their EU headquarters and book their profits there rather than higher tax member states where revenues were earned. Globally, countries with low corporate taxes and weak regulations have served as tax havens for major corporations, thereby depriving government treasuries (including the US and many European countries) of revenues necessary to fund public spending.

Prior attempts to reach a global agreement were unsuccessful. However, the Biden administration, with its more committed approach to multilateralism, took steps to address this by proposing a minimum corporate tax at the June 2021 G-7 meeting, with the expectation that this action would be expanded to OECD member countries and the G-20. In October 2021, 130 countries agreed a 15 per cent minimum tax on the world's largest companies (Rappeport and Alderman 2021). Significantly, the agreement also requires corporations to pay taxes in countries where their goods or services are sold, even if they are not physically located there. This is aimed particularly at technology companies like Amazon, Apple and Meta that earn revenue throughout the EU, but book their profits in low-tax member states like Ireland and Luxembourg. Given the challenges related to changing domestic tax laws, it is not yet clear when this agreement will fully come into effect.

Competition policy

As trade barriers come down and FDI increases, competition policy enforcement becomes important in shaping the domestic economy. Foreign rivals enter the market and erode the market power of incumbent domestic firms – assuming these foreign firms are able to effectively contest the market. This is the first area where competition policy enforcement becomes important under liberalized trade. Fred Bergsten highlighted that several 'trade' disputes between the United States and Japan during the 1980s and 1990s, such as those concerning auto parts, photographic film and semiconductors, were really about alleged anti-competitive activity by firms and not trade regulations (Bergsten 1998). Foreign firms must be able to compete effectively; evidence suggests that once firms are established in a jurisdiction they tend to stay (Evenett, Lehmann, and Steil 2000: 12). Thus, effective competition policy has the long-term benefit of making markets more contestable. If foreign firms are significantly larger than domestic firms, a second threat is that they may gain too much of the market, thereby enabling them to use their market power to keep rivals out; antitrust law is thus important in maintaining a competitive market. The rise of network industries, such as social media, telecommunications and e-commerce, also poses problems for the international coordination of competition policy. In industries where the utility of a product is a function of how many other people have it, a firm that establishes leadership can quickly dominate a market, as consumers 'coalesce' around the product (Evenett, Lehmann, and Steil 2000: 15). In software, there is an additional opportunity for market dominance since the marginal cost of producing an additional copy is so low (and indeed can be transmitted at virtually no cost through the internet), thus making it exceptionally difficult to dislodge dominant firms. Though early fears that antitrust legislation designed for the industrial era would not be able to cope with the new economy have appeared slightly exaggerated, the increasing level of economic interdependence epitomized by firms like Amazon, Alphabet, Microsoft and Meta offers increased chances of regulatory conflict.

Finally, the expansion of FDI across the globe to developing states provides an additional rationale for further development of competition policy. Many developing states have few if any antitrust rules and the further development of these economies – and the firms that invest there – may hinge on the creation of robust competition policies. Though the EU dropped competition policy from its list of Doha Round negotiating objectives (see Chapter 4), it was instructive that Brussels warmed to the idea of a multilateral competition policy as European firms began to invest more in developing economies.

Competition policy enforcement has become more important because of increased FDI flows. However, as a policy area it is distinct from investor protection agreements, which are enshrined internationally in bilateral investment treaties (BITs). Competition policy sets out the parameters of how private parties interact with one another; it is about regulation of the marketplace. Investment protection, by contrast, is concerned with the relationship foreign investors have with the host government. Host governments will often, in an attempt to gain further from an initial investment by a firm, make continued operations contingent on compliance with regulations relating to sourcing of parts, employment of the local population and other performance requirements. The ultimate sanction for a non-complying firm is expropriation. BITs seek to constrain the ability of host governments to impose and enforce performance requirements (Bora 2004).

They have become an important element of US regional trade agreements; the EU does use them, but has paid more attention to the international dimensions of antitrust (Gagne and Morin 2006).

The salience of international antitrust measures – whether pursued through multilateral or bilateral means – has increased in recent decades. In 1986, there were only 2,676 global mergers (Statista 2023). Interest in international antitrust measures first gained prominence in the 1995–2002 period when a global mergers boom (there were 39,783 mergers in 2000) seemed to signal the need for international coordination of policies, if only to reduce transaction costs. However, several high-profile EU–US disputes, discussed later, seemed to signal a greater need for international cooperation beyond that of saving firms money on compliance costs. Since then, the number of global mergers has ranged from a low of 27,201 in 2002 to a high of 57,958 in 2021. The European Commission received notification of 11 mergers in 1990, when its power to vet mergers began, growing to 110 in 1995, and 300–400 per year since 2014, signifying the importance of the EU market for global companies and the regulatory reach of the EU (European Commission 2023b). Yet competition policy has not resumed its place on the international policy agenda as an area of controversy, despite the dramatic increase in FDI flowing to developing states where the risk of anti-competitive practice ought to be the greatest because of a wide range of disagreement on whether and how to do so.

Evolution of EU competition policy

It is important to understand at the outset that many of the roots of competition policy in the EU owe much to existing US antitrust measures (see later). American influence on European competition policy began immediately after the Second World War II, when the United States insisted that West Germany adopt strict anti-cartel legislation to prevent the re-emergence of the Nazi-era industrial combines such as Farber (Devuyst 2001). However, in marked contrast to their American counterparts, it took many decades for European-level competition authorities to make a significant policymaking impact, the key catalyst being the Single Market Programme (SMP) of the late 1980s and early 1990s. As European companies aggressively pursued M&As to prepare for the single market environment, the early and mid-1990s saw something of a boom in EU competition policy development. However, a series of high-profile cases in the late 1990s and early 2000s fuelled the impression that the Commission was overextending itself and exerting influence over business that went beyond its mandate. After a slight retrenchment, the Commission appeared re-energized to take on cases, particularly in the 'new economy' of high technology, in the 2010s and early 2020s when competition policy was under the direction of Commissioner Margrethe Vestager (Aydin and Thomas 2012).

Like the trade directorate, competition authorities in the EU enjoy relatively high levels of authority and autonomy vis-à-vis national governments. Though trade policy authority owes much to the enhanced leverage gained by pooling sovereignty for trade negotiations, the nature of the Commission's dominance in competition policy owes more to internal European factors. From the outset, developing a common economic area was bound to require the development of a competition authority:

> The Treaty of Rome's aspirations to prevent any such distortions to trade and to create a complete and genuine common (and later single) market were inconceivable without the application and enforcement of rigorous competition rules. (McGowan and Cini 1999: 176–7; see also Todorov and Valke 2006; Wilks 2005)

The Commission enjoys clear primacy in the development and implementation of competition policy, with the Council of Ministers and the European Parliament finding themselves 'on the sidelines' (McGowan and Cini 1999: 177). That said, the Commission's competition enforcement activity was not particularly prominent in the early years of the Communities. This was partly because national-level policy frameworks seemed adequate for the task and because some member states were adamantly opposed to further extensions of Commission power. It was also due to the fact that the Commission's authority resided largely in the domain of price collusion and abuse of dominant position. Mergers and acquisitions (M&A) – two key methods firms use for entering new markets – were not included in the list of powers. Mergers were not under Commission remit until the Merger Control Regulation of 1989, though various European Court of Justice (ECJ) decisions had helped enhance the Commission's powers in this area. The 1973 Continental Can judgment reinforced the Commission's assertion that it could use its existing – albeit limited – powers to regulate the competitive effects of mergers (McGowan and Cini 1999: 179).

The adoption of the Merger Control Regulation finally affirmed the Commission's primacy where mergers were concerned and coincided with a clear neo-liberal shift in European politics towards more competitive markets and in turn the need for a robust competition policy. The SMP would not work if local collusive practices were tolerated. Successive competition commissioners used the bureaucracy's powers with considerable zeal, making the directorate among the Commission's most activist and internationally well-known bureaucracies (McGowan and Cini 1999; Damro 2001). By taking authority over M&A, the Commission was now the key regulator for the prime method of entering new markets – and not just in Europe. Since the 1990s M&A have boomed, and business demands for a single regulator to oversee all this merger activity were also key to the success of Brussels in extending its powers in this area. Indeed, the European-level process of developing a single regulatory body – with its attendant reduction in transaction costs for firms – has rather prefigured and informed current debate about the wisdom of an international competition policy. The Merger Task Force (MTF) was set up within DG Competition to attend to the expanding case-load falling under the Merger Control Regulation.

Though the Commission is now recognized and generally praised as one of the world's leading antitrust authorities, its activities have not been uncontroversial. As the merger boom of the late 1990s and early 2000s pressed on the Commission's resources, a series of questionable decisions began to undermine business confidence in the process. A small set of these decisions involved the United States (see later), but most referred to mergers among European firms. In a series of decisions, including Lafarge and Airtours, outside experts and business people began to question some of the underlying practices of the MTF. They noted that in contrast to American practice, there is no separation of powers among bureaucracies: DG Competition was the investigator, judge and jury for merger cases. From a practical standpoint, critics wondered how a relatively small staff could cope with the number and complexity of merger cases coming before them. By contrast, American antitrust authorities operate with much greater resources. Further damage on the MTF's credibility was inflicted in 2002 at the Court of First Instance (the EU's court of appeal for mergers) when the judges overturned the MTF's decision to block the merger of two UK travel firms – First Choice and Airtours. It was the first time a Commission decision in the area of mergers had been overturned and was described at the time as a 'hammer blow' to the Commission's standing (Veljanovski 2004: 154). Two further cases were lost and more appeals filed – crucially including the controversial General Electric–Honeywell case (see later).

In response to these criticisms, and adverse judgments at the ECJ, the Commission launched an extensive review of merger regulations. The MTF was disbanded and its functions spread across other units in the Competition Commission. There is now much bolstered economic analysis thanks to increased resources, including the creation of the post of chief economist. A key reform in the substance of merger policy was the greater acceptance that mergers can generate considerable economic efficiencies – even if the combined group has a significant market share. This reform, which owes much to the General Electric–Honeywell case, moves the EU merger rules away from a central concern about market structure towards a more American-style interest in market operations (European Commission 2004; Todorov and Valke 2006).

Upon taking office in 2004 Commissioner Neelie Kroes signalled changes in the policy trajectory (European Commission 2007). These included a greater emphasis on consumer welfare in relation to competition, thus signalling a slight shift away from the producer orientation taken by EU authorities over many decades. Among the key shifts was the desire to pay more attention to the anti-competitive consequences of state aids, amid continuing evidence that member states were reluctant to let market forces work where politically sensitive (automobiles) or prestigious (airlines) sectors were concerned. Whereas competition policy in the EU in the 1980s was concerned with creating a competitive marketplace, attention now is focused on the EU's lagging productivity and poor record on innovation. The Competition Directorate, no less than other Brussels bureaucracies, has been keen to develop its own policy role in respect of the Lisbon Agenda. 'Strong competition, encouraged and protected by EU competition policy, is rightly regarded as instrumental for achieving the competitiveness objective of the European Union and the Lisbon Strategy' (European Commission 2004). In this respect EU policies do reflect traditional American beliefs and policy that innovation is best secured through fiercely contested markets. In fact, there is growing evidence that the EU has, in many cases, surpassed the United States in the competitiveness of its markets. Philippon (2019) argues that many markets, including airlines and telecommunications, are more competitive in Europe than in the United States, due to a stronger EU antitrust policy and fewer opportunities for companies to influence regulation and policymaking through 'regulatory capture' and campaign finance donations. A key question and difference between US and EU approaches is how best to create and maintain contested markets.

Evolution of US antitrust law

The American preference for fierce competition in the marketplace has a long lineage, though it was not present at the creation of the United States, as some of the mythology would have us believe (Matthijs and Parsons 2022). As Peter

Gourevitch (1996) noted, American economic policy took a pro-market turn in the late 19th century that fundamentally altered the relationship between market and state. Until this turn, America shared more than is commonly believed with continental European economies with their more corporatist, social market orientation. This mercantilist economic tradition, championed by the country's first Secretary of the Treasury Alexander Hamilton, has tended to be forgotten in commentaries on American economic policy until recently, when increasing foreign competition led some policymakers to call for a renewal of the Hamiltonian tradition of state involvement in the economy.

America's turn towards the open, competitive market we saw during most of the 20th century took place in the late 1800s amid increasing public disquiet – anger even – over the anti-competitive activities of large firms such as the Standard Oil Trust. The Sherman Act of 1890 is one of the best-known pieces of American legislation and was passed in response to public concern about the activities of 'large industrial conglomerates' in rigging markets (Devuyst 2001). That said, it was not immediately obvious that the act would work to encourage fair, market-based competition. This was because one consequence of the Sherman Act – and its active interpretation by the courts – was to spark a merger boom between 1895 and 1904. As Mowery and Rosenberg point out, since the Sherman Act prohibited rigging markets via cartels and informal arrangements, firms simply internalized the market via mergers. The Supreme Court's subsequent decisions reduced the attractiveness of mergers and indeed created incentives to diversify product portfolios so as to avoid the legal scrutiny that came with dominance of one industry (Mowery and Rosenberg 1998: 14–15). The Clayton Act passed in 1914 is less known to many but is arguably the more important element of US competition policy legislation. This is because it deals with the forms of collusion and sharp practice and does so by forbidding price collusion, supplier agreements and other restraints on trade. As such, it sought to protect small businesses by ensuring that no company could through its activities substantially reduce competition in the marketplace. The Clayton Act is the foundation of US merger law to this day (Devuyst 2001: 128).

More merger legislation was passed in subsequent years, often with the intention of preserving small businesses in the face of larger competitors. Though it will strike many as odd given the numerous large multinationals domiciled in the United States, competition policy in the United States has long been shaped by a fear of large business units. US antitrust policy is generally more active than comparable bodies of merger and competition control. Nonetheless, the aggressive promotion of competition by American authorities in the early part of the 20th century may have had one paradoxical side effect: it allowed some

US firms to become very large. By forcing firms away from collusion, legislation induced a form of natural selection into the market; those firms able to manage a portfolio of activities thrived, as did those able to harness gains from in-house innovations. Firms that did not develop excellent in-house management failed. Antitrust policy was central to the growth of the modern – large – American firm that dominated 20th-century business around the world (Mowery and Rosenberg 1998: 16).

The United States was one of the first nations to create and implement competition policies; indeed, it was decades ahead of other states. Until the early 2000s, relatively few states had antitrust policies in place, reflecting perhaps different views on the nature and desirability of competitive marketplaces. US antitrust policy was also notable for its early acceptance of extraterritorial application of competition law. In 1945, the US Supreme Court ruled that existing provisions outlawing anti-competitive behaviour, though intended for domestic application, could be applied irrespective of the location of the firms involved, provided their activities had an effect on the American market. This was an extremely controversial aspect of American law, and one fiercely resisted by other states. The EU adopted the effects doctrine in its Dyestuffs case, where it sought to fine several international firms for price collusion in the industrial dye market even though those firms were domiciled outside the EU, and this also became an issue in the cases centring on Boeing–McDonnell Douglas and General Electric–Honeywell during the early 2000s (see Box 6.1 for in-depth discussion on how EU and US authorities handled these two highly controversial merger cases).

Like any other body of law, American antitrust law has evolved in response to changes in the political and economic environment. In the 1980s, for example, concerns about the competitiveness of American semiconductor firms in the face of Japanese competition resulted in antitrust waivers for several government-brokered research consortia, via the National Cooperative Research Act (1984) (Fox, Peritz, and Sullivan 2004). Likewise, authorities' views on agglomeration have altered in the face of evidence that efficiency gains can be extracted even from mergers that result in a more concentrated industry. However, some features have stood the test of time. Compared with European conceptions of antitrust policy, US enforcement traditionally gave primacy to consumer – as opposed to producer – welfare and has been more concerned with market efficiency than industry structure *per se* (Fox, Peritz, and Sullivan 2004). Politics has also been a factor, with the Republican administrations of Ronald Reagan, George W. Bush and Donald Trump less inclined to pursue antitrust cases, while Democratic Party presidents Barack Obama and Joe Biden investigated antitrust allegations more aggressively.

Box 6.1 The Boeing–McDonnell Douglas and General Electric–Honeywell cases

The Boeing–McDonnell Douglas and GE–Honeywell mergers showed how, from time to time, there are significant differences of view across the Atlantic. It is no accident that these two controversial mergers arose in one sector (aerospace) where transatlantic foreign direct investment is low and political sensitivities high (Guay 1998). In the first dispute, the Commission threatened to block Boeing's acquisition of its American-based rival, McDonnell Douglas (MDC). The Commission was widely seen as acting on behalf of Boeing's European rival, Airbus, in opposing the merger. There was concern that the merged company would enjoy lock-in effects as airlines chose to update their fleets with the group's aircraft rather than incur switching costs by moving to Airbus. Boeing had indeed secured long-term aircraft purchase deals from two US airlines, American and Delta, that appeared to confirm these fears.

European Competition Commissioner Karel Van Miert voiced his concerns about the proposed merger by arguing that the combined group would enjoy a dominant position in the commercial aerospace market. Van Miert's view was that the combined market shares would augment Boeing's existing command of half of the market by adding customers. The American view could not have been more different. MDC's 10 per cent market share provided a rationale for the US Federal Trade Commission to approve the deal. They argued that MDC's market share was minimal, was likely to decline and indicated that the company was no longer a viable competitor in the market (Damro 2001: 214). The Commission's concerns reflected a greater emphasis in EU merger regulations on market structure, rather than economic efficiency.

The Boeing merger controversy was eventually settled via negotiations and the company agreed to two main concessions. First, Boeing agreed it would not enter into any new exclusive agreements with airlines; and second, the company agreed to publish data on US-government-funded corporate R&D, a concession clearly informed by the long-running rivalry with Airbus, where both companies accused the other of receiving illegal government subsidies (see Chapter 4).

The GE–Honeywell merger controversy was altogether more fraught. The Commission's particular complaint concerned the ability of a combined GE–Honeywell to 'bundle' aerospace products and services together and in so doing diminish competition across markets. GE made jet engines and also enjoyed a significant share of the global airliner-leasing business. Honeywell enjoyed a strong market presence in avionics as well as products in the small aircraft engine market. The Commission voiced anxiety over the ability of the merged group to offer both products and related financing packages that competitors could not beat.

The analysis that underpinned the Commission's view came in for considerable criticism, and not just from GE (Morgan and McGuire 2004). The MTF's economic analysis was regarded as flawed and the product of outdated economic theory and analytical tools. The Commission's impartial handling of the case was called into question as it became clear how it relied on an economic analysis of the merger produced by Rolls-Royce, a GE competitor. These criticisms dealt with process and drew attention to the considerable concentration of authority in a small section of one directorate within the Commission. More general criticism was reserved for the MTF's views on the relationship of mergers to economic efficiency. In the United States it is recognized that mergers can enhance economic efficiency and consumer welfare. On this view, the fact that GE could bundle products and offer them at more attractive prices was an argument in favour of the merger. In the end, GE failed to placate the Commission's concerns and the merger was blocked.

After the GE controversy had subsided, the Commission announced a reorganization of the merger and antitrust bureaucracy. The MTF was disbanded and its responsibilities handed to several other bureaucracies. The Commission enhanced its much-criticized analytical capacity with the appointment of a head of economic analysis.

The GE and Boeing cases were important in highlighting procedural and substantive differences between the United States and the EU. Moreover, the GE case highlighted weaknesses in the Commission's processes that were addressed under Neelie Kroes's commissionership. It is also important to note that controversies are exceptional. Full substantive convergence between the partners seems unlikely given the different policy trajectories followed by Europe and America. Though the new merger regulations pay attention to economic efficiency, the Commission has not abandoned its interest in market structure, particularly as smaller national markets remain susceptible to market distortion. European regulators also take a more sceptical view of vertical restraints, for the similar reason that creating the single market required the breaking down of nationally based practices (Melamed 1998). The United States, with its well-established single market and cultural acceptance of competition, does not need the same focus on industrial structure.

Coordination and conflict

Transatlantic relations in competition policy are mostly harmonious and illustrative of the kind of policymaking characterized by expert dominance of a technical process, shared understandings among these experts and the relative lack of political salience and visibility of the competition policy area (Damro and Guay 2012). This has produced a policy area characterized by relatively high degrees of cooperation among American and European authorities in relation to procedures and, to some extent, the substance of competition policy. This is partly a concession to the realities of enforcement. Devuyst notes that very often information crucial to the prosecution of an antitrust case lies in another jurisdiction. Thus, effective enforcement requires healthy degrees of inter-agency cooperation (Devuyst 2001: 132). Competition policy, in common with a number of other regulatory policy areas, has thus been central to the development of what we described in Chapter 2 as 'transatlantic governance'.

Competition policy relations are a stark contrast to trade:

> In comparison with the 'conflict management' focus of trade negotiators trying to protect their own domestic producers' interests, the EU-US competition relationship is characterized by a culture of genuine 'regulatory cooperation' with antitrust agencies trying to increase the effectiveness of their common enforcement task. (Devuyst 2001: 127)

Eleanor Fox, in testimony to the US Congress, highlighted the successful nature of most EU–US competition enforcement when faced with the merger of WorldCom and MCI in the late 1990s: 'Enabled by confidentiality waivers, the agencies [DoJ and the Commission] coordinated requests for information, jointly met with the parties, and concluded settlements that met the concerns on both sides' (Fox 2006b: 3). Her comments draw attention to the centrality of procedure and day-to-day management in the smooth running of transatlantic competition policy relations.

This propensity to collaborate is also bolstered by the strong business links across the Atlantic, including the significant amounts of FDI that flow between the partners (see earlier). Foreign investment can take the form of portfolio investment (i.e. buying shares of another company but in an insufficient amount to have a controlling interest), but the purchase of assets in the other economy is a major route to market for American and European firms. As such, competition policy compliance can be an important issue and a transaction cost for firms. Thus, firms have an interest, if not in convergence of regimes, at least in the development of transparent and predictable policy systems. That said, business interest tends to be confined to input on an ad hoc basis. Devuyst explains this by pointing out that antitrust regulators are supposed to supervise businesses in the marketplace and as such are careful about the form and amount of firm-level influence allowed into the process (Devuyst 2001: 138).

Some political issues, because of their very technical nature and their distance from the consumer, remain the preserve of a relatively small group of technical experts and are rather immune from the populist pressure politics seen in areas like consumer health and agriculture. A similar argument can be made about competition policy: officials on both sides of the Atlantic have succeeded in keeping this considerably depoliticized. In part, this reflects the arcane and specialist nature of the policy area. Moreover, notwithstanding its interest in consumer welfare, most consumers are blissfully unaware of the effect of competition policy enforcement on their lives. However, Damro notes that regulators in Washington and Brussels have been keen to preserve their power and autonomy vis-à-vis political authority. Thus, they have exhibited a strong preference for bilateral linkages at the official level, partly in an effort to head off more onerous, formal political agreements that might impinge on their autonomy. By taking it upon themselves to promote cooperation, regulators 'reduce the likelihood of politicians becoming involved in competition cases and linking outcomes to trade policy' (Damro 2006: 872).

The basis for European–American cooperation on competition policy is the 1991 agreement which set out a framework for transatlantic cooperation (and which reflected the bargaining power acquired by the EC through the development of the SMP at that time). The agreement is illustrative of the deep and rich set of relationships that characterize transatlantic economic relations. It commits each party to consider the interests of the other in pursuing enforcement activities and formalizes this with comity provisions. Exchanges of information and the cultivation of a culture of cooperation were embodied in commitments among officials to regular, bilateral meetings. Finally, the accord called on each party to cooperate and coordinate with the other to the greatest extent possible without prejudicing or impairing domestic enforcement of competition laws (Janow 2000: 32). The agreement was an important milestone in the development of international efforts to coordinate antitrust enforcement. Nonetheless, the agreement had significant limitations; it was designed mainly to avoid jurisdictional conflict via the timely exchange of information; it is not equipped to resolve conflicts once they arise. The agreement lacks a dispute settlement mechanism and does not impose limitations on the ability of one party to exercise its rights to investigate a particular merger if it feels it is in the national interest to do so. There is nothing unusual per se about these arrangements; they reflect the reality of the 1991 agreement as an international agreement between sovereign nation states (with the EU acting on behalf of members) rather than a supranational treaty (Damro 2004).

In addition to the direct, bilateral relationships between Washington and Brussels, both participate in an array of multilateral forums, which aim to foster closer ties and more effective cooperation among numerous competition agencies. This network of organizations is not particularly new, reflecting the realization some years ago that extraterritorial application of competition laws was fraught with controversy. In the wake of the 1945 Alcoa decision, the United States began a period of 'aggressive extraterritorial enforcement' in areas such as international shipping, the petroleum industry and watchmaking (Guzman 1998: 1507). As early as the 1940s, consideration was given to an international competition policy, packaged as part of the Havana Charter that was to have given birth to the International Trade Organization. As with the rest of the Havana process, the competition policy proposals were shelved in the face of American uncertainty over the implications for US sovereignty.

As it did in other spheres of policymaking, the OECD assumed a role as key facilitator of cooperation on antitrust measures. In 1967 the organization's members agreed a series of recommendations on antitrust policy in the context of increasing international trade (Damro 2004: 271). Gradually, through the successive issuing of recommendations, the level of cooperation among OECD member countries in respect of competition policy has increased. Originally designed to facilitate information-sharing, later versions of the OECD agreements allow states to request investigations by another member and make greater calls on members to actively assist in each other's enforcement proceedings (Damro 2004: 272). The organization has developed a particular niche role in respect of cartels. The OECD Hard Core Cartel Recommendation was an effort to develop OECD-wide agreement on the identification and prosecution of cartels in member states. This particular agreement owes much to the United States, which has a tradition of fierce prosecution of cartel behaviour; indeed, the US extraterritorial application of its laws was typically in aid of anti-cartel activity. The OECD anti-cartel guidelines, agreed in 1998, were pursued by the United States because the OECD was seen as an effective platform for progress – in contrast to the World Trade Organization (WTO) – and because of the lack of a binding enforcement mechanism (Damro 2004: 273).

Cooperation at the international level does have its limits. With the rise of technology, e-commerce and social media companies during the early decades of the 21st century has come increased interest in regulating them. The reasons include tax avoidance (as discussed earlier), but also data privacy and abuse of their dominant positions. However, US and EU regulators have approached these subjects differently. The disagreements began with Microsoft in 1993, when both the European Commission and the US Department of Justice under the

Bill Clinton administration began investigations on whether Microsoft's licensing practices inhibited the ability of competitors to sell their operating systems to personal computer manufacturers (Litan 2000). Antitrust authorities in the United States and EU coordinated their investigations and agreed that Microsoft's licensing procedures were effectively exclusive dealing as a monopolist. The company agreed to a settlement. In 2000, the European Commission initiated a new investigation that Microsoft withheld interoperability information from competitors who produced operating systems for computers, and that the company was bundling its own applications like Windows Media Player into its operating system, thereby depriving competitors of market opportunities. Further penalties were applied in 2013 for Microsoft's failure to offer an alternative to Internet Explorer for web browsing, as it had agreed to do in 2009. The company ultimately paid over €2.2 billion in fines to the EU (Chee 2023). This time, however, the United States under the George W. Bush administration took a lighter touch. The EU's more aggressive response was labelled a 'dangerous precedent' and a 'new form of protectionism' by Representative Robert Wexler, chairman of the US House Foreign Affairs Subcommittee on Europe (Forelle 2007). Damro and Guay (2016) contend that the EU's prolonged case against Microsoft and the severity of the fines imposed gave other antitrust regulators, including South Korea and Japan, sufficient confidence to bring similar cases against the company.

The EU's broad success in bringing antitrust cases against Microsoft perhaps bolstered the Commission's decisions to take subsequent actions against a range of 'Big Tech' firms, including Advanced Micro Devices, Intel and Google, for similar concerns that these companies were abusing their dominant position, and that a truly competitive market required them to make fundamental changes in the ways they do business. Perhaps the most consequential step to regulate Big Tech to date has been the EU's 2022 Digital Markets Act. Aimed at large gatekeeper platforms, which include Alphabet, Amazon, Apple, Bytedance, Meta and Microsoft, the Act puts strict limits on what companies can do with peoples' online data. It also prohibits these companies from using strategies to block rivals from competing, requiring, for example, Apple to offer alternatives to its App Store and Apple Pay, and barring Amazon from collecting data from independent sellers to offer competing products (Satariano 2022). Penalties could be imposed up to 20 per cent of the offending company's global revenues. Although the Act, and the EU's treatment of Big Tech for the past couple of decades, is viewed by some critics as anti-American, given that this global industry is dominated by US companies and very few European ones, these policies also can be seen as representative of a different values system – one that prioritizes the protection of personal information and a wariness of dominant companies. Once investigations are started by the US and EU authorities, companies have the option of permitting the regulators to share information and exchange views on key issues. EU Competition Commissioner Margrethe Vestager suggests this is beneficial for all parties.

> For the companies, if it's something that can be remedied, then maybe one remedy will work on both sides of the Atlantic. We're different democracies, but we are democracies, and we can do more to work together to set the standards for how technology is being used and developed. There's a need for that globally. (Conrad 2022)

A second major, but more recent, controversy between the EU and United States is in the area of state aids, or subsidies to industries. In the EU, responsibility for the review of state aid falls within the Competition Commission (Cini and McGowan 2009). The general principle is that financial support given by a member state government to a domestic company represents an unfair advantage. This is particularly important for the proper functioning of market competition within the EU SMP. If one member gives aid to favoured domestic companies, then firms from the other 26 member states are disadvantaged. EU law does permit state aid under some circumstances, for example financial support for the general economic development of a member state region that is available to all companies.

The United States treats state aid somewhat differently. At the national level, Washington funds certain industries such as agriculture or energy either through direct expenditure or tax policy (e.g. providing tax breaks to activities such as oil exploration). The 50 states and their local governments are permitted, even encouraged, to offer subsidies, tax holidays and other financial incentives to court investment (domestic or foreign). There is no equivalent of the EU's Competition Commission barring, say, South Carolina from offering financial incentives to BMW to build a factory. State aid becomes a problem at the international level, especially with respect to trade. Many of the trade disputes adjudicated by the WTO derive from claims that governments are providing financial support to domestic firms to the detriment of foreign companies, thereby distorting global trade flows.

In the past, the main disputes between the United States and EU with regards to state aid revolved around aerospace and defence (see Chapter 4) and agriculture, since both Washington and Brussels have historically provided considerable financial support to farmers. But more recently, the intersection of state aid, green energy and national security has raised transatlantic tensions

(Kamin and Kysar 2023). In 2022, the Biden administration enacted two pieces of legislation: the Inflation Reduction Act (IRA) and the CHIPS and Science Act. The IRA provides tax credits to incentivize and accelerate the adoption of electric vehicles totalling $369 billion over ten years on climate change and energy security. However, as enacted, the IRA tax credits only apply to vehicle and battery production in the United States, thus placing electric vehicles produced in Europe at a disadvantage. Similarly, the CHIPS Act aims to move semiconductor production away from Asia, and primarily China, by providing subsidies for the building of such factories within the United States. The Act provides $52.7 billion of spending on semiconductor manufacturing and $24 billion on tax credits for chip production (McKinsey 2022). Advocates see both acts as key 21st-century strategies to revitalize American manufacturing, create good-paying middle-class jobs, reduce reliance for key technologies on adversaries like China and jump-start decarbonization initiatives that will make the United States a leader in electric batteries and vehicles and green technologies (Khanna 2023). Europeans, not surprisingly, feel differently. French president Emmanuel Macron said that the IRA was 'super aggressive' towards European companies (Rose and Mason 2022). The European Commission responded to these US initiatives with the Temporary Crisis and Transition Framework, which will allow member states to subsidize sustainable technologies, including batteries, solar panels, heat pumps, wind turbines and other green production (Allenbach-Ammann 2023). Given the stakes involved in these sectors, including the ability to become a market leader for products that will likely be in high demand in the coming decades, it is highly likely that a state aid/subsidy arms race between the United States and EU will ensue, with other competitors including China, Japan and India following suit.

Applying Euro-American policies to the world

The dramatic growth of investment as well as trade has led somewhat expectedly to increasing calls for the internationalization of competition policy and the expansion of investor protection regulations. As in other policy areas, there is a perceived mismatch between the increasingly global operations of firms and heightened interdependence of economies, and the location-bound nature of most economic governance structures. International competition policy would seem to offer a way of enhancing trade policies designed to open markets. Trade policy has traditionally focused on 'at-the-border' issues, so removing or reducing these barriers opens trade. But the removal of trade barriers does not guarantee that a market is contestable – and this is where competition policy is important. In the absence of trade restrictions, incumbent firms might still collude with each other and government to hamper new competitors. For some observers, the best way to address this level problem is to create supranational governance structures which would provide common regulations for all. The attraction to firms is the reduction in transaction costs; compliance with one set of rules is cheaper – and should be easier – than compliance with multiple sets of regulations across the many countries where they do business. The riposte, however, is that any international effort should focus on coordination and transparency rather than on convergence on a single set of regulations. It is not obvious that formal multilateralization would be any better than the existing practice of bilateral agreements in preventing market abuses (Fox 2006a). However, the issue is not so clear-cut and it would be wrong to frame it as a stark choice between maintaining competing national systems of enforcement and a global agreement under WTO auspices. In fact, both the United States and the EU use both the WTO and regional trade agreements to plurilateralize various policy areas not formally part of the WTO agenda. The difference is that the EU is more comfortable doing so in the field of antitrust measures; the United States, by contrast, has placed more emphasis on investor protection legislation.

As in the trade policy area, the Union's comfort with a multilateral process has its roots in the European political economy. The experience gained by the Commission in the creation of the Single Market has made it comfortable with, and experienced in, the creation and implementation of supranational public policy. Deep integration of this sort can reduce transaction costs associated with multiple policy regimes, but it is invasive and can create tensions in member states, with politicians and voters alike resenting Brussels' interference in national affairs.

Arguably, however, the EU's warm regard for international competition policy is informed by norms and not just by the experience of European integration. The EU more than any other member of the WTO had been keen to include 'trade-and' topics for negotiation during the Doha Round. The Singapore issues of government procurement, trade facilitation, competition policy and trade and the environment owed their inclusion on the agenda to the insistence of the EU. It is true that from time to time the United States has also raised these – or related – issues, but in Washington this is more to do with placating domestic constituencies. Bill Clinton's ill-advised suggestion about linking trade and labour standards was an example. The comments, made at the start of the disastrous Seattle WTO ministerial in 1999, were designed to reassure his Democrat-voting labour activists but succeeded in merely outraging swathes of the WTO delegates. Though American politicians sometimes repeat the language, the United States has not adopted linkage politics to the same extent as the EU. Why is Brussels so interested? For Sally (2004), it is because the EU seeks to recreate the EU at the multilateral level, by fostering the creation of the WTO that emphasizes regulatory harmonization as its core operating principle. Earlier chapters suggest an additional, more values-based explanation that the EU, as a civilian superpower, demonstrates a comfort with, indeed enthusiasm for, multilateralism as a mechanism for solving problems not shared by other actors, most notably the United States.

The Singapore issues proved controversial at subsequent WTO ministerials. Developing countries disliked the linkages drawn between trade and other issues, and the issue of competition policy was not an important item on their agendas. For many smaller states, the resource implications of the adoption of an international competition policy are serious, requiring numerous trained staff (economists and lawyers) as well as a judicial system capable of handling antitrust cases. Many developing states already find compliance with WTO agreements complex and onerous. Poor economies are likely to have greater needs than creating a competition authority. In 2004, competition policy multilateralization was formally dropped as a Doha negotiating item, to the relief of most developing states (Bhattacharjea 2006: 293). With no prospect of a new WTO trade agreement for the foreseeable future, given the lack of global enthusiasm for trade agreements in general and the WTO in particular (as discussed in Chapter 4), it is safe to say that the diffusion of competition policies through multilateral fora is dead. That said, the EU, before and since the dropping of competition as an agenda item, has demanded the inclusion of antitrust commitments in bilateral and regional preferential trade agreements (Bhattarchajea 2006: 273–4). The price of access to the EU market is to participate in and accept elements of the EU *acquis*, without the actual benefits of membership.

The United States' ambivalence towards multilateralized competition policy is, like the EU position, explained partly by an appeal to history. The United States is historically concerned about the constraints that might be imposed by an international organization and, as such, is generally drawn to bilateral initiatives in response. Among American policymakers, there was acknowledgement that international antitrust cooperation and coordination were necessary and desirable; it did not follow that the answer was a single global competition authority. In response to EU initiatives, the United States created the International Competition Policy Advisory Committee (ICPAC), designed to inform and advise American policymakers. For the United States, it represented an effective way to maintain interest and influence in the evolving debate about international antitrust policy without actually committing to a binding agreement. The EU accepted, indeed welcomed, the creation of ICPAC, but viewed it as 'complementary, not as an alternative to the WTO proposal' (Devuyst 2001: 133). ICPAC was wound up in 2000, but American interest in the international dimension of antitrust regulations was maintained by the International Competition Network (ICN), an organization comprising 141 competition policy authorities from 129 jurisdictions that drew directly out of the recommendations of ICPAC's final report (ICN 2023). Membership of ICN is voluntary and the organization does not make rules, but it does foster knowledge-sharing and 'best practice'. Central to the ICN is the freedom it gives to members to implement ideas as they see fit (ICN 2007).

Investor protection

Investor protection is a closely related policy area that has also been the subject of negotiation at the multilateral and regional level. Broadly, regulation in this area is designed to protect investors from what they would regard as arbitrary treatment by the host government. Examples of such treatment might be onerous local sourcing requirements or expropriation of assets without compensation. For firms, limits on the ability of governments to interfere with their operations reduce the political risk associated with an investment, which should result in greater levels of investment in a given economy. However, from the perspective of governments, such constraints may prevent governments from acting in good faith for the benefit of their society. As such, the extension of investor protection requirements has been highly controversial. The Doha Declaration included investment protection in response to complaints from European and American business that the existing Trade-Related Investment Measures (TRIMs) were not able to offer adequate protection. To the extent this is true, it is partly down to the inability of firms – and government policymakers – to agree on the precise scope and extent of investment provisions.

Another factor militating against strong investor protection provisions was the operation of the disputes settlement process in the North American Free Trade Agreement (NAFTA) in respect of the rights accorded to firms to sue foreign governments in their home jurisdiction (Bora 2004: 213–13; Gagne and Morin 2006). Critics charged that NAFTA set an unwelcome precedent for the ability of firms – as private parties – to make claims that affected the sovereignty of nation states. Bora argues that these fears contributed to the collapse of OECD-sponsored negotiations on the Multilateral Agreement on Investment (Bora 2004: 214).

However, American interest in securing a more predictable international environment for its firms to operate in meant that the issue was raised again in advance of the Doha Declaration in late 2001. The declaration acknowledged the link between trade and investment, noting that 'transparent, stable and predictable conditions' assist in encouraging foreign direct investment and expanded trade (WTO 2001b). The United States pressed for a broad agreement covering the widest possible forms of investment (Bora 2004). In the event, the text offered considerable scope for member states to regulate investment matters 'in the public interest', reflecting the fierce resistance the American proposals generated among other states (WTO 2001b). The Doha language was sufficiently ambiguous for the United States, while pursuing the Doha Round negotiations, to have sought to include investor protection provisions in its bilateral and regional trade pacts. However, even the United States seems to have pulled back from far-reaching investor protection towards a model that preserves flexibility for states to act in the national interest. American policymakers drew lessons from the unhappy experience of the operation of the NAFTA's provisions, which led to the American government having to defend its investment policies in court (Gagne and Morin 2006). NAFTA's chapter 11 gave corporations the ability to demand arbitration where national law is deemed to have injured the firm: this represented a break from the legal tradition that only states had 'standing' before disputes processes (Capling and Nossal 2006). By the time the United States and Australia began to negotiate a bilateral free trade agreement, the Americans had succeeded in getting NAFTA-like investor protection language in several bilateral free trade agreements. However, to the surprise of many observers, investor protection did not appear in the final text of the Australian-US Free Trade Agreement (Capling and Nossal 2006). American policymakers themselves were surprised by the potential for NAFTA-style language to constrain their ability to implement policy for environmental and health standards (Capling and Nossal 2006). The American government has reverted to a less ambitious formula, using bilateral investment treaties (BITs) that are not part of broader free trade agreements. The model that forms the basis of all US BITs was created under the 2002 Bipartisan Trade Promotion Authority Act (US Department of State 2006). The United States has 39 BITs in force, virtually all with developing countries (US Department of State 2024).

Until recently, the EU has not shown the same enthusiasm for BITs, preferring instead to use the OECD and WTO processes to achieve internationally agreed levels of investor protection. As was seen in Chapter 4, the EU placed trade and investment regulations among the Singapore issues on the Doha agenda. However, the EU used bilateral initiatives in this area while still pursuing the Doha objective. Thus, Brussels started the EU down the road followed by Washington: the inclusion of investor protection rules as part of bilateral and regional trade agreements. Both the EU-Mexico trade agreement, which entered into force in 2000, and the EU-Chile Association Agreement signed in 2002 included a range of investor protection clauses that, at least in the Chile case, are designed to go beyond 'existing WTO commitments'. But it wasn't until December 2009, when the Lisbon Treaty went into effect, that the EU became the sole negotiator of international investment treaties, removing the legal ability of member states to negotiate their own international agreements on FDI (Basedow 2020).

In the years since 2009, the EU has sought to forge BITs with key economic partners. But attempts to do so with its two most important economic partners (and rivals) – China and the United States – failed quite spectacularly. Earlier in the chapter it was noted that European concerns over human rights and political issues derailed the EU-China CAI. The EU-US Transatlantic Trade and Investment Partnership (TTIP) aimed not only to further reduce trade barriers (discussed in Chapter 4) but to promote investment. One of the key components of the latter aspect was the Investor-State Dispute Settlement (ISDS) mechanism, which permits investors to opt for private arbitration tribunals in lieu of domestic courts to resolve legal issues that could impact their investment. While such panels may have helped to reassure investors, they were a lightning rod of criticism, mainly on the European side, where opponents argued that ISDS favoured the interests of multinationals, that cases were not transparent because they were reviewed and decided behind closed doors and that ISDS made it difficult for governments to make new policies regarding health or the environment because companies could argue the additional costs of compliance made their investments less profitable (Ames 2015). Such public opposition by many civil society groups, as well as some politicians in member states and the European Parliament, presented negotiating challenges for the EU. In the end, the Trump administration solved this dilemma by withdrawing the United States from TTIP negotiations.

Overview and conclusion

Competition and investment policies attract virtually none of the headlines that trade and monetary policy matters do, but that is not because these areas are unimportant. Competition policy remains a cornerstone of any properly functioning market economy and it is significant that as the process of globalization has unfolded, it has been accompanied by a growing interest in, and adoption of, competition rules by policymakers around the world. However, the area is technical, and so tends not to be as politicized as other policy spheres. The transatlantic relationship is marked by considerable cooperation among regulatory agencies. European and American influences on international competition policy are considerable – and sometimes controversial.

Investment issues are somewhat more problematic. First, the overlap between national security and economic development has brought FDI from certain investors, mainly Chinese, to the forefront of policymaking. For Europe, that means the adoption of ISMs (Meunier and Chan 2022, Meunier and Nicolaidas 2019), while for the United States this has led to divergent interests from Washington (emphasizing the security dimension) and state and local governments (which tend to prioritize economic growth). While the United States has encouraged European and other allies to ban investment by, and contracts with, companies feared to be too close to their home governments (such as China's Huawei), it is not practical to approach initiatives like this multilaterally or in trade agreements. Second, to the extent that investor protection rules appear to place the policy preferences of multinational companies above those of the local population, they become a target for protest. Moreover, concerns that the widespread adoption of investment protection could have unintended consequences for the United States and Europe have also tended to dampen enthusiasm. Fear that the US federal or state governments could find themselves sued by firms for enacting environmental legislation under NAFTA led the United States to move away from the inclusion of investor protection language in later bilateral free trade agreements. The United States Mexico Canada (USMCA) agreement, negotiated under pressure from the Trump administration to replace NAFTA, removed the ISDS mechanism between the United States and Canada and a revised arbitration agreement with Mexico (Bernasconi-Osterwalder 2018; CRS 2020). In this context, the main arguments made in this chapter are:

- First, in both America and Europe, competition policy has been a key element of market-friendly regulation, promoting economic growth. European conceptions of competition have differed from the American, but this gap is narrowing.
- Second, in contrast to the area of international trade, competition and investment politics are much less contested at the transatlantic level, but increasingly so vis-à-vis rivals, mainly China and Russia. This is due largely to the fact that policymaking – particularly in competition policy – remains very technocratic, with the key stakeholders sharing similar views about the purpose and content of policy.

- Third, the EU has shown more enthusiasm for developing an international competition policy, perhaps because the Commission has greater experience with international regulatory issues, while the United States is more concerned that its own tough competition laws will be weakened by any international agreement. As such, though both the EU and the United States are members of ICN, the organization owes its modus operandi to American preferences for looser forms of multilateralism.

As Europe and America become more interdependent, not merely with each other but with the rest of the world, agency cooperation has become an important element of the relationship. In the case of competition policy, some substantive differences remain between Washington and Brussels that reflect differing historical traditions and the salience of different economic and political issues. That said, in this, a technical area where enforcement agencies share a common interest in minimizing political interference, cooperation has been prevalent. Both Washington and Brussels have an interest in extending this cooperation globally. As with the substance of policy, the mechanisms for achieving this are disputed. However, in the absence of viable WTO-based or other multilateral solutions, the EU has found the American-inspired ICPAC a very useful forum.

Investment regulation has not had the same profile as competition policy, but is nonetheless an area that features many of the same characteristics. European and American firms remain advocates of multilateralized regulatory solutions, but there is significant disagreement over the precise reach and content of such regulation. The US government has successfully implemented a bilateral and plurilateral solution in the form of renewed and updated investment agreements. Europe has not pursued bilateral investment agreements with the same vigour, but like the United States has used bilateral and regional negotiations to press for enhanced protection on matters like investment. The EU-Chile Association Agreement seems certain to be a model for further developments.

To the extent that competition and investment policies tend to be packaged as part of trade negotiations, both policy areas could be affected by the diminished ability of Europe and America to translate their preferences into outcomes in the WTO. As we noted in Chapter 4, the dramatic rise of the developing world in the organization – and the dramatic economic growth of these economies – illustrates the growing confidence of states to resist what they regard as the imposition of inappropriate policies by the EU and the United States. Some of this reflects political linkage among negotiating issues in the WTO rather than opposition to the ideas per se. China, as noted earlier in this chapter, has seen a surge of inward and outward FDI since WTO accession and is no doubt aware of the 'market credibility' signalled by membership and adherence to rules. Nonetheless, as WTO negotiations have all but ended between Washington and Brussels, it makes sense to shift the level of negotiations down the hierarchy to the bilateral level, where their economic power counts for much more.

Chapter 7

Power and security in EU–US relations

Introduction

One of the consequences of the EU's growing international presence and activity, and of the extension of its reach into new areas such as foreign and defence policy, has been a growing concern with issues of power and security. For the United States, this has been a preoccupation since the beginning of the 20th century, as the United States became a world power, and particularly during the Cold War and its aftermath, when the United States was either one part of a superpower duopoly or (in the immediate post-Cold-War period) 'the only superpower'. More recently still, as noted elsewhere in this volume, the effects of global power-shifts, of rising powers and their interaction with the United States have become a key dimension of global change.

In this chapter, the focus is on the ways in which the European Union and the United States approach issues of power, and on how their distinct approaches come together when they are dealing with questions of security and insecurity in the world arena. The chapter thus links with many of the issues discussed in previous chapters, both those chapters that deal with particular areas of policy and those such as Chapters 3 and 4 that are more concerned with the intersection of domestic, regional and global processes. It also develops several of the key themes identified in Chapter 2 – specifically, those dealing with the processes of EU and US policymaking, the impact of change and the coexistence of markets, hierarchies and networks. One of the key focuses of this chapter is what might be seen as fundamental conflicts between the EU and the US approaches to matters of power and security, and the ways in which these seem to be expressed in a variety of arenas. Another key theme is the changing nature of security in the post-Cold-War and post-9/11 era, which has greatly broadened the notion of 'soft security' as opposed to traditional military 'hard security' and has led to fluctuating perceptions of threat and vulnerability.

In confronting and responding to these developments, the EU and the United States have brought to bear very different predispositions, resources and strategies. Indeed, it has been argued that the two entities live almost in two different worlds when it comes to issues of power and security in the new millennium, with the EU pursuing negotiation, multilateralism and 'soft power' while the United States has espoused coercion, unilateralism and the massive deployment of 'hard power' (Kagan 2003; M. Smith 2004; Lindberg 2005). The purpose of this chapter is to explore this general assertion, to arrive at an assessment of the extent to which the EU and the United States live in different worlds of power and security and to discuss the implications of their mutual relations for global security issues. As in previous chapters, we shall examine first the EU's approach to power and security, then that of the United States, and then the implications for the relationship. These implications will then be examined to highlight the ways in which the EU and the United States relate to each other in matters of global power and security.

Power and security in EU external action

In confronting the 'new world' created by the end of the Cold War, the European integration project and its leaders were not concerned solely with external policy developments. It is important to remember that the fall of the Berlin Wall and the end of the Soviet Union occurred alongside (and often intersecting with) institutional and policy developments in European integration – the very developments, in fact, that created the European Union itself and gave it a new range of institutional and policy resources (Laffan, O'Donnell, and Smith 2000). Thus, between 1990 and 1995 the European Union was set in place, a Common Foreign and Security Policy was established and Economic and Monetary Union was put in motion with its projected completion date the turn of the millennium. The first question we must address in relation to these developments is, what motivated them? What predispositions in Europe and in the EU did they reflect, and how can we see these in relation to broader questions of power and security?

One way of engaging with these questions is to cast them in terms of the nature of the European project, and the kinds of underlying orientation towards power and security that it reflects. It is thus important to understand that the EU is a kind of 'trading state', whose original impetus drew upon cooperation in the commercial and economic fields, and whose institutions were profoundly shaped by this fact. Trading states, as Richard Rosecrance has argued (1986, 1993), pursue characteristic policy aims, centred on stability and the pursuit of commercial advantage. True to its underlying character, the EU thus pursues essentially conservative international policies, aimed at creating forms of 'negotiated order' in the world arena. At the same time, these policies are also predominantly 'civilian', using diplomatic and commercial devices to establish and maintain a predictable international setting and valuing these almost as ends in themselves. The EU's diplomacy is based also on reciprocity, a process of give and take which sees international order as centred on the exchange of rewards and the granting of incentives. The objective is to create a set of international structures that engender stability and enable the EU to carry on its international business (M. Smith 2004: 107–11), consolidating its status as a 'market power' (Damro 2012). The EU thus presents a long-term attempt to promote 'soft security' and use 'soft power', but it must not be forgotten (see Chapter 1) that it was also established within the framework of the Cold War, in which 'hard security' was the key area of confrontation between the United States and the Soviet Union.

This focus on 'soft power' and 'soft security' can be observed throughout the life of the European project; although individual EU member states might take a more martial line in particular circumstances, they all subscribe to these assumptions for matters where the EU is the central focus of their activities. In the post-Cold-War world, however, these assumptions came under severe strain, for a number of reasons. First, the end of bipolarity and subsequent changes created for the Union a much more unpredictable international context, in which tensions and conflicts could flare up suddenly and in which 'civilian' issues such as trade could become very closely linked with political or military activities through processes of 'politicization' or 'securitization'. Second, this has been added to by the impact of globalization, through which the impact of shocks in one part of the world arena is transmitted very rapidly to other parts. This is not a world in which it is easy to establish stability or predictability, and thus the EU has come under pressure from a number of sources. As a result, the EU has become engaged (as one would expect) with key issues of power and security in areas such as the environment, development and human rights, but has also had to contend with the essential unmanageability of many of the tensions and conflicts that surround them. We shall see in later parts of this chapter what this might mean in specific conflict situations. Third, the Union, as might be expected, makes policy in what might be described as a 'negotiated' or 'deliberative' way, having to take into account the needs and preferences of member states and of the 'European' institutions as well as the 'European interest' (Elgström and Smith 2000), but this is not on the face of it a very efficient way of responding to the unpredictable and interconnected crises that have erupted in the post-Cold-War era and the 21st century.

The picture of the EU's motivation towards issues of power and security is thus at least partly cloudy. Yet at the same time, the changing circumstances of the post-Cold-War era prompted the EU to develop significant new resources with which to confront such issues. Most importantly, the Union has provided itself with new institutions in the field of foreign, security and defence policy that have moved it at least in principle away from purely 'civilian' power (M. Smith 2001b). In the Maastricht Treaty of 1991, which entered into force in 1993, the Common Foreign and Security Policy (CFSP) was a major feature; it was then added to by the Amsterdam Treaty of 1997 and the Nice Treaty of 2000, so that by the beginning of the new millennium there was a complex institutional structure, supported by growing budgetary resources and by activities that seemed to integrate more than ever before the wide range of interests that the Union had in the world arena (Vanhoonacker 2005). From 1998 onwards, the development of the European Security and Defence Policy (ESDP, later relabelled the Common Security and Defence Policy, or CSDP) created an embryonic military dimension to the Union's external policies, and by 2007 there were established 'battle groups' bringing together contributions from many EU member states (Howorth 2005, 2007), as well as an increasing number of military and civilian missions outside Europe (Howorth 2014: Chapter 5). The Constitutional Treaty of 2004 would have gone even further down this track, by providing for a Union 'foreign minister' and for the creation of long-term mechanisms for ensuring the resources necessary for foreign policy activities. But, as was noted in Chapter 1, the Constitutional Treaty was never ratified.

In 2009, the ratification of the Lisbon Treaty, which contained many of the innovations proposed in the Constitutional Treaty, laid the institutional foundations for a much more coordinated approach to EU external action. The creation of a European External Action Service (EEAS), headed by the High Representative for International Affairs and Security Policy, who is also a Vice-President of the European Commission (HRVP) and working with a semi-permanent President of the European Council, seemed to give the Union a much more coordinated external image and diplomatic 'voice', along with the potential for further development of security and defence policies (Keukeleire and Delreux 2014, 2022; Hill, Smith, and Vanhoonacker 2023; Howorth 2023).

The Union's institutional development since the end of the Cold War has thus been dramatic, and in precisely those areas where the EU was previously lacking as an international actor – diplomacy and security/defence policy. In a sense, this can be seen as a direct response to the challenges posed by the end of superpower bipolarity. The disappearance of the Soviet Union created a need for imaginative initiatives in Europe (see Chapter 8), but it also created both challenges and opportunities in the rest of the world. The emergence of the CFSP and then the CSDP, and later the production of the Lisbon Treaty, reflected in part a recognition by EU member states that a collective EU presence was essential in order to spread the risks and take advantage of some of the opportunities created by the new world situation (Ginsberg 2001). Clearly, however, there are limits on this set of developments, emerging both from divisions between member states and from the fluid nature of the world arena itself. The EU is thus still limited in its external defence activities to what are called the Petersberg tasks – essentially conflict prevention, peacekeeping and peace-building, aligned to post-conflict reconstruction and the creation of effective government – although aspects of crisis management have been added to these.

Box 7.1 CFSP and CSDP from Maastricht to the Lisbon Treaty

Maastricht

Establishes Common Foreign and Security Policy, with the eventual possibility of European defence policy and 'European defence'. New instruments: Common Positions (from EPC) and Joint Actions. Possibility of Qualified Majority Voting (QMV), limited Commission power of initiative. Some budgetary provision. Association of the Western European Union (WEU) with CFSP. Remains essentially intergovernmental.

Amsterdam

Further extension of QMV, introduction of Common Strategies and possibility of 'constructive abstention'. Incorporation of 'Petersberg tasks', further linkages with WEU (eventual merger). Establishment of high representative supported by Policy Planning and Early Warning Unit. Further budgetary regularization. Still largely intergovernmental.

Nice

Incorporation of ESDP agreements from St Malo to Helsinki and establishes CSDP: includes new Political and Security Committee (COPS), Military Committee and Military Staff. Consolidation of proposals for rapid reaction force based on 'headline goals' of 50,000–60,000 troops, focused on Petersberg tasks.

Constitutional Treaty

Establishment of European Union foreign minister and External Action Service. New provisions for crisis management (beyond Petersberg Tasks) and for 'enhanced cooperation' among sub-groups of member states. Solidarity clause against military attack and terrorist action. Creation of European Armaments Agency to coordinate national arms procurement policies and (in the longterm) bring them into EU framework.

Lisbon Treaty

The Constitutional Treaty was rejected in referenda in France and the Netherlands in 2005. In 2007, it was agreed that a revised 'reform treaty' should be negotiated, containing most of the above provisions relating to foreign and security policy. The result was the Lisbon Treaty, which was ratified in 2009 and entered into force in 2010. Lisbon established the European External Action Service (EEAS) headed by the High Representative for Foreign Affairs and Security Policy (HRVP), who is also a Vice-President of the European Commission and is appointed by the member states for a five-year term. It also established a semi-permanent President of the European Council, who is appointed for two-and-a-half-year terms and who has responsibilities for external representation of the Union.

Added to this set of 'harder' resources, the Union has substantial and long-established resources in the economic and commercial fields, which can be brought to bear on questions of power and security through trade policy, development policy and the like (see Chapters 4–6). In this way, it can be seen, the Union has added considerably to its resources during the period since the end of the Cold War, but it is not always clear how they can be deployed to deal with issues of power and security in a globalized world. There is a persistent gap between the multilateral institutional level at which the EU can be effective on the basis of its role as a 'trading state' and the essentially confused and dynamic situations in which the Union might need to deploy its security and defence resources.

One response to the critique outlined earlier has been the development of EU strategies, which aim to establish the principles for 'European foreign policy' and link it to the pursuit of power and security. The Union has for a long time had many strategies, whether towards individual international partners or on specific international issues, and thus in a way it is easy to discern the principles of 'European foreign policy'. Such principles would include multilateralism, dialogue, negotiation, the use of international institutions and the promotion of 'global civil society' including such aspects as human rights and good governance. It is only since the end of the 1990s that the Union has attempted to set these out in terms of its explicit commitments and objectives. In particular, in 2003 the Union agreed the European Security Strategy (ESS), which brought together a wide range of world order objectives with the more specific interests of the Union itself, and set out how these should be pursued (Council 2003; Howorth 2007: Chapter 6). This document was the first to fully encapsulate the Union's commitment to conflict prevention, crisis management and the pursuit of 'effective multilateralism' through channels such as the United Nations (see Box 7.2). The document in effect set out what it means to be a 'trading state' in the new post-Cold-War world, and by so doing revealed that 'civilian power' was no longer enough to protect and promote the Union's interests. The EU's security required the development of a 'harder' or more martial strategy, and the deployment of different types of resources, while retaining the broad commitment to multilateral means and civilian priorities (Dannreuther and Peterson 2006: Chapter 1; M. Smith 2006b). This might have been a source of regret, that the Union was losing its 'unique selling point' in the pursuit of international order, but in many ways it was a logical response to the nature of the post-Cold-War world (Manners 2006; K. Smith 2000, 2005c).

Although the ESS was reviewed in 2008, it was another eight years until the next attempt to produce a comprehensive statement of the EU's external goals and methods. The Global Strategy (European Union 2016; see also Tocci 2017) set out the key aim of 'strategic autonomy' for the Union (a phrase fraught with implications for transatlantic relations), and proposed a global approach in two senses: first, that its scope applied to the whole world, and second, that it encompassed all of the external actions and capabilities of the Union. Key aspects of the strategy included a commitment to the enhancement of the Union's 'strategic autonomy', a comprehensive approach to conflicts and crises, the encouragement of resilience (and thus the promotion of stability) in key regions and the formation or consolidation of 'strategic partnerships' with a range of states and international organizations (see also Chapter 8). The strategy proposed a 'joined-up' approach to policymaking, designed to make the most effective use of the Union's resources and thus to maximize the Union's influence on the global stage while not jettisoning the established EU commitment to multilateral methods and the use of non-military power. In 2022, the Global Strategy was supplemented by the 'European Strategic Compass', which was designed to put flesh on the bones of the broad strategy and to map out a course for the development of the EU's resources and commitments in a more focused and substantive way (European Union 2022).

Does this development of a new strategic focus and (at least in part) a new 'strategic culture' (Cornish and Edwards 2001; Duke 2017; Biscop 2019) provide the EU with a good basis on which to exercise new forms of power and pursue issues of global security? In a world where the oddly reassuring presence of two super-powers is long gone, but where there are new protagonists and new challenges, there is still a clear need to project ideas about what a European identity and European interests might add up to (Manners and Whitman 2003; Whitman 1998; Biscop 2019). There is also a need to bring together the commercial and economic interests of the EU with the 'harder' security interests that are increasingly linked to them. In a globalizing world, the increasing politicization and securitization of the commercial is a key point of reference (as we have noted in many of the previous chapters in this book), and the EU seems well placed to respond to it. But the pursuit of strategic visions, and of the aims set out in the Global Strategy and the Strategic Compass, is limited by the institutional and other constraints noted earlier in this chapter. It is both a strength and a weakness of the EU that it is not a state in the conventional meaning of the word: a strength, because it can generate among its member states a normative consensus that goes beyond purely national interests and provides a strong basis for the extension of European power in the non-military arena; a weakness, because the EU is in no position at present to guarantee that its stance on security issues can be backed up with the 'hard power' that is sometimes required to make diplomacy or negotiation more effective. It is also important to note that in the area of 'hard security' the EU does not possess the institutional dominance that is a feature of its engagement with some areas of 'soft security'; quite simply, the density of the institutional arrangements surrounding 'hard security', with NATO and a range of other bodies playing active roles and actively involving the United States, means that the EU still has to proceed with acute awareness of its institutional limitations (Cameron 2007: Chapter 5; Howorth 2007, 2014, 2023).

Box 7.2 The European Security Strategy and the Global Strategy (extracts)

ESS

In a world of global threats, global markets and global media, our security and prosperity increasingly depend on an effective multilateral system. The development of a stronger multilateral society, well functioning international institutions and a rule-based international order is our objective.

It is a condition of a rule-based international order that law evolves in response to developments such as proliferation, terrorism and global warming. We have an interest in further developing existing instruments such as the World Trade Organization and in supporting new ones such as the International Criminal Court. Our own experience in Europe demonstrates that security can be increased through confidence building and arms control regimes. Such instruments can also make an important contribution to security and stability in our neighbourhood and beyond.

There are few if any problems we can deal with on our own. The threats described above are common threats, shared with all our closest partners. International cooperation is a necessity. We need to pursue our objectives both through multilateral cooperation in international organizations and through partnerships with key actors.

Source: A Secure Europe in a Better World. European Security Strategy, Brussels, 12 December 2003.

GS

As Europeans we must take greater responsibility for our security. We must be ready and able to deter, respond to, and protect ourselves against external threats. While NATO exists to defend its members – most of which are European – from external attack, Europeans must be better equipped, trained and organised to contribute decisively to such collective efforts, as well as to act autonomously if and when necessary. An appropriate level of ambition and strategic autonomy is important for Europe's ability to foster peace and safeguard security within and beyond its borders. Europeans must be able to protect Europe, respond to external crises, and assist in developing our partners' security and defence capacities, carrying out these tasks in cooperation with others. Alongside external crisis management and capacity-building, the EU should also be able to assist in protecting its Members upon their request, and its institutions.

When it comes to collective defence, NATO remains the primary framework for most Member States. At the same time, EU-NATO relations shall not prejudice the security and defence policy of those Members which are not in NATO. The EU will therefore deepen cooperation with the North Atlantic Alliance in complementarity, synergy, and full respect for the institutional framework, inclusiveness and decision-making autonomy of the two. In this context, the EU needs to be strengthened as a security community: European security and defence efforts should enable the EU to act autonomously while also contributing to and undertaking actions in cooperation with NATO. A more credible European defence is essential also for the sake of a healthy transatlantic partnership with the United States.

Source: Shared Vision, Global Action: A Stronger Europe. A Global Strategy for the European Union's Foreign and Security Policy. Brussels, June 2016.

If we look at the record of EU engagement with issues of power and security since the end of the Cold War, this paradoxical situation becomes clearer, especially in the case of global security. The Union has been relatively effective on those issues and processes that give maximum leverage to its 'civilian power', for example the building of institutions to deal with global problems such as environmental change or sustainable development (see Chapter 10), and it has become a significant presence in the United Nations and related bodies through the capacity of its member states to coordinate their positions, including those on conflict prevention and management (Sbragia 1998; Laatikainen and Smith 2006; Holland and Doidge 2012; Koops and Macaj 2015; Vogler 2023). It has also taken an effective stand on questions such as those of land-mines or so-called 'dual-use weapons', where its member states can readily agree on the priorities. There are also examples in Europe of conflicts where the EU has taken an effective collective stance, within the limits set by member state agreement (see Chapter 8). But in situations where the demands are more urgent, where the likelihood of violence is higher and where major state interests are engaged, the EU is (maybe not surprisingly) markedly less effective, and other organizations such as NATO become more salient. Such characteristics have been especially marked in the period since 9/11 – an event that marked a coming together of a new set of security threats, and led to responses across the spectrum of 'hard' and 'soft' security measures, challenging the EU's capacity to maintain solidarity and to muster its institutional resources in a variety of areas (see later) (Gnesotto 2004; Hill 2004). They have also been demonstrated in no uncertain fashion through the EU's engagement with the 'Arab Spring' from 2011 onwards and with conflicts in Georgia, Ukraine and elsewhere since 2008. This is a reflection of the fact that whatever its institutional development, and however apparently strong the commitment of member states, the centre of gravity of the EU is still in its nature as a 'trading state'. The likelihood or the actual use of force is still not something on which the Union and its members are effectively 'integrated', despite progress in the coordination of armaments programmes and the initiation of 'permanent structured cooperation' in defence since the Lisbon Treaty. In fact, it can lead to the opposite, to forms of fragmentation and disintegration. Thus in the Middle East, or the Persian Gulf, the Union can become involved but seems unable to move beyond a presence and into purpose or impact (Crowe 2003; Ortega 2003; Youngs 2006: Chapter 1; Duke 2017: chapters 5 and 6). Despite the declaration by the incoming President of the European Commission, Ursula von der Leyen, in 2019 that the EU would pursue a new 'geopolitical' role in its external action, and the subsequent development of the 'Strategic Compass', it was not clear that this would lead to a transformation of the Union's limited role in 'hard security' or the use of 'hard power' (Biscop 2019; Rachman 2019; Blockmans 2020).

Power and security in US foreign policy

As noted in the introduction to this chapter, the United States has been integral to world order since the beginning of the 20th century, and a leading if not the dominant member of the world arena since at least 1945. During the Cold War, the United States was one of the two 'superpowers', existing in an often uneasy state of 'adversarial partnership' with the Soviet Union and dominating the 'western alliance' of which the European Communities were a subordinate part (Mandelbaum 2022: Chapters 7–9). With the end of the Cold War and the disappearance of the USSR, the United States assumed a position of unchallenged predominance in terms of 'hard power' at the global level, simply being able to do things that no other power – or even combination of powers – could do (Mandelbaum 2022: Chapter 10). But this did not make for an easy relationship between the United States and issues of power and security: the 'only super-power' could often seem the 'lonely superpower' without a near rival; the management of predominant power could be as challenging as the management of subordination (Ikenberry 2002; Daalder and Lindsay 2003; Held and Koenig-Archibugi 2004); and the emergence of new challengers could throw into question the assumptions of US policy. This means that we can ask the same questions about power and security in US foreign policy as we did in the preceding section about the EU and external action: what predispositions does the United States bring to questions of power and security? What motivates US policy? What resources do they deploy? What strategies do they pursue? And what does the record say about the relationship between the United States and questions of power and security since the end of the Cold War?

US policymakers have more often than not approached issues of power and security with a 'vision' of how they should be dealt with (Daalder and Lindsay 2003; Lieven 2004; Mandelbaum 2005; Ikenberry 2006; Deudney and Meier 2018). The notion that the United States is an exceptional country, with a mission to bring its form of democracy to as many of the world's peoples as possible, was integral to US foreign policy during the Cold War and beyond (and indeed since the beginning of the 20th century, when the United States first became a global power) (Lieven 2004: Chapter 1; Deudney and Meier 2018; Mandelbaum 2022). But alongside this notion of 'American exceptionalism' there has normally gone a more pragmatic or 'realist' strand to US policies, especially when the

United States was locked into the contest with the Soviet Union for Cold War predominance. This realism often combined with elements of liberalism to support a US commitment on pragmatic grounds to multilateral institutions and principles (Ikenberry 2006: Part one). There is also a third strand: the persistent tendency among some Americans to hanker after various forms of isolationism, to withdraw from the world and cultivate the perfect democracy, insulated from the grubby dealings of the world (and especially of Europe, at least in the past).

This set of coexisting tendencies is backed up by an acute awareness in the United States of the merits of 'hard power', and of the need to back up the US vision with muscle, especially military muscle, in order to promote the hardest possible security perimeter. It can readily be seen that this interaction between vision and muscle might take three distinct patterns: when power is aligned with 'exceptionalism' it can lead to a form of crusading foreign policy; when linked with 'realism' it can lead to a search for international primacy and alliances, and to qualified support for multilateral institutions; and when linked with isolationism it can lead to a policy centred on 'fortress America'. In contrast to the EU, this gives the United States the character not of a 'trading state' but of what might be termed a 'warrior state'; even when it wishes to back away from the world, the role of 'hard power' and military capability is central to US policies (M. Smith 2004). This central element is accompanied by a strong preference for the use of economic power as an adjunct to 'hard power', which has been modified from time to time both by the growth of economic interdependence and by forms of economic 'isolationism' in the form of 'America First' policies (Cox 2018).

None of these strands in US foreign policy have gone away in the post-Cold-War period, but they have been present in a markedly new type of international structure, characterized by major power-shifts and a changing policy agenda. The disappearance of the Soviet Union instantly gave the United States a position of international primacy that was unprecedented in the modern era, based not only on military power but also on economic leadership (partly expressed through globalization) and 'ideological' primacy centred on ideas of liberal democracy. But the absence of challengers created as many problems as it solved for US policymakers. Where 'hard power' is effectively unlimited, as in the case of the United States after the end of the Cold War, all other countries in the international system have a problem: how are they going to deal with the predominant power? But the predominant power also has a problem: how can this unlimited power be managed politically, in a situation where it seems that it has only to be applied to prevail? The Clinton and George W. Bush administrations that led the United States in the decade after the end of the Cold War had to grapple continually with the problem of political management of power, and while their solutions to the problem were often different in detail they reflected essentially the same underlying question: how do you adjust to a world in which you have no effective rivals and in which you can apparently act unilaterally as often as you want? While the Clinton administration generally came down in favour of multilateral action and coordination with allies, the George W. Bush administration generally came to a different conclusion: that there was no compelling case for multilateralism, especially when the vital interests of the United States were at stake. Such a position was crystallized by the events of 9/11 and was pursued through the 'war on terror' and then the war in Iraq (Daalder and Lindsay 2003: Chapters 6–11; Halper and Clarke 2004: Chapters 7–9; Kaldor 2004).

One of the reasons for this unique position, in which the United States could effectively define its own interests as equivalent to those of the world community and impose its vision of power and security on its allies as well as its adversaries, lay in the resources the United States was able to apply. Particularly in the area of military resources, the United States was theoretically capable of prevailing over almost any conceivable combination of other countries in the world arena. This predominance reflected the massive investment that had been made in military capabilities during the later stage of the Cold War – in this respect, George W. Bush was the principal legatee of Ronald Reagan (M. Smith 2004, 2009). Whether on land, in the air, at sea or even in outer space, the United States was technologically dominant and apparently invincible.

As 9/11 showed, however, this apparent invulnerability could be challenged dramatically by those such as Al-Qaeda practising 'asymmetric conflict' and effectively operating in a different world of power. Economically, the United States was not so unchallengeable in the first post-Cold-War decade: the existence of major competitors such as the EU and the emergence of new economic powers such as China and India made the post-Cold-War global political economy a much more complex place (see Chapter 4), and the need for collective management was necessarily more apparent in this area. Although the United States might be seen as the progenitor of globalization, that does not mean that American leadership was easy to establish or to maintain in the global economic arena. In the area of political ideas, resistance to US attempts to extend the 'free world' was widespread and often effective. This might be seen in terms of a global 'clash of civilizations' (Huntington 1993), but it could also be interpreted in terms of imperialism, domination and resistance – a relationship with a long historical tradition (Ikenberry 2006: Chapter 9; Mann 2003; Todd 2003).

The replacement of George W. Bush with Barack Obama as US president, and his foreign policy between 2009 and 2017, signalled a significant change of tone in the US approach to matters of power and security. Whereas his immediate predecessor and his key advisors had subscribed to the idea of a 'new American century' and to the use of 'hard power' as the key means of response to external challenges and opportunities, the Obama administrations adopted a seemingly much more pragmatic view of the world. In this view, the United States should where possible reduce its external interventions, without sacrificing its predominance: that predominance would be used in different ways, to shape global institutions and to exercise 'soft power' or 'smart power' – the latter referring to a sophisticated combination of means to achieve US objectives and to adjust to processes of global change (Nye 2018). This made Obama the president that all Europeans wanted, but it did not reduce the complexities of the US search for a role in the world. The Obama administrations experienced a paradox: in order to re-shape the US role, there might be a need for increased use of 'hard power' and new means of warfare to create the conditions for withdrawal. Thus, in Iraq and Afghanistan, the US engagement was intensified before eventual retreat or adjustment, and the United States became the world's premier exponent of drone warfare, using new technologies to replace 'boots on the ground' (Woodward 2010). At the same time, the need to counter economic challenges, especially from China, in the aftermath of the global financial crisis, meant that the Obama administrations were caught between the politics of interdependence and the need to defend US interests in a more hard-nosed and confrontational way, for example through economic measures against China or other 'unfair traders'.

While the Obama administrations were thus confronted with a series of tensions and contradictions in their approach to questions of power and security, the presidency of Donald Trump, who took office in January 2017, seemed to reject such complexities. As expressed in his inaugural address, the new president's aim was to put 'America First', and to do so by confronting both allies and adversaries in new ways. From the outset, it was clear that US power was to be used in the service of US domestic politics, and especially the re-election of the president. Multilateral institutions were to be downgraded, and subject to the withdrawal of US support if they did not serve American interests. Diplomacy would no longer be influenced by notions of broader US leadership and responsibilities; rather, it would be conducted on severely 'transactional' lines, in which the key test for agreements was the extent to which they served US interests (M. Smith 2021). Such policies had strong elements of isolationism, in the sense that they emphasized the idea of 'Fortress America' in economic and military terms and subjected all international engagements to the test of their benefits for the American people. There was still an emphasis on the availability of 'hard power', but military means were in many cases sidelined, with economic sanctions and economic warfare becoming a key tool of US policies. Existing military engagements were subject to review and to rejection if they were seen as not serving the interests of the United States; thus, involvement in Afghanistan and in the Middle East was reduced, and the challenges of conflicts in Syria and elsewhere were met with US abstention rather than further engagement. The contrast to both the George W. Bush and the Obama administrations was striking, but the elements of 'Trumpism' in foreign policy were not wholly unprecedented.

As can be seen from this discussion, the post-Cold-War world has been a much more complicated place to manage than some US policymakers have been able to admit. Unilateralism and the deployment of 'hard power' can achieve spectacular results in the short term, but this does not guarantee success in the longer term. The most dramatic demonstration of this problem is to be found in the invasion of Iraq, and the subsequent inability of the United States to control the insurgency that then followed (Woodward 2006). The 'war on terror' itself did not require simply the application of massive military power; rather, it demanded long-term planning and the application of a wide range of political, legal, administrative and other measures as well as force. Equally, an 'America First' policy requires extensive deployment and coordination of a range of economic, military and diplomatic instruments if it is to be more than a simple policy of isolationism. The United States has very large 'hard-power' resources, and the capacity to deliver them to many parts of the world, but the need to apply these in a complex, globalized and crisis-ridden context places unprecedented demands on the US political and administrative system as well as on its armed forces. Not only this, but the frequent resort to 'hard power' can have the result of reducing the credibility of US 'soft power' and making it much more difficult to bring others along with US international initiatives (Nye 2002, 2004a). Not coincidentally, the concept of 'smart power' was developed partly as a reflection of these contradictions and the Obama administration's attempts to grapple with them (Nye 2018).

The management of power and security is thus not a simple problem for the United States. Power and resources are available, but their impact and their relationship to political objectives are not predictable. One way of attempting to deal with this problem is through the development of 'grand strategy', and this has been a characteristic feature of US foreign policy during the post-1945 period (Kupchan 2002; Lieber 2007). While during the Cold War the centrality of the contest with the Soviet Union provided the core of such 'grand strategy', the post-Cold-War period has not been so easy to cope with. The Clinton administrations of the 1990s generally pursued a strategy based on the interrelated concepts of 'engagement' and 'enlargement' – engagement with both allies and adversaries, enlargement of the zone of freedom and democracy – a strategy which reflected a broadly multilateralist approach but which was accompanied by the willingness to use force if necessary, as in Bosnia and Kosovo (see Chapter 9). The George W. Bush administration after 2000 adopted a posture based much more closely on the exercise of 'hard power' at an early stage, pre-emptively if necessary. The National Security Strategy of 2002, adopted immediately after 9/11, focused almost exclusively on the need to prevent challenges to the United States and to use force in this cause. Engagement with allies as an end in itself was marginalized; in the words of US Secretary of Defense Donald Rumsfeld, 'the mission determines the coalition, rather than the coalition determining the mission'. But as time and the consequences of US interventions unfolded, things began to look much more complicated and intractable. In this sense, the Obama administrations of 2009–17 were partly a response to this set of obstacles and partly a reversion to the politics of the Clinton administrations, with the emphasis on the need for cooperation and attention to the need for readjustment of US ambitions, while the Trump administration was a rejection both of the expansive aims of the George W. Bush years and of the 'pragmatic realism' practised by Obama. When the Trump administration was replaced in 2021 by the administration of Joe Biden, there was an immediate change of tone, with much more emphasis on multilateralism and the regeneration of US leadership, but this did not mean the problem of managing power had been resolved. Indeed, the continuation and intensification of tensions with China, and then the outbreak of large-scale warfare in Europe after the Russian invasion of Ukraine, meant that it would emerge in new and even more challenging forms between 2021 and 2024.

Power and security in EU–US relations

Although both the EU and the United States have a persistent interest in issues of global power and security, they approach them from markedly different positions and with markedly different resources and strategies. In this part of the chapter, we look at the ways in which these different approaches have intersected or collided in the post-Cold-War world and at the ways in which they have contributed to broader changes in the world arena. As noted at the beginning of the chapter, it has been argued that the EU and the United States exist in 'separate worlds' when it comes to their roles in the global arena, but self-evidently this is true only at the most abstract level. As might be expected, the pursuit of power and security by the EU and the United States has several dimensions. Here we will look at two of them: the management of power, and the changing security agenda. The argument will be illustrated first by reference to key cases relating to the uses of power at the global level: the 'war on terror' that ensued after the attacks of 9/11, the Iraq War and occupation, and the problem of Iranian nuclear intentions. A second set of cases will deal with the ways in which EU–US relations reflect the changing security agenda. In Chapter 8, security issues in Europe will be addressed in the light of problems of order and change.

The management of power

Both the EU and the United States confront problems emerging from the management of power. The EU experiences the continuous need to manage American power, since the United States is a dominating feature of the external environment for European integration. Since the end of the Cold War, this problem has taken successive forms, and the EU has had to deal with a United States that is itself searching for an appropriate role in world order. In this respect, it was rather easier for the Union to come to terms with the Clinton administrations than with those of George W. Bush since the Clinton years saw at least an attempt by US leaders to use the institutions and mechanisms that might channel or contain their power (Smith and Woolcock 1994; Peterson 1996b). The George W. Bush administrations had a different view of American power: they wanted to use it, and to demonstrate their primacy as well as to assert it in the cause of global democracy. This, not surprisingly, created pressure on the EU and its member states, and made collective action by the Union much more difficult in areas where the United States took an assertive position (M. Smith 2005a). The Obama administrations posed a different challenge: while they had been overwhelmingly the preference of Europeans, the 'pragmatic realism' of US policies did not provide EU leaders with an endorsement of 'civilian' or 'normative' uses of power, and instead demanded that Europeans step up to the plate in support of continued US engagement with a number of significant conflicts (M. Smith 2011a). The Trump administration, which described the EU as a 'foe' in economic and political terms, and which took unilateral actions to an extreme, was easier for the EU to stand against but represented a new dynamic not only in transatlantic relations but also in the global arena – for example through its use of 'economic warfare' measures against China. The Biden administration from 2021 onwards in many respects continued Trump's policy of confrontation with China, while attempting to regenerate the 'western alliance' and exploit its connections in the Indo-Pacific through links with Japan, Australia, India and others.

The attacks of 9/11 provided a catalyst for many of these underlying tensions in EU–US security relations. In one sense, the fact that the attacks reflected a novel, transnational and non-governmental form of violence seemed to play to some of the strengths of the EU: this was a problem that demanded cross-national coordination, often by non-military means, to preserve economic and social structures in the face of a broad and often ill-defined threat (M. Smith 2001b; Nye 2004b). Thus, the EU collectively could respond with statements of support and with economic and diplomatic measures. But the 'war on terror' as it developed faced the EU with a different challenge, as US forces led the move into Afghanistan during 2001–2 with the aim of deposing the Taliban regime that had harboured Al-Qaeda. This pushed EU solidarity beyond the limits of sustainability, and leading members of the coalition that led the Afghan campaign, such as the British or the Dutch, acted much less as members of the Union than as allies of the United States; there was also a tendency among the larger member states to take on a special role in the crisis, as for example when the French, the Germans and the British met separately before the European Council meeting of October 2001, or when British prime minister Tony Blair convened a meeting of those who had committed themselves to military engagement in Afghanistan, without inviting Javier Solana, the EU's high representative for Common Foreign and Security Policy (Cameron 2007: 32–4).

In the longer term, however, the EU could play a role in organizing the reconstruction effort and coordinating financing – areas that played into the 'soft-power' resources of the Union. In the same way, the EU could provide support for the 'war on terror' through its developing responsibilities for 'justice and home affairs': a category of activities that was greatly extended with the need to exchange information and coordinated intelligence in the aftermath of 9/11 (den Boer and Monar 2002; Monar 2004). Thus the EU was able, for example, to promote a pan-European arrest warrant, measures to promote transport and data security and regulations to deal with the financing of terrorist groupings. The Union was also able in some areas to resist US policies, for example where conceptions of human rights differed between the two sides of the Atlantic (see later). Not only this, but it could be argued that new areas of European foreign policy cooperation were made possible, not in the classic collective foreign policy mode but through the emergence of new potential coalitions within the EU and through their interaction with NATO and other security organizations to address shared problems (Hill 2004; M. Smith 2006b).

Whereas the 'war on terror' saw strains but also new forms of solidarity within the EU, the invasion of Iraq was clearly opposed by a number of leading EU member states, and was not seen by them as part of the response to 9/11. Thus, as the United States moved towards war with Iraq during 2002–3, it was effectively impossible for the Europeans to maintain unity; a number of countries such as the UK, Spain and Italy defected from any common position on the ground that they must support the United States, while others such as France and Germany attempted to maintain solidarity around resistance to the looming invasion and full use of the United Nations (Lindstrom 2003: Chapters 1–2; Gordon and Shapiro 2004; Peterson 2004a). The particular issue of 'weapons of mass destruction' (WMD) and their presence or absence in Iraq saw a fundamental divergence between those within the Union who supported a multilateral, UN-based approach (and who suspected the issue of being a cover for 'regime change') and those who espoused a more coercive military approach. This created a position of considerable internal crisis within the EU, and led Donald Rumsfeld to identify a division between what he termed 'old' and 'new' Europe (see Chapter 1, Box 1.8).

While Rumsfeld's division was simplistic and provocative (and referred to the enlarged NATO as well as to the EU), the wounds opened by the Iraq crisis did lead to a proliferation of efforts to form more partial 'European' caucuses and to express difference or convergence between European and US positions. In many of these initiatives, the EU institutions themselves seemed likely to be marginalized; thus in the months before the invasion, the French and the Germans took measures to increase their cooperation in resisting US and British pressures; in January 2003, the leaders of eight EU member states or soon-to-be member states signed an open letter supporting US policies without consulting other member states or candidate members, and in February the so-called 'Vilnius Group' of Central and East European countries (including seven candidate EU members hoping to accede in 2004) pledged support for the United States in a letter published in the *Wall Street Journal*. Only with difficulty was a position reached in the Council of Ministers that allowed the EU as a whole to state a common position on the humanitarian and related aspects of the conflict, while maintaining an uneasy silence on the war itself. Although tensions arising from these events persisted in the EU for several years, threatening to make it much less easy to undertake security initiatives in other areas, there was a gradual process of repair (Lindstrom 2003; Peterson and Pollack 2003; Lindstrom and Schmitt 2004; Peterson 2004a; Pond 2004). The issue of relations between the EU's defence identity and other defence organizations also persisted; in February 2005 German Chancellor Gerhard Schroeder suggested that NATO was no longer the appropriate forum for discussion of transatlantic security issues (Cameron 2007: 86), and although not many other EU leaders would have agreed with him then, the question still lingered as the CSDP developed further.

The divisions within the EU and between the EU and the United States over war in Iraq were also responsible for one of the more notable transatlantic debates during the early 2000s. In 2003, arising directly out of the buildup to the war, Robert Kagan published an article and then a book dealing with what came to be known as the 'Mars/Venus' problem (Kagan 2003; see also Lindberg 2005). In Kagan's view, the United States had not fully come to terms with its preponderance of 'hard power', but had (as noted earlier) a tendency to resort to coercive solutions even where others might work. On the other hand, the Europeans emphasized the use of 'soft power' and resistance to military solutions, partly as a rationalization of their military weakness but also because of historical experience with the use of force. To put it in the terms used by a popular American self-improvement book on the differences between men and women, 'Americans were from Mars and Europeans from Venus'. In various forms, this debate came to encapsulate not only a political but also an institutional and cultural difference between the two sides of the Atlantic. This difference was not absolute – the British, for example, looked more like Martians than Venusians on many occasions – but it came to stand as a metaphor for the EU–US divergence on 'hard-security' issues (Cox 2003; M. Smith 2004; Forsberg and Herd 2006). The key question is how much this presumed difference constituted a fundamental and lasting rift in EU–US security relations (Andrews 2005: Part III; Lindberg 2005; Zabarowski 2006a).

Does this difference over the management of power and the pursuit of security reflect broader differences over the utility of unilateral and multilateral approaches? One example that can help to answer this question is that of EU and US responses to fears that the Iranians would pursue and obtain a nuclear weapons capability. Coming alongside the war and insurgency in Iraq, this challenge represented for some American neo-conservatives an extension of the problem that had led to US intervention in the first place – an extension to which the remedy might be 'more of the same' in the form of the use of force against Iran. The European analysis differed: there was a consensus within the Union that the Iranian problem was not only distinct from that of Iraq (although it had become entangled with it partly as a consequence of US intervention in Iraq) but also that it should be dealt with diplomatically, using the EU's 'soft power' in the form of potential partnership and cooperation agreements. During the period 2003–7, the EU developed a mechanism for pursuing a diplomatic solution through the so-called 'EU-3' (France, Germany and the UK), which maintained diplomatic contact with the Iranian government and which was able to put together successive packages of measures to present to the government in Tehran (Everts 2004; Posch 2006; Youngs 2006: Chapter 3). This did not prevent the Iranian government from making moves towards the production of the raw materials for a nuclear device, but it did preserve a diplomatic linkage and prevent the taking of pre-emptive military action. Perhaps surprisingly, the United States went along with this diplomatic strategy, but it should be noted in this context that the growth of the insurgency in Iraq between 2004 and 2006 and the consequent growth in domestic opposition to US interventions would have made any unilateral American action difficult in any case.

The EU's preference for using multilateral channels coupled with internal divisions among European foreign policy actors seemed unlikely to lead to EU–US convergence over Iran even after Obama took office in 2009. During his campaign, Obama stressed the importance of abandoning the Bush administration's policy of isolation in favour of diplomatic engagement with states such as Iran. In early 2010, however, the EU and the United States were still divided on how to approach Tehran after Iran publicly defied the international community with a series of weapons tests. After months of going back and forth over the need for diplomacy through the UN, it was announced in March that consensus was reached on the need for a new UN-led action. Failed UN talks resulted in both the EU and the United States imposing sanctions in 2010 followed by more sanctions and an EU oil embargo in 2012 (Sauer 2015). In July 2015, a deal was finally reached in the form of the Joint Comprehensive Plan of Action (JCPOA), which the EU quickly approved. The Obama administration also approved the deal, was unable to convince Congress to support it, but could implement it through executive order.

In February 2016, the US Congress voted to impose new sanctions on Iran, thereby undermining the credibility of Obama's position. At that time, it was already apparent that a Trump administration would take a radical line. True to his promise, Trump declared Iran in violation of the JCPOA and followed this by ratcheting up sanctions on a bilateral basis, while also professing to want a deal with the Tehran regime. This placed the EU in a difficult and potentially dangerous position. On the one hand, the Union's commitment to multilateral diplomacy conducted under the auspices of UN resolutions, which had led to the JCPOA, was viewed as a victory for the new diplomatic mechanisms established by the Lisbon Treaty. This view strengthened the EU's opposition to Washington's newly aggressive posture. Moreover, the Trump administration was suspected of wanting to achieve regime change in Iran, as it explicitly linked the use of sanctions and the underlying threat of the use of force to the viability of the Iranian government. But, on the other hand, regime change was profoundly at odds with the multilateral diplomacy practised by the Union (Geranmayeh 2017; Litwak 2019). As a result, the years 2017–19 were taken up with attempts by the EU to reinforce its commitment to the JCPOA and to restrain Iran from reacting forcefully to US measures, while US policymakers attacked the Union regularly for what they saw as a form of appeasement. The resulting loss of trust between Washington and EU leaders was not simply a one-off event. Rather, it seemed to reflect a cumulative trend towards the divergence of the EU and the United States on matters of regional security in the Middle East and the Persian Gulf (Sanger 2019). For some in Washington, when the chips were down, differences over Iran equalled the marginalization of the EU (Erlanger 2019b). Although the Biden administration came into office with a stronger commitment to the JCPOA and a multilateral solution, little movement had occurred on this front by 2023.

The changing security agenda

Each of the examples referred to earlier has contained major elements of 'hard security'. But as noted earlier in this chapter, there are many current issues between the EU and the United States that are predominantly if not entirely of a 'soft-security' type, reflecting a changing security agenda. The notion of 'soft security', as noted earlier, relates to the preservation of economic security, environmental security, energy security and what has come to be termed 'human security' in the broad sense. In the post-Cold-War era many of these areas have become newly or increasingly 'securitized': that is to say, they are presented by governments as questions relating to the preservation of national security (or EU security) in the face of new threats and risks. They are also used by some if not all governments as weapons in their relations with others, through the manipulation of dependencies (for example, on supplies of oil or gas or technical assistance) and consequently vulnerabilities. The EU and the United States are bound together by their status as rich countries or groupings in dealing with these problems, but this has not prevented the emergence of significant tensions between them. In the context of this argument, the important question is: to what extent do these differences betray different fundamental perspectives on the use of 'soft power' in the search for 'soft security'?

The first case to examine is 'economic security'. Since the 1970s, as indicated in Chapter 1, there have been differences between the US and the European views of economic security, if by that is meant the preservation of economic stability and the pursuit of economic growth and prosperity, for example through trade and the management of the currency. The US economy remains the single largest national economy in the world (although increasingly challenged by China), and thus there is a historic tendency among US policymakers to stress the ways in which growth and prosperity depend upon national initiatives and national instruments. During the 1990s and 2000s, there were variations in the stances of successive administrations (see Chapters 4–6), but these have been variations around a fairly consistent tendency to prioritize national measures and to downplay the prospects of multilateral cooperation. Thus although the United States is a leading member of the G-7 industrial countries, which meet annually to coordinate national economic policies, Washington has been reluctant to allow its national economic strategy to be constrained by international action. The EU's stance is different: long experience with coordination and integration within Europe itself has created a predisposition to multilateralize economic security issues, and to search for means of collaboration. Although again there are variations around this trend line, the tendency to prioritize collaboration and multilateralism is evident (Pollack 2003a). It is also difficult in this area for the United States to 'divide and rule', since unlike areas of 'hard security' there are stronger institutional arrangements and a predisposition in the Union to agree on matters of 'economic security', even where there are sharp differences among member states on the specifics.

These contrasting stances were severely challenged by the economic and financial crisis of 2008 and after. That crisis, which was linked to the development of new forms of debt instruments in the United States and then globally, and which led to a near-collapse in banking arrangements throughout the western world, led to new forms of global cooperation, in the shape of the G-20, which brought together the leading economies of the world, but also highlighted the divergence of views between leading economic powers on how to combat the crisis (Jokela 2011; see also Chapter 5). As might have been expected, the US solution was to focus primarily on the recovery of its domestic economy, which might then stimulate growth in the rest of the world economy. Despite this tendency, the Obama administration did enter into multilateral cooperation, but with the unstated assumption that the United States was the leading economic power and that others had to show they could punch their weight in the recovery process. At the same time, the EU was challenged by its own increasingly severe internal financial crisis, reflecting the economic divergences between member states and the threat that Economic and Monetary Union might collapse. Finally, the crisis highlighted the emergence of new centres of economic and financial power, especially China, which came to play a growing role in the provision of global economic security but on different terms from those pursued by either the EU or the United States. These issues remained contentious with the growth of 'economic warfare' between the United States and China under the Trump administration, as already noted (and see Chapter 4), and the competitive pursuit of economic security remains at the centre of EU–US security relations. Although the Biden administration set out to cooperate more consistently with the EU, its continued focus on competition with China, and its determination to promote its domestic economic security, created new challenges for the Union.

While there is a long tradition of European solidarity on matters of 'economic security', albeit challenged severely since the global economic crisis, the second example, environmental security, is less longstanding. Significantly, however, the EU's acquisition of competence in areas of environmental policy during the late 1980s and 1990s coincided with growing awareness of the ways these issues needed to be managed at the multilateral level (Sbragia 1998). The EU has thus had an incentive (through the European Commission) to pursue a leadership role in environmental security, and to create a distinctively 'European' definition of interests, focused (for example) on the adoption of binding targets for reductions in carbon dioxide emissions and on the development of emissions trading schemes. Despite a great diversity of views within the EU on most environmental issues (notably between some of the less developed new member states and the older-established and richer members), there has been a capacity to collaborate around common positions in international organizations, often in distinct opposition to US views (Vogler and Bretherton 2006; Vogler 2023; Wurzel and Connelly 2010). On the American side, while the United States has led in some areas of international environmental regulation, there is more of a predisposition to allow market forces to operate, and to initiate action at the national level. This has been particularly the case in the area of climate change, where the United States opposed binding targets for reductions in carbon dioxide emissions (as symbolized by the commitments in the 1999 Kyoto Protocol) and instead argued for the development of new technologies through market incentives and at the national level. Such contentious relations continued throughout the George W. Bush period, but were replaced by a greater degree of cooperation during the Obama administrations, eventually finding expression in the Paris Accords of 2015, which set wide-ranging targets for environmental action. Under the Trump administration, the pendulum of US policy swung dramatically back towards unilateralism, with repudiation of the Paris Accords and an attempt to revive industries such as coal-mining in defiance of global norms and commitments. The Biden administration's major efforts to promote 'green industry' through its Inflation Reduction Act and other measures continued a major trend towards 'domesticism' in the management of environmental issues (see also Chapter 4).

These are thus not mere differences of detail: they betray a basic difference between EU and US perspectives on environmental regulation that emerges as much from cultural predispositions or the relationship between government and society as from government tactics (Bodansky 2003, Vogler 2016, 2023). Nevertheless, setting aside the rhetoric on both sides, there is a good deal in common between the EU and the United States, since both of them share the problems of rich industrialized areas that need to find a way to preserve their standards of living and levels of consumption in a world where others (such as India or China) are seeking to emulate them. In this sense, the question is one that squarely confronts the themes of this book: there is a great deal of overt competition between the EU and the United States, but a large amount of common interest arising out of their shared predicament and an inescapable engagement with both short-term and long-term crises in the global arena.

The third example that can be examined here is that of energy security. During the 2000s, both the Europeans and the Americans have become more sensitive than at any time since the 1970s to the price for and the supply of oil and gas. Neither the EU nor the United States could until recently satisfy its own energy needs from domestic sources, and thus both have been heavily dependent on supplies from the Middle East and Persian Gulf, the former Soviet Union (particularly Russia) or Latin America. The impact of conflict in the Middle East and the Gulf during the early years of the 21st century was severe, and drove up oil prices in general to historic highs. At the same time, the newly assertive Vladimir Putin government in Russia tried to use the 'energy weapon' as a means to restore its international status and to make others take notice of its priorities (see Chapter 8). In Latin America, the Chavez government in Venezuela made it its business to provoke Washington and to use its oil resources as a means of forming new international alliances (for example with Cuba and Iran). Both the EU and the United States thus came under pressure to address problems of energy vulnerability, without being able in the short term to avoid reliance on imported oil and gas supplies (Musu and Wallace 2003).

The situation changed radically after 2010, with the growth of production of oil and gas from shale deposits in the United States creating a new self-sufficiency, and thus fundamentally changing the relationship between the EU and the United States at a time when energy security was called into question more generally. Although the EU – and particularly certain member states – was able to develop alternative sources of energy such as wind or solar power, these did not in the short term promise to become dominant sources. The issue of differential vulnerability became especially pressing after the crisis in Ukraine during 2014–15, was underlined further by the policies of the Trump administration, which were based on the assumption that the United States was essentially invulnerable in this area and could thus pursue much more aggressive policies against a variety of targets, and fed into a crisis when Russia invaded Ukraine in February 2022, provoking sanctions on its exports and radically increasing the price of oil and gas on world markets.

This is an inherently political issue, one where 'hard power' is not to be relied upon as a means of dealing with it, but also one in which EU and US perceptions of security have diverged increasingly during the 21st century. Whereas for the EU there is little room for manoeuvre, since they cannot intervene forcibly in the absence of 'hard-power' resources and in the presence of divergent views among member states, the United States has assumed a position in which there is no need for it to pursue active policies in the Middle East and elsewhere – both because those policies led to complications in the past, and because of its own perceived self-sufficiency. The result has been a state of flux in EU–US energy relations, which has been compounded by the volatility of oil prices in the context of the US shale revolution and of challenges such as the COVID-19 crisis. The Ukraine war beginning in 2022 crystallized many of the contradictions outlined here, since it entailed the use of oil and (especially) gas as economic and political weapons by Russia, and created new challenges of policy development for the EU given the varying levels of exposure and vulnerability among member states.

Finally, there is the issue of 'human security'. During recent years there has been growing attention to the combination of regional conflicts, development issues and human rights issues that clusters around the security of individuals or groups within or across national jurisdictions. The plight of refugees from a great variety of civil conflicts, but now also from a growing range of environmental disasters, is perhaps the most obvious example of a wide-ranging problem. In terms of world order, it is clear that the EU places a much larger emphasis on cooperative solutions to such problems, embodying multilateral principles and inclusive characteristics, while the United States (perhaps inevitably as a dominant power) has tended to look for exclusive coalitions and 'special relationships', if necessary rejecting efforts at multilateral management (Kaldor, Martin, and Selchow 2007). Thus, the European Union has been a strong supporter of United Nations management of regional conflicts, while the United States has been much more equivocal about it; equally, the EU has strongly supported the International Criminal Court as a means of pursuing and punishing those involved in civil conflicts, while the United States has rejected it and specifically attempted to undermine the EU's collective position by concluding agreements with EU member states to exempt US forces from its application. Until recently, the EU has had little capacity to intervene in civil conflicts or regional conflicts that cross national boundaries, but the development of CSDP since the early 2000s has given it at least some significant instruments in this area (Howorth 2014, 2017). As a result, the EU has become involved in Central Africa, in dealing with conflicts involving Rwanda and the Democratic Republic of Congo, and in a variety of other conflicts ranging from the Horn of Africa to the Maghreb. The United States, on the other hand, has largely remained uninvolved on the ground, reserving its interventions for those areas in which it has a direct strategic interest, such as the Middle East or the Gulf, and withdrawing even from those to a degree under the Trump administration, only to be dragged back into intensive Middle East diplomacy by the 2023–4 Israel-Gaza war. The EU, it might appear, has a winning combination of assets that can be used in the African context particularly: emerging military capacity (limited as noted in Box 7.1 to the 'Petersberg' and associated tasks); a long-standing engagement with international development in Africa; historical and cultural ties due to colonialism; and a commitment to the achievement of 'human security' through multilateral action, which might enable it to develop a form of 'burden-sharing' with the United States (Lindstrom 2005; Carbone 2013).

But the dynamics of 'human security' are not so simple. When the crisis in the Darfur region of Sudan emerged in the late 1990s, both the EU and the United States described the actions of government-backed militias as 'genocide', but neither was willing to intervene with the requisite force or economic support for the affected areas. Given that other factors also operate in Central Africa – particularly the recent discovery and exploitation of large oil reserves, and the increasing presence in the region of China as an aid donor and oil buyer – it might be suspected that attitudes both in the EU and the United States could have changed rather rapidly, but that is to underestimate the public (and in the case of the EU, member state) opposition to renewed intervention in the wake of Iraq and Afghanistan. Equally, when conflicts in the Middle East led to mass involuntary migration from 2015 onwards, the EU, which was the target for many such migrants, found it almost impossible to develop a coordinated policy for dealing with them, despite its existing role in the region and its clear strategic interests in conflict management. Faced with similar flows of migrants from Central America, the United States adopted a much harder stance, eventually constructing a border barrier between itself and Mexico to stem the flow and repatriating a large number of migrants under the Obama, Trump and Biden administrations. Here, then, a 'soft-security' issue is strongly linked to considerations of 'hard power' and domestic political calculations, and this problem afflicts both the EU and the United States. As with the issue of energy security, however, there is a key role for divergent perceptions of interest and vulnerability on both sides of the Atlantic, which constrain effective cooperation in the face of continuing crises.

Overview and conclusion

This chapter has focused on the ways EU and US views of power and security can be explored and evaluated, and on the ways they can be observed in action within EU–US relations. A key aid to understanding these issues is an awareness of processes of change, both within the EU and the United States and in the broader global context within which they conduct their relations. This is not a new theme in this book – indeed, it is one of the core themes that run through the whole of our analysis. Here, it has a global scale and a connection with key aspects of the approaches to the world on both sides of the Atlantic. The chapter has argued as follows:

- First, the change from the Cold War world to the post-Cold-War world created new challenges and opportunities for both the EU and the United States, to be followed by major shifts in the international structure of power and security. Their responses to these challenges, opportunities and structural shifts reflect a combination of pragmatic, institutional and cultural understandings about the way the world works and the way it should look.
- Second, and more specifically, the chapter has characterized the EU as a form of 'trading state', emphasizing the search for stability, the use of multilateral strategies and the exploitation of 'soft power' based on reciprocity and problem-solving. Although the EU's external actions have acquired more of a 'hard edge' as time has passed, these basic preoccupations have persisted.
- Third, the United States, on the other hand, can be characterized as a 'warrior state', searching for advantage, prepared to act unilaterally and to use 'hard power', particularly military force, in pursuit of national advantage. While there have been variations around this central position, it still constitutes a basic point of difference from the EU.
- Fourth, in matters of global power and security, the EU and the United States represent different responses to the issue of managing the changing global power structure, and these responses are crucial for the management of global power and security as a whole. The relationship between 'hard power' and 'hard security' and 'soft power' and 'soft security' is crucial here, but it is also complex and does not produce a clear-cut distinction between EU and US positions.

The discussion in this chapter reveals that the EU and the United States have differences over power and security at three levels. In the first place, they have pragmatic and practical differences about the 21st-century world, in economic, security and defence issues, which arise out of their mutual interactions and which in principle are susceptible to management through a process of negotiation and problem-solving. Many of the economic issues that arise between the two partners are of this kind, but so also are a number of security issues which reflect the broader conception of security that has grown in the post-Cold-War era. Often these disputes arise within a framework of shared understandings and expectations and can be very effectively managed. But there are other differences that emerge out of a kind of competition between the EU and the United States to 'sell' or establish their models of economic and political organization to potential converts in the post-Cold-War context (Sbragia 2010). Into this category fall a number of 'big-picture' trade and development issues, as well as some questions to do with human rights and the management of international conflicts. The processes of interaction here are those of hard bargaining and the exercise of muscle, rather than negotiation and problem-solving. The final type of difference is much less amenable to either problem-solving or bargaining since it depends upon fundamental differences of culture and assumptions about the nature of power, sovereignty and international order itself. We can expect that in the future these three strands will continue to characterize the respective EU and US approaches to issues of power and security, and that the result will continue to be an uneasy and shifting set of complex compromises.

Chapter 8

The EU, the United States and European order

Introduction

This chapter has two key dimensions. First, it is centred predominantly on the evolution of the post-Cold-War order in Europe, as opposed to the largely global emphasis in Chapters 4 to 7 and 9–10. Second, it focuses primarily on security and diplomacy, providing additional focus to the more general discussions of power and security in Chapter 7 and regional crises in Chapter 9. In terms of the argument put forward in Chapter 2, the discussion is thus firmly in the area of 'high politics' as opposed to 'sectoral' or 'low' politics. In this way, the chapter takes forward key themes about the nature of power and security but relates them to the particular issues arising in post-Cold-War Europe.

Chapter 1 gave an outline of the qualities of EC–US relations during the Cold War, specifically as they affected roles in Europe. It explored the nature of US power, its predominance in the security domain and the ways the United States could be seen as exercising hegemony over both Europe in general and the European integration project in particular. This hegemony was qualified during the 1970s and 1980s and to some extent undermined as the shape of post-Cold-War Europe began to be established. It was at this time that a number of questions emerged that were to become more pointed and a focus of recriminations in the post-Cold-War period. Also at this time, the ideology of 'civilian power Europe' was developed and became a key element in the EC's self-perception in international relations.

Chapter 1 also dealt with a number of specific questions that arose for EC–US relations at the end of the Cold War, and the ways they found expression. The chapter examined the outlines of the emerging 'new Europe' or 'new Europes' and asked whether the EC or the United States was better qualified to act as the guarantor of the emerging post-Cold-War order. The answer, of course, is that this was a hotly contested and variable issue, which intersected with the emergence of new ideas about the nature of Europe and European identity, as well as with the changing nature of the European integration project. It also intersected with the ways Americans saw their role in the world and the ways they felt they should be able to influence events in Europe (Treverton 1991; Smith and Woolcock 1993: Chapters 1–2; Gompert and Larrabee 1997).

In this chapter, as in Chapters 4 to 7 and 9–10, the argument follows a common general pattern. First, the chapter will deal with the EU's role or roles in the 'New Europe' that emerged from the end of the Cold War. Second, it will deal with the equivalent questions for the United States: how did the Americans respond to the 'New Europe', and also to the EU's roles within it? Third, the chapter will explore the ways in which competition and convergence between the EU and the United States in respect of the 'New Europe' have expressed themselves since the early 1990s, and how the intersecting EU and US roles have been managed through the key changes of the post-Cold-War era, including a number of European crises. The concluding section will outline the 'new Euro-American system' in respect of the European order, which seems to have emerged from these developments, will explore the challenges posed by changes in EU and US policies and will suggest some possible future developments. In Chapters 9 and 10, the focus will shift to pursue a number of these questions in terms of regional order, global order and global governance, building on the arguments made here and in Chapter 7.

The EC/EU and post-Cold-War Europe

Although the end of the Cold War is well symbolized by the fall of the Berlin Wall from the autumn of 1989 onwards, the process had begun long before. The dim outlines of a possible 'new Europe' in which the EC would play a central role had been discernible for several years, and this had also begun to raise questions about the continuing roles of the United States and of NATO. The developments of the period 1989–91, though, raised the issues in inescapable form and are crucial to an understanding of the ways in which the EC/EU and the United States approached the creation of 'new Europe(s)' (Story 1993; M. Smith 2000; Laffan, O'Donnell, and Smith 2000; Niblett and Wallace 2001).

Three key features of the process should be identified from the outset. First, the ending of the Cold War was in many ways an essentially 'European' process, arising from the increasing pressures from newly mobilized groups within Soviet bloc countries and from the crumbling of established institutions both in those countries and in the USSR itself. There is substantial debate about the part played in the process by US policies, including a large increase in defence spending, and by the pressure exerted by US imposition of sanctions and other measures during the 1980s, but it seems clear that the radical changes of the late 1980s and early 1990s did have authentically European roots (Alting von Geusau 1993; Story 1993; Laffan, O'Donnell, and Smith 2000; Niblett and Wallace 2001). A second feature of the process was that although it could be defined as a series of changes in 'high politics' – the nature of alliances, the control of nuclear weapons, the creation of 'grand bargains' about the future architecture of Europe – it also brought together in potent form all three of the 'baskets' of issues dealt with in the 'Helsinki process': security and defence, economic issues and human social and cultural questions. The Cold War had effectively compartmentalized these issues, giving automatic priority to questions of 'hard power' and 'hard security', but such a compartmentalization was no longer possible. Third, the end of the Cold War raised immediate and pressing questions about the institutional 'architecture' of the changed continent, and about the ways in which institutions might have to change to reflect and encourage new forms of political and economic alignment (Keohane and Hoffmann 1993).

Key to all of these general features was the presence and the potential of the EC. For those countries and social groupings pressing for a 'return to Europe' in the ruins of the Soviet bloc, one of the primary objectives was close association and eventually membership of the EC (Nello and K. Smith 1998; Henderson 1999; A. Smith 2000). This was seen as a means of guaranteeing economic and social reconstruction and thus also as a way of enhancing the security – in the broadest sense – of the new or newly liberated regimes. The Community responded initially by creating new programmes of economic and humanitarian assistance, particularly the Phare programme for the reconstruction of Central and East European economies and institutions, and by taking the lead in the group of G-24 countries giving aid to Central and Eastern Europe (a lead encouraged by the United States). But the diplomacy of the end of the Cold War in other respects remained on relatively traditional tracks: the 'grand bargains' at the Paris Conference of 1990 and elsewhere that might be seen as the end-of-Cold-War 'settlement' were bargains between the members of NATO, led by the United States, and the ex-members of the Warsaw Treaty Organization (Keohane and Hoffmann 1993; Lundestad 2008: Chapter 8). The EC was associated with these, albeit indirectly, and it might play a key role in practical reconstruction or political stabilization, but this was still confined effectively to the 'civilian power' realm that had been characteristic of EC policy for years if not decades.

There is no doubt however that between 1989 and 1991 the EC became central to the process by which the Cold War was ended. The new institutional 'map' of Europe saw the EC and then the EU installed as a central pillar of the European order, with responsibilities going far beyond those purely of market reforms and economic reconstruction. At the same time, it created doubts about the continued existence of NATO, despite continuous attempts to extend new forms of association and partnership to the countries of the former Soviet bloc and the Soviet Union itself (Sloan 2005: Chapters 5–8). As Figure 8.1 shows, this new Europe was one in which a number of potentially complementary (but also potentially competing) organizations occupied the landscape. Some of them included the United States and Canada; others did not. Some focused especially on the 'high politics' of alliance and armaments; others did not. Not surprisingly, there was the potential for what has been called 'institutional overcrowding', with uncertainty about which institutions could or should take the lead in dealing with the new range of security issues. These issues themselves

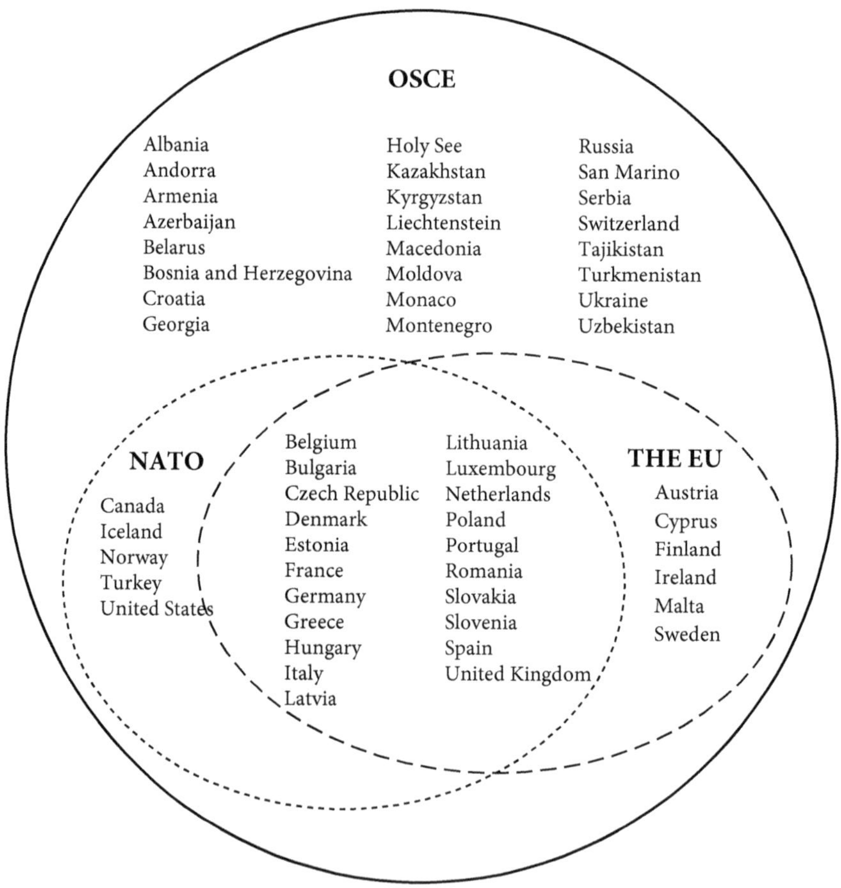

Figure 8.1 Membership of major security organizations in Europe, 2007.

linked together military, diplomatic, economic and humanitarian dimensions in new and often unpredictable ways. Not only this, but they created or underlined areas of tension between the EC and its member states, which had often strongly divergent views on the implications of German unification, the expansion of NATO and other questions. This was to be a constant underlying theme in the politics of European order during the following 30 years.

One consequence of the crumbling of the Cold War order for the EU was in effect its own creation, through the Maastricht Treaty. The Common Foreign and Security Policy established by the treaty can be seen in some ways as a response to the fall of the Berlin Wall, and the desire of other EC member states to create a political framework for the 'containment' of the new Germany after unification in 1990 (Keohane and Hoffmann 1993; Niblett and Wallace 2001: introduction). But it also contained both the legacy of European Political Cooperation and the seeds of more far-reaching change which were to come to fruition in the late 1990s. The CFSP itself after Maastricht remained largely procedural, in the sense that the framework provided for additional types of collective decision-making by EU member states, but not for the really concrete types of foreign policy action that some might have hoped for (M. Smith 2001b). Its institutional and financial basis was still unclear, and subject to a process of 'learning by doing' that gave it an experimental air, especially in areas of crisis such as the former Yugoslavia (see later). Nonetheless, the CFSP did provide for enhanced levels of collective action by EU member states in respect of a wide range of security policies – especially if security was defined in its broader 'soft' sense rather than simply in terms of military action and concerns. Combined with the Single Market Programme and the prospect of EMU, this gave the EU an air of dynamism and a predominant role in the shaping of European order from within Europe, notwithstanding the persistence of NATO. If there was a burden to be borne in the 'new Europe', the EU seemed to be an obvious if not *the* obvious candidate to bear it (Allen and Smith 1991–92).

For the EU, therefore, the shape of the post-Cold-War European order was not a distant ambition: it was and is central to the immediate environment of the Union, and presented immediate problems of management within the 'near neighbourhood'. It also presented the EU with a demand that can never be faced by the United States: the demand for membership, and thus for the reshaping of the EU itself, not simply its external environment. While in the early 1990s there were those who felt the Central and Eastern European countries might be kept at arm's length with only the distant prospect of membership, it rapidly became clear that the pressure to open membership negotiations could not be resisted (Nugent 2004: Chapters 1–3; K. Smith 1999, 2005a). It was a question not of whether but of when as many as ten new countries from Central and Eastern Europe might be admitted, along with two Mediterranean countries, Cyprus and Malta. This is in itself a complex story of institutional change, of negotiations and of 'winners and losers' which is still not complete, even after the entry of Bulgaria and Romania in January 2007 and Croatia in 2013 – and of course, the departure of the UK as a result of Brexit (see Figure 8.2)

It might be thought that the new, enlarged EU would presage a fundamental shift in the global power structure. While this conclusion has not been borne out, it is clear that EU enlargement during the period since 1990 created a basically new power structure in Europe itself. The EU (once memorably described by the *Economist* as 'the club that swallowed a continent' – see Figure 8.2) had to re-shape its own internal order and institutions at the same time as it had to take on the implications of its geographical (geo-economic and geopolitical) dominance in almost the whole of the European continent – a problem often summed up by the tension between 'deepening' and 'widening' (M. Smith 2000, 2008; Wallace 2000). The Constitutional Treaty designed to produce some of this reshaping was put into limbo during 2005 by negative French and Dutch referendum results, but then many of its provisions re-emerged in the Lisbon Treaty of 2009, with particular resonances in the field of external action and Common Foreign and Security Policy (see Chapter 7, Box 7.1). The reshaping of internal institutions and significant parts of external policy was not simply a matter of treaty provisions. External policy had to be re-shaped in the form of the EU's 'neighbourhood policy', first declared in 2008 and then developed into a set of 'Eastern' and 'Southern' Partnerships in the subsequent period. As will be seen later in this chapter, these partnerships and the EU commitments they have entailed are central to some of the most challenging crises of the post-Cold- War period. Designed to bring together the 'ring of friends' with which the Union wanted to surround itself (Aliboni 2005; Dannreuther 2003; White, McAllister, and Light 2002; Sedelmeier 2004; K. Smith 2005a, 2005b), some have seen them as creating a 'ring of fire' which has challenged the EU's role as a shaper of regional order. At the same time, the extension of NATO through new arrangements with Russia and other states of the former Soviet Union as well as through the admission of states from Central and Eastern Europe created a new institutional architecture in which the EU and the United States remain implicated, and which implied their mutual entanglement in regional and subregional crises (Webber 2007: see also later).

We should not forget here that although it is tempting to cast the EU's roles in the 'new Europe' in terms of geopolitics and political influence, there is a highly significant geo-economic story to be told as well. The 'return to Europe'

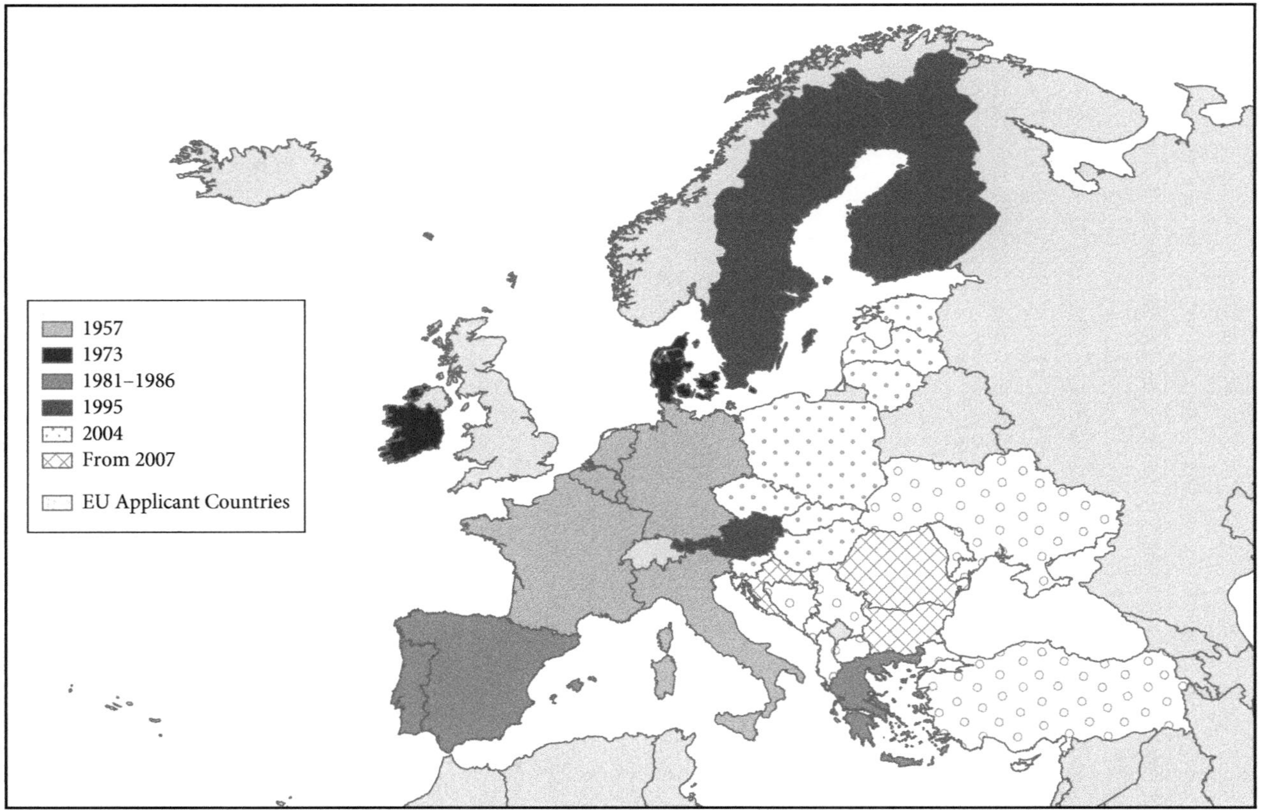

Figure 8.2 Map of the member states of the European Union, 2024.

for Central and Eastern European states was certainly motivated by key security considerations, namely protection from a potentially resurgent Russia, but it was driven also in large measure by the desire for shared prosperity within the EU (Faini and Portes 1995; A. Smith 2000). The redirection of trade and investment flows within and between the states of the former Soviet bloc, to produce an overwhelming focus on the EU, was one of the key shifts in the international political economy of the 1990s, and its results echoed into the 21st century. In similar fashion, the economic and financial crisis of 2008 and after created major challenges for the EU's capacity to fund ambitious partnerships in the wider Europe and the Mediterranean, and intensified disparities within the Union itself between those countries such as Germany that were capable of shaping major policy initiatives and those that were subject to financial discipline at the European level, such as Greece (see Chapter 5).

A further dimension of both security and political economy is added by the fact that the expansion of the EU, its absorption of many former Soviet bloc states and its creation of eastern and southern partnerships brought the Union into ever more direct contact with Russia as not only the key former Soviet state but also a potential key actor in Middle East policy. Thus the growing post-Cold-War trade between the EU (especially certain EU member states) and Russia – particularly the growing energy dependence of EU members on Russian oil and gas – was not just an economic matter: it could be seen as a matter of political and economic vulnerability, exemplified indirectly by the political use of the energy weapon against the government of Ukraine during 2005–6 and later, and the Belorussian regime in early 2007. Equally, the later construction of the 'eastern partnership' was bound to create frictions and potential conflicts with Moscow, as were European initiatives in the Middle East and elsewhere.

The US and post-Cold-War Europe

In the immediate aftermath of the fall of the Berlin Wall, the United States through the administration of George H. W. Bush made it perfectly clear that they saw the EC and European integration as a key building-block of post-Cold-War Europe. This met a ready response in Brussels, at least at the level of general policy direction, although at an early stage there were doubts voiced by some member states about the desirability of major enlargement (Allen and Smith 1991–2; Smith and Woolcock 1993: Chapter 2). The economic reconstruction of the Central and Eastern European states was led by the EC and then the EU, but the diplomacy of the end of the Cold War in other respects remained on relatively traditional tracks: as noted earlier, the United States and NATO member states were key actors in the post-1990 bargains that framed the end of the Cold War. American policy and policymakers were also central to the process of German unification (see for example Zelikow and Rice 1995), although it must be noted that the absorption of the former German Democratic Republic into the EC, through 'enlargement without accession', was also a crucial part of the process (Spence 1991). The EC's impact was thus still confined effectively to the 'civilian power' realm that had been characteristic of EC policy for years if not decades. In terms of the arguments made in Chapter 2, therefore, the United States remained structurally dominant in the broad security architecture that emerged from the end of the Cold War in Europe.

Despite this apparent continuing dominance, the end of the Cold-War division in Europe was greeted with a mixture of sentiments in Washington. On one hand there was a tendency to assume that the job was done, and that the time had come to reap the 'peace dividend' and to retire from direct involvement in Europe. But this was countered by an equally if not more powerful desire to retain political leverage in Europe and to prevent the development of a 'European foreign policy' that would deviate from that of the United States – not only in Europe but also in the wider world (Smith and Woolcock 1993; Peterson 1996b). Thus as noted earlier the attempts by US leaders in the early 1990s to define the parameters of a new world order had direct implications for the nature of the anticipated new European order. The George H. W. Bush administration that ended in January 1993 laid the foundations for this by calling for the EU to assume the burden of financing reconstruction in Central and Eastern Europe, and by also calling for rapid and wide enlargement of the EU (Peterson 1996b; Guay 1999). In this way, it might be argued, the EU was to become 'America's European pacifier', a channel for the stabilization of the new Europe and for the extension of market economies, the rule of law and western liberal ideas into the former Soviet bloc.

When the Clinton administration took office in January 1993, it did not repudiate this perception of the EU's role, but embedded it into a wider national security strategy of 'engagement and enlargement' – engagement with both allies and adversaries, and enlargement of the zone of peace and democracy. In this, the EU was seen as an invaluable prop, but predominantly in its 'civilian power' manifestation, partly because of the unproven nature of the CFSP but also because of the continued assumption that NATO was the primary channel of US influence in the security and defence domain. This assumption was also fed by key EU member states such as the UK, which had a distinct interest in maintaining its 'special relationship' with the United States (most obviously in areas such as intelligence-gathering) and which used this and the NATO dimension to balance against the more enthusiastically 'European' of its EU colleagues (Niblett and Wallace 2001).

A key focus of evolving US attitudes during the 1990s was the enlargement process. This was a compelling feature of the policy context for the EU. But it is also of fundamental importance that this was a game into which the United States could not enter directly, and in which the resources, the magnetism and the structural power of the EU were key factors in producing the eventual enlargements of 2004 and 2007 (and later the accession of Croatia in 2013). This is not to say that the United States did not try to influence the process: its perception of likely costs and benefits to the US economy (and especially to US farmers as a result of the extension of the CAP) ran alongside its acute awareness of the potential consequences to the United States' position in European security and diplomacy (Asmus 1997; Baun 2000; M. Smith 2005c). One manifestation of this was the persistent and at times strident US insistence that negotiations should be opened for Turkish membership of the EU – an extension that could be seen as benefiting the United States through insertion into the Union of a major NATO ally and one with a key geostrategic position on the eastern edge of the 'new Europe' (Buzan and Diez 1999; see also later). Another symptom was the US effort to make sure that new Central and Eastern European member states recognized the benefits they could gain from membership in NATO as well as in the EU, and the recognition that such countries as Poland would if anything add leverage to US positions and preferences in the enlarged Union (Bugaski and Teleki 2007). As Chapter 7 showed, this could lead to tensions and recriminations in time of broader global crisis.

It must be re-emphasized, however, that although both the EU and the United States were implicated in these arrangements and in the broader architecture of the 'new Europe', their impact on and significance for the EU was of a different order than for the United States. While it would be both inaccurate and unfair to say that the United States was a bystander in many of these processes, it clearly approached them from a very different perspective both under the Clinton and the George W. Bush administrations. While the Clinton administration wished to pursue 'engagement and enlargement' within the context of a changing European order (and as we shall see later, became directly involved in European crises and conflicts), the George W. Bush administration after the 2000 presidential election was immediately concerned not with Europe itself but with a far broader view of global order in which Europe – at least initially – rated a relatively low level of attention. The notion that the United States had an opportunity to re-shape the global order was given additional weight by the 9/11 attacks and then by the

US invasion of Iraq – two episodes in which the EU (as opposed to specific EU member states) could only ever play a marginal role.

This tension between two images of US engagement with the European order – and their links to challenges outside Europe – persisted throughout the presidencies of Barack Obama and Donald Trump, but in very different forms. Obama's commitment to withdrawal from a number of key conflicts and to a foreign policy of 'pragmatic realism' meant that US attention was focused largely either domestically or on areas beyond the EU, such as Afghanistan and Iraq. In 2012, the proclamation of a 'pivot' to the Asia-Pacific by the administration also highlighted an increasing preoccupation with the rise and impact of China, which had both an economic and a security manifestation (Jing Men and Wei Shen 2014). With the inauguration of Donald Trump in January 2017, US foreign policy took a different direction again, but it did not eliminate the tensions between European engagement, global commitments and US domestic politics: in fact, the Trump administration intensified the challenge for the EU by pursuing new relationships with Russia, by confronting China and by presenting the EU and its focus on multilateralism and 'soft power' as a barrier to effective US leadership (M. Smith 2021). In this febrile atmosphere, it was clear that the EU's primary 'geopolitical' focus on its neighbourhood was likely to put it at odds with Washington.

The EU, the United States and European order: Competition, convergence and crisis

Do the tensions outlined earlier mean that there has been an open confrontation between EU and US ideas of 'Europe' and of European order during the early 21st century? It certainly appears that the predominantly geopolitical conception of Europe held by a number of policymakers in the George W. Bush administrations elected in 2000 and 2004 was in direct contrast to the more intimate, subtle and complex conceptions of Europe that resulted from the processes of EU enlargement and of the recognition that the 'neighbourhood' was of prime concern to European policymakers (Peterson and Pollack 2003: introduction). Although the Obama administrations between 2009 and 2017 had a more nuanced and 'Euro-centric' approach to common challenges, they actually continued with the key lines of tension that had been established in the early post-Cold-War years, between the regional and the global, for example in their increasing focus on security in East Asia. There was also more than a hint of competition between the gospel of free-market, neo-liberal ideas preached not only by the US government but also by a burgeoning range of

American non-governmental organizations in the former Soviet sphere, and the more restrained ideas encapsulated by the EU in the shape of a social market economy – but it must be remembered that there was considerable divergence of views on this question within the EU itself, so the competition is more complex than it might appear. There was certainly institutional and policy competition, often muted but often more overt, in security matters between the growing European security and defence apparatus and NATO, not to mention the US defence establishment (Howorth 2003; Dannreuther and Peterson 2006: introduction and conclusion). But again this was moderated by the close links between EU member states and the United States, whether in the context of NATO or in their bilateral relationships. On the whole, the picture within Europe was one in which EU member states agreed on the key architectural features and could act collectively although there were disagreements on specific issues, for example between France, Germany and the UK over approaches to Russia. The Trump administration did not create these tensions and cross-cutting alignments, but it did give them an added twist through its downgrading of diplomacy and of institutions, both in Europe and more broadly, whereas the Biden administration from 2021 onwards promised a return to processes of cooperation and a renewed concern with European stability. The chapter will now explore the extent to which this mixed image of competition and convergence is true in the context of conflicts and crises within Europe itself.

The EU, the United States and the management of crises in post-Cold-War Europe

The chapter has been concerned up to now with the ways in which the European order broadly defined has been re-shaped, and the roles that the EU and the United States have played in that process, but such a treatment needs to be accompanied by recognition that specific conflicts and crises may show a very different picture, as they engage not only the broad preferences of European and American governments but also their specific capacities to act or to influence events in particular circumstances. In this section the focus is on conflicts and crises in post-Cold-War Europe, with the aim of identifying the ways they have impacted on EU–US relations and of exploring their impact on the complex balance between competition and convergence in EU–US relations. The section deals first with the conflicts in former Yugoslavia, and then the conflicts and tensions that have emerged from the collapse of the Soviet Union, in both Eastern Europe and the Caucasus–Central Asia.

Former Yugoslavia: towards a new EU–US division of labour?

It is clear that the collapse of the Yugoslav Federation during the 1990s started some time earlier, after the death of President Tito in 1980. Throughout the 1980s, the increasing economic and political tensions within the multinational federation intensified, bursting out into the open with the ending of the Cold War (M. Smith 2001b). There followed four main phases of conflict, leading to the dissolution of the Yugoslav Federation: in 1990–1 Croatia and Slovenia claimed their independence; between 1991 and 1995 Bosnia-Herzegovina experienced a bloody civil war the effects of which are still felt in the early 21st century; in 1999, there was further conflict over the status of Kosovo; and the final phase, still unfinished, centred on the stabilization of Macedonia (now known as North Macedonia), on continuing reconstruction in the other areas of earlier conflict and on the accession of some countries to membership of the EU itself. The latter process came to initial fruition in 2004 with the accession of Slovenia, to be followed in 2013 with the accession of Croatia, but the process for others has been lengthy and at times stalled. Each of these phases created specific patterns of opportunities and challenges for the EU, and each of them brought the EU and the United States into close proximity with each other in an often uneasy partnership (Zucconi 1996; Owen 1995).

The declaration of independence by Croatia and Slovenia in mid-1990 was followed by short-lived but intense fighting. Significantly, both of the defecting republics expressed their wish to join the EU, and this underlines the ways in which the EU was seen as a model for stability in the post-Cold-War context. But the crisis also found the EU locked into a debate about its own role, and in particular about the qualities and instruments of the nascent CFSP. The EU was therefore trying to establish its own set of foreign policy directions at the same time as it was facing the challenge of conflict in the Balkans – a conflict in which different EU member states had different stakes and expectations (Crawford 1996). At the same time, US policies were pulled in the direction of more global challenges, especially the Gulf crisis of 1990–1 caused by Iraq's invasion of Kuwait and a disastrous 1992–4 humanitarian mission in Somalia. Not surprisingly, there was an inclination in Washington to see the EU as the key channel for conflict management in the Balkans, especially since US public opinion was still hankering after a withdrawal from all but the most pressing global commitments (Smith and Woolcock 1993: Chapters 2, 4). As the conflicts developed, these pressures led first to a series of tensions within the EU especially over the recognition of Croatian and Slovenian independence, and then to pressures on the United States for more active intervention – which were resisted.

While Croatia and Slovenia tested the internal solidarity of the EU, and also the level of US commitment, it was the war in Bosnia-Herzegovina between 1992 and 1995 that provided the sternest examination of their ability to work together in a situation of crisis and violence. While the EU was initially still seen as a significant diplomatic actor, it was progressively marginalized as the conflict intensified. Its diplomatic representative, David Owen, the former British foreign secretary, was both active and committed, and in 1993 was the joint progenitor with Cyrus Vance, the UN representative, of the Vance–Owen plan (Owen 1995: Chapter X). The Plan, though, depended for its implementation on the availability of large numbers of US troops, and Washington was less than enthusiastic about the prospect in the face of domestic opposition and military reluctance.

After the failure of Vance–Owen, the diplomacy of the Bosnian war was dominated by three processes, none of which included the EU as an integral part. The first process centred on the Contact Group composed of the United States, Russia, Britain, France and Germany (with Italy added later) and was effectively a form of old-fashioned 'concert diplomacy' among the relevant 'great powers'. It pursued a peace plan modelled in part on Vance–Owen, but with an implied possibility of the use of force if the parties refused to comply with it. Alongside this process went a gradual process of engagement by the United States, not only through the Contact Group but also through bilateral diplomacy both with partners on the ground and with the Russians, who had special links with the leadership of Slobodan Milosevic in Serbia. Of all the potential 'peacemakers', only the United States could really muster an effective and credible threat of the use of force. The final process, in 1995, was one of direct military intervention through NATO, with US leadership but also with the active participation of several leading EU member states.

In the final Dayton Agreement of 1995, which established the basis for the future consolidation and reconstruction of Bosnia-Herzegovina, the EU played the part of an observer, but it also had a potentially key role as the coordinator of the economic and social reconstruction processes that were to last for years if not decades. Some drew the conclusion from this that there was an emerging 'division of labour' between those who did the fighting (the United States and NATO members) and those who provided the longer-term reconstruction and 'peace-building' efforts, such as the EU and the OSCE (Hoffmann 1996; Peterson 2003). This analysis could also be supported from studies of the EU's impact on the conflict in former Yugoslavia during the early 1990s, which showed significant influence in these longer-term and 'structural' areas (Ginsberg 2001: Chapter 4).

The third phase of the conflicts in former Yugoslavia centred on the fate of Kosovo. While Kosovo itself was internationally recognized as part of Serbia, escalating Serb repression of the Albanian majority there created a threat to the stability of the Western Balkans as a whole, and thus could provide the basis for active if not forcible intervention. The negotiations that took place in 1998 and early 1999 under the aegis of the Contact Group, in an attempt to resolve the issue peacefully, thus took place in the shadow of NATO threats to intervene (Gow 1997; Weller 1999). This made it appear that the EU had been marginalized right from the start, although this was a somewhat misleading impression, given that it was recognized from the outset that the Union could play a major role in post-conflict reconstruction and in the diplomacy of the crisis.

These features of the situation meant that although NATO – and by implication the United States – dominated the headlines as conflict escalated, the EU became important in plans for the final resolution. One significant aspect especially was the search for a regional solution, and the injection into this of a 'membership perspective' for those local entities seeking membership of the Union. During the Kosovo conflict, the EU proposed the idea of a 'stability pact' for the Balkans, through which peacekeeping, economic reconstruction and regional cooperation would be developed under the aegis of the Union (Friis and Murphy 2000). On the basis of performance within the proposed 'stability and association agreements', regional entities could then be considered as potential EU members. When violence erupted in Macedonia in 2000, the Macedonian government was actively engaged in negotiations for its own stability and association agreement with the EU, and this arguably gave the Union significant leverage in practising a form of 'coercive diplomacy' to bring the situation back to a stable basis. EU involvement in Macedonia also led in March 2003 to the first operational deployment of EU forces, Operation Concordia. In its turn, Concordia was supplanted in December 2003 by an EU policy mission, Operation Proxima, and in late 2004 the EU took over responsibility for supervision of the Bosnia-Herzegovina settlement through what became known as the European Union Force (Eufor), giving itself a significant military presence in the Balkans for the first time (Howorth 2005, 2007). In the longer term, the stabilization of what became known as the Western Balkans has reflected not just this injection of EU 'hard power' but also the structural forces set in motion by processes of association and accession: thus the membership of Croatia, the stabilization of relations with Serbia, (North) Macedonia and Montenegro and the recognition of Kosovo by at least some EU member states show this significant longer-term perspective – a perspective the United States has been unwilling and unable to match.

From this outline of the developments in former Yugoslavia, it seems clear that despite a number of false starts the EU managed between 1991 and 2004 to develop a substantial role as a diplomatic and then eventually as a military actor; in the decade and a half since the major crises were stabilized, the EU has also exercised a key structural role in the Western Balkans. It is also clear that the EU's engagement in the Balkans fed directly into the moves that took place from 1998 onwards to develop a Common European Security and Defence Policy (ESDP, later CSDP). This reflected a broad (and still evident) feeling that the United States should not be relied upon as the 'stabilizer' of post-Cold-War Europe – and as we have seen it also corresponded to US preferences for a reduction in its military commitments in Europe, which persisted through the Obama and Trump administrations.

This did not mean that the Clinton administration and its successors did not have an interest in maintaining US leverage in Europe; indeed, Secretary of State Madeleine Albright, while welcoming the moves towards ESDP in 1998–9, made it clear that these must not lead to what were described as the 'three Ds': decoupling, duplication and discrimination (Albright 1998: see Chapter 1, Box 1.7). Successive secretaries of state have supported what is now the CSDP, but with these caveats never far from the surface, and EU member states have generally been anxious to explain that the aim is not to replace US influence but rather to provide a means whereby EU member states and others could act collectively in situations where the Americans were unable or unwilling to lead. In this sense, the Western Balkans provided a laboratory for the development of a new EU–US division of labour, in which the EU itself added a hard edge to its 'soft power'. One key question, though, was whether the EU could build on this set of developments in respect of the broader European order.

The broader European 'neighbourhood'

Any discussion of EU–US relations in relation to European order would be incomplete without consideration of the ways 'non-EU Europe' enters into the relationship. For the purposes of this chapter, 'non-EU Europe' is taken to mean the constituent parts of the former Soviet Union (some of which are part of wider Eurasia and extend to the Russian Far East and into Central Asia) and Turkey (which in turn borders on areas of continuing EU concern in the Middle East). As noted earlier in the chapter, these are areas in which the United States, as a superpower and a key interlocutor of governments and other groups, has a strong and consistent interest. They are also areas which in most cases are unlikely to become candidates for full EU membership; even Turkey, at long last given candidate status and then the opening of negotiations in the early 2000s, has effectively ceased to be a credible candidate for EU membership (see later). As noted earlier, the EU in the early 2000s developed an extensive 'Neighbourhood Policy' to pursue its aims in areas extending from the Mediterranean to the Arctic, expressed particularly in terms of partnership and cooperation mechanisms and new forms of association agreement (Dannreuther 2003; Batt et al. 2003; Weber, Smith, and Baun 2007). These areas engage both the EU and the United States in terms of key security interests, as well as presenting economic challenges and opportunities. So there is much for both the EU and the United States to play for, but also an unpredictable political and economic context in many of the areas concerned. These are also areas in which for obvious reasons the EU and the United States are competing more in terms of traditional international instruments, given the lack of the 'membership perspective' and the strong gravitational pull of American political and economic resources.

The challenge of Russia

During the Cold War, although there had been differences between European and US policies – particularly during the early 1980s in relation to sanctions imposed in the wake of the declaration of martial law by the Communist government of Poland, US missile deployment in Europe and over US attempts to impose controls over technology transfers to the Soviet bloc – there had generally been agreement, or at least compliance, among EC member states to US policy preferences. The end of the Cold War removed what has been described as the 'security overlay' that had muted differences of view both among EC member states and between them and the United States, and this has had a series of important consequences for their approaches to common problems. As a preliminary to the discussion of these problems, it must be noted that as with the Central and Eastern European countries, Russia stands in a different geopolitical and geo-economic relationship to the EU from that which it enjoys with the United States. Large parts of Russia are European, and even though the Russian Far East may seem a long way away from Western Europe, there are substantial (though often submerged) elements of common culture and experience. Not only this, but the process of enlargement discussed earlier had to pay continuous attention to the 'Russian dimension', given the previous status of many of the countries involved and the closeness of Russian territory (part of it, in the case of Kaliningrad, surrounded after 2004 by EU member states). For obvious reasons, the US experience with Russia has been more distant and more clearly defined in terms of strategic competition, and this has been a key element in the management of both EU and US relations with Moscow since 1990 (Allen 1997; Light, White, and Lowenhardt 2000; Webber 2000; Haukkala 2010, 2021).

The EU's strategies towards Russia have thus been shaped by a combination of broad interests (for example, in Russia's adoption of democratic institutions and peaceful means for the resolution of disputes) and more immediate or tangible pressures created by the economic needs of member states, the consequences of the enlargement process or the handling of conflicts in Europe and beyond. These are issues on which EU member states themselves have often been divided: for example, even before enlargement took place, there were clear differences between German or Finnish attitudes, shaped by geographical proximity and economic dependence (for example, on energy supplies from Russia), and those of Spain, Portugal and the UK. After enlargement, with the accession initially of eight and later of ten countries that had either been members of the Soviet bloc or (as in the case of the Baltic states) part of the Soviet Union itself, it became clear that this dispersion of preferences among EU member states had increased. The net result has been that it has often been difficult to discern any kind of EU collective strategy towards Moscow (Allen 1997; Light 2003; Haukkala 2010, 2021), and that European positions have been pushed and pulled around by an uneasy mixture of ideological and material forces.

Nonetheless, the EU in the late 1990s developed a policy framework for dealing with Russia, based on a series of agreements and also on the Common Strategy adopted by the European Council in June 1999. The Partnership and Cooperation Agreement was concluded in June 1994, but it came into force only in 1997, having been delayed as a consequence of Russian actions in Chechnya (Light 2003: 74). At the same time, the Technical Aid to the Commonwealth of Independent States (TACIS) programme provided key elements of support for democratic transition. Tellingly, though, despite occasional Russian claims that they would wish to be EU members, there was no move towards including a 'membership perspective' in any of the main EU–Russia agreements. These were designed to establish an arm's-length relationship, with the key aim of stabilization and furthering democratic transition but without pushing so hard on the latter that material aims were jeopardized. The formal agreements were supplemented by the growth of regular dialogues and consultations, and not least by the deepening of private investment and other ties between the EU and Russia.

This process of engagement was especially intense with respect to energy, where the fluctuating price of oil and gas and the political risks associated with energy supplies at the global level created a political dilemma for the

Europeans. European oil corporations (for example, BP and Total) were among the leading participants in exploration and exploitation in the Russian context, and key EU member states such as Germany were particularly dependent on supplies from the former Soviet Union, so there was a very strong set of forces tending towards accommodation with whatever regime was in power in Moscow. In October 2000, this was formally expressed in an EU–Russia Energy Partnership. But at the same time Russian policies in Chechnya and elsewhere created opposition in the EU, and added to the pressures on EU member states to take punitive measures. Not surprisingly, these were not forthcoming on any significant scale, either in the cases noted here or in the later cases of Georgia, Ukraine and Belarus, until the major crises and conflicts of 2014 and after (see later).

At the same time as generating tensions both within and outside the Union, Russia occupies a key position in EU thinking about the emerging European order, and about EU international strategy. Sometimes this is a very immediate consideration – for example, the historic links between Russia and Serbia were a factor in EU policies towards the Balkans, especially in the Kosovo conflict, and as will be seen later, the Ukraine crisis and Russian intervention of 2014 and after created a major challenge for the Union. As we saw in Chapter 7, the Russian position on global conflicts and the War on Terror has also been a key influence on the thinking of EU member states. More generally, though, Russia is important to the kinds of 'structural diplomacy' in which the EU seems to specialize (Keukeleire 2003, Keukeleire and Delreux 2014, 2022), through which the Union has set out to provide collective regional and interregional agreements with the aim of enhancing stability and institutionalizing cooperation. Thus, the Union set out in the early 2000s to construct a jigsaw of agreements – later formalized in the Eastern Partnership – with countries of the former Soviet Union, and to balance in this context between their relationship with Russia and the desire to promote the independence and stability of other, often fragile, states. Equally, the EU's strategy towards Russia in security terms was shaped by the European Security Strategy of 2003, with its emphasis on 'effective multilateralism' and broad international order considerations, but it also had to adapt to the development of the CSDP and the complex coexistence between CSDP and NATO (Webber 2001; Howorth 2014, 2017). Russia's emphasis on maintaining and if possible enhancing its great-power status led it to exert considerable pressure on the EU for recognition of that status, and to try to exert influence through not only diplomatic but also other means, including the 'energy weapon' – in other words, exploiting the dependence of Germany and other EU member states on supplies of gas from Russian sources.

Crises in Eastern Europe

EU strategies have also been conditioned by the ways in which the international politics of the Soviet 'successor states' have been conducted (Webber 1996, 2000). While the Baltic states have been successfully incorporated into the Union, albeit with some remaining tensions over the treatment of Russian-speaking populations in these countries, and more recently fears of Russian expansionism in the wake of the Ukraine crisis and war (see later), the 'near neighbours' Ukraine, Belarus and Moldova, along with a number of states such as Georgia, Azerbaijan and Armenia in the Caucasus, have until recently had no prospect of EU membership, but are clearly vital to what might be described as the EU's 'security perimeter' (M. Smith 2006b). They are also incidentally in several cases vital to the flow of oil and gas to Western Europe. Not surprisingly, these countries have been central to the EU's development of its 'Eastern Partnership' (EaP), which relies upon a combination of trade and association agreements and support for democratization to achieve the overall aim of stability. From the beginning of this process in the early 2000s, the EU has come up against the diverse pressures caused by (1) local desires for greater independence from Russia (in the case of Ukraine and Georgia especially, also linked with a desire for EU membership, particularly in the case of Ukraine), (2) continued authoritarian rule and dependence on Moscow (Belarus in particular) and (3) local or regional antagonisms (in the Caucasus especially, often mixed with Russian intervention). Many of the tensions noted earlier, between ideals and self-interest, can be seen at work here: the 'Orange Revolution' in Ukraine which toppled a pro-Russian regime in 2004–5 and the apparent triumph of pro-western forces in Georgia in the period 2003–8 led to Russian retaliation, and to consequent hard choices for EU member states, often creating the kind of divergence that has typified many EU policies towards Russia itself. The perceived attractiveness but also insecurity of energy supplies from the Caucasus that have to transit Russian territory has been a further key geopolitical consideration.

From the EU perspective, what had appeared to be a fragile but cumulative process of stabilization between 2003 and 2008 was transformed into a period of outright crisis between 2008 and 2015. First, in 2008, open conflict between Georgia and Russian-backed separatists posed an immediate problem for EU solidarity: while some member states led by France actively pursued a diplomatic solution, others distanced themselves from the conflict, while a third group argued for a 'western' intervention via NATO. At the same time, Russian intervention in a smouldering conflict in Moldova challenged another area in which the EU was committed to stabilization processes. In a wide range of ex-Soviet countries from Eastern Europe to the Caucasus and beyond, the idea of an eastern partnership came into collision with the 'new geopolitics' of Russian resurgence under the regime of Vladimir Putin (K. Smith 2023).

These trends initially came to a head between 2013 and 2015, in the case of Ukraine – a country seen by many in Russia as the foundation of Russian civilization. The Orange Revolution of 2004–5 had seemingly changed the course of Ukrainian foreign and domestic policies, shifting their centre of gravity from east to west and creating the conditions for a sustained EU effort to create structural and political change. But this came up against the facts that a large part of the Ukrainian population was culturally and politically aligned to Russia, and that Russian policy was geared increasingly towards (re)establishing its geopolitical and economic dominance over the Ukrainian regime. In 2013, as the government in Kiev seemed to be on the verge of signing a Deep and Comprehensive Free Trade Agreement and Association Agreement with the EU, the crisis escalated. The Ukrainian government was progressively destabilized, indirect (but often scarcely concealed) Russian military involvement led to the effective secession of parts of eastern Ukraine, and Russia effectively annexed the Crimea, using the fig-leaf of a referendum to claim it as a legitimate move in response to popular opinion. This was naked geopolitics, and it proved a very difficult challenge for the EU to meet, since it attacked the Union's policies at their weakest spot – the lack of 'hard power' and of internal consensus on what power to use, combined with EU dependence on energy supplies from Russia. The use of increasing levels of economic sanctions coupled with diplomatic measures was central to subsequent EU policies, but proved incapable of reversing the *fait accompli* in the Crimea and of creating unity in the face of continuing Russian use of the energy weapon. Although Ukraine did eventually sign the Association Agreement in 2014, and it was implemented in 2017, this could not conceal the diplomatic and military realities and thus the limitations of EU influence in the former Soviet sphere (Haukkala 2016).

While EU policies towards Russia and the former Soviet Union have thus been characterized by tensions and often 'lowest-common-denominator' policy outcomes, US policies often seemed likely to create open conflict after the end of the Cold War. One source of this latent conflict was the structural reality of the United States as the 'only superpower', dominating the global military scene and capable of intervening in ways Russia initially could not contemplate. Another source was the ways in which, in the immediate aftermath of the collapse of the USSR, the United States did intervene both economically and politically in Russia. As Margot Light pointed out, this created a high level of anti-Americanism since it became associated with economic instability, with the iniquitous privatization of major state industries and with a feeling of national humiliation against which the later policies of the Putin regime can be seen as a reaction (Light 2003). Much of the feeling at the diplomatic level became concentrated on responses to the enlargement of NATO and the military intervention of the United States in the Balkans, both in the Bosnian conflict and in the Kosovo crisis. Although the Clinton administration between 1993 and 2001 made efforts to counter this by attempting to engage Russia in a variety of diplomatic contexts – including making special arrangements for the relationship between Moscow and NATO (Larrabee 1997) – this was not true of the George W. Bush administration from 2001 onwards. The unilateralist tone of much US diplomacy, and the commitment of the administration to major developments in nuclear weapons, missile defence and related policies meant that there was little prospect of major advances in US–Russian relations.

At the same time as the diplomatic landscape of US–Russian relations remained 'frozen' for much of the George W. Bush period, there was also evidence of increasing intervention by the United States through 'private' channels in Russia and former Soviet states. In contrast to EU policies, which were often unavoidably conservative, those of the US regime could be described as radical or even revolutionary in nature. Private religious or political groups were encouraged to become involved in reform movements in Russia and elsewhere, and to provide financial and logistical support to civil society organizations working against the incumbent governments. Such groups were influential in encouraging the 'revolutions' in Ukraine and Georgia, and were active despite efforts to ban them in Russia and Belarus. When combined with the distinctly unilateralist posture of the administration itself in respect of Russia, they created a sense of continuing tension between Washington and Moscow, which was if anything exacerbated by the globally interventionist policies of the George W. Bush government. These chimed badly with Russian sensitivities about the maintenance (or the recreation) of great-power status and arguably contributed to the more abrasive Russian stance on European issues in relations with the EU.

Whereas the George W. Bush administrations effectively confronted Moscow, this was not so clearly the case under the Obama administrations. Indeed, the initial foreign policy of the first Obama administration focused partly on a 'reset' of policy towards Russia as a reflection of the 'pragmatic realism' noted earlier. For the EU and its member states, this was in many ways a disconcerting development, since it confronted them with the possibility that the United States and Russia might reach agreements affecting them without their participation – a problem familiar from the Cold-War years and processes of *détente* under the Nixon administrations. The desire for a 'reset' did not survive the evidence of

Russian expansionism and intervention from Georgia to Ukraine, but it was clear that while the Americans were ready to impose economic and diplomatic sanctions on Moscow, they would go no further. This reflected not only the resurgence of Russia as a force in European geopolitics, but also the broader effects of the global power-shifts that were seen to be in train with the rise of China and the BRICS grouping more generally.

With Donald Trump's inauguration in 2017, the process was accentuated: the president expressed his admiration for President Putin (as he did for many authoritarian rulers), was not anxious to protect Europeans who did not pay their dues in NATO and saw the Ukrainian crisis mainly through the lens of domestic politics (where it became part of the process leading to his impeachment in 2019–20). When this was combined with his presentation of the EU as a 'foe' at least in economic terms, and with his denunciation of key post-Cold-War agreements on nuclear weapons and 'open skies' monitoring processes, it became clear that the Union was on its own in trying to forge a stable European order, but it was also clear that this was a coming together of some longer-term trends in US policy, which would not necessarily disappear if the president failed to be re-elected in November 2020.

With Trump's defeat in the 2020 presidential election, there was the prospect of re-invigoration for EU–US relations, and especially of the US commitment to order and stability in Europe. Indeed, the EU delivered even before the inauguration of President Biden a proposal for a wide-ranging 'new agenda' in transatlantic relations, and the Biden administration was quick to declare the EU as a key partner in its pursuit of a 'summit for democracy' (Joint Communication 2020; White House 2021). As noted in Chapter 7, this did not immediately transform the EU–US relationship in substance as opposed to rhetoric and atmosphere, but from late 2021 onwards the escalation of tensions between Russia and Ukraine, and the eventual Russian invasion of Ukraine in February 2022 created a major crisis in the heart of the EU's 'neighbourhood'. The Biden administration made it clear that in no circumstances would they initiate the use of military force, and that they would place the emphasis on economic and diplomatic sanctions in response to Russian threats. In such a process, the EU was actually an indispensable partner, and as a result it played a continuing and significant role as long as the discussion remained centred on diplomacy and economic pressure. Inevitably, the outbreak of war generated large flows of refugees into nearby EU member states, and the Brussels institutions played a key role in their support and distribution among member states (despite resistance from some). Not only this, but for the first time the Union was able to commit funding to the purchase of weapons which could then be supplied by member states to the Ukrainian forces, through the use of its European Peace Facility. EU member states generally showed solidarity in confronting Russia, but there were inevitable tensions between those that depended heavily upon Russian oil and gas supplies and thus were cautious about escalation of the Union's measures, and those who might still be dependent but placed a higher priority on the defence of Ukraine and European order. While the United States (along with the UK) was not only willing but able to provide very large amounts of military support to Ukraine, the geopolitics and geo-economics of European order were again evident in the constraints placed upon EU actions despite a substantial 'hardening' of the measures that were taken. As the war proceeded, the pressure to provide a 'membership perspective' for Ukraine, and for Moldova and Georgia, became intense, leading to the formalization of candidate status for Ukraine and Moldova in 2023. At the same time, two EU member states, Finland and Sweden, applied for membership of NATO, with Finland admitted in 2023 and Sweden in early 2024.

The Turkish conundrum

Further evidence of the uneasy balance between EU and US attitudes in respect of the EU's 'neighbourhood' can be found in the handling of Turkey's attempts to start accession negotiations with the Union in the late 1990s and early 2000s (Aydin-Düzgit and Tocci 2015). Turkey had had an association agreement with the EC and then the EU since the 1960s, had initially applied for membership in 1987 and had agreed to establish a customs union with the EU in the mid-1990s. On the other hand, it had been a member of NATO, and a key element in the United States' preferred 'security architecture' for the Black Sea region since the early 1950s. So there is a lot of history on all sides to this relationship. Since the Turkish application for membership in the late 1980s, US support for Turkish accession to the EU – essentially on geostrategic grounds – has been constant, while within the EU there have been distinct differences of opinion leading to a succession of attempts to put off the time at which any decision might have to be made (Buzan and Diez 1999). Thus during the 1990s it became almost a ritual for the EU (and especially members such as France or Austria) to express grave doubts about the Union's capacity to absorb Turkey, while US representatives pressed privately (and often not so privately) for Turkey to be granted candidate status. At the Helsinki European Council of 1999, where major decisions about the mode and timing of accession negotiations were made, the Turks were consigned to a 'waiting room' constituted by a 'European Conference'. US pressure for active negotiations continued, to the irritation of

President Chirac of France in particular, coming to a head in late 2002 when US intervention in the run-up to the Copenhagen European Council meeting, in the form of demands for an opening of accession negotiations with Turkey, led to strong condemnation by the French and the Germans. Maybe it was not a coincidence that within the following three months the French and the Germans in particular were among those most solidly opposed to US intervention in Iraq (although the Turks themselves refused permission for US forces to enter Iraq via their territory – see Chapter 7).

While formal accession negotiations with Turkey eventually began in 2005, they made very slow progress, and during the period 2005–20, there were some fundamental shifts in the Turkish position – increasingly authoritarian leadership, alignment with Russia, engagement in Middle Eastern crises and perhaps most dramatically entanglement in the refugee crises precipitated by the post-Arab Spring conflicts in Syria, Libya and elsewhere – that created a very challenging prospect for EU diplomacy. US policies under the Obama and Trump administrations were of little assistance to the EU, consisting as they did of strictly limited engagement and ultimately under Trump effective abdication of leadership responsibility in the eastern Mediterranean, accompanied by escalating tensions between Washington and Ankara. Rather than consolidating a new order based on an EU–US division of labour, this was a recipe for continuing instability and contention, with high stakes. The onset of war in Ukraine in early 2022 saw further tensions, as the Turkish government positioned itself as a potential mediator between Russia and the 'west' and abstained from sanctions imposed on Moscow. In terms of EU–US relations, this meant that Turkey was effectively outside the democratic 'club', but that it remained a key geostrategic actor – and thus a continuing source of uncertainty in the broader European order, both in terms of values and in terms of policy (Toygür 2022).

A new Euro-American order?

The issue of Turkey encapsulates what some might see as fundamental differences in the style and purpose of EU and US policies on European order after the Cold War. On the one hand, the immediacy and material nature of the stakes for the EU clearly conditioned attitudes towards Turkish membership – as they had attitudes towards the former Soviet Union and conflict in the Balkans. For Europe, these were not notional issues to be dealt with in a broad strategic fashion: they were and are issues relating to the immediate environment within which the Union operates, and they also intersect with internal divisions within the Union. In the same way, EU enlargement is about the very essence of the

Union itself, engaging deep cultural and ideological issues as well as major substantive interests in economic and other matters. While it would not be accurate to claim that the United States has no such immediate interests in European order, it is possible to draw a distinction between views and actions in the United States and in the EU. Back in the 1970s, in his 'Year of Europe' speech (see Chapter 1), Henry Kissinger attracted European ire by asserting that European interests were regional while those of the United States were (and had to be) global, concerned with the shape and future direction of the international system as a whole. If anything, the aftermath of the Cold War, with EU enlargement, regional conflict, political and economic reconstruction and the building of new institutions, has underlined both parts of Kissinger's statement: the EU has become deeply entangled with the politics of the continent in a way not possible before, while the United States as a superpower has been led into renewed global interventionism and then a spasmodic process of global retreat.

Something else has also happened, however. Because of the enlargement of the EU, and its diplomatic activism in the wider Europe, the Union has extended its reach and its grasp – to such an extent that it is no longer entirely fanciful to talk about the Euro-American system as an EU–US system (as suggested in Chapter 2). To be sure, the continued claims of Russia to great-(European) power status, the continued existence of NATO and its re-invigoration as a result of the Ukraine war, and the uncertain impact of Brexit dilute this claim to a degree, but they cannot dispose of it. The consequences of this for the EU–US relationship are likely to be substantial, and arguably already are. In terms of the mechanisms discussed in Chapter 2 – transatlantic governance, 'hard' and 'soft' balancing and crisis management – it can be seen that the scope of these mechanisms has expanded, and to some extent the room for manoeuvre around them has decreased as the EU has come to fill up the European end of the 'transatlantic space'. Does this make transatlantic governance more effective (because of the greater scope of the EU's authority in many matters of 'low politics'), or does it make it more difficult (because of the raising of stakes in governance disputes)? Does it create a situation in which 'soft balancing' by the EU may increasingly 'harden' as its defence capacities expand and as the stakes are raised both by US policies and by greater policy competence in Brussels? Finally, does it mean that crisis management, which has been a pervasive feature of EC–US and EU–US relations for 50 years, has become more difficult if not impossible given the lack of 'ways out' within an increasingly polarized Euro-American system, or does it mean that crises will be less frequent because of the development of 'early-warning mechanisms' and continuing dialogue between the two partners?

Overview and conclusion

As can be seen from the discussion in this chapter, there are many unanswered questions about the developing roles of both the EU and the United States in European order. This chapter has attempted to provide a framework for consideration of such questions by exploring EU–US relations in respect of post-Cold-War Europe. The following conclusions can be drawn:

- First, the transition from Cold War to post-Cold War saw the coming together of a series of potent factors that continue to condition relations between the EU and the United States. Some of these were inherent in EC and EU–US relations, others were generated by the emergence of a new European order, while others still reflected broader international change (see Chapter 9).
- Second, EU and US responses to the challenges posed by post-Cold-War Europe were conditioned by the nature of the perceived stakes, the immediacy or 'distance' of challenges and the internal politics both of the EU and of the United States. The 'regional–global' dichotomy is one way of expressing this, but reality also reflects a series of different levels of engagement and response feeding into broad patterns.
- Third, the challenges of conflict in the Balkans, the Caucasus and Eastern Europe, and of the politics and economics of the former Soviet Union, have evoked distinct patterns of response from the EU and the United States, reflecting not only the broad strategic postures noted earlier but also particular patterns of preferences or 'governmental style'. These patterns have changed and been adapted over a period of 30 years or more, but were thrown into very sharp relief by the Russian invasion of Ukraine in early 2022.
- Finally, the expansion of the EU and its predominant position in terms of the 'European architecture' have changed the dynamics of EU–US relations as much as they have the European order itself, and they will continue to do so. This poses a continuing challenge for analysis and for evaluation.

A number of these issues relate strongly to the discussion of power and security in Chapter 7 and to broader regional issues as will be described in Chapter 9. In Chapter 10, we will explore these and related issues in respect of global governance – that is to say, the creation of institutions and order in the broader global arena beyond the transatlantic and the European orders.

Chapter 9

Regionalism, interregionalism and partnership diplomacy

Introduction

The European Union is a regional as well as a global power. It is indeed the most richly developed, complex and successful regional political arrangement in existence. The United States too is a regional and global power; its regional relationships are constructed differently from the EU's but both actors have sought to develop a complex web of geographically defined economic, political and – in the broadest sense – security relationships. Some of these owe their existence to history, while the new regionalism of recent years, and the new forms of partnership explored in this chapter, owe a great deal to both actors seeking to maximize their access to markets, secure foreign policy goals and consolidate their global roles in the post-Cold-War and crisis-prone world. For the EU, such goals have been formalized firstly in the European Security Strategy adopted in 2003 (European Council 2003), and more recently by the Global Strategy of 2016 (European Union 2016), which made an explicit case for a 'joined-up' approach deploying all of the Union's economic, political, cultural and other assets. For the United States, as we shall see, there has been constant attention to the need for US leadership and intervention, expressed in successive National Security Strategies, but also the need to adjust to changes at the domestic and the global level.

The international system is often less globalized than commonly thought – or at least differently globalized – with distinct regional and bilateral political and economic arrangements surviving and indeed thriving in this age of the global (Gamble and Payne 1996; Hettne, Inotai, and Sunkel 1999; Schirm 2002; Payne 2004). It is to be expected that large entities like the United States and the EU have policies tailored to specific regions or strategic partners. However, there has been something of a renaissance in the use of region-specific and targeted bilateral politics in recent years, partly out of frustration with multilateralism at the global level but also as a reflection of the important historical and cultural realities that shape and constrain policy choice (see also Chapter 4). As power in the international political economy has shifted away from Europe and America and towards Asia, both the EU and the United States have relied on regional or bilateral pacts where their bargaining power is significant. There is however an important point of contrast in the manner in which the EU and the United States engage regionally. In the regional sphere the EU is clearly the civilian superpower: both within Europe itself, and on the broader global plane, EU leaders have forged a series of powerful but essentially diplomatic and commercial arrangements (Edwards and Regelsberger 1990; Alecu de Flers and Regelsberger 2005; M. Smith 2018b; Ferreira-Pereira and Smith 2021). Despite possessing substantial and growing leverage in these contexts, the Union has limited abilities to use coercion or force and prefers not to. The EU also has a distinctive approach to issues of regional development, preferring to use aid as well as preferential trade agreements in its regional policies (Feinberg 2003; Holland and Doige 2012; Carbone 2023). This reflects the 'civilian superpower' status of the Union (and also consolidates it) but also arises from a European political economy tradition not so convinced of the efficacy of market-based solutions for development problems and wedded to institutional forms of cooperation.

By contrast, the United States as a military as well as political and economic superpower is much more willing to use the full range of policy tools – including military force – to attain goals, and more likely to adopt a security-focused approach to relationships with regional partners (M. Smith 2021). American policies at the interregional level and in 'partnership diplomacy' also reflect a more overt commitment to market-based solutions, and often also entail the use of development policies for political or security ends (Hamilton 2014).

European and American regional and partnership policies are thus different in important and obvious ways at the level of mechanisms and motivations. They also contrast in terms of their regional and bilateral focus. It is unsurprising that the United States takes a keen interest in its Latin American neighbourhood, or in the Indo-Pacific region, in the same way that the EU devotes considerable energy to relations with Eastern Europe and Turkey. However, at the broadest level, both actors have over the long term been motivated by similar desires and beliefs: that economic liberalization is good for all countries and makes for more peaceful relations; that regional policies and bilateral partnerships can be used to promote good governance and the rule of law in developing states; and that these policies must be multifaceted rather than reliant on single policy tools.

This chapter explores these issues first by assessing the growth of regionalism and regionalization in the global arena. It goes on to explore the ways in which the EU and the United States can be seen as regional powers, and by evaluating their respective approaches to interregionalism and strategic partnerships. Finally, it investigates the impact of competition, convergence and crisis in this context, with the aim of providing insight into how the EU–US system is evolving in the 21st century and may continue to evolve in the 'post-COVID era'. By doing so, the chapter contributes a specific perspective on the roles of the EU and the United States as 'powers', complementing the discussion of European order in Chapter 8 and of world order in Chapter 10 and taking further the discussion of power and security in EU–US relations.

Regionalism and regionalization in the global arena

The growth of regionalism, interregionalism and 'strategic partnerships' alongside pressures for globalization can be seen in two main dimensions. First, regional trade agreements exploded in popularity in the 1990s and 2000s, partly out of frustration with the slow progress of WTO multilateral talks (see also Chapter 4) but also out of recognition that some regional arrangements were necessary to accommodate dramatic new growth in areas of the world – and that states (and their firms) cannot risk exclusion. Japan and South Korea for example embraced the regional trade agreement path, both having been staunch advocates of an exclusively multilateral path in the past. Both did so for a mix of reasons: Japanese firms were very angry at efforts to handicap their operations in NAFTA through complex local content requirements, while the Koreans saw a free trade area with the United States as an important bulwark to the increasing presence of China. Both states are relative newcomers to the regional game: the same cannot be said for the United States and the EU. The WTO now estimates that over 350 agreements of varying membership, scope and complexity are in existence (see Chapter 4).

Given the problems with the multilateral level negotiations, many states have opted for restricted, regionally defined or bilateral arrangements. Some critics have opposed these arrangements, and see in them the potential for a stalling, if not a rolling back, of the gains made from trade liberalization or broader areas of global governance over the past several decades. There are several attractions of regional and bilateral trade agreements, ranging from specific economic gains to more political goals such as satisfying domestic constituencies. There is a view that regional integration and the pursuit of bilateral agreements represent important stepping-stones on the route to larger, multilateral economic and political arrangements. This argument disagrees with the view that regional, bilateral and multilateral arrangements are somehow in conflict, instead asserting an essential complementarity. There are several reasons for this. First, regional and bilateral arrangements feature a smaller set of negotiating partners, and all other things being equal, it seems easier to conclude an agreement among a limited group of states. The very difficult Doha negotiations (see Chapter 4), or climate change negotiations (see Chapter 10), to say nothing of the increasingly fraught internal politics of the EU, would be cited by many as illustrative of the diminishing ability of ever-larger groupings to come to meaningful agreements.

The second area of change and development at the regional and interregional levels is that of security. During the Cold War, as noted in Chapter 1, there had grown up a network of regional security pacts focused on Europe (especially in the form of NATO) and other regions where the threat of communism was seen as pressing, such as South-East Asia and Latin America. Not surprisingly, the United States was at the core of all of these arrangements, but they progressively collapsed as the needs of American diplomacy and the impact of regional conflicts fluctuated. In the wake of the collapse of the Soviet Union, security pacts associated with the USSR also disappeared – but that did not mean that regional security needs had disappeared. In the post-9/11 environment, many existing regional arrangements took on new security aspects, reflecting the expanding conception of security itself in the context of the 'war on terror' and concerns over issues as diverse as migration and the environment. This means that in this area, the EU and the United States have had to adjust to new security needs, to reflect these in a new generation of regional and interregional agreements, and above all, in the context of this book, to address a series of issues and potential crises in which they are both entangled.

Such processes of linkage and entanglement are inextricably linked with the broad structural shifts in power and leverage dealt with in Chapter 1 and Chapter 7. Since the global financial and economic crises of 2009 and after, the presence of 'rising powers' such as China, India and Brazil, and of 'resurgent powers' such as Russia has profoundly re-shaped the context in which both the EU and the United States pursue 'partnership diplomacy' (Alcaro, Peterson, and Greco 2016). The linkages between economic and commercial leverage and perceptions of regional and global security challenges have become ever closer, and when these are combined with the internal preoccupations of Brussels and Washington, there is a strong series of pressures to reassess and restructure at the national, regional and interregional levels. The economic, political and security ramifications of the COVID-19 pandemic from 2020 onwards have only served to sharpen the resulting dilemmas.

The European Union as a regional power

One of the key motivations for setting up the European Communities during the 1950s was connected with 'regional power'. To put it simply, the aim of many of those involved in the European project was to create a 'zone of peace' in Western Europe, which would make the recurrence of general war impossible and which would use economic and political means to create a form of 'security community'. For some, this was also accompanied by a broader aim: to create a European regional power which could exert influence on the broader international level, and which might ultimately rank alongside the two 'superpowers' – the United States and the Soviet Union. The two aims were in principle complementary, since a successful regional community in Europe could act as the base for projection of a distinctively European identity and European priorities in the global arena. During the 1950s and 1960s, the most determined proponents of such a view were the French Gaullists, who were in turn resisted by others with a more regionalist or even 'Atlanticist' point of view (see Chapter 1). The consolidation of the Communities saw in turn a consolidation of regional power, such that increasingly they became seen as an anchor of stability in a changing Europe, but progress on the broader global level appeared less impressive – both to its supporters within the Communities and to those outside who might have been threatened or supported by it.

A major factor in the growth of the EU as a regional power, if not a 'regional superpower', is thus clearly the expansion of the Union itself. As was seen in Chapter 8, the enlargement and the 'deepening' of the EU have given it an extraordinary amount of structural power in the European continent, both by reason of its own internal development and because of the attractions of membership (Keukeleire 2003; M. Smith 2008; Keukeleire and Delreux 2014, 2022). The Union exercises a magnetic force within the continent of Europe, engaging not only potential members but also those in the 'European neighbourhood' who have to adjust their politics and policies to the presence of the EU. The power thus achieved and exercised, however, remains essentially civilian: it depends upon the institutional strength, the commercial weight and the diplomatic leverage that emerge from the development of the European integration project. In many ways also, the power is 'unconscious', reflecting not so much a grand strategy for the exercise of power over the continent as the implications of the EU's dominant presence. Where the power is exercised more self-consciously, it is also subject to important internal restrictions imposed by the 'division of powers' within the Union between the member states and European institutions (see Chapter 3). Other limitations emerge from the impact of history: from the longstanding connections of individual member states with 'outsiders' within Europe, and from traditional alliances and alignments. During the post-Cold-War period, the most notable of these challenges has come from a resurgent Russia, with far-reaching implications for the EU's capacity to manage the changing European order (Haukkala 2010, 2021; K. Smith 2023; see also Chapter 8).

Despite these limitations, the EU can rightly be described as a 'civilian superpower' with a dominant regional role in Europe – a role that combines economic, social, cultural and political dimensions, and that has important security implications. The Global Strategy of 2016, with its call for 'joined-up' policymaking and the coordinated use of all of the Union's resources, was a logical response to this role, and an attempt to formulate it in terms suitable for a changing and more challenging global arena. The EU can also be described as a 'trading state', in the sense that its collective concerns are predominantly commercial and diplomatic, with the diplomatic and security domains closely linked with commercial interests and preoccupations (M. Smith 2004; see also Chapter 10). The Union does not deal in the 'harder' end of coercion and force, but this does not mean that it is easy to ignore or to resist the incentives or possible penalties that it can offer or impose. These incentives and rewards are clearest in the case of EU enlargement, but there has also grown up in and around Europe a series of arrangements designed to create a regional order centred on Brussels. The Union's 'neighbourhood policy' has come to encompass countries ranging from the Arctic to the Mediterranean, and has generated a complex web of civilian agreements covering not only commercial concerns but also questions of governance, human rights, the environment and migration – questions that in the 21st century are unquestionably linked to security (Dannreuther 2003; K. Smith 2005b, 2023; see also Chapter 8).

From the 1960s onwards, the EU and its predecessors have thus clearly reflected the growth of European integration as the basis for regional power. For the EU in its region, this has generated a web of new relationships, including strategic partnerships, which have been continuously adjusted and renegotiated in line with both regional and global changes. There has also emerged a series of broader strategies, aimed at key regions or groupings outside Europe. Sometimes, these strategies have a global reach, as with the Lomé and later the Cotonou Agreements setting up trade and development links with the African, Caribbean and Pacific (ACP) countries, which were first established in the 1970s and have been renegotiated several times since (Holland 2000, 2002; Lister 1999; Holland and Doige 2012; Carbone 2023). Other such agreements are more 'continental' in character, setting up broad arrangements between the EU and Latin America, Asia (including South, East and Southeast Asia) and Africa (see later). A third group of agreements is more restricted, establishing what might be described as 'privileged partnerships' between the Union and individual countries or groups of countries from other parts of the world. These will be dealt with in more detail in the next section, but it is important to note here that all of these arrangements reflect a complex mixture of motivations and pressures: historical ties between EU member states and other regions, commercial needs, political ambitions connected with the need to establish the EU as a 'presence' in other parts of the world and increasingly the need to ensure security in terms of resources, political stability and other, broader aims (Teló 2001; Aggarwal and Fogarty 2004; Alecu de Flers and Regelsberger 2005; Soderbaum, Stalgren, and van Langenhove 2005; Teló 2013; Ferreira-Pereira and M. Smith 2021).

Another vital aspect of the EU's assertion of its regional power is that it brings the Union inevitably into contact with the United States. Indeed, for some European leaders, the development of regional and interregional policies and of strategic partnerships has been a core element in a global competition with the United States, in which the Union is seen as having a kind of comparative advantage because of its 'civilian' status and its links to 'normative power' (M. Smith 2010). The increasing range and scope of the EU's regional and interregional links has thus extended its global reach but has also brought it into a new kind of relationship with the United States. Discussion later will explore how this has impacted upon specific interregional and bilateral relationships, especially where the engagement of the United States has been accompanied by increasing politicization and 'securitization' of the relationships in question.

The European Union, the new regionalism and partnership diplomacy

The end of the Cold War, as noted earlier, created a new dynamism in respect of the EU's position in the wider Europe (Laffan, O'Donnell, and Smith 2000: chapter 8). As described in Chapter 8, this led to substantial enlargement of the Union itself, and to a broader set of strategies relating to broader European order, including the 'neighbourhood policy' embracing countries in Eastern Europe, the former Soviet Union and the Mediterranean, which later was reformulated as a series of regional partnerships. The concern here is with the global implications of the Union's development during the post-Cold-War period, with the ways it has intersected with new regional developments and with the growth of interregional and bilateral strategic partnerships as a central feature of the EU's external relations. This has been a salient and evolving aspect of the EU's global role in the 21st century, and as noted earlier it has brought the EU directly into contact – or collision – with the United States. The drive to establish new interregional arrangements reflected a number of forces, not all of them pointing in the same direction (Teló 2001, 2013; Aggarwal and Fogarty 2004: Chapter 1; Alecu de Flers and Regelsberger 2005). First, the increasing self-confidence of the Union arising from its pursuit of the Single Market Programme in the early 1990s, and from the institutional changes embodied in the Maastricht Treaty of 1991, gave it a new impetus towards involvement in global order and thus generated a search for new partners. At the same time, this was accompanied by a second and less positive motivation: the desire to avoid being excluded from new and dynamic regions as the United States and (to a more limited extent, in political economy) Japan extended their own global reach. The 'triangle' of the EU, the United States and Japan understandably preoccupied many EU policymakers as they pondered how to make the most of the post-Cold-War world. A third force operating on EU policies was the desire to create or reinforce an image for the Union as a 'world partner', one that did not carry with it the baggage associated with the United States and Japan in specific regions of the world.

In developing a strategy – or rather, a set of strategies – the EU was not starting with a blank sheet of paper. There had been interregional arrangements with countries in Africa, South-East Asia and Latin America since the 1980s, and the Lomé Conventions had set in place a wide-ranging economic partnership between the EU and the African, Caribbean and Pacific (ACP) countries which had in its time been hailed as a revolution in relations between rich and poor countries (Edwards and Regelsberger 1990; Holland 2002; Holland and Doige 2012; Carbone 2023). Member states of the Union had also in many cases had close relationships with other regions over a period of centuries, in the form of colonial domination, and from the 1960s onwards, the establishment of interregional partnerships can be seen as an important element in the process of decolonization – but also as a means for the French especially to retain influence in their ex-colonies, and for the British, when they joined the EC in 1973, to create a post-colonial network for aid and development as well as trade. The Lomé framework can thus be read either as a progressive expression of economic partnership or as a means of perpetuating post-colonial influence by some of the EU's member states.

The first extensive attempt beyond Lomé to form a new sort of partnership was focused on the Asia-Pacific region – an area where the EU and its member states have extensive historical and commercial ties, but from which they seemed in danger of being excluded in the early 1990s. In 1994, the Commission published a communication calling for a new Asia strategy, and setting out the broad framework for a new type of relationship with the countries of the Asia-Pacific region (European Commission 1994). A key reason for this strategy was the fear of being excluded from the world's most dynamic region. After all, the EU had no real claim to being a major Pacific presence, but it did have many links that might be drawn upon to bolster its involvement. The result was the Asia-Europe Meeting (ASEM) – an umbrella conference between heads of state and government from the EU and (at that time) ten Asia-Pacific countries consisting of the members of the Association of Southeast Asian Nations (ASEAN) plus China, Japan and South Korea (Forster 1999, 2000; Gilson 2004; McMahon 1998). The ASEM met first in Bangkok in 1996 and has since met on a biennial basis alternately in Asia and Europe. The ASEM itself has also spawned a series of economic, administrative and cultural networks, and a number of action plans in such areas as investment and trade facilitation. But it has also found difficulty in dealing with more 'political' issues, such as whether the 'pariah' government of Burma (Myanmar) should be allowed into the ASEM when it joined ASEAN. What the ASEM has done is partly to remedy the absence of the EU from formal Asia-Pacific forums: whereas the United States has excellent Pacific credentials and was a founder member of the Asia-Pacific Economic Cooperation forum (APEC) during the early 1990s, the EU collectively has only made the effort to establish a continuous link since the mid-1990s.

The EU has also pursued new interregional agreements with the ASEAN countries – both collectively through the development of a strategic partnership, and individually with its member states – and with the countries of the South Asia Association for Regional Cooperation (SAARC) grouping. These are groupings with which the EU and its member states have a strong historical link (and crucially, in which the link to the United States has been rather less prominent). These efforts have gone alongside the development of strategies for the key bilateral relationships with China and India, and with other emerging powers such as Indonesia; both China and India, but especially China, have massively increased trade and investment links with the EU since the mid-1990s, and in addition both countries are crucial to the broader security and stability of their regions (Renard and Biscop 2012). In the case of China, the growing economic weight of Beijing was also demonstrated by its increasing engagement in the Union itself after the onset of the economic and financial crisis in 2008–9, and has since been translated into the Belt and Road Initiative (BRI) which spans the Eurasian land mass and the associated sea routes (see also Chapter 4). As a result, China was at an early stage (in 2003) designated as a 'strategic partner' by the EU, with India at a later stage, both attracting special political and economic attention and frequent contacts at the highest levels (Allen and Smith 2004, 2005; Zabarowski 2006b; Grevi and de Vasconcelos 2008; Ferreira-Pereira and Smith 2021). By the early 2020s there had accumulated a wide range of EU strategic positions and organizational forms relating to Asia as a whole, both bilateral and multilateral. The European Security Strategy of 2003 explicitly referred to these and other strategic partnerships as the basis for an expanded EU security role, while the Global Strategy of 2016 was explicit on the need for an active 'partnership diplomacy' as part of the EU's contribution to stabilization and the enhancement of resilience in a wide range of regions.

The EU also developed a stronger interregional relationship with Latin America during the post-Cold-War period (Faust 2004). As noted earlier, this was not done from a standing start. As early as the 1960s, relationships with some of the early attempts at Latin American economic integration had been established by the EEC. During the 1970s and especially the 1980s, these had persisted and had been given new strength by the membership of Spain and Portugal in the EC from 1986 onwards. They had also become politicized, in particular because of the ways in which they cut across US relationships with Latin American countries. During the Ronald Reagan administrations (1981–89), the Community actively participated in relationships with groupings such as the San José grouping of central American states which put them on the side of resistance to US domination, and this was one of the early manifestations of a distinct 'European foreign policy' (H. Smith 1995, 1998). The late 1990s saw a new drive to establish an intercontinental relationship, rather in the same form as the ASEM relationship with Asia-Pacific countries: biennial meetings were established in 1999, covering both economic and political aspects of the EU – Latin American partnership. At the same time, the EU pursued free trade arrangements both with Latin American groupings such as MERCOSUR (the 'southern Common Market', with which final agreement was reached in 2019) and with key partners such as Chile, Mexico and later Brazil (Faust 2004; Müller-Brandeck-Bocquet 2000; Dominguez 2021). Mexico was a member of the NAFTA grouping – and now of its successor, the US-Mexico-Canada Agreement (USMCA) – and thus a free trade agreement with Mexico in principle offered access for EU firms to the North American market via a route different from that offered by bilateral EU–US relations.

Box 9.1 EU bilateral and multilateral strategic partnerships as of 2021

Bilateral

Brazil
Canada
China
India
Japan
Mexico
Russia (suspended in 2014)
South Africa
South Korea
United States

Multilateral

African Union
Association of Southeast Asian Nations (ASEAN)
Gulf Cooperation Council
Latin America and the Caribbean
Mediterranean countries (Union for the Mediterranean)
Middle East and North Africa (MENA)
NATO
The United Nations

Africa is the third key continental grouping which has attracted the EU's attention since the end of the Cold War. Once again, as noted earlier, there is a history, both colonial and through the EC's Lomé Conventions, which were first negotiated in the mid-1970s (Holland 2002; Ravenhill 2004; Holland and Doige 2012; Carbone 2013, 2023). A number of key EU member states, such as France and Britain, remain deeply involved through investment and bilateral political links with sub-Saharan African countries. Significantly, until recently the United States and other major non-European actors such as China have been rather less directly engaged in sub-Saharan Africa, and the EU has had a dominant role in many parts of the region. As in the cases of Asia-Pacific and Latin America, the chief innovation in the post-Cold-War period was a series of biennial Euro–Africa meetings, commencing in 2000 and providing the same kind of 'umbrella' as the ASEM and the EU–Latin America meetings. This process has led to the establishment of a wide-ranging strategic partnership between the EU and the African Union. Alongside this have gone the Lomé and Cotonou Processes, through which a complex set of institutions has been set up to provide a framework for negotiation and for the management of development aid and trade. The Cotonou Process, agreed in 2002, set out a general framework within which a series of Economic Partnership Agreements have been negotiated between the EU and either individual countries or regional groupings (Holland 2000, 2002; Holland and Doige 2012); a new series of agreements within the Cotonou framework was due to be concluded in 2021–2. As in the cases of Asia and Latin America, there has been a process of 'politicization' in respect of the EU's relations with Africa, based on democracy promotion and conflict prevention (Olsen 2002); this has increased in intensity since the injection of Chinese influence into sub-Saharan Africa and the upsurge in support for radical Islamist groups in several African states (Carbone 2013).

The net result of these and other interregional activities conducted by the EU has been the creation of a carefully differentiated system of intercontinental, subcontinental and bilateral agreements, which in turn has created a continuous process of negotiation between the EU and a wide range of partners (Alecu de Flers and Regelsberger 2005; Teló 2013; Baert, Scaramagli, and Söderbaum 2014). Typically, the 'umbrella' intercontinental agreements focus on broad-ranging dialogue and global issues, while more specific commercial and political issues are dealt with at the subcontinental or the bilateral level, and bilateral strategic partnerships where they exist are conducted separately again. It is clear that over time there has been a growing political and security content to these relationships, and that this has accelerated since approximately 2010: the EU has pursued 'conditionality' relating to good governance, human rights and other issues, and has attempted to use its economic muscle (including both access to the EU market and other mechanisms such as development aid) to raise its profile and promote the interests of European firms and other groupings within the regions concerned. It has also increasingly taken an activist diplomatic stance on issues such as migration or Islamist insurgencies, and even deployed military capabilities, for example in the Horn of Africa when seeking to counter piracy. The one thing it has not done – and cannot collectively do – is to assert overtly coercive power as a means of pursuing its aims. Although the Union has used economic sanctions in a number of cases (most comprehensively against Russia after the 2014 crisis in Ukraine and then the war of 2022 and after, but also for example against the Mugabe regime in Zimbabwe, or the military regime in Myanmar after the coup of early 2021) (K. Smith 2006b; Meixier and Creery 2022), and indeed has sent military, police or observer contingents (for example to the Congo or to Indonesia) during the past 20 years (Howorth 2014: Chapter 5), these have been essentially dedicated to political objectives, associated with UN mandates and (in the case of military contingents) severely limited as to their aims and terms of engagement. Although over time the EU has assumed a 'harder' edge to its power projection in interregional relations, the process has been an extended one and has not been without its setbacks.

The United States as a regional power

The renewed interest in the development of regionally oriented policies and strategic partnerships should not blind us to the historical reality: both Europe and America have long had such policies. Both actors have taken keen interest in particular areas of the world and developed specific policies – though perhaps within a broader foreign policy framework – to engage with those regions and with key players within them. As noted earlier, the EU's engagement with Africa and Asia has often reflected the long and tangled history of colonialism and thus the interests of member states such as France, Britain, the Netherlands, Belgium, Portugal and Spain. In the case of the United States, regional policies mixed with imperial pretensions a mere few years after the founding of the United States, with extensive American involvement in Latin America and the Caribbean and in the Pacific – most notably the Philippines. American interest and involvement in Latin America represents by some measure the most durable US regional policy. American interest in Latin America today owes much to these early experiences of state rivalry in South and Central America. In the first decades of the founding of the United States, efforts to evict the Spanish from Florida and South America were justified on security grounds and, in the latter case, economic ones as well. 'Why should European powers be the sole beneficiaries of the gold and other treasure flowing from Mexico and Peru?', asked Alexander Hamilton in 1799, articulating a mercantilist view of international relations that would have been familiar to many European diplomats (Chernow 2004: 567).

The Monroe Doctrine of 1823 articulated the view that the United States had significant economic and security interests in South and Central America that justified intervention if necessary. American policies towards Latin America thereafter were informed by the view that no foreign power should be able to exercise such influence as to threaten US interests. The United States was not concerned about the domestic policies of Latin American states provided they were friendly to American interests. This has always meant, among other things, the maintenance of economies friendly to American investment. After the Second World War, it was the spectre of Soviet influence in the Americas that provided the rationale for a series of controversial interventions. American support for the military in Guatemala in 1956 resulted in decades of repression – but with an economy friendly to American investment. From the late 1950s, the United States took a strongly anti-communist stance in relation to Cuba, including military intervention (the unsuccessful 1960 Bay of Pigs operation) and a comprehensive embargo. In 1962, the Cuban missile crisis was precipitated by the installation of Soviet missiles on the island and brought with it the risk of nuclear escalation. Anti-communist policies also led to American support for Augusto Pinochet's bloody overthrow of the democratically elected, left-leaning regime of Salvador Allende in Chile in 1973. Likewise, the Reagan administrations in the 1980s authorized covert military support for opponents of Nicaragua's leftist Sandinista regime. This support was both controversial – its execution broke US law – and ultimately a failure; the Sandinista regime was eventually replaced not by the gun but by losing elections. More recently, the fraught relationship between the United States and radical regimes in Venezuela has led to the imposition of diplomatic and economic sanctions. The cumulative effect of American interventions in Latin America has left policymakers and the general public deeply suspicious of American motivations and activities. Yet the economic ties remain strong. Brazil has succeeded in penetrating selected US markets for aircraft and fruit and has emerged as a potentially important supplier of the gasoline replacement, ethanol, while Mexican and Brazilian firms became active investors in the United States by the early 21st century (Santiso 2007).

American interest in regional trade and security policies increased in the 1980s, when two distinct developments together provided a powerful case for a foreign policy more attuned to regional developments. On the economic front, the slow and uncertain progress of the Uruguay Round negotiations added to the perception that the multilateral trade system that the United States had done so much to develop was no longer serving American interests. Though the Uruguay Round was eventually concluded in 1994, the United States began to embrace regional trade agreements with enthusiasm. This represented a dramatic shift in US foreign economic policy, which had since 1945 been firmly multilateral in orientation. As recently as 2001, the United States was party to only two regional trade agreements, though over 130 existed worldwide (Feinberg 2003: 1019). The United States began to play the bilateral or regional trade agreement card in the 1980s, with the Uruguay Round at its nadir. The first was a small but significant agreement with Israel, negotiated in the early 1980s. In 1988, the Canada–United States Free Trade Agreement (CUSFTA) was signed and could be seen in two ways: on the one hand, it embodied a view of the opportunities provided by regional agreements, but on the other hand, it could be seen as an implicit threat to the broader multilateral system, with the potential for further such agreements taking the United States further from the WTO and related bodies.

In the 1990s, however, the Clinton administration showed renewed interest in multilateral arrangements – or at least large-scale regional trade agreements – and other forms of partnership as the best mechanism for achieving US objectives. In 1994, having successfully passed the NAFTA agreement through Congress, albeit with last-minute concessions to environmental and labour lobbies, the president sought to expand trade liberalization through the twin tracks of the WTO and a hemispheric trade agreement. The WTO track consisted mainly of allowing the new Uruguay Round settlement to bed in, and the United States did not press for a new round of WTO talks until late in the Clinton presidency. Even then, the American preference was for a limited round, addressing some of the unfinished issues of the Uruguay settlement (like agriculture) but not envisaging major new negotiations (in contrast with the EU, which preferred a comprehensive negotiation including such areas as investment and environment). In respect of a trade agreement for the Western hemisphere, with NAFTA safely passed, the Clinton White House looked for a quick expansion of the agreement via an agreement with Chile, long the most liberal and open of the major South American economies. The timing seemed propitious, as many South American states had begun to embrace neo-liberal economic reforms (often referred to as 'the Washington consensus' due to pressure applied by the International Monetary Fund and US government bodies to adopt them) such as selling off state-owned enterprises, budget and monetary discipline and greater openness to trade. Indeed, the pressure for an expanded and evolved NAFTA came principally from Chile, and by the turn of the decade even traditionally protectionist Brazil was warming to the idea of an ambitious, hemispheric project.

Gradually, however, the momentum for large-scale liberalization faltered. Argentina's economic crisis of 2001 deeply undermined faith in the durability of economic liberalization in Latin America. Argentina's difficulties in turn caused considerable problems for important trading partners like Brazil, as international investors turned away from Latin America, having piled in during the 1990s. In the United States, the ending of the internet and dotcom economic boom also signalled a more sceptical congressional view of trade agreements. As protectionist sentiment gained ground, the possibilities of American concessions on market access for Latin American goods receded, and with them the rationale for entering talks in the first place. Instead of pursuing grander visions, the Bush administration and then the Obama administration pushed for less ambitious proposals for FTAs with selected partners. The Trump administration, pursuing its transactional trade diplomacy, succeeded in obtaining Mexican and Canadian agreement to a revised version of NAFTA, the US-Mexico-Canada Agreement (USMCA), which was explicitly rationalized on the basis that it was a 'win' for the United States against its partners, and which entered into force in 2020.

The United States, the new regionalism and partnership diplomacy

Though he was disinclined to enter into grand multilateral or regional trade deals, President George W. Bush's regional policies, not merely in Latin America but more widely, were shaped by two events: the terrorist attacks of '9/11' and the collapse of the Cancún ministerial of the WTO in September 2003. When Bush became president, there was a widespread expectation that South America would be the focus of regional initiatives; indeed Bush himself indicated as much and made good on this with Vicente Fox of Mexico becoming the first foreign leader to meet the newly inaugurated president in February 2001. In addition to Mexico, Brazil was singled out as a country that would receive special attention, with the aim of repairing the strained relations between the two states (Hakim 2006: 40). Brazil was South America's largest economy but its relations with the United States had long been contentious, with Brazil suspicious of American overtures – particularly on trade – and Washington impatient with a long list of alleged unfair trade practices by Brazil.

The events of 9/11 quite understandably caused the Bush administration to focus on the Middle East and Southwest Asia to the exclusion of other regions – but also signalled a shift in the type of policies pursued. In doing so, the Bush administration committed the United States to policies of regime change and democratization that were at odds with much of America's diplomatic tradition. Post-1945 US policies had been conservative, in the sense that they sought to maintain the system largely created by US power (Jervis 2005). Though lip-service might have been paid to the importance of democracy and the universality of human rights, the United States supported undemocratic and authoritarian regimes when it suited. Jervis notes how much this changed during the Bush administration: 'insufficient attention has been paid to the odd fact that the United States . . . is behaving more like a revolutionary state than one committed to preserving arrangements that seem to have suited it well' (Jervis 2006: 8; see also M. Smith 2009). American policy shifted to one based on firm belief in the importance and feasibility of the extension of democracy.

Though much emphasis was placed on military interventions in Afghanistan and Iraq, and on related strategic partnerships with Central Asian countries such as Kazakhstan, Kyrgyzstan and Uzbekistan, the United States also used economic leverage with several free trade agreements being signed with Middle Eastern states. These agreements were meant to perform two functions. First, they were an element of the administration's strategy of opening up markets for US goods. But with, for example, US exports to Morocco amounting to $475 million per year, such liberalization measures were marginal in global terms (USTR 2004). The second function was security-related. Bahrain, Morocco, Oman and Jordan – to name the counterparties to a number of US FTAs in the Middle East – are small states in a volatile part of the world; they have broadly pro-Western governments in place; and are all potentially vulnerable to extremists. Offering free trade agreements was seen as a way of insulating these regimes from political instability flowing from religious extremism or social unrest.

As a result of these diverse pressures, the Bush administration embraced regional and bilateral initiatives to a degree not previously seen in US economic policymaking. In 2002, George W. Bush gained important trade promotion authority (TPA) from Congress, which allowed the president to conclude trade agreements and place them before Congress for an up or down vote on the entire package. In the wake of 9/11, it was relatively easy for the president to convince Congress that rapid progress on trade liberalization, with or without the WTO, was a necessary element of US security. Robert Zoellick, the US trade representative, aggressively pursued bilateral deals with a wide range of trade partners. Chile, which had been the target of a larger, NAFTA-based agreement, eventually signed a bilateral pact. Other partners in Africa, Asia, the Middle East and Latin America were also brought into the ever-expanding list of American preferential trade partners (see Box 9.2). US business played its part in developing these deals. Like members of the US administration, American business leaders had grown weary of the complex and bewildering machinations at the multilateral level. Moreover, the anti-globalization movement, by focusing so much attention on the WTO, had convinced business leaders that a more conducive and less controversial avenue for liberalization lay with bilateral deals (Drahos 2007).

Relations with China have crept up the US policymaking agenda for several years, with the most noteworthy aspect being the increasing importance of economic relations in addition to the growing military rivalry. China finally achieved normal trade relations – the granting of US most-favoured nation status – during the Clinton presidency. This development owed a great deal to the persistent lobbying of American multinationals worried that the withholding of NTR status impaired their ability to tap the burgeoning Chinese market. Eager as US firms were to expand their relations with China, the expanding Chinese trade deficit – discussed in Chapter 4 – provoked Congressional anger amid the perception that China was trading unfairly by manipulating its currency (see Chapter 5). Other critics also drew attention to China's poor human rights record, which in the eyes of a number of politicians demanded an American response. While US policy responses were relatively muted during the Obama presidencies, the Trump administration between 2017 and 2021 took aim at China and effectively declared a trade war, while the Biden administration after 2021 continued and expanded measures to 'contain' China.

As with other regions of the world, the Asia-Pacific saw considerable US efforts aimed at developing bilateral trade agreements in the early years of the 21st century. Singapore, Australia and South Korea were three of the most important such agreements. Trade-dependent Singapore has always, like Hong Kong, been seen as a key advocate of the multilateral trade process, so its willingness to enter into a bilateral agreement was met with some concern. For the United States, by contrast, it was evidence that its policy of competitive liberalization paid considerable dividends. The US–Singapore Free Trade Agreement provided more indications that the United States was succeeding at gaining concessions at the bilateral level that it could not gain at the WTO level. In this case, Singapore's willingness to enhance provisions relating to the protection of intellectual property (IP) were a key part of the package for the United States. The same was true of the Australian–American pact signed in 2004. Critics were concerned that Australia's ability to develop and implement its own IP regulations was being constrained. This, and a view that Australian negotiators did not gain enough access to America's markets – especially in areas like sugar – made for a lukewarm reception for the pact among Australians (Thurbon and Weiss 2006).

These trends towards bilateralism, both in the economic and in the political arena, continued under the presidency of Barack Obama, from 2009 onwards; the continuation of attempts to consolidate interregional relationships went alongside an increasing preoccupation with the impact of 'rising powers', as already noted in the case of the EU, and with the need for partnerships with a wide range of regional actors (Hamilton 2014). Above all, the focus on China as an emerging economic and potentially strategic superpower conditioned the approach of the Obama administrations. Whereas during the first Obama administration between 2009 and 2013 the global financial and economic crisis was the central focus, and priority was given to domestic recovery, by the time of Obama's second term between 2013 and 2017, there was a strong emphasis on a strategic re-focusing of US policies towards the Asia-Pacific region (now also described as the 'Indo-Pacific' to include South Asia). This took two predominant forms. First, there was a strategic 'pivot' in foreign policy and diplomacy, with a renewed prioritization of disputes in the South China Sea and the East China Sea, where China was becoming increasingly assertive. While this was accompanied by continued reliance on multilateral mechanisms such as the International Court of Justice for legal judgements, it was also the focus for a significant military (and especially naval) buildup. Second, there was a move to initiate a form of 'economic containment', in the shape of the proposed Trans-Pacific Partnership (TPP) – an arrangement between the United States and a dozen Pacific countries in Latin America and East Asia (but not China) to undertake trade liberalization and other forms of multilateral cooperation (see also Chapter 4).

At the same time, there was a search for strategic partnerships with a range of other countries in the 'Indo-Pacific' region, especially India (where partnership had been initiated by the preceding George W. Bush administration), in order to consolidate the US position in Southern and Southwest Asia as its presence in Afghanistan was wound down. In all of these initiatives, it was easy to see from the Brussels perspective that there were potential implications for the EU, and for the overall nature of the EU–US partnership (Ross, Tunsjø, and Zhang 2010; Jing Men and Wei Shen 2014; Duke 2017: chapter 7). If US attention and resources were directed towards the Asia-Pacific and the Indo-Pacific, how would that impact the economic and security relationships that lie at the heart of transatlantic relations? This question remained unanswered as the Obama administration left office after the 2016 presidential elections.

Box 9.2 US strategic partnerships and dialogues (selected)

[These are in addition to formal treaty arrangements such as NATO and the US–Japan treaties.]

Formal strategic partnerships

Mexico
Poland
Ukraine
Egypt
Israel
Kenya

Australia
India
Vietnam
Chile
Uzbekistan

[Total formal strategic partnerships numbered 31. Most but not all of these were complemented by strategic dialogues.]

Strategic dialogues

Russia (now suspended)
Tunisia
South Africa
China
[Total strategic dialogues numbered 41.]

Source: Hamilton (2014) pp. 22–3.

Whereas the Obama administrations had retained a strong nominal commitment to multilateralism and to the development of bilateral and interregional partnerships within a global framework, the same was not true of the Trump administration that came into office in 2017. For the president, the focus as stated in his inaugural address was firmly on 'America First' and gaining advantage through an essentially transactional and predominantly bilateral diplomacy (M. Smith 2021). This did not rule out partnerships – but it did mean that any partnership would be entered into on US terms, and with a firm eye on what was in it for Washington, rather than on the basis of mutual gains or more generalized cooperation. Initially, the Trump administration's focus was firmly on two areas: NAFTA, which the president condemned as the 'worst trade deal ever', and the relationship with China, which degenerated into a trade war with security and ideological overtones. Between 2017 and 2019, NAFTA was renegotiated as effectively two linked bilateral deals, with Canada and Mexico, entailing concessions from both of the partners, and collectively labelled the US-Mexico-Canada Agreement (USMCA – see also Chapter4).

At the same time, US policies towards China became more confrontational and revolved around successive waves of US economic sanctions in retaliation for what were seen in Washington as unfair trading practices. While such tensions were not unprecedented (see earlier), their intensity and scope were novel and challenging at the global level. Another early casualty of the Trump administration's policies was the TPP, whose demise was accompanied by the 'freezing' of negotiations for a Transatlantic Trade and Investment Partnership (TTIP) (see Chapter 4). As noted earlier, the Biden administration kept up the pressure on China in relation to trade and also began to build what could be seen as a set of strategic partnerships in the Indo-Pacific area: first by revitalizing the so-called Quad (the United States, India, Japan and Australia), then through the AUKUS agreement between Australia, the United States and the UK, then with a trilateral agreement with Japan and South Korea, and finally in 2023 by agreeing an enhanced partnership with Vietnam.

Competition, convergence and crisis in a changing world

As with other aspects of the relationship, EU and US relations with other regions of the world are characterized by a mix of competition, convergence and crisis. In the area of trade and commerce, preferential trade agreements (PTAs) raise concerns among business that they will be excluded or disadvantaged. Hence both America and Europe have tended to follow a 'me-too' pattern, pursuing the logic of 'competitive interdependence' (Sbragia 2010) where one actor will negotiate a PTA in response to the success of the other. European efforts to develop a network of Latin American agreements were clearly motivated by concerns that US firms would enjoy all the advantages of a growing South American economy; in similar fashion, EU links with Asia-Pacific have grown at least in part because of a desire to prevent exclusion from a region where the United States is influential if not dominant. Rivalry also explains some of the interest of both parties in developing relations with southern Africa. Yet cooperation is seen across the globe too. Though the EU's relations with China are less fraught than those of the United States, it is the case that both Brussels and Washington have shared a belief in the importance of encouraging progressive Chinese engagement with the world. Both share a view that economic development is not an end in itself, but will help catalyse changes within China, including enhancing human rights and the rule of law (Wan 2007) although this view has been sorely tested in recent years with the growth of a more assertive and confrontational Chinese diplomacy (M. Smith 2014). Likewise even in areas where competition seems to be the defining element of the relationship both actors move from similar motivations. Both believe that the best way to secure the economic development of South America and Africa is through trade liberalization and the evolution of democracy – and both the EU and the United States use aid and trade as mechanisms for encouraging this (for an example relating to EU and US relations with Mercosur in Latin America, see Box 9.3).

As well as engaging in this process of 'competitive cooperation' in the sphere of trade and development, the EU and the United States have been affected by processes of politicization and securitization in pursuing their interregional ambitions. It was noted at the beginning of the chapter that the post-Cold-War context has lent a strong security tinge to the development of interregional relations in general, and that since the year 2000 there has been an increasing influence of the 'new geopolitics' and geo-economics. For the EU and the United States, the events of 9/11 underlined this dimension of their engagement in Asia, Latin America and Africa, and were followed by increasing engagement with the turbulent political and security dimensions of the Middle East, the Asia-Pacific and the Indo-Pacific. The longstanding and continuing mutual engagement of the EU and the United States in the Middle East has always had a major security component, and the EU has seen this as a regional arena (very close to home in geopolitical terms) in which it might develop a meaningful foreign and security policy role (Ortega 2003; Youngs 2006). In a different way, the shifting structures and resulting crises of international politics and economics in Eastern Europe, the Caucasus and Central Asia have offered both challenges and opportunities for the EU and the United States, of which the most dramatic have been those emerging from the Russian invasion of Ukraine in 2022. The result is an emerging – if often implicit – competition between the EU and the United States in terms of regional security and crisis management, which is likely to be shaped by the distribution of (for example) energy resources, environmental challenges and human rights issues (see Chapters 7 and 8 for further discussion of this in terms of power, security and order). Box 9.4 provides a summary of some of the areas in which this interregional security competition might arise.

Box 9.3 The EU, the United States and Mercosur

In 1991, four South American states, Argentina, Brazil, Paraguay and Uruguay, agreed to create Mercosur (Common Market of the South), one of the world's largest regional trade agreements. The agreement is a customs union, meaning that trade is meant to flow freely among members and all member states adopt a common set of trade instruments. The new grouping was in some sense the culmination of efforts to move South American states away from economic nationalism and spur economic growth through regional integration. Argentina and Brazil were the two main actors in Mercosur, with Brazil alone accounting for almost 73 per cent of Mercosur's exports in 2005 (WTO 2006).

Though much smaller than either the European Union or NAFTA (Canada, Mexico and the United States), Mercosur was large enough in world trade terms to merit attention. In the late 1990s, Argentina and Brazil in particular were seen as promising emerging markets and foreign investment, notably from the United States and Spain, poured in. As with all regional trade agreements, firms often prefer to invest rather than risk remaining outside the agreement, potentially facing discriminatory tariffs and other barriers. Throughout the 1990s and early 2000s attempts were made to bring NAFTA, Mercosur and other Western hemisphere states into a grand regional grouping, the Free Trade Area of the Americas. Such efforts foundered for many reasons, not least the difficulties that Brazil and the United States had in managing their bilateral relationship. Brazil had long attracted American criticism for its nationalist economic policies in areas as diverse as civil aircraft production, pharmaceuticals and citrus production. Brazil, for its part, objected to American trade protection laws, which it regarded as unfair barriers preventing Brazilian goods from gaining market share in the United States.

The European Union opened negotiations about a European–Mercosur tie in 1992, shortly after Mercosur's creation, and a wide-ranging political dialogue developed thereafter. The EU offered a range of technical assistance, as well as financial support for Mercosur's secretariat. For some observers, the EU's approach of bundling together economic, political and social issues into a regional cooperation agreement reflected the EU's emphasis on normative power projection, in contrast to the American preference for rules-based agreements that emphasize trade (Grugel 2004). We should also be clear, however, that European firms were concerned that any US–Mercosur tie might affect their access to the market. Moreover, European negotiators were as unwilling as their American counterparts to consider a dramatic liberalization of agricultural markets, a central goal for Mercosur, particularly Brazil (Doctor 2007). After more than 25 years of negotiation, with many false starts and periods of stagnation, the negotiations finally bore fruit in 2019, with the provisional conclusion of an agreement, but there was widespread opposition in the EU to its ratification.

How are we to explain this complex picture of interlocking and intersecting interregional and partnership relations? And was it overturned or otherwise transformed by the impact of the Trump administration with its emphasis on 'America First' and transactional diplomacy? Four potential explanations can be outlined here, none of which captures the whole picture and each of which contributes to it. The first potential explanation lies precisely in the fact that both the EU and the United States are regional powers. Both of them have developed means of pursuing stability and order within their regions, and this inevitably has an external impact. To put it simply, it may be that both the EU and the United States have created 'spheres of influence' in their respective regions, and that this has contributed to an emerging international division of labour between them: not a complete or even clear-cut division of labour, but one that reflects certain ground rules for engagement in each other's sphere. At present, there is also clearly an unevenness in this division, since the EU does not possess and is unlikely to possess the 'hard power' to which in principle the United States can resort (see Chapters 7 and 8). Yet the United States does not resort to hard power very readily, despite appearances: where it has done so, it has been largely in areas outside its own sphere of influence, where the ground rules are even less clear. Leaving this issue aside, it seems clear that both the EU and the United States as regional powers have an impact on the outside world as well as within their neighbourhoods, and that this inevitably brings them into contact or collision with each other.

The second potential explanation is that in a world characterized by coexisting globalization and regionalization processes, there are ample opportunities for both the EU and the United States to inject their presence into new and 'unclaimed' regions. This in turn leads to EU–US 'encounters' which can be both competitive or cooperative – or both at once, with elements of 'competitive cooperation' for example in relations with China or other actors in the Asia-Pacific, or in parts of Eastern and Central Europe. The EU's and the United States' interregional strategies are interdependent, and they are bound to create some uncomfortable episodes as both 'powers' try to assert themselves in new regions or in new relationships.

Linked to this is the third potential explanation: that different regions of the world become more or less significant over time, and that this creates changing incentives and risks for both the EU and the United States in their interregional strategies, especially when it comes to practices of crisis management (Alcaro, Peterson, and Greco 2016; Brown 2020). A case in point is that of sub-Saharan Africa, where for many years the United States did not see a compelling reason for involvement either bilaterally or at the interregional level, except when there were fears of Soviet influence. The discovery of new energy reserves in Central Africa, the intervention of China and the occurrence of internal conflicts with associated human rights questions have changed the calculus for regional intervention in Africa, with effects that will be felt over the next decade at least. The EU has an established interregional relationship in this region, but it is unclear how that might respond to the increased interest not only of the United States but also of other external powers.

Box 9.4 The EU, the United States and regional security: Issues and cases

The EU and the United States either have found or might find themselves in competition in areas such as the following:

- The Middle East: here, the central focus has been the Israel–Palestine issue, but this is accompanied by (1) a series of broader security issues relating to the geopolitics of the 'greater Middle East', such as the politics of the Gulf subregion and the problems associated with Iraq, and (2) a series of cross-regional security issues relating to energy supplies, human rights, democratization and development. The United States is engaged primarily at the level of regional stability and security, while the EU through its 'EuroMediterranean partnership' and its links with organizations such as the Gulf Cooperation Council has a wider range of organizational connections. All of these coexisting involvements were given a new focus after 2011 by the crises and conflicts associated with the 'Arab Spring'. Both the EU and the United States have encountered severe difficulties in managing their presence in the MENA region as a result: the EU has been effectively marginalized in conflicts such as that in Syria, but has experienced the consequences in terms of migration pressures and other human rights issues; the United States under both the Obama and Trump administrations found itself unable to determine the course of regional and domestic conflicts, and as a result has withdrawn from active and continuous military engagement. One consequence has been the injection of Russian power into Syria and the broader region. In October 2023, the Israel–Palestine conflict erupted into open warfare, and while the United States played a central part in the surrounding diplomacy, the EU was again in a marginal role.
- Central Africa: the EU and its member states have strong historical links to Central African countries, and have been involved in many of the conflicts that have occurred in this region during the post-colonial era. Over the period 2000–21, the EU has sent some of its most significant military contingents to Central Africa, especially in relation to the conflicts surrounding Rwanda and the Democratic Republic of Congo, while EU member states such as France have remained active in countering regional insurgencies, many of which are shaped by radical Islamic movements. The EU also has a broader interest in development and stability in the region through the operation of the Cotonou Convention which sets the framework for EU cooperation with the African, Caribbean and Pacific countries, and through its strategic partnership with the African Union. US interest has historically

been more distant, but this has changed because of the coincidence of greater Chinese engagement with Central Africa, the discovery of extensive oil reserves in a number of Central African countries and the presence in conflicted regions such as the DRC of significant deposits of 'rare earths' used in advanced technologies such as mobile phone and electric car batteries.

- South-East Asia: both the EU and the United States have important strategic interests in the stability and prosperity of South-East Asia. The EU is engaged through its longstanding cooperation agreements with the ASEAN, including its observer status at the ASEAN Regional Forum for security issues and through the ASEM and its associated economic, cultural and diplomatic networks. The EU has also been actively engaged in monitoring a number of regional conflicts, most notably that in Aceh (Indonesia) where it established an EU observer mission. The US interest is pursued through bilateral channels and through its engagement with the Asia-Pacific Economic Cooperation forum; it is also an observer at the ARF, but it has not actively intervened in the management of recent subregional conflicts, possibly as part of the legacy of its Vietnam entanglement during the 1960s and 1970s. There are, though, some areas in which the United States has high stakes: Taiwan, the Philippines and others that could become matters of intense concern as the role of China changes. Both the EU and the United States have been concerned if not alarmed by the emergence of a more assertive Chinese policy in the region, potentially affecting key maritime supply routes, although the pressure is most significant for the United States in military terms. As noted earlier, the Biden administration has pursued an active diplomacy in the area, including the conclusion of a strategic partnership with Vietnam.

The fourth and final dimension of competition, convergence and crisis as they relate to the EU and the United States in interregional relations is linked inextricably to the global system. If there are EU and US 'spheres of influence', or if there is a growing potential competition between the two in key regions, this has repercussions for global institutions and global order. Chapters 8 and 10 deal in more detail with these issues of European and world order, but it should be noted here that (for example) trade relationships at the interregional level between the EU, the United States and key regions such as Asia-Pacific are directly related to issues arising in the WTO or in key global institutions dealing with environment, development, energy and other urgent issues. Indeed, one dimension of growing EU engagement with regions such as Asia-Pacific has been the desire to generate support for EU positions in trade negotiations or other global issues, while the United States has benefited from support from regions such as Latin America in many global arenas. However, such support cannot be guaranteed, particularly in the context of political and other changes within the relevant regions; here, there is another dimension to the interregional question, since it appears that in some respects the EU and the United States might be played off against each other by regional actors.

How, and how much, was this picture of complex EU–US relationships in the changing international structure challenged if not transformed by the impact of the Trump administration? It is important not to overstate the novelty of Trump's approach to the international arena: as noted at several points in this chapter, and earlier in Chapter 1, his was not the first administration to give priority to US domestic interests, or to threaten retaliation against what were seen as unfair trading practices or processes of political subversion. Nor was it the first to see the EU as an economic and political rival rather than as a natural partner. But as has been emphasized throughout this and other chapters, the Trump administration operated with a confrontational style in a transformed global political and economic structure, in which the world outside transatlantic relations posed new challenges and created new opportunities. For the EU, the implications of the Trump trade war on China were disturbing, since the deepening of a US–China 'cold war' would have repercussions for the Union both economically and politically. Security issues relating to the South China Sea, Taiwan and more broadly to the Indo-Pacific were also of concern to EU leaders aware of their limitations in a more geopolitical and geo-economic world characterized by increased competition and confrontation. Not surprisingly, the incoming European Commission in autumn 2019 committed itself to fostering a more 'geopolitical' approach to its key international partnerships (Blockmans 2020) – aimed at the United States as much as at other targets – and this general approach was only moderated by two factors: first, the impact of the COVID-19 crisis, which revealed the fragility of the internal foundations for an assertive international role, and second, the defeat of Donald Trump in the elections of November 2020, which led to the installation of a less openly confrontational (but no less challenging in other ways) US administration headed by Joe Biden. For the EU, its approach to interregional relations and partnership diplomacy has been partly shaped by the development of its own strategic consciousness, as expressed in the Global Strategy and other frameworks, but also by the ways in which domestic and international crises have changed perceptions of the EU's roles and capabilities.

Overview and conclusion

This chapter has added the regional and interregional dimension as well as a consideration of 'partnership diplomacy' to our understanding of EU–US relations, and has focused on a number of key policy and analytical issues. In particular, the chapter has argued that:

- Both the EU and the United States can be seen as 'regional powers', each with its own characteristic features and priorities. In addition, one way of conceptualizing EU–US relations is in terms of the building of regional systems or 'spheres of influence', which in both cases have long historical antecedents.
- Both the EU and the United States have developed systems of interregional relations, with both bilateral and multilateral elements, embodying historical relationships but also reflecting recent and current policy priorities. Whereas the EU's system of interregional relations reflects the nature of the EU as a 'civilian superpower', and is based on negotiation and institution-building, the US system reflects the fact that American policymakers can have recourse to 'hard power', and is based more often on strategic priorities such as the 'war on terror' or the putative US–China 'cold war'. This is not to ignore the fact that EU interregional policies can have a 'hard edge' to them, or that US policies can place emphasis on negotiation and agreement; it is rather to identify a divergence in the central trend lines of policymaking.
- The intersection of EU and US interregional policies can be evaluated in terms of competition and convergence, with important trends emerging from the fact that both the EU and the United States are regional powers and that their policies have different tendencies or mechanisms. The coexistence of tendencies towards regionalization and globalization in the world arena means that the EU and the United States will encounter each other in a variety of regional and interregional contexts, and that in turn these encounters will be reflected at the global level. The encounters themselves – in common with the interregional involvements of both the EU and the United States – have become more 'politicized' and 'securitized' during the post-Cold-War period.
- A key dimension of the interaction between EU and US policies in the 21st century has been their responses to a series of regional crises, a number of which have had major global implications. In the Middle East, Southwest Asia, East Asia and sub-Saharan Africa, these crises have been defined predominantly in terms of security and 'high politics', but it is also important

to note that there has been a series of regional economic and commercial crises, in Europe itself, Latin America and Asia, which have engaged the attention of both the EU and the United States. Very often, the economic and security aspects of such crises have been mutually reinforcing, and tracing the shifting interests of the EU and the United States in this context constitutes a major contribution to understanding their interactions in many policy areas.

In this context, it is reasonable to ask, what might the future hold for the EU and the United States? Will it be characterized by increasing interregional competition and 'competitive interdependence', by the building and reinforcement of spheres of influence, or by a form of global division of labour in which both the EU and the United States will play their parts? This question is raised by many of the chapters in this book, and it will be taken up explicitly in Chapter 11, which evaluates the changing relationship in general.

Chapter 10

The EU, the United States and global governance

Introduction

As noted in Chapter 1, the evolution of relations between the European integration project and the United States must be seen in the perspective of at least 70 years, if not longer. Vital to this long process of development in EU–US relations has been the related process of development in global governance. The Bretton Woods system of international financial institutions established in the wake of the Second World War was fundamental to the ways in which European integration and EC–US relations evolved. The achievement of international financial stability and the convertibility of currencies between the western industrial countries that was finally achieved in the late 1950s was essential to the recovery of Western Europe and thus to the progress of European integration (Diebold 1960; Krause 1968). In like fashion, the reconstruction and liberalization of world trade in the context of the General Agreement on Tariffs and Trade (GATT) was fundamental to the expansion of US commercial influence but also key to the establishment of the European Economic Community in the late 1950s – indeed, without Article XXIV of the GATT, which permitted the establishment of customs unions, there is a case for saying that the EEC might never have seen the light of day. As the Bretton Woods institutions came under increasing pressure in the late 1960s and 1970s, this also reflected the strains already referred to in EC–US relations, and in the early 1970s, the strains simply became too great for the system to withstand. As a result, the floating of major currencies and the reform of the global trading system that went alongside it during the 1970s and 1980s saw the EC and the United States playing central roles. Indeed, it can be argued that through the 1970s and 1980s, the transatlantic partners and rivals were at the core of the continuing hard-fought liberalization of world trade and payments that lay behind the later emergence of large-scale globalization processes (Tsoukalis 1986; Woolcock and Van der Ven 1986; Patel and Weisbrode 2013).

It was this intersection – between the development of EC/EU–US relations and the process of global liberalization that powered globalization – that continued to drive forward key institutional and political developments in the world arena during the 1990s. At the EU level, after the broad completion of the Single Market Programme and the establishment of Economic and Monetary Union as a key policy objective, a host of other developments in policy areas such as environmental regulation, food safety, communications and information technology and transport became salient, while the initiation of the Common Foreign and Security Policy gave the EU a stake in what came to be termed 'security governance' (M. Smith 1998) and in the application of global norms such as those dealing with human rights. At the same time, the Clinton administrations between 1993 and 2001 provided a broad framework of multilateralism for US policies, which was able to accommodate at least some of the major developments in global governance that emerged during the decade after the end of the Cold War. Not only this, but at the transatlantic level, there was established during the 1990s an increasingly complex and wide-ranging set of EU–US partnership agreements – the Transatlantic Declaration of 1990, the New Transatlantic Agenda of 1995 with its accompanying Action Plan, and the Transatlantic Economic Partnership first mooted in 1998 (Pollack and Shaffer 2001; Steffenson 2005) and then extended in 2007 with the creation of the Transatlantic Economic Council. An unprecedented level of transatlantic economic and regulatory cooperation developed during these years, notwithstanding the persistence of important trade and other disputes (Petersmann and Pollack 2003; Pollack and Shaffer 2001; Peterson 1996b; Steffenson 2005; Pollack 2005), enhancing what can be thought of as a common transatlantic economy (Hamilton and Quinlan 2021). For some during the Obama administrations, this created the basis for an ambitious and wide-ranging Transatlantic Trade and Investment Partnership (see Chapter 4). While it was much more difficult and contentious to try and develop transatlantic security cooperation at the EU–US level, there was nonetheless tangible progress towards transatlantic security consultation not merely through NATO but also between the EU and the United States (Howorth 2014; Rees 2009).

The result of this long evolutionary process can be summarized quite readily at one level. The evolution of EU governance reflected at many stages – and in at least some of its core institutions – important US influences and the broader context of the Cold War and after (see also Chapter 3). At the same time, there had developed a complex set of partnership arrangements that could be seen as the basis for a new system of 'transatlantic governance'. Finally, the EC/EU and the United States had over a long period been key components of processes of global governance, reflected especially in the Bretton Woods institutions but also in the ways those institutions adapted to new economic challenges between the 1970s and the 1990s (M. Smith 2011b). But this relatively clear-cut summary becomes markedly less clear when one considers the continuing tensions at all levels between the process of European integration and the pursuit of US leadership, and when one considers the greatly extended role for processes of global governance in the later years of the Cold War and thereafter. The chapter goes on, as in earlier chapters, to explore the EU and US approaches to global governance, and then to examine a number of cases from the post-Cold-War period to illustrate and evaluate the course of EU–US relations in respect of global governance.

The European Union, 'effective multilateralism' and global governance

Almost from the outset, as noted earlier, the development of the European integration project has been closely linked to the broader development of global governance. Indeed, the nature of the Union as a particularly intense form of regional governance can be seen as a major building-block of global governance mechanisms more generally. As can be seen from Box 10.1, the EU has explicitly recognized this relationship in the 21st century and has built it into its approaches to world order and international cooperation.

Box 10.1 The EU and processes of global governance

The European Commission's White paper on Governance, published in 2001, presented the link between the EU's internal governance structures and processes in very clear terms:

> The objectives of peace, growth, employment and social justice pursued within the Union must also be promoted outside for them to be effectively attained at both European and global level. This responds to citizens' expectations for a powerful Union on a world stage. Successful international action reinforces European identity and the importance of shared values within the union.
>
> (European Commission 2001; cited in Ortega 2007, p. 92)

This was further underlined by the European Security Strategy of 2003:

> In a world of global threats, global markets and global media, our security and prosperity increasingly depend on an effective multilateral system. The development of a stronger international society, well-functioning international institutions and a rule-based international order is our objective.
>
> (European Council 2003, p. 11)

And it was further amplified by the EU's Global Strategy in 2016:

> Without global norms and the means to enforce them, peace and security, prosperity and democracy – our vital interests – are at risk. Guided by the values on which it is founded, the EU is committed to a global order based on international law, including the principles of the UN Charter, which ensure human rights, sustainable development and lasting access to the global commons. . . . The EU will strive for a strong UN as the bedrock of the multilateral rules-based order, and develop globally coordinated processes with international and regional organisations, states and non-state actors.
>
> (European Union 2016, p. 39)

'Effective multilateralism' has become a recurring element in the rhetoric of EU foreign and security policy and is key to the analysis of the EU's role in global governance. First explicitly presented in the European Security Strategy of 2003 (European Council 2003), it has since been repeated in a wide variety of contexts and has been a part of the Union's self-definition as an international actor – not only in the sphere of security policy, but also in the context of global governance more generally. As Caroline Bouchard and her co-authors have argued, the concept of 'effective multilateralism' keys into a general growth in the demand for multilateralism at the beginning of the 21st century (Bouchard, Peterson, and Tocci 2014), but raises important questions both about the contours and content of multilateralism and about the EU's commitment to it. Although the Union can be presented as a compulsive multilateralist, on grounds both of its internal make-up and its self-conception as an actor in the world arena, it is often not clear what the extent and consistency of the EU's commitment is, and what the notion of 'effective multilateralism' amounts to in practice. The strategic review of the EU's external action, and the subsequent Global Strategy (EEAS 2015; European Union 2016) attempted to address the gap between the aspiration to effective multilateralism, the attempt to achieve it and the reality of persistent bilateralism and plurilateralism (relations between limited groups of actors). There is thus a continuing puzzle about the widely accepted view of the EU as an 'effective multilateralist' and the ways in which this view takes practical effect in EU external policies, and this puzzle is central to the recent and current evolution of global governance institutions and processes

Multilateralism is said to be in the EU's DNA, and to be the means not only by which the EU can exert its influence in the world but also establish its legitimacy as an international actor (M. Smith 2011a, 2011b, 2018b). This can be connected to the idea that the EU is a 'post-modern' international actor

(Cooper 2000), based on post-sovereign values and in a sense pathologically committed to the pursuit of multilateral solutions to shared problems. But this is not the only possible perspective on the EU's approach to multilateralism. Others have proposed a more instrumentalist view, which treats the EU as an 'emerging international actor' committed to multilateralism because that is the route to the kinds of rules and institutional frameworks within which it can prosper. The extent to which the EU actually lives up to its own propaganda as a multilateralist can also be questioned, by showing the extent to which EU behaviour deviates from the kind of liberal internationalism to which it expresses its commitment, for example in trade or development policy (Youngs 2011; Youngs and Smith 2018). It can also be argued that whatever its approach to multilateralism, the EU lacks credibility when it fails to speak with one voice in multilateral arenas or groupings, and when the persistent (and subversive) influence of the member states is in evidence.

How can we relate this discussion to the idea of the EU as an 'effective multilateralist'? Since the phrase first emerged, there have been numerous attempts both to clarify the phrase itself and to locate the EU in relation to the notion it embodies. The effective practice of multilateralism, both within the global order in general and by individual actors, can be understood as the promotion of substantive rules and adherence to them, the application of principles of reciprocity and inclusiveness, and the devotion of resources to the building of institutions embodying those rules and principles. Caroline Bouchard and her co-authors, drawing upon the work of Laatikainen and Smith (2006), identify four different dimensions of effectiveness in the case of the EU: internal (the generation of effective collective action at the EU level), external (centred on the perceptions of the EU's role, either as leader, promoter or exemplar, in multilateral contexts), what might be termed institutional (expressed in terms of the EU's contribution to international organizations) and finally the ways in which the organizations in which the EU is engaged themselves achieve effectiveness within the global arena. On this basis, they conclude that the EU, despite being good at writing multilateral principles into treaties and other key declarations of intent, is relatively ineffective at translating these into practice, especially in contexts where there is not a high level of institutionalization to start with, for example in dealing with international migration or a range of environmental issues (Bouchard, Peterson, and Tocci 2014: 285 et seq). Such a conclusion reflects in many ways the elements of contestability in the EU's approach to multilateralism as outlined earlier.

A specific manifestation of the tensions and ambiguities inherent in the EU's approach to multilateralism can be found in the Union's relationship to global governance frameworks, and especially to international regimes, for example those relating to environmental, energy or human rights issues (Smith and Elgström 2013).International regimes are symptomatic of the commitment to multilateralism in a wide range of issue areas, and the establishment, evolution and impact of regimes have been a long-standing feature of work in core areas of international political economy, diplomacy and security studies. The classic definition of international regimes by Stephen Krasner is that they embody 'principles, norms, rules and decision-making procedures around which actor expectations converge in a given issue-area' (Krasner 1982). In other words, they are fundamental to the idea of a 'rules-based international order' which lies at the heart of the EU's approach to global governance. The intensification and extension of international regimes have in many respects gone alongside the EU's search for channels through which to exploit its commitment to multilateralism, and the EU has made much of its engagement with major international regimes in trade, the environment, development, security, communications, human rights and other areas (Jørgensen and Laatikainen 2013: Part V). But this engagement carries with it a series of potential contradictions, which go to the core of the EU's international roles and influence, and also carry important implications for EU–US relations (see later). The EU's participation in a wide range of regimes is shaped by the influence of EU member states and the Brussels institutions, and by the interplay between them; inevitably, there are differences of view which affect the capacity of the Union to commit to any given set of ideas and institutions. This means that any EU commitments will result from some kind of compromise between 'European' and national preferences. As a result, there will also be a fluctuating balance between internal bargains and the need for external commitment, and between the 'logics of appropriateness' at EU and regime levels – in other words, there is a process of continuous negotiation between the various actors within the EU framework, as well as between the EU and other countries or institutions.

The EU's presence in a given regime is also shaped by a mixture of internal and external normative forces. On the one hand, the regime will be seen as an arena for projection of the EU 'voice' and consolidation of an EU identity, and as a vehicle for the projection of EU norms. For example, the EU's role in the World Trade Organization has been foundational to its identity as a 'champion trader' and a 'trade superpower', but more broadly also to its role as a 'civilian power' in the world arena. At the same time, it is clear that there can be important tensions between EU policies in different but linked issue-areas – for example, trade and development or trade and environment – where different sets of EU institutions and priorities come into collision. This means that there is no simple answer to the questions 'how far is the EU an effective multilateralist?' and 'how far can the EU lead in providing effective multilateral solutions to global governance?' As has been shown in studies of the EU's engagement with the United Nations system and other bodies (Laatikainen and Smith 2006; Kissack 2010; Orsini 2014), intersecting processes of multilateralism and governance can lead to a complicated balancing act for the Union. As the scope of the EU's external action has expanded (see also Chapters 8 and 9), this balancing act has become more challenging, as was acknowledged in the EU's Global Strategy: the commitments made in the strategy to 'principled pragmatism' and to the pursuit of 'strategic autonomy', but also to the continued pursuit of multilateralism and the promotion of global governance, represent in many ways an attempt to square the circle between 'world partner' EU and 'world power' EU. They also represent a potentially new and challenging basis for relations with the United States, and the later parts of this chapter will relate these questions to EU–US relations in a variety of issue areas.

The United States and global governance

Very often, a sharp contrast is drawn between the EU's commitment to multilateralism, negotiation and 'civilian power' and the United States' practices of unilateralism, coercion and the deployment of 'hard power', especially in the military domain (M. Smith 2004; Pollack 2003a; see also Chapter 7). This contrast has important implications for the study of EU–US relations in the context of global governance. To put it crudely, American policymakers are likely to put the pursuit of global governance 'for its own sake' in a subordinate position on their list of global priorities. For them, the key is material interest, shaped by perceptions of the United States' predominant position in the global arena. These interests and perceptions are often seen as reflecting an 'American exceptionalism', which is a consistent thread running through US foreign policy since at least the late 19th century (Deudney and Meiser 2018; Mandelbaum 2022). The United States is seen as a power unlike any other, not only because of its exceptional material power, but also because of its embodiment of a certain form of government – liberal democracy. In a way, of course, this can be seen as matching the form of 'European exceptionalism' embodied in some of the EU assumptions outlined earlier, but it leads in markedly different directions when it comes to the conduct of practical policy (M. Smith 2010).

Such an orientation gives the United States a particular position on matters of global governance. To put it simply, international cooperation, seen by the EU and generally its member states as a matter of necessity (both for the sake of the EU and for the broader global good), is seen by US policymakers as a matter of choice. The use of global governance processes and institutions is conditioned by considerations of US 'grand strategy', and occupies a largely instrumental position within the conduct of US international policies. While different US administrations will vary in the vehemence with which they state this position, the central tendency is towards the instrumentalization if not the marginalization of those institutions that the EU often sees as central to its international presence and identity. As a result, the United States can exercise its raw power in relation to institutions of global governance not only by using them as instruments of active policy, but also by ignoring them and exercising its power of defection (Foot, McFarlane and Mastanduno 2003; Barnett and Duvall 2005; Keohane 2003b).

This does not mean that US administrations are against the governance of international transactions per se. But it is important to note that when Americans talk about the governance of international affairs, they often see the United States as the 'governor' – and equally often can see the institutions and rules that are at the core of global governance as threats to the position of the United States. A very clear statement of this position can be found in the work of Michael Mandelbaum (2005), who argued forcefully that the United States is effectively 'the world's government', providing essential public services for the global community through its provision of leadership and its deployment of material power, for example by safeguarding shipping lanes through use of its global naval presence. Crucially, Mandelbaum argued also that the EU was in no position to challenge the United States in this domain, and that it suffered from disabling internal limitations that effectively precluded it from ever posing such a challenge:

> The most consequential problem [emerging from what he describes] in European-American relations is not the failure of the United States to consult with European governments but rather the failure of those governments to muster the resources to make major contributions to global governance. Their failure means that when the United States acts unilaterally, it does so as much by default as by design. The Europeans endeavour to produce good behaviour on the part of potentially dangerous countries by the force of their example, not by force of arms. They see their global mission as embodying civilisation but not defending it. (2005: xx–xxi)

This quotation is significant not only for the obvious attack on the collective action capacity of the EU, but also for its interpretation of 'global governance', which is ultimately defined in terms of security and the countering of key threats from 'dangerous countries' (see also Foot, MacFarlane and Mastanduno 2003: Introduction and Conclusion). As such, it accurately reflects two of the key assumptions that lie at the centre of US policies on global governance issues: first, they are about vital national interests defined in terms of power, threat and security; second, they demand 'real' power, and not the kind of abstractions such as 'civilian power' or 'normative power' that have been seen as central to the EU's pursuit of global governance. Put simply, the idea that the EU is a 'model' or an effective participant in global governance would be met with considerable scepticism by Americans (and others) holding this more 'power-centred' or 'realist' position on global governance more generally. As was noted in Chapter 7, this links with a range of general differences between the EU and the United States on matters of international power and security.

The United States might thus be seen as the ultimate 'selective multilateralist', enabled by its power and its position to practice 'multilateralism *à la carte*'. This expresses the nature of the United States not only as a hegemonic but also as essentially a 'modernist' actor, focused on sovereignist assumptions about the way the world works and the way in which its interests can be defended (M. Smith 2004, 2011a). But this image of the United States as multilateralist can be overstated; moreover a series of correctives might be applied. One of these relates to the changing power position of the United States and the need to prepare for a world in which American power is markedly less predominant. From this perspective there is a strong link between US assumptions about multilateralism and its uses and the broader arguments about power-shifts in the global arena that have brought rising powers such as China to the fore (Alcaro, Peterson, and Greco 2016; Brown 2018). Such a linkage seemed to be borne out at least in part by the Barack Obama administration's adoption of a pragmatic realist approach to its international commitments and its pursuit of multilateral solutions to some of its key international dilemmas (M. Smith 2011a), and featured in the Biden administration's initial approaches to foreign policy. Nonetheless, it is still fair to identify the US posture on multilateralism as essentially selective and 'domesticist', focusing on the needs of the United States first. Such a judgement was reinforced by the Trump agenda (see later). Box 10.2 sets out some of the key statements about multilateralism made by the United States since the Clinton administration.

Box 10.2 Key US statements on multilateralism and global governance

The Clinton administration's national security strategy emphasized 'engagement and enlargement' with a firm focus on US leadership:

> Our nation can only address this era's dangers and opportunities if we remain actively engaged in global affairs. We are the world's greatest power, and we have global interests as well as responsibilities. As our nation learned after World War I, we can find no security for America in isolationism nor prosperity in protectionism. For the American people to be safer and enjoy expanding opportunities, our nation must work to deter would-be aggressors, open foreign markets, promote the spread of democracy abroad, combat transnational dangers of terrorism, drug trafficking and international crime, encourage sustainable development and pursue new opportunities for peace.
>
> President of the United States, A National Security Strategy of Engagement and Enlargement. The White House, February 1996 iv

Under George W. Bush, the strategy was focused much more on US power and the assembling of coalitions in a variety of contexts:

> We are . . . guided by the conviction that no nation can build a safer, better world alone. Alliances and multilateral institutions can multiply the strength of freedom-loving nations. The United States is committed to lasting institutions like the United Nations, the World Trade Organization, the Organization of American States, and NATO as well as other long-standing alliances. Coalitions of the willing can augment these permanent institutions. In all cases, international obligations are to be taken seriously. They are not to be undertaken symbolically to rally support for an ideal without furthering its attainment.
>
> America will implement its strategies by organizing coalitions – as broad as practicable – of states able and willing to promote a balance of power that favors freedom. Effective coalition leadership requires clear priorities, an appreciation of others' interests, and consistent consultations among partners with a spirit of humility.
>
> President of the United States, National Security Strategy of the United States of Americas. The White House, September 2002: 3, 25

For the Obama administration, there was more emphasis on multilateral cooperation related to global issues, within a focus on US interests:

> The United States will protect its people and advance our prosperity irrespective of the actions of any other nation, but we have an interest in a just and sustainable international order that can foster collective action to confront common challenges. This international order will support our efforts to advance security, prosperity, and universal values, but it is also an end that we seek in its own right. Because without such an international order, the forces of instability and disorder will undermine global security. And without effective mechanisms to forge international cooperation, challenges that recognize no borders – such as

> climate change, pandemic disease, and transnational crime – will persist and potentially spread.
>
> President of the United States, National Security Strategy. The White House, May 2010: 40

The Trump administration stressed US dominance and the determination to reflect US priorities at the multilateral level:

> The United States must lead and engage in the multinational arrangements that shape many of the rules that affect U.S. interests and values. A competition for influence exists in these institutions. As we participate in them, we must protect American sovereignty and advance American interests and values. . . . Authoritarian actors have long recognized the power of multilateral bodies and have used them to advance their interests and limit the freedom of their own citizens. If the United States cedes leadership of these bodies to adversaries, opportunities to shape developments that are positive for the United States will be lost. All institutions are not equal, however. The United States will prioritize its efforts in those organizations that serve American interests, to ensure that they are strengthened and supportive of the United States, our allies, and our partners. Where existing institutions and rules need modernizing, the United States will lead to update them. At the same time, it should be clear that the United States will not cede sovereignty to those that claim authority over American citizens and are in conflict with our constitutional framework.
>
> President of the United States, National Security Strategy of the United States of America. The White House, December 2017: 40

If we link these characteristics and statements to the criteria for 'effective multilateralism' put forward by Bouchard et al. (see earlier), it is clear that the United States operates on an essentially different approach to multilateralism and global governance from that adopted by the EU. Internally, US administrations have adopted a broadly sovereignist view of international engagement, both within the international political economy and on international security issues. This has been subject to relatively little contestation. Externally, the United States has adopted a position that pays little attention to detailed multilateral engagement, preferring to focus on the domestic roots of its power and reputation and on its external strength (Mandelbaum 2005, 2022; Nau 1990, 2002). Institutionally, the United States limits its commitments in light of domestic constraints and a belief that at least some multilateral institutional mechanisms constitute unacceptable interventions in US sovereign concerns. This feeling is reflected in evaluations of effectiveness on the part of the institutions themselves – the key test is, do those institutions enable US leadership and serve US interests broadly defined?

This viewpoint was reinforced by Donald Trump's election in 2016, which strengthened the link between US diplomacy and transactionalism and explicitly challenged the notion of global governance. Central to the Trump campaign was a sovereignist assumption that the United States was free to abandon multilateral commitments if they did not meet American needs – an assumption aimed primarily at a domestic audience that saw the United States as a victim of globalization and, by extension, the multilateral system or liberal order that gave rise to globalist challenges (Ikenberry 2018; Patrick 2017; Peterson 2018). Trump's contentions echoed Reaganite arguments that the primary task for the United States was to be strong and act as an example to the rest of the world (Nau 1990, 2002), rather than be a leader in multilateral governance and negotiation. However, Trump added a twist by focusing on himself and his personal relationships with other leaders. During the first year of the Trump presidency, this focus led to a US denunciation of the 2015 Paris climate change agreement, an abandonment of the efforts to conclude a Trans-Pacific Partnership, a freezing of efforts to negotiate a Transatlantic Trade and Investment Partnership, the withdrawal from UNESCO and a refusal to certify Iranian compliance with the 2015 multilateral agreement on its nuclear programme (see Chapter 7 and later). The declaration of a trade war in US–China relations and the weaponizing of the US economy as a tool of transactional diplomacy, deployed not only in trade wars but also in the use of economic sanctions, further created an atmosphere in which many of the United States' most long-standing allies were disconcerted (Verola 2019).

Trump's tendency towards unilateralism and disruption was underlined by the administration's approaches to North Korea, which alarmed allies and revealed the limitations of diplomacy centred on the interaction of individual leaders. This was a paradigm case of transactional diplomacy: bilateral if not unilateral, focused on the president as an 'audience of one' for foreign policy advice, and above all aimed at the conclusion of sequential deals without an overarching strategy or set of principles. The approach created new elements of risk by simultaneously raising the stakes attached to individual encounters between the president and his interlocutors and separating them from the support mechanisms provided by the diplomatic establishment. It also challenged the established regime relating to nuclear non-proliferation, to which the EU has consistently subscribed.

There was strong resistance to these steps by the 'globalist' elements in Washington, especially those reflecting the interests of US business, transnational corporations and those with a liberal approach to global political economy and global governance. This meant that US diplomacy became characterized by uncertainty and by unpredictability, creating a situation in which hegemonial assumptions were questioned and in which it was difficult to know which United States to relate to or respond to. The impact of the Trump administration's transactional approach destabilized not only relations with major allies and adversaries but also the diplomatic machine of the State Department and allied agencies, which found themselves in many instances marginalized by the president's initiatives. Not least among those discomfited by US diplomacy after 2016 was the EU itself, not to mention major EU member states. Indeed, President Trump pronounced that the EU was a 'foe', especially in economic terms (Contiguglia 2018), and he rejected significant multilateral agreements such as those on climate change and Iran (both of which were intimately connected with EU diplomacy – see later). This, in turn, led to a situation in which German chancellor Angela Merkel and other leaders proclaimed their distrust of Washington while at the same time making firm commitments to the 'strategic autonomy' of the Union as set out in the Global Strategy and, as noted earlier, a new commitment to multilateralism (see also Chapters 7 and 8).

The United States thus represents a distinctive approach to the institutions and rules of global governance; although the Trump administration challenged these in a very explicit way, it was in many ways a crystallization of trends that have appeared in US policies over an extended period, and of pressures of change that have led to important shifts in the global arena, with implications for the status of the United States more generally. Significantly, the Biden administration in 2021 proclaimed that 'the US is back' in the game of global governance, but related this strongly to US leadership in a way that had echoes of earlier 'exceptionalist' statements (Schade 2023; Olsen 2022). In terms of the three elements discussed earlier in relation to the EU, the United States has displayed long-term doubts about the effectiveness and utility of the institutions of global governance; this has in turn reflected the persistence of sovereignist and 'exceptionalist' norms in US foreign policy, and it has led successive administrations to reject or attempt to bypass global negotiation processes. There have clearly been variations in the extent to which these challenges pervade US policies, but there is little doubt that they stand in strong contrast to the assumptions and practices displayed in EU external action. The final section of this chapter explores a number of cases in which these contrasts can be seen playing out, and assesses their implications.

The EU, the United States and global governance

The contrast between the EU and the United States over multilateralism and unilateralism in issues of security reflects a broad difference of view on the utility of international cooperation and institutions. As we have seen, the EU places great store in the need for global governance, not least because of its experience with multinational governance in Europe itself (see Ortega 2007). Although there are differences between EU member states, they all share this broad commitment to the management of international order, and to the role of institutions in that process. The Americans, on the other hand, see international cooperation as a matter of choice rather than of necessity: where US interests are served, the cooperation is acceptable, but where international cooperation threatens what are seen as US vital interests, the country retains the right to opt out, to oppose and to undermine such efforts. As Robert Keohane points out (2003a), this reflects an attachment to the Westphalian view of sovereignty which has largely disappeared under the impact of interdependence and integration in the EU. Thus when the United States opposes the International Criminal Court, as it has since its establishment in the early 2000s, it is not merely on grounds of practicality; rather, it is on grounds of underlying attachment to a view of sovereignty that is at odds with any such effort at international management. Likewise, EU support for the Paris Accords on climate change is partly a reflection of recognition of environmental threats, but also a reflection of deep-rooted views about the necessity for international cooperation itself.

The EU has been very active in promoting multilateral institutions and rules, not least because it is through some of them that the EU can maintain and enhance its international legitimacy and status. The EU is itself an example of governance at the continental level, and some have argued that this gives the Union a special role in promoting and defending the mechanisms of global governance. The United States has historically taken a different perspective arising from its emphasis on sovereignty and its national interests but has had to take into account the need for management of the globalizing world. During the post-Cold-War period there have been many instances in which these different approaches have come to the fore, and here we will present six examples to illustrate this phenomenon (drawing on M. Smith 2005b, 2010).

Trade and the Doha Round

The first case is the process by which the agenda for the Doha Development Round was established and pursued within the WTO during the period 1998–2003 (see also Chapter 4). A number of forces contributed to the initiation of a process that led first to the Seattle ministerial meeting of 1999 and later to the Doha ministerial meeting in 2001, the Cancún ministerial meeting of 2003 and the Hong Kong ministerial meeting of 2005. In Seattle, the presence of thousands of anti-globalization protestors added drama to the ministerial meeting, which failed to set an agenda for a new round of trade negotiations; the EU blamed the United States for the failure, and the United States blamed the EU. The Doha ministerial meeting agreed an agenda focused especially on the needs of developing countries and was hailed as an example of the international community working together in the aftermath of the 9/11 attacks. After two years of tortuous negotiations, in which both the EU's Common Agricultural Policy and US farm export subsidies came under sustained attack, the Cancún meeting failed to meet its deadline to agree detailed negotiation processes and targets. Two years later, the Hong Kong ministerial also failed to make significant progress, and again the intransigence of the EU and the United States was blamed, especially by the so-called G-20 of large developing exporters (which should be distinguished from the G-20 of the most powerful economies, set up in the throes of the post-2008 financial crisis). In all of these stages, the participation of the EU and the United States was seen as essential at the multilateral level; equally, in all of them there was a strong EU–US bilateral agenda in which the existence of 'competitive co-operation' was apparent (Allen and Smith 2002, 2003, 2004; Baldwin, Peterson, and Stokes 2003; M. Smith 2005b). In what ways can this be seen as contributing to 'global governance'?

Throughout the buildup to the various ministerial meetings, the EU and the United States were active in establishing their own negotiating positions, but also in attempting to have these accepted as the focus for the multilateral process. In areas such as agriculture and the broad 'development' agenda, the EU and the United States vied for influence and were also frequently engaged in intense bilateral exchanges. As the Cancún meeting approached, the EU and the United States produced on a bilateral basis a key document dealing with agriculture, which aroused intense suspicion among other members of the WTO and arguably contributed materially to the collapse of the Cancún meeting. But the Cancún debacle also revealed other aspects of the negotiation process: while the EU and the United States had been mutually absorbed in their bilateral context, the growth of the G-20 developing countries had led to the emergence of a powerful caucus dedicated to resisting any EU–US bilateral stitch-up. Pursuit of the agenda for the Doha Development Round thus involved structured negotiation occasions between the EU and both the United States and other WTO members, but also a host of less formal and structured encounters. Arguably, the focus on EU–US bilateral concerns and their projection onto the multilateral arena meant that important signals about changes in the negotiation context were ignored and the 'Cancún surprise' reflected this. It is a moot point as to whether global governance was enhanced or undermined by this example of EU–US 'bi-multilateralism'.

China and the WTO

A second and closely related case is provided by the negotiation of China's admission to the WTO, which was achieved formally at the beginning of 2002 (Allen and Smith 2001, 2002, 2003). For our purposes, the key feature of this process is that both the EU and the United States had a major stake in getting the Chinese into the multilateral trade regime, and that in accordance with the rules of the WTO the Chinese had to negotiate deals with all of the existing WTO members before they could enter. Both the EU and the United States were thus negotiating bilaterally with the Chinese, while the result would be a major change in the scope and membership of the multilateral trading regime. What emerged during the latter part of 2000 was a kind of 'negotiation race' in which the respective offers made by the Chinese to the EU and the United States generated a competitive dynamic in areas such as financial services, fed by the demands in both the EU and the United States of major interest groups – particularly those related to the financial services industry. In the terms proposed by this chapter, here there was a process underway that promised to extend and enhance global governance, but because of the rules and conventions built into the WTO, there was an incentive for major stakeholders to conclude advantageous bilateral deals – and to renegotiate them, indeed, if the opposition seemed to have stolen a march at any given stage. All of the parties at various stages could take advantage of linkage strategies, with uncertain consequences for the WTO regime in general. After the Chinese entered the WTO, they continued to exert this paradoxical influence on EU–US relations: both the EU and the United States experienced large and growing trade deficits with China, which led to appeals for protection from industries such as apparel, and which in turn led the EU both to impose unilateral quotas on the Chinese and to threaten complaints against China in the WTO (Allen and Smith 2006); but both the EU and the United States preferred to act bilaterally to negotiate with China in the shadow of WTO action, a tactic that appeared to bring some results in at least the short term. The United States also tried to get the Chinese to revalue their currency, and thus to reduce the price advantage held by their products, but with little immediate success.

Here, we can perceive the tensions built into global governance mechanisms when major members (in this case of the WTO) can see advantage in dealing bilaterally with others, or acting unilaterally against them. In this case, the EU and the United States initially preferred not to invoke the most punitive WTO measures against the Chinese; was this a victory for global governance or for bilateralism? Such a question has only increased in importance during the past two decades, with increasingly unilateral measures adopted by the United States both under the Obama administrations and most explicitly under the Trump administration (Larres 2018). By taking unilateral actions against China in what came to be labelled a trade war, the United States not only diverged from the processes enshrined in the WTO, but also put pressure on its international partners, among them the EU, to follow suit. When this was allied to US moves against the WTO in general (see Chapter 4), it could be argued that global governance in international trade issues had been effectively subverted by a combination of US policy and broader shifts in global geopolitics. This was not a comfortable position for the EU, which despite its increasing recourse to regional or bilateral free trade agreements (see Chapters 4 and 9) remained staunchly committed to the use of WTO or WTO-compliant methods for handling trade disputes.

Global environmental negotiations

A third case raising questions about the EU, the United States and global governance is provided by the EU–US tensions that emerged in the late 1990s and persisted into the new millennium, centred on the ratification and implementation of international environmental agreements. This tension was focused initially on the Kyoto Protocol (Allen and Smith 2000, 2001, 2002; Bodansky 2003; Bretherton and Vogler 2006), but continued through a series of attempted global agreements including the Paris Accords of December 2015 which have formed the context for subsequent negotiations. This process was discussed earlier in the context of 'soft-security' issues (see Chapter 7), and this dimension is relevant to its fate in global governance terms.

The Kyoto Protocol dealt with the emission of greenhouse gases and the consequent phenomenon of global warming, and it established a framework for dealing with successive reductions in emission of the damaging gases. The United States was initially supportive of the process, but at the end of the Clinton administration it reversed its position and refused to ratify the protocol – a major problem for its implementation, since the United States accounts for a larger proportion of emissions of greenhouse gases than any other country (though rising powers such as China, India and Brazil have transformed the overall global balance in the past two decades). Through the early years of the new millennium, there was a succession of EU–US bilateral efforts (mediated especially by the UK) to rescue at least part of the deal, with notably more commitment on the

EU side than on that of the George W. Bush administration after 2000. At the same time, the EU set out to establish what can only be described as an anti-US coalition in the context of continuing efforts to achieve multilateral ratification of the protocol – an effort which attracted the lasting hostility of the Bush administration but which also brought to prominence the role of other major players such as Russia (whose ratification was vital to the implementation of the protocol). For the EU, the position was complicated further by the need to negotiate emissions trading procedures within the Union itself, while at the same time trying both to deal with the United States on a bilateral level and with the rather unruly remainder of the Kyoto coalition in the multilateral arena (Vogler and Bretherton 2006).

This problem of positioning had clear roots in the 'bi-multilateral' nature of the negotiation process, in which the bilateral relations between the EU and the United States were related strongly to the progress of multilateral efforts to deal with climate change, and meant that particularly for the EU the problem of creating and maintaining a credible posture was especially difficult (M. Smith 2005b). Although the Protocol came into force in February 2005, following Russian ratification in November 2004, the United States then proceeded to sponsor alternative international efforts to try to arrive at more flexible targets – efforts that were eventually if reluctantly accepted by the EU, while the Union maintained its commitment to the more prescriptive Kyoto model.

Through a series of climate change negotiations between 2008 and 2015, this underlying, and increasingly explicit, tension between the EU and the US approaches to global cooperation assumed a central importance. The Union continued to argue for the maximum level of coordination, and for explicit and binding targets for the reduction of greenhouse gas emissions, while the United States, primarily under the Obama administration between 2009 and 2017, sought to moderate the extent of any commitments, and also to ensure that those commitments did not place the United States at what was seen to be a competitive disadvantage. The Copenhagen Conference of Parties (COP) in December 2009 was instructive in this respect: the EU attempted a bold and comprehensive plan, which aroused resistance among many of the negotiating parties, and then found itself outflanked by a US initiative which had the effect of diluting the potential agreements. After a series of conferences in which halting progress was made, matters came to a head at the Paris COP in December 2015, where the final agreements were both more binding than US administrations had traditionally wanted and less comprehensive than those pursued by the EU. In the final stages of the negotiations, it became apparent that the United States had assembled a coalition of countries that supported their version of the final agreements, and that the EU had effectively been marginalized. Thus, the United States had committed itself to more in the way of global governance on climate issues than had previously been expected, but had also by-passed full cooperation with the EU in favour of a broader-based coalition with countries such as China. This underlying tension persisted in climate change negotiations as far as the 2021 COP26 meetings in Glasgow, which again saw bilateral deals, for example between the United States and China (despite their other differences), in uneasy coexistence with multilateral commitments.

This seems to present a clear example of the ways in which competition – in this case between two models of the global governance of climate change – and convergence can and do coexist in EU–US relations, and also of the ways in which this feeds into attempts to manage the climate crisis. Again, the issue for global governance is whether the EU–US relationship has contributed materially to advances in the multilateral management of climate change issues. Perhaps significantly, the convergence of views that did take place in 2006 and 2007, and then under the Obama administrations, was reflected not specifically in EU–US actions, but in the different institutional contexts of the G-8 leading industrial countries (the United States, Canada, France, Germany, Italy, Japan, Russia (before its expulsion from the grouping after 2013) and the UK), the G-20 of leading economies (set up during the global economic and financial crisis of 2008 onwards) and an ad hoc coalition of industrial and emerging powers in the run-up to the Paris Conference in 2015.

The road to effective convergence between the EU and the United States on global governance issues can thus take several routes depending on the subject at issue and the institutional resources available. But it becomes a much more difficult prospect if one of the parties explicitly defects from attempts at international cooperation. This was the case under the Trump administration between 2017 and 2021. In line with its general rejection of multilateral solutions to global problems, the administration set its sights on the Paris Accords at an early stage, and in June 2017 formally announced its intention of withdrawing from them, thus precipitating a transatlantic crisis. This was a continuation of the 'America First' positions adopted in a number of other areas, and it led to a basic divergence between the EU and the United States on matters of climate change. The US withdrawal was set to become complete in December 2020, just after the presidential election of that year, and if completed it would have marked a major split between EU and US conceptions of global governance. As it happens, the defeat of Trump and the installation of the Biden administration created a new US commitment to global governance, but as already noted this was to be on terms set in Washington rather than negotiated in multilateral contexts.

Governing global energy

A further case study is provided by the pursuit of energy security and the governance of the global energy markets. The picture presented by this fourth case is rather different. On trade and commercial policy, the EU and the United States operate on relatively equal terms and have learned certain lessons of cooperation. On environmental issues, the EU seems to have been able to take an effective lead, although the United States remains crucial to the process – especially in the critical stages of negotiations as in Copenhagen, Paris or Glasgow, or when it attempts to undermine global cooperation as in the case of the Trump administration. When it comes to energy – and especially energy security – the mechanisms of global governance in general are far less well-developed, and there is still an atmosphere of 'every country for itself' in relation to crises of supply or price, further complicated by the presence of major multinational oil companies, some state-owned and some private. This is not to say that energy security is unimportant to the EU and the United States: in fact, since the year 2000 there has been constant attention by both to the issue in the light of major increases in price and accompanying concerns about the politics of supply (see Chapter 7). The EU has spent a lot of time and effort on trying to stabilize its energy supplies, with particular reference to relations with Russia and countries in the former Soviet Union, and has produced successive programmes for the promotion of energy security, including those seeking to promote an 'energy union' (Vogler 2023). At the same time, the United States became increasingly concerned in the first years of the new century about security of supply from the Middle East and the Persian Gulf, which for them is linked closely with other security preoccupations. More recently, and with major political effects, the 'fracking revolution' in the United States has created a new self-sufficiency in energy supplies, which the Trump administration in particular used to exert political pressure on the Europeans and others. Such pressure was also closely linked to the US posture on environmental issues: the Trump administration had promised to re-invigorate indigenous energy industries, including not only oil and gas but also coal, as part of its programme to 'make America great again'.

The result of these coexisting pressures and priorities was a classic confrontation between the EU approach, based on negotiation and the conclusion of supposedly binding supply agreements, and the American approach, based on domestic priorities and internationally at least partly on the use of coercion and if necessary force. While it is misleading to argue that the only motivation for US intervention in Iraq during 2003 was security of oil supplies, this was clearly a significant aspect of US policymaking. Another example is provided by the crises surrounding supply of gas from Russia via the Ukraine to EU member states, which came to peaks initially in 2007 and 2009; here, the solution was sought, primarily by the EU, in terms of monitoring arrangements and the search for binding supply and transit undertakings. At the same time, there were accusations from Moscow that the United States had intervened to bolster the Ukrainian position and in pursuit of a kind of 'containment' policy. Calls for a Transatlantic Energy Security Dialogue from the EU were initially met with silence from Washington.

These tensions over the management of Russian oil and (particularly) gas supplies were given a dramatic twist by the Ukraine crisis of 2013–14, when the imposition of sanctions by the EU and the United States in the wake of Russian annexation of Crimea and its installation of proxy regimes in parts of eastern Ukraine led to further threats by Moscow to limit gas supplies to EU member states. While this crisis did not immediately lead to open conflict between Russia and the 'west', the Russian invasion of February 2022 ratcheted up the tensions to the point at which such conflict was at least possible. The imposition of yet more sanctions by Brussels and Washington, and the provision of major aid to the Ukrainian military, led to Russian threats to cut off gas supplies to EU member states, several of which were heavily dependent on such supplies. While the United States and others were able to compensate in part for the shortfall, they could not immediately or fully do so; when this was allied to a major spike in prices for what gas was available, it created intense pressure on governments in the EU, and on the UK, which was the second-largest supplier of military assistance to Ukraine. The asymmetrical impact of the crisis created tensions both within the EU and across the Atlantic, but the nature of the Russian threat provided a major incentive for transatlantic solidarity, at least initially.

Human rights

The fifth case concerns an area in which global governance mechanisms and power and security considerations overlap: the protection of human rights in the 'war on terror' and subsequent conflicts. As noted in Chapter 7, the EU has positioned itself in general as a form of 'normative power' concerned to defend and promote a particular perspective on human rights and related issues. By doing so, it has aligned itself with a host of intergovernmental and non-governmental bodies, ranging from the United Nations to Amnesty International, which are concerned with the rights of individuals or groups and their defence against encroachments from 'national security' and other areas (K. Smith 2006a, 2006b,

2015; Kissack 2015). The European Security Strategy of 2003 and the Global Strategy of 2016 placed such considerations at the core of the EU's international objectives, and also linked them strongly with its commitment to multilateral solutions for international issues in general. This normative commitment has been seen as a core element of the EU's development as an international actor, and it is key to the evolving narrative of the EU's external action. As noted in Chapter 7, though, there is a problem for the EU in implementing such a commitment: there is no 'hard power' involving military force that can be called upon by the Union to enforce its decisions. There is, however, a wide range of sanctions short of force – economic, diplomatic, cultural – with which the Union can attempt to influence the actions of those it targets.

The United States, on the other hand, has historically seen human rights at least partly as an instrument of foreign policy, subject to the demands of national security; thus, they have tended to align themselves with regimes that promise stability but do not put human rights at the top of their list of priorities, while rhetorically endorsing a vision of international democracy (Halper and Clarke 2004: Chapter 1). These two approaches – one seeing human rights as an end in themselves, the other seeing them as part of the search for security – were brought out in a sharp form by the conduct of the 'war on terror' after the attacks of 11 September 2001, and they have persisted in one form or another at the core of EU–US relations from George W. Bush to Donald Trump. For the Bush administrations between 2001 and 2009, the central focus was on the pursuit of rogue regimes (the so-called 'axis of evil' constituted by Iraq, Iran and North Korea) and their associated clandestine operations conducted either directly or via cross-national terror organizations. For the Obama administrations between 2009 and 2017, the focus was on different forms of confrontation, often seen as the precursor to a reduction in the United States' entanglements in regional conflicts, such as those in Iraq or Afghanistan – often with new means, such as the use of drones, which raised their own issues of human rights and the conduct of conflicts. For the Trump administration after the 2016 elections, the process of withdrawal from entanglements was central to an 'America First' policy, but was also accompanied by a desire on the part of the president to establish close relationships with a number of authoritarian rulers – for example, Vladimir Putin in Russia, Recep Tayyip Erdogan in Turkey, Xi Jinping in China and Kim Jong-Un in North Korea. This created problems when those rulers showed themselves to be heedless of the demands of international human rights frameworks, for example in the cases of China, Turkey and Russia, and also inevitably created tensions with the EU when priorities and practices clashed.

Some examples will sharpen the focus here. One concerns the demand by the United States – most obviously during the height of the 'war on terror' – that terrorist suspects should be extradited from the EU to face charges that might imply a death sentence. The EU consistently resisted this demand, on the grounds that its member states had abolished the death penalty and that they could not extradite individuals to face even the possibility of execution. A second example concerned the holding of terrorist suspects by the United States at its base in Cuba, Guantanamo Bay. The US defined many of these as 'unlawful combatants' and thus not subject to the humanitarian provisions of the laws of war as set out in the Geneva Conventions. Once again, opinion in the EU was strongly opposed to this interpretation, although individual member states such as the UK found it more difficult to resist the US position. There was also a continuing tension between the EU and the United States over the process of 'extraordinary rendition', through which the CIA allegedly transported terrorist suspects to countries (including, again allegedly, some in the EU itself) where they faced severe interrogations leading to claims of torture. The EU, and especially the European Parliament, took a strong stand against such processes and in favour of the various investigations that took place into them (Allen and Smith 2006, 2007). Each of these cases shows the symptoms of 'bi-multilateral' governance processes, in which the EU and the United States are linked to broader processes of global governance and to the regimes and rules that characterize a globalizing world.

Beyond the 'war on terror', there have been consistent tensions between the EU and the United States over the use of new forms of warfare (for example, drones) and over the general issue of human rights in military interventions, on which the European Parliament has taken a strong stand. These have been balanced by US accusations that for the EU, commercial considerations tend to predominate over the protection of human rights where major markets are concerned: for example, the EU's stance on trade with China was presented, especially but not only by the Trump administration, as playing down Chinese violations of human rights in the case of the Uighur population of Xinjiang, or in the case of Hong Kong – although the United States, under the Trump administration in particular, was not immune from the temptation to let commercial objectives overrule a concern with human rights, for example in its dealings with Saudi Arabia and its reluctance to take punitive measures in the wake of the murder of Adnan Khashoggi, a US-based critic of the Saudi regime. A number of other rights-related disputes have emerged over the use of information and intelligence: in the period of the 'war on terror', there was constant US pressure for the EU to provide it with information about air passengers, while there have been continuing tensions about the security of electronic information. Most notably, during the later years of the Obama administrations, there was a major transatlantic crisis about the ways in which the United States had (over a period of many years) gathered intelligence about EU citizens and governments, by means including the hacking of government communications. A particularly sharp dispute arose between Germany and the United States over the penetration of secure communications, including the monitoring of Chancellor Angela Merkel's telephone and email systems. Many of these tensions were essentially bilateral, but as in other areas, the bilateral tensions and crises that emerged in EU–US relations have tended to raise the issues of global governance and the role of global norms.

The COVID-19 crisis

In early 2020, global governance issues were crystallized by an unprecedented crisis in the governance of global health and related questions: the COVID-19 or coronavirus pandemic. The initial outbreak of a novel disease in late 2019 occurred in China, but it rapidly spread to Europe and the United States, as well as other regions, enabled by the speed and intensity of international travel. In both the United States and the EU, the pandemic created a challenge to a fundamental requirement of good governance – that it should keep its people safe – but it also precipitated an economic crisis, as the resources of government and industries were stretched to the limit, and a crisis of political legitimacy, as the capacity of governments and other institutions across the world was tested. For the purposes of discussion here, the pandemic created – or rather accentuated – a crisis in transatlantic relations which threatened to dissolve the glue of the 'western alliance' and to underline the divergence between the commitments of the EU and the United States to the promotion of global governance.

The roots of the transatlantic – and by implication the global – COVID crisis were to be found at a very local level in China, but from an early stage they implicated the institutions of global health governance, specifically the World Health Organization (WHO), which has the responsibility to identify health problems of global concern. There has been much debate about how efficient and effective the WHO was at the outset of the pandemic, but it was also clear from an early stage that there was the potential for clashes between the interests and demands of national governments, whose capacity to fight the pandemic varied greatly according to levels of economic development, scientific sophistication and governmental resources. These variations made themselves felt in the EU, creating major difficulties in arriving at common responses to a novel threat, but EU member states were able to agree during 2020–1 on some far-reaching proposals to raise resources and respond in joint ways, to such an extent that some commentators talked in terms of a 'rebirth' of the EU (Alcaro and Tocci 2021). This set of EU responses was linked also to a willingness to share supplies of the potential vaccines with less developed regions, although this was another focus of intense debate in the Brussels institutions and among member states.

The response from the Trump administration in Washington was markedly different, leading some to talk of an intensified transatlantic crisis within the broader global context (Arvanitopoulos 2020). As is evident from the earlier cases, tensions between the EU and the Trump administration were well-recognized before COVID struck, but the US response was a further escalation of the president's 'America First' strategy. After initially refusing to recognize the Covid threat, Trump then initiated a series of measures that, while not aimed only at the EU, had an instant impact upon it and on its member states. These included a travel ban, attempts to ban the export of vital medical supplies such as face-masks and further attempts to pre-empt production of vaccines in favour of the United States. Since many aspects of medical industries are effectively globalized, such attempts promised fundamentally to disrupt relations between US and EU partners, such as those involved in producing the innovative Pfizer/BioNTech vaccine both in the EU and in the United States. Not only this, but the Trump administration defined the COVID crisis in terms of its ongoing confrontation with China, creating further tensions around not only US but also EU contacts with Beijing (including, in the case of the EU, their negotiations for a bilateral investment treaty with China) (Scazzieri 2020).

The implications of these tensions for global health governance were profound. The efforts of the WHO to create global awareness of the COVID threat were hampered by US policies in particular, while its efforts to investigate the origins and spread of the pandemic were constrained by the politicization of relations between the 'west' and Beijing as well as by the Chinese government's inevitable resistance to external intervention. The distribution of vaccines and other resources to countries in Africa and Latin America was slowed, and partly as a result, new variants of the COVID virus were able to develop and then spread, both globally and to Europe and North America. Global governance in issues of public health was not destroyed by these problems, but its effectiveness and its legitimacy were severely restricted, not only in the short term but also arguably for the medium and long terms. While the EU made significant contributions to the distribution of medical resources such as vaccines on a global basis, the policies of the Trump administration did not treat this as a priority. The Biden administration elected in 2020 was far more inclined to multilateral solutions, but the legacy of 'Trumpism' would linger in this area of global governance; the question was, did it reflect a permanent shift in the foundations for the US approach to such issues?

The balance sheet of EU–US relations in terms of global governance, on the basis of these examples, is decidedly mixed. It is not a case of 'EU good, US bad' (on the grounds that the EU presents itself as being in favour of increased global governance and indeed a model for it, while the United States resists it and preaches national self-sufficiency). Rather, it seems to be the case that the EU and the United States have fundamentally mixed attitudes towards the establishment and the extension of global governance mechanisms, and that this reflects mixed views on particular areas of competition or convergence. Such complex and mixed views can lead and have led to a number of confrontations and crises, in which the differing EU and US attitudes to global institutions, norms and negotiations have become apparent. It is not possible to arrive at a simple overall judgement, but the aim of the cases presented here has been to show the ways in which the roles of the EU and the United States in global governance might be explored and evaluated.

Overview and conclusion

This chapter has focused on the ways in which EU and US views of global governance can be explored and evaluated, and on the ways in which they can be observed in action within EU–US relations. A key aid to understanding these issues is an awareness of processes of change, both within the EU and the United States and in the broader global context within which they conduct their relations. This is not a new theme in this book – indeed, it is one of the core themes that run through the whole of our analysis. Here, it has a global scale and a connection with key aspects of the approaches to the world on both sides of the Atlantic. The chapter has argued as follows:

- First, the change from the Cold War world to the post-Cold-War world created new challenges and opportunities for both the EU and the United States, and their responses to these challenges and opportunities reflect a combination of pragmatic, institutional and cultural understandings about the way the world works and the way it should look.
- Second, and more specifically, the chapter has explored the evolution of the EU's approach to issues of multilateralism and global governance. While there are variations both between issue areas and between the EU and

member states, it is clear that the centre of gravity in EU external action lies in a positive promotion of multilateral solutions and a commitment to global institutions, norms and negotiations.

- Third, the United States, on the other hand, can be seen as a 'selective multilateralist', with attitudes rooted in its approach to sovereignty and its reluctance to accept global commitments. These attitudes relate closely to the issues of power and security explored in Chapter 7, and they form a constant set of foundations for US foreign policy despite variations between administrations. They lie at the centre of US challenges to global institutions, norms and negotiations, and were displayed most dramatically by the Trump administration after 2017.
- Thus, in matters of global governance there is considerable evidence of a different balance between the EU and the United States, giving the EU a form of comparative advantage in institution and regime-building, but both the EU and the United States are essential components of global governance mechanisms. There is also evidence of the impact of competition and convergence between the EU and the United States, and significant evidence that each of them subscribes to global governance in ways that are modified by their own interests and internal politics. Transatlantic crises involving the EU and the United States, often connected to global challenges, have embodied these different understandings of the priority to be given to multilateralism and global governance mechanisms, and there is no sign that this tendency is decreasing.

The discussion in this chapter reveals that the EU and the United States have differences over global governance and broader world order at three levels. In the first place, they have pragmatic and practical differences about the post-Cold-War world, in economic, security and defence issues, which arise out of their mutual interactions and which in principle are susceptible to management through a process of negotiation and problem-solving. Many of the economic issues that arise between the two partners are of this kind, but so also are a number of security issues which reflect the broader conception of security that has grown in the post-Cold-War era. Often these disputes arise within a framework of shared understandings and expectations and can be very effectively managed. But there are other differences that emerge out of a kind of competition between the EU and the United States to 'sell' or establish their models of economic and political organization to potential converts in the post-Cold-War context. Into this category fall a number of 'big-picture' trade and development issues, as well as some questions to do with human rights and the management of international conflicts. The processes of interaction here are those of hard bargaining and the exercise of muscle, rather than negotiation and problem-solving. The final type of difference is much less amenable to either problem-solving or bargaining since it depends upon fundamental differences of culture and assumptions about the nature of power, sovereignty and international order itself. We can expect that in future these three strands will continue to characterize the respective EU and US approaches to world order.

Chapter 11

Competition, convergence and crisis

The Euro-American system in a turbulent world

Introduction

This concluding chapter has its starting point in two linked views of European Union (EU)–United States (US) relations. The first view rests on the historical development of the relationship between European integration and the United States, charting a number of key themes and points of major change (see Chapter 1; see also for example Winand 1993; Lundestad 2005: 201; Patel and Weisbrode 2013; Sloan 2016; Larres 2022). The second addresses the notion of the 'Euro-American system' – a structured set of relations involving not only the European integration process and the United States but also the networks, institutions and processes of policymaking in the transatlantic area, of which EU–US relations have been a growing if not now dominant part (as outlined in Chapter 2; see also for example Pollack and Shaffer 2001; Peterson and Pollack 2003; Steffenson 2005; Alcaro, Peterson, and Greco 2016; Smith and Steffenson 2023). The Euro-American system and EU–US relations must be viewed in the context of broader processes of global change and transformation, to which EU–US relations contribute at the same time as they are affected by them. How much of what was established in the 1950s and 1960s is still recognizable in EU–US relations, how much has been changed, and how much has the relationship been transformed into something fundamentally different from what it was at its origins? The purpose of this chapter is to explore these key questions, and to identify a number of key current trends that may point towards different futures for the Euro-American system. The underlying argument in the chapter is that new patterns of competition and convergence characterize EU–US relations in the 2020s, and that these are intimately linked to patterns of change and crisis at three levels: domestic order, European order and world order (for related arguments, see M. Smith 2023a and 2023b).

The European–American relationship has been central to international relations and international political economy for most of the last century. The relationship is a network of dense and well-developed relationships among a myriad of actors – politicians, officials, military bodies, regulators, corporations, international institutions and, increasingly, non-governmental organizations. Relations among these actors have been underpinned by shared assumptions about the importance of democracy as the best means of allocating political power, and of the market as the optimal means of allocating economic resources. They have also historically been founded on shared perceptions of the key security challenges and of the nature of a desirable European and world order. Europe and America have disagreed about the wisdom of particular foreign policy decisions – and about the extent to which the free market should govern all aspects of economic life – but the basic ideational consensus has proven to be remarkably durable. As EU–US relations have developed and deepened, they have come to comprise the key component of transatlantic relations in general, and to subsume a growing proportion of the key interactions between the many groupings involved in the Euro-American system. They have also engaged with 'domestic' politics in both the EU and the United States, and with the broader development of diplomatic patterns and partnerships in the global arena (as discussed in Chapters 3 and 9).

The global impact of the EU–US relationship cannot be exaggerated. For most of the post-1945 period, it has been central to the global economy (Smith and Steffenson 2023). The United States in the immediate period after the Second World War accounted for half of the global economy, and even now the United States remains the world's largest national economy by a considerable distance. The EU, taken as a single economic entity, is one of the world's two largest traders, exporting goods and services across the globe; its affluent and open market, like America's, is a magnet for investment. Both actors have a substantial role in the management of the global economy. Some functions, like that of the US dollar as the *de facto* global currency, are obvious but others are not. Throughout the world, Euro-American standards and regulations are the benchmark against which other national and regional systems are measured. The World Trade Organization (WTO) owes much of its structure, processes and substance to successive generations of American and European diplomats, who worked hard to overcome domestic opposition to trade liberalization, motivated by the belief that economic nationalism rarely ends well. The effect is subtle, but important, because it forces other states to play the game according to a set of rules created by others – specifically, the EU and the United States. Thus, when China is accused of breaching international agreements on intellectual property, those agreements are deeply informed by European and American understandings of the desirability of intellectual property protection and of the importance of enforceable contracts. A signal feature of the international political economy has been the extent to which shared understandings of how economic life should be conducted owe everything to Europe and America. It is hegemony in its clearest, yet most subtle form, extending beyond the WTO into the international monetary institutions and into the management of a vast range of international transactions and communications (see for example Foot, MacFarlane, and Mastanduno 2003; Ryner and Cafruny 2017).

In the realm of international relations more broadly conceived, the Euro-American system has been central as well. The components of this system are states, intergovernmental institutions and an increasing array of private actors, such as firms and a variety of groups from civil society, constituting overlapping systems at the intergovernmental, transgovernmental and transnational levels (see Chapter 2; see also for example Pollack and Shaffer 2001; Steffenson 2005; Alcaro, Peterson, and Greco 2016). Thus, the intergovernmental aspects of transatlantic relations, carried on by a growing range of states since the end of the Cold War, have a clear impact not only on those states directly involved but also on the broader balance of power in the world arena. Not only this, but the EU has come to perform a range of economic and diplomatic roles not unlike those of many states (operating alongside and coordinating while not replacing its member states in crucial areas) (Genschel and Jachtenfuchs 2014). Both the EU and the United States use international organizations as an instrument of state power, though the United States has a more durable scepticism about this route and the EU has to work in coordination with its member states in crucial areas such as monetary, development, environmental and security policy. While many EU leaders proclaim the primacy and the desirability of multilateral action through international institutions, many American politicians and commentators are vocal critics of the United Nations and prefer to use multilateral organizations only as a last resort. Both the EU and the United States have used unilateral and multilateral mechanisms to advance the rule of law internationally – an often overlooked achievement. The United States, more so than the EU, is prepared to use force to attain its goals, but this should be placed into a broader historical context and understanding of the roles played by both the EU and the United States more generally. Thus, for example, criticism of Donald Trump's conduct of foreign policy has focused to a considerable extent on its departure from American norms, while the notion of the EU as a 'civilian power' guided by multilateralism is in tension with some of the policies adopted by key member states, not to mention some of the challenges faced in Europe and elsewhere (M. Smith 2018, 2021).

Despite the enduring influence of intergovernmentalism and 'state power' in EU–US relations, international organizations exert influence themselves. The international trading system works – albeit imperfectly – according to rules manifest in WTO agreements, backed up by a disputes process. As with any regime, international organizations work to structure actor expectations and inculcate norms of behaviour. Though they remain, ultimately, vulnerable to state indifference or hostility, they are not empty vessels for preferences of the powerful. Most importantly, the picture is one that emphasizes the persistence of different layers of interaction between and within international institutions. The EU itself is an object lesson in this respect: as noted by many commentators, the EU presents a hybrid organization, with aspects of supranational authority and collective action existing alongside intergovernmental coordination and sometimes conflict to present a picture of complex multi-level political and economic activity (see Chapters 2 and 3: see also M. Smith 2012).

It is important to note the central role of private actors in the Euro-American system. In several spheres of economic activity, private organizations provide critical expertise that informs debate and influences policy. For example the EU's adoption of international accounting standards during the late 1990s relied heavily on private sector efforts to develop internationally agreed rules, and the search for solutions in the area of cyber-security during the 21st century has engaged a wide range of public and private bodies, while responses to the COVID-19 pandemic during 2020 and 2021 especially demonstrated the powerful and sometimes unpredictable interactions between the EU, the United States, national governments within the EU and a range of scientific actors on both sides of the Atlantic (see Chapter 10). American trade policy is deeply influenced – some say dangerously so – by lobbyists from both organized labour and corporate interests – but then, so is trade policy in the EU. Indeed, many influential US lobby groups are prominent in Brussels as they target EU legislation and policy initiatives (see for example Coen, Katsaitis, and Vannoni, 2021). In similar fashion, the international community of monetary and financial experts has strong bases both in the EU and in the United States, and dominates thinking about the structure and the restructuring of the international financial system. Even in the areas of 'high politics' encapsulated by activities in international security and related policy domains, the transatlantic influence of communities of experts and private industry has come to be a significant factor in the generation of transatlantic policy initiatives.

We can thus discern a system founded on multiple levels of activity, demonstrating the presence of markets, hierarchies and networks, and revolving around a form of multi-level politics in 'high', 'low' and 'sectoral' policy arenas, as outlined in Chapter 2. A variety of policy domains demonstrate the varying patterns that these political and economic processes take, and the ways they intersect with each other to create new challenges and opportunities both for the EU and for the United States. One feature that has become very apparent is that quite apart from the interactions between the EU and the United States, it is important to take into account the domestic politics of policymaking and political and economic change: on both sides of the Atlantic, the influence of powerful forces is evident, whether it is the member states and a variety of transnational forces in the EU or the Congress and other parts of the federal system in the United States (see Chapter 3 especially, but also many other chapters). Another feature that has become salient is the coexistence of competition – sometimes threatening open conflict – and convergence between the EU and the United States.

Competition and convergence

One conceptualization of the post-1945 world was the gradual convergence of the global economy and society towards an American model of free-market economics and democratic government. This view enjoyed particular prominence in the wake of 9/11 among neo-conservative US commentators (Krauthammer 2002). But we adopt a different view, based on the evidence in this book. Convergence does occur in the EU–US relationship, but it is not necessarily towards an American ideal, and this convergence can only be understood fully in terms of its relationship with broader challenges posed by change in the wider global arena. The terms competition and convergence suggest polar opposites, but the reality of politics in the Euro-American system is that issues can feature complex *blends* of competition and convergence. Moreover, issues evolve and competition or convergence can arise as one or both – or many – actors alter their policy preferences in reaction to changing circumstances. Despite their shared preferences on many issues, the EU and the United States have thus disagreed, and continue to offer up alternative solutions across a range of issue areas. These disagreements reflect deeply held differences informed by history and society, often sharpened by the evolution of the broader world arena. They can in principle be managed through a number of processes: transatlantic governance, balancing – 'hard' or 'soft' – and crisis management, but it is clear again that these cannot be fully understood unless they are related to the broader context of change, challenge and crisis in the global arena (see Chapter 2: see also Alcaro, Peterson, and Greco 2016).

Competition between the two actors is seen most clearly in the economic realm, where despite a shared preference for the market economy, alternative visions of the extent and operations of that market persist – given added point by the ways in which European integration has shifted the balance of economic power in the direction of the EU since the late 1960s. Europe remains much more attached to a social market conception of capitalism, with relatively higher taxation and a larger role for the state. Extensive state intervention in health care, for example, is a signal feature of most European states, even the UK (and this despite the UK's departure from the EU through the process of 'Brexit') (as noted in Chapter 3 and elsewhere). Yet even here EU–US convergence on some issues can be seen. Across policy areas, developments push both actors towards not so much a common solution but more a consensus about the general way to tackle the issue. In competition policy, for instance, European practice became more American-like in the early 21st century, thanks partly to the controversial performance of the Merger Task Force in the 1990s (McGuire and Smith 2008: Chapter 5; see also Damro 2004, 2006). In financial services regulation, Europe appeared to be setting the pace, for a more complex set of reasons to do with the Lisbon Agenda and the unintended consequences of American legislation, while more recently the issue of data privacy created new tensions and adaptations (Fahey and Terpan 2021). In respect of innovation, the development of transnational industrial structures and processes of exchange within industries had made the structure of competition and convergence complex and thus regulation more challenging; the notion of 'national' or 'European' champions is misleading in the era of the global corporation, and this has led to new processes of 'competitive cooperation' involving both state and EU authorities and private entities (McGuire and Smith 2008: Chapter 6; see also Chapter 7 in this volume).

Processes of competition and convergence are also discernible in the broader world arena, where the search for order and for structure entails not only economic and commercial relations but also those of diplomacy and of security policy. As in more purely 'economic' transactions, here we find competition not only at the level of day-to-day activity but also at the level of models and values. The competition between the EU and the United States for 'presence' in major regions such as Asia, Latin America and Africa is often informed by the idea that Brussels and Washington are in a competition for global advantage, based in their contrasting attitudes towards economic organization, political order and the pursuit of values such as security or development (as discussed in Chapter 9:

see also Sbragia 2010). Yet this interregional competition and its accompanying 'partnership diplomacy' also gives evidence of a common set of EU and US interests centring on stability, market economics and democratic politics. This coexistence of competition and convergence is equally discernible in the pursuit of European and world order, but here there is a key set of differences to be taken into account. Within Europe, the EU has been able to bring to bear a preponderance of structural power based on its economic, institutional and legal order (Keukeleire and Delreux 2022: chapter 10; see also Weber, Smith, and Baun 2007). This holds true even in countries that openly challenge the EU's order like Hungary, although the need to deal with these internal challenges has had effects on the EU's internal balancing processes (Keleman 2020). The mere fact that many of the EU's neighbouring countries wish to become part of it has given the Union a substantial set of resources and has given the 'EU model' an advantage. This advantage, though, remains largely 'civilian', based on 'soft power', and it dissipates the closer events move towards the use of coercion or 'hard power', as we shall see later. The pursuit of world order encapsulates this problem for the EU. The Union's capacity to threaten or to reward declines rapidly as it moves away from the European neighbourhood, while the US preponderance in military power and the instruments of coercion becomes more substantial (Smith 2004: see also Chapters 8–9). This does not always mean that the core preferences or priorities of the EU and the United States diverge, but it does mean that the chosen instruments for pursuit of those preferences and priorities can be markedly different. It might be supposed that this is a fundamental structural difference between the EU and the United States, in which the United States is dominant and the Union essentially dependent, but there is some evidence that the 'hardening' of EU security policies during the early years of the new millennium has changed the terms of EU–US engagement. This, though, is only the beginning of what might be a very long story.

What does this mean for the mechanisms of management noted earlier: transatlantic governance, balancing and crisis management? As with the presence of competition and convergence themselves, it is clear that the mechanisms of management coexist more or less comfortably, and that they are deployed in situations where policy requires a complex blend of qualities. Thus, in the area of political economy, there is considerable evidence of transatlantic governance in action, but it is also clear that this often takes place at the global level, through bodies such as the WTO or other international regimes. Governance itself in areas of political economy can often be accompanied by considerable evidence of balancing through the exploitation of international 'institutional opportunities' such as those presented by negotiations on the global environment or energy security, and there is also evidence of the need for crisis management in a rapidly changing global political economy. When the story turns to diplomacy and security, we would expect to find more evidence of balancing and crisis management, and this is borne out both by the historical and by the more recent record; often, the occasions for crisis emerge from outside the Euro-American system and create a demand for imaginative responses in situations where the use of 'hard power' is a possibility. The incidence of crisis is dramatic and threatening, both in general and to EU–US understandings of their respective roles, but it must be placed into the context of the broader balancing between the EU and US 'models' in the longer term, and of the persistence of governance mechanisms even where the competition and conflict seems at its height.

EU–US relations in a new age of crisis

It is possible to trace the competition and convergence theme through various issue areas: trade, finance, investment and competition, security, European order and global governance. A key element that emerges from these areas is the extent to which the EU and the United States have both been challenged by globalization – ironically, a process of which they have been the major originators – and reactions against globalization in the 21st century (see Riddervold and Newsome 2018; Schade 2023). The international system is moving towards a multipolar structure, where the Euro-American system, while still prominent, is no longer so powerful that it can develop and implement policies irrespective of the wishes of other actors. The globalization of economic activity owes much to Europe and America; their belief in rules to structure markets is manifest in the myriad of international organizations that work to facilitate trade and exchange. Yet other states, particularly China, have learned to play the globalization game well, and the liberalization of markets became an increasing source of controversy in Europe and America during the early 21st century, as workers were squeezed while corporate profits soared (Reich, 2020). This trend was hugely underlined by the global financial crisis starting in 2008, which accentuated the ongoing power shift in the global political economy; while the EU and the United States recovered more or less painfully and more or less completely, the rise of China and other 'emerging powers' contributed to a major shift in the challenges and opportunities faced on both sides of the Atlantic (Renard and Biscop 2012; *International Affairs* 2013). This shift generated competing policy responses – ranging from the declaration of trade wars to a search for new rules and institutions – from the EU and the United States which continued to cause friction into the 2020s. Here again, the COVID-19 pandemic brought to the fore not only tensions at the global level, centring on the role of China, but also transatlantic tensions over the control of intellectual property, the imposition of travel controls and other aspects of public health governance.

At the same time, the globalization of security concerns has posed new challenges and creates new opportunities for the EU and the United States as they move further into the 'post-post-Cold-War period'. While in the early 21st century these challenges and opportunities were focused on the Persian Gulf and Southwest Asia, there has since been a series of regional and other related crises that have contributed to the sense of an 'omni-crisis' surrounding both the EU and the United States. There are two major theatres of this crisis in the realm of security: first, the Middle East and North Africa, following the 'Arab Spring' of 2011 and after and encompassing vicious conflicts in Libya and Syria and between Israel and Palestinians, most recently in 2023–4, and second, the EU's 'eastern neighbourhood', beginning with the crisis over Georgia in 2008 and continuing with intervention, crisis and eventually full-scale war in Ukraine. Both of these theatres have been crucial tests of the EU's belief that in some way, civilian and institutional power could be mustered to generate stability and reform; at the same time, they have tested the US commitment to continued engagement in matters of global security, and its willingness to invest resources in the management of regional conflicts with global ramifications. Another such theatre of crisis – currently more potential than actual – is the South China Sea, where competing claims and the assertiveness of China have created a potentially toxic brew of military presence and economic tensions, and where the link to possible Chinese military intervention in Taiwan has been highlighted by the Russian invasion of Ukraine. These developments are bound to engage both the EU and the United States, but on very different terms and in very different degrees, given the US position as a Pacific power and the limitations of EU engagement outside the realm of political economy.

Towards the future in a turbulent world

European–American relations in the first quarter of the 21st century present us with something of a paradox. On the one hand, the dominance of the Atlantic area is eroding – across a number of issue areas. The world of the 21st century is moving rapidly towards a multipolar system, where Europe and America play leading roles but arguably are no longer dominant (Alcaro, Peterson, and Greco 2016). This is most apparent in the global political economy, where the centrality of the EU–US relationship can no longer be taken for granted in a wide range of issue areas. In terms of global security, the Iraq conflict signalled – as did the

Vietnam War in the 1970s – that the United States was not guaranteed to dominate, because of the increasing prominence of 'asymmetrical' conflicts where formal military firepower is not the only determinant of outcomes. Such a judgement was further borne out by the vicissitudes of American engagement with the Middle East and Afghanistan under the Obama and Trump administrations. The impact of Iraq on the EU's collective view of its 'security future' raised key issues about the EU's role as a 'partial superpower', issues which have been underlined in the subsequent two decades by the interaction between the EU's incremental development of security and defence policies and the occurrence of violent conflict in the eastern neighbourhood, culminating in the Ukraine war (M. Smith 2023a). For the United States itself, recent experience in the Middle East and in Afghanistan has repercussions throughout the world, not least with America's traditional allies asking themselves about the solidity of American commitment. America now shares global commercial and financial power with Europe, yet it is in Asia that the largest trade surpluses and foreign exchange reserves now lie. China in particular, despite the vicissitudes of COVID, has demonstrated an ability to integrate into the world economy and begin to shape its future much more quickly and successfully than many had anticipated, with India not far behind.

Yet it is significant, as noted earlier, that in the global political economy both China and India are still playing a game whose rules were 'written' by the European–American relationship. The structure of the global economy, from its liberalized capital flows to its increasing constitutionalization in the form of the WTO, owes everything to Euro-American diplomacy, business and conceptions of how world affairs ought to be conducted. Even patterns of business–government interactions in forums like ASEAN are imitations of consultative practices that have been hallmarks of Euro-American relations for years. In sum, Europe and America remain central to the global political economy, though not always in ways that are appreciated. In the global diplomatic system, the EU and the United States are still near to the core of world events, and their diplomatic dealings with each other are still influential. In terms of global security, we can see that the United States remains more central than the EU, if only on the basis of its 'hard-power' credentials, but its position is challenged by new or sometimes resurgent powers, not all of them states. One of the effects of the Russian invasion of Ukraine has been to demonstrate how deep and wide the resources of the United States in defence and security still are, and the ways in which they continue to shape the development of the EU's foreign and security policies (Streeck 2022). At the same time, the continuing and deepening tensions between the United States and China promise a wider set of geopolitical and geo-economic confrontations.

A theme raised throughout this chapter (and in Chapters 7 and 10) has been the relative willingness of the EU to adopt multilateral approaches to international relations in both security and economic spheres. For some observers in the early 21st century, the evolution of a multipolar world was likely to suit Europe much more than America, for the latter was seen as a unilateralist first, using international organizations or coalitions only as a last resort (M. Smith 2018). These arguments were given added force by the ways in which US foreign policy under the Trump administration focused on transactional and unilateral diplomacy rather than multilateralism (M. Smith 2021). Such views are not so much wrong as lacking in nuance. For many developing states, the EU is not a paragon of 'give-and-take' multilateralism; it is a bully that uses its market dominance to gain policy preferences, just like the United States. The EU's fondness for regulation and standards, though highly successful in some spheres, is deeply opposed by some states, who despair at the demands this would place on their governments and societies. Though the EU's internal market is large and affluent, on most measures of productivity, innovation and wealth, it still trails the United States. The United States has indeed been highly unilateralist in recent years, even under the Obama administration, but this period may draw to a close. The Biden administration's espousal of a 'new multilateralism', especially among liberal democracies, emphasized the need for reciprocity, but this was still framed by assumptions of US leadership (Olsen 2022). Yet the world's most sophisticated armed forces backed by the world's largest military budget were unable to quell unrest in Iraq and Afghanistan, with consequent impacts on the credibility of US commitments in the global context. At the same time, the American public, no less than the European, has seemed completely unwilling to contemplate the kind of protracted conflict, demanding a combination of military resources with diplomacy and economic or social interventions, that might defeat persistent insurgents or adversaries. In this context, the Russian invasion of Ukraine constitutes an acid test, since as of the time of writing, it seems likely to give rise to a protracted and costly entanglement on the borders of the EU itself, with a major commitment by both the United States and NATO. All of this might change radically if Donald Trump were to be re-elected as President in November 2024 – potentially demonstrating once again the intimate link between US domestic politics and the future of transatlantic relations.

Overview and conclusion: What kind of Euro-American system?

It is possible to see EU–US relations in four overlapping ways: as a system based on power and security, on US dominance and the rise of the EU as a challenger to it, on interdependence and integration and on institutions and cooperation. From the discussion earlier, it can be seen that each of these elements is present in the current Euro-American system. Rather than separate systems, they represent four coexisting tendencies within one complex system of relations, responding both to change within the EU and the United States and to change within the broader world arena. This coexistence of qualities and tendencies is what helps us to understand the functioning of the system, and to evaluate the impact of change in any of its components or in its broader environment. The key point of this approach is to advance a set of analytical questions with which we can penetrate the complexities of the system and its significance for the world arena. It is possible, though, to arrive at five broad conclusions from this discussion:

- First, there is evidence to support the argument that the Euro-American system is one in which economic, political and security issues occur at a number of intersecting levels, and in which both the EU and the United States are effectively part of each other's policymaking processes. State policies and 'state functions' remain important if not central, but they are surrounded by a constellation of other actors and factors.
- Second, the system does show the presence and the interaction of markets, hierarchies and networks, and policymakers are at their most effective when they recognize the varying configurations these elements can take. Many areas demonstrate these interactions and configurations, but the key word is 'varying'; we have provided evidence for at least some of the ways in which this variation occurs, and for some of its consequences both for the EU and the United States and for the rest of the world.
- Third, the system has generated an increasingly dense set of institutions, many of which have become dominated by the EU–US relationship as the EU has expanded to become in some ways synonymous with the broader European order. Increasingly, the key transatlantic institutions and practices are those generated around the EU and the United States, with other organizations such as NATO and the OSCE occupying reduced roles. But here again, there are variations, especially between the political economy of EU–US relations and the diplomatic or security dimensions of the relationship; and the Russian invasion of Ukraine has arguably changed the balance again, with as yet uncertain implications.
- Fourth, the system has been crucially impacted by change: change within the EU and the United States, and change within the broader world arena.

Many of the areas we have explored in this chapter show the significant impact of processes such as globalization or the ending of the Cold War. More specifically, they suggest that the world around the Euro-American system is changing in ways that present major challenges as well as major opportunities for policymakers, and that are likely to impact on the mutual EU and US understandings of the changes taking place. Uncertainties and tensions in both EU and US policies in the 2020s bear witness to this assessment.

- Fifth, the system is not one of 'either/or'. It is not one that can be turned on or off by policymakers either in the EU or in the United States. Its extended history, its institutional density, the shared experiences of transatlantic elites and the sheer self-interest embodied in the world's closest economic and security relationship mean that it is robust and resilient. But it is not immortal. It is not impossible to conceive of circumstances in which the boundaries of the system are exceeded, and in which the conventions of crisis management that have grown up over 70 or more years might be discarded. In this case, we would be talking not of 'competition and convergence' but of 'confrontation and conflict'.

In addition to these general conclusions, a major analytical and policymaking question arises from our argument: given the shocks administered since the beginning of the 21st century, how might the Euro-American system and its key participants be re-shaped for the longer-term future? Throughout the chapter, we have emphasized the interplay between continuity, change and crisis both within the Euro-American system and around it, in the broader European and world orders. There is a temptation – not resisted by all commentators – to argue that a combination of COVID-19, environmental and energy crises and the return of violent geopolitics has completely overturned what previously had evolved over a period of decades – in a fashion not dissimilar to that established in the early post-Cold-War years. Our argument is more nuanced: that it is important to retain a sense of the interplay between continuity and change not only in thinking about the past and present of EU–US relations, but also in approaches to the future of the Euro-American system.

In this context, it is important to explore the relevance of a number of scenarios, and here we suggest three. A first scenario would (perhaps optimistically) emphasize the robustness of the Euro-American system derived from its internal pluralism and the continuing resilience of the liberal international order. In this context, the roles of the EU and the United States as repositories of multilateralist thinking and practice would re-emerge from a period of upheaval, leading to a re-invigoration of global governance and of a global negotiated order. But that scenario would be directly contradicted by a second: the creation of a new bipolarity between status quo and revisionist powers (that is, between the EU and the United States and certain other countries, and the resurgent and expansionist forces led by Russia and China). This scenario would imply a restructuring of the Euro-American system to reflect the US dominance in 'hard-power' domains and the EU's dependence; some would argue that this process is already well under way in the early 2020s, and that it is not restricted simply to the domain of 'hard power' given the impact of the US Inflation Reduction Act and other measures of economic nationalism. A variation on this essentially geopolitical and geo-economic perspective would place the emphasis on the growth of 'European sovereignty' and the EU's strategic autonomy, and thus on a kind of differentiated partnership between the EU and the United States within a broadly bipolar world order. Finally, a third scenario would reflect a deeply pessimistic view of the Euro-American system, in which the fragmentation of authority both at the international and at the domestic level leads to forms of isolation and/or paralysis, and in which opportunistic alliances or alignments might lead to a form of international anarchy familiar to students of the 1930s. In that dystopian scenario, all bets would be off both for the Euro-American system and for its principal participants.

Ultimately, there is no answer to the question of future Euro-American order, although elements of each of the three scenarios explored earlier are likely to feature in what emerges from the crisis of the 2020s. This chapter, and the book as a whole, has attempted to sharpen appreciation of what lies behind the EU–US relationship, how it relates to the institutions and policy processes of both the EU and the United States and how the Euro-American system relates to the broader world arena. We have aimed to show the complexity of the relationship, the variations that occur within it and the ways in which the relationship is managed through good times and bad. Analytically, it is our conviction that an appreciation of different perspectives on the relationship, and their links to different narratives of its development and future course, is the best way in which to construct a rich view of what matters in EU–US relations. But the result is a series of more sharply defined and well-illustrated questions, not a single answer to the question 'what kind of Euro-American system?'

References

Abelson, D. and S. Brooks, eds (2022), *Transatlantic Relations: Challenge and Resilience*, London: Routledge.

Acemoglu, D., D. Autor, D. Dorn, Gordon H. Hanson and B. Price (2016), 'Import Competition and the Great US Employment Sag of the 2000s', *Journal of Labor Economics*, 34(1): S141–98.

Aggarwal, V. and E. Fogarty, eds (2004), *EU Trade Strategies. Between Regionalism and Globalism,* New York: Palgrave Macmillan.

Ahearne, A. and B. Eichengreen (2007), 'Europe's External Monetary and Financial Relations Since the Euro: A Review and a Proposal', Paper presented at *the Conference, Bruegel Project on Europe and the Global Economy*, 12–13 October 2006. Available online: http://www.nuigalway.ie/staff/alan_ahearne/documents/ahearne_eichengreen.pdf (accessed 15 June 2007).

Albert, M. (1992), *Capitalisme contre capitalisme,* Paris: Seuil.

Albright, M. (1998), 'Statement to the North Atlantic Council, Brussels', 8 December 1998. Available online: http://secretary.state,gov/www/statements/1998/981208.html (accessed 20 July 2007).

Alcaro, R., J. Peterson and E. Greco, eds (2016), *The West and the Global Power Shift: Transatlantic Relations and Global Governance,* Basingstoke: Palgrave Macmillan.

Alcaro, R. and N. Tocci (2021), 'Navigating a Covid World: The European Union's Internal Rebirth and External Quest', *The International Spectator*, 56(2): 1–18.

Alecu de Flers, N. and E. Regelsberger (2005), 'The EU and Inter-Regional Cooperation', in C. Hill and M. Smith (eds), *International Relations and the European Union*, 317–42, Oxford: Oxford University Press.

Aliboni, R. (2005), 'The Geopolitical Implications of the European Neighbourhood Policy', *European Foreign Affairs Review*,10(1): 1–16.

Allen, D. (1997),'EPC/CFSP, the Soviet Union and the Former Soviet Republics: Do the Twelve have a Coherent Policy?', in E. Regelsberger, P. de Schoutheete de Tervarent and W. Wessels (eds), *Foreign Policy of the European Union: From EPC to CFSP and Beyond*, 219–37, Boulder: Rienner.

Allen, D. (1998), 'Who Speaks for Europe? The Search for an Effective and Coherent External Policy', in J. Peterson and H. Sjurse (eds), *A Common Foreign Policy for Europe? Competing Visions of the CFSP*, 41–58, London: Routledge.

Allen, D. and A. Pijpers, eds (1984), *European Foreign Policies and the Arab-Israeli Dispute*, The Hague: Nijhoff.

Allen, D. and M. Smith (1982), 'Europe, the United States and the Middle East: A Case Study in Comparative Policy-making', *Journal of Common Market Studies*, 22(2): 125–46.

Allen, D. and M. Smith (1989), 'Western Europe in the Atlantic System of the 1980s: Towards a New Identity?', in S. Gill (ed.), *Atlantic Relations: Beyond the Reagan Era*, Brighton: Harvester Wheatsheaf.

Allen, D. and M. Smith (1991–2), 'The European Union in the New Europe: Bearing the Burden of Change', *International Journal*, 47(1): 1–28.

Allen, D. and M. Smith (2000), 'External Policy Developments', in G. Edwards and G. Wiessala (eds), *The European Union: Annual Review of Activities, 1999/2000*, 101–20, Oxford: Blackwell.

Allen, D. and M. Smith (2001), 'External Policy Developments', in G. Edwards and G. Wiessala (eds), *The European Union: Annual Review of Activities, 2000/2001,* 97–115, Oxford: Blackwell.

Allen, D. and M. Smith (2002), 'External Policy Developments', in G. Edwards and G. Wiessala (eds), *The European Union: Annual Review of Activities, 2001/2002,* 97–116, Oxford: Blackwell.

Allen, D. and M. Smith (2003), 'External Policy Developments', in L. Miles (ed.), *The European Union: Annual Review of Activities, 2002/2003,* 97–114, Oxford: Blackwell.

Allen, D. and M. Smith (2004), 'External Policy Developments', in L. Miles (ed.), *The European Union: Annual Review of Activities, 2003/2004*, 95–112, Oxford: Blackwell.

Allen, D. and M. Smith (2005), 'External Policy Developments', in L. Miles (ed.), *The European Union: Annual Review 2004/2005*, 109–26, Oxford: Blackewell.

Allen, D. and M. Smith (2006), 'Relations with the Rest of the World', in U. Sedelmeier and A. Young (eds), *The European Union Annual Review 2005*, 155–70, Oxford: Blackwell.

Allen, D. and M. Smith (2007), 'Relations with the Rest of the World', in U. Sedelmeier and A. Young (eds), *The European Union Annual Review 2006*, 163–82, Oxford: Blackwell.

Allen, D. and W. Wallace (1977), 'European Political Cooperation: Procedure As a Substitute for Policy?', in H. Wallace, W. Wallace and C. Webb (eds), *Policy-Making in the European Communities*, Chichester: Wiley.

Allenbach-Ammann, J. (2023), 'EU State Aid: The Good and the Bad of Opening the Floodgate', *Euractiv*, 13 March. Available online: https://www.euractiv.com/section/economy-jobs/news/eu-state-aid-the-good-and-the-bad-of-opening-the-floodgates/ (accessed 3 October 2023).

Allgeier, P. F. (2005), 'Implementation of the Dominican Republic-Central America Free Trade Agreement (DR-CAFTA)', U.S. Government Printing Office. Available online: https://www.govinfo.gov/content/pkg/CHRG-109hhrg23918/html/CHRG-109hhrg23918.htm (accessed 9 October 2023).

Alter, K. J. (2008), 'The European Court and Legal Integration: An Exceptional Story or Harbinger of the Future?', in Keith E. Whittington, R. Daniel Kelemen and Gregory A.

Caldeira (eds), *The Oxford Handbook of Law and Politics*, 209–28, Oxford: Oxford University Press.

Alting von Geusau, F. (1993), *Beyond Containment and Division: Western Cooperation from a Post-Totalitarian Perspective*, The Hague: Nijhoff.

Ames, P. (2015), 'ISDS: The Most Toxic Acronym in Europe', *Politico*, 17 September. Available online: https://www.politico.eu/article/isds-the-most-toxic-acronym-in-europe/ (accessed 13 October 2023).

Andrews, D., ed. (2005), *The Atlantic Alliance Under Stress: US–European Relations after Iraq*, Cambridge: Cambridge University Press.

Aoyama, R. (2016), '"One Belt, One Road": China's New Global Strategy', *Journal of Contemporary East Asia Studies*, 5(2): 3–22.

Arslanalp, S., B. Eichengreen and C. Simpson-Bell (2022), 'The Stealth Erosion of Dollar Dominance: Active Diversifiers and the Rise of Nontraditional Reserve Currencies', *International Monetary Fund Working Paper WP/22/58*, March. Available online: file:///C:/Users/trg12/Downloads/wpiea2022058-print-pdf.pdf (accessed 10 October 2023).

Arvanitopoulos, C. (2020), 'Transatlantic Relations after the COVID-19 Pandemic', Wilfried Martens Centre for European Studies *European View*, 19(2): 164–71.

Ashbaugh, H. (2001), 'Non-US Firms' Accounting Standard Choices', *Journal of Accounting and Public Policy*, 20(2): 129–53.

Asmus, R. (1997), 'Double Enlargement: Redefining the Atlantic Partnership After the Cold War', in D. Gompert and S. Larrabee (eds), *America and Europe: A Partnership for a New Era*, 19–50, Cambridge: Cambridge University Press.

Aydin, U. and K. Thomas (2012), 'EU Competition Policy in the 21st Century', Special Issue of *Journal of European Integration*, 34(6): 531–681.

Aydin-Düzgit, S. and N. Tocci (2015), *Turkey and the European Union*, Basingstoke: Palgrave Macmillan.

Baert, F., T. Scaramagli and F. Söderbaum, eds (2014), *Intersecting Interregionalism: Regions, Global Governance and the EU*, Dordrecht: Springer.

Baily, M. N. and J. K. Kirkegaard (2004), *Transforming the European Economy*, Washington: Institute for International Economics.

Baldwin, M., J. Peterson and B. Stokes (2003), 'Trade and Economic Relations', in J. Peterson and M. Pollack (eds), *Europe, America, Bush: Transatlantic Relations in the Twenty-First Century* , 29–46, London: Routledge.

Barnett, M. and M. Duvall, eds (2005), *Power in Global Governance*, Cambridge: Cambridge University Press.

Basedow, R. (2020), 'The EU's International Investment Policy Ten Years On: The Policy-Making Implications of Unintended Competence Transfers', *Journal of Common Market Studies*, 59(3): 643–60.

Batt, J., D. Lynch, A. Missiroli, M. Ortega and D. Triantaphyllou (2003), *Partners and Neighbours: A CFSP for a Wider Europe*, Chaillot Paper 64, Paris: EU Institute for Security Studies.

Bauer, Michael W. and Jarle Trondal, eds (2015), *The Palgrave Handbook of the European Administrative System*, Houndmills, Basingstoke: Palgrave Macmillan. .

Bauerle Danzman, S. (2022), 'Is the US Going to Screen Outbound Investment', *Atlantic Council*, 10 January. Available online: https://www.atlanticcouncil.org/blogs/econographics/is-the-us-going-to-screen-outbound-investment/ (accessed 29 September 2023).

Baun, M. (2000), *A Wider Europe*, Lanham: Rowman & Littlefield.

Baylis, K., S. Peplow, G. Ruasser and L. Simon (2008), 'Agri-environmental Policies in the EU and United States: A Comparison', *Ecological Economics*, 65(4): 753–64.

BBC. (2016), 'Trump would "Cancel" Paris Climate Deal'. Available online: https://www.bbc.com/news/election-us-2016-36401174 (accessed 23 June 2021).

BBC. (2018), 'Donald Trump: European Union is a Foe on Trade', 15 July. Available online: https://www.bbc.com/news/world-us-canada-44837311 (accessed 9 October 2023).

BBC. (2020), 'A Quick Guide to the US-China Trade War', 16 January. Available online: https://www.bbc.com/news/business-45899310 (accessed 9 October 2023).

BBC. (2021), 'Boeing-Airbus Trade Row Set to End after 17 Years', 15 June. Available online: https://www.bbc.co.uk/news/business-57484209 (accessed 9 October 2023).

Begg, I. (2009), 'Regulation and Supervision of Financial Intermediaries in the EU: The Aftermath of the Financial Crisis', *Journal of Common Market Studies*, 47(5): 1107–28.

Beloff, M. (1976), *The United States and the Unity of Europe*, Westport: Greenwood.

Berger, A., A. F. Cooper and S. Grimm (2019), 'A Decade of G20 Summitry: Assessing the Benefits, Limitations and Future of Global Club Governance in Turbulent Times', *South African Journal of International Affairs*, 26(4): 493–504.

Bergsten, F. (1998), 'Competition Policy and the World Economy', speech to the *World Economic Forum*, Davos, Switzerland, 30 January. Available online: https://www.piie.com/commentary/speeches-papers/competition-policy-and-world-economy (accessed 2 October 2023).

Bernasconi-Osterwalder, N. (2018), 'USMCA Curbs How much Investors can Sue Countries – Sort of', *International Institute for Sustainable Development*. 2 October. Available online: https://www.iisd.org/articles/usmca-investors (accessed 2 October 2023).

Bernhard, L. and H. Kriesi (2021), 'Populism in Election Times: a Comparative Analysis of 11 Countries in Western Europe', M. Caiani and P. Graziano (eds), *Varieties of Populism in Europe in Times of Crises*, 48–68, Abingdon: Routledge.

Bertoldi, B., C. Giachino, S. Bernard and V. Prudenza (2015), 'Fiat-Chrysler Deal: Looking for a Good Return from M & A', *Journal of Business Strategy*, 36(4): 23–33.

Bhattacharjea, A. (2006), 'The Case for a Multilateral Agreement on Competition Policy: A Developing Country Perspective', *Journal of International Economic Law*, 9(2): 293–324.

Biscop, S. (2019), *European Strategy in the 21st Century: New Future for Old Power*, London: Routledge.

Bistline, J., N. Mehrote and C. Wolfram (2023), 'Economic Implications of the Climate Provisions of the Inflation Reduction Act', in *NBER Working Paper* 31267. Cambridge, MA: National Bureau of Economic Research.

Blais, André and Peter John Loewen (2009), 'The French Electoral System and its Effects', *West European Politics*, 32(2): 345–59.

Blockmans, S. (2020), *Why the EU needs a Geopolitical Commission*, Brussels: Centre for European Policy Studies, 15 September. Available online: https://www.ceps.eu/why-the-eu-needs-a-geopolitical-commission/ (accessed 4 December 2020).

Bodansky, D. (2003), 'Transatlantic Environmental Relations', in J. Peterson and M. Pollack (eds), *Europe, America, Bush: Transatlantic Relations in the Twenty-First Century*, 59–68, London: Routledge.

Boeing. (2023), 'Commercial Market Outlook'. Available online: https://www.boeing.com/commercial/market/commercial-market-outlook/ (accessed 9 October 2023).

Bora, B. (2004), 'Investment Issues in the WTO', in B. Hocking and S. McGuire (eds), *Trade Politics*, 2nd edn, London: Routledge.

Bouchard, C., J. Peterson and N. Tocci, eds (2014), *Multilateralism in the 21st Century: Europe's Quest for Effectiveness*, London and New York: Routledge.

Bradsher, K. (2023), 'How China's Property Crisis is Testing its "too-big-to-fail" Banks', *New York Times*, 30 September. Available online: https://www.nytimes.com/2023/09/30/business/china-evergrande-banks-property.html (accessed 29 January 2024).

Bremmer, I. (2009), 'State Capitalism Comes of Age: The End of the Free Market?', *Foreign Affairs*, 88(3): 40–55.

Bretherton, C. and J. Vogler (2006), *The European Union as a Global Actor*, London: Routledge.

Brooks, E. and R. Geyer (2020), 'The Development of EU Health Policy and the Covid-19 Pandemic: Trends and Implications', *Journal of European Integration,* 42(8): 1057–76.

Brown, C. P. (2020), 'Trump's Trade Policy is Hampering the US Fight against COVID-19', *Peterson Institute for International Economics*, 13 March. Available online: https://www.piie.com/blogs/trade-and-investment-policy-watch/trumps-trade-policy-hampering-us-fight-against-covid-19

Brown, C. P. and M. Kolb (2020), 'Trump's Trade War Timeline: An Up-to-Date Guide', *Peterson Institute for International Economics*, 13 March. Available online: https://www.piie.com/blogs/trade-investment-policy-watch/trump-trade-war-china-date-guide (accessed 9 October 2023).

Brown, S. (2018), *Power, Perception and Foreign Policymaking: US and EU Responses to the Rise of China,* London: Routledge.

Bugaski, J. and I. Teleki, eds (2007), *Atlantic Bridges: America's New European Allies*, Lanham: Rowman & Littlefield.

Bulmer, S. and L. Quaglia (2018), 'The Politics and Economics of Brexit', *Journal of European Public Policy*, 25(8): 1089–98.

Busch, M. and E. Reinhardt (2006), 'Three's a Crowd: Third Parties and WTO Settlement', *World Politics*, 58(4): 446–77.

Buzan, B. and T. Diez (1999), 'The European Union and Turkey', *Survival*, 41(1): 41–57.

Cafruny, A. and M. Ryner, eds (2003), *A Ruined Fortress? Neoliberal Hegemony and Transformation in Europe*, Lanham: Rowman & Littlefield.

Calingaert, M. (1996), *European Integration Revisited: Progress, Prospects and US Interests*, Washington, DC: Brookings Institution Press.

Calleo, D. (1970), *The Atlantic Fantasy: The US, NATO and Europe*, Baltimore: Johns Hopkins University Press.

Calleo, D. (1981), *The Imperious Economy*, Cambridge, MA: Harvard University Press.

Calleo, D. and B. Rowland (1973), *America and the World Political Economy: Atlantic Dreams and National Realities*, Bloomington: Indiana State University Press.

Cameron, F. (2007), *An Introduction to European Foreign Policy*, London: Routledge.

Camps, M. (1960), 'Britain, the Six and American Policy', *Foreign Affairs*, 39(1): 112–22.

Camps, M. (1967), *European Unification in the Sixties: From the Veto to the Crisis*, Oxford: Oxford University Press for the Royal Institute of International Affairs.

Capling, A. (2004), 'The Politics of Intellectual Property', in B. Hocking and S. McGuire (eds), *Trade Politics*, 2nd edn, 179–93, London: Routledge.

Capling, A. and K. M. Nossal (2006), 'Blowback: Investor-State Dispute Mechanisms in International Trade Agreements', *Governance*, 19(2): 157–72.

Carbone, M., ed. (2013), *The European Union in Africa: Incoherent Policies, Asymmetrical Partnership, Declining Relevance?* Manchester: Manchester University Press.

Carbone, M. (2023), 'The European Union and International Development: Evolving Tensions and Contested Transformations', in C. Hill, M. Smith and S. Vanhoonacker (eds), *International Relations and the European Union*, 4th edn, 236–58, Oxford: Oxford University Press.

Chase, J. and E. Ravenal, eds (1976), *Atlantis Lost: The United States and Europe after the Cold War*, New York: New York University Press for the Council on Foreign Relations.

Chee, F. Y. (2023), 'Microsoft Offers to Charge for Teams to Address EU Antitrust Concerns', *Reuters*, 5 May. Available online: https://www.reuters.com/technology/microsoft-offers-charge-teams-address-eu-antitrust-concerns-sources-say-2023-05-04/ (accessed 3 October 2023).

Chernow, R. (2004), *Alexander Hamilton*, New York: Penguin.

Chien, Y. and P. Morris (2017), 'Is U.S. Manufacturing Really Declining?' *Federal Reserve Bank of St. Louis*, 11 April. Available online: https://www.stlouisfed.org/on-the-economy/2017/april/us-manufacturing-really-declining (accessed 9 October 2023).

Chin, G.T. (2016), 'Asian Infrastructure Investment Bank: Governance Innovation and Prospects', *Global Governance*, 22: 11–26.

Cini, M. and L. McGowan (2009), *Competition Policy in the European Union*, 2nd edn, Basingstoke: Palgrave Macmillan.

Cleveland, H. (1966), *The Atlantic Idea and its European* Rivals, New York: McGraw-Hill for the Council on Foreign Relations.

CNN. (2016), *Trump on Brexit: America is Next.* https://edition.cnn.com/2016/06/24/politics/us-election-brexit-donald-trump-hillary-clinton/index.html (accessed 23 June 2021).

Coen, D., A. Katsaikis and M. Vannoni (2021), *Business Lobbying in the European Union,* Oxford: Oxford University Press.

Cohen, S. D., R. A. Blecker and P. D. Whitney (2003), *Fundamentals of U.S. Foreign Trade Policy: Economics, Politics, Laws, and Issues,* Boulder: Westview Press.

Congressional Research Service (CRS). (2020), 'USMCA: Investment Provisions', 8 January. Available online: https://crsreports.congress.gov/product/pdf/IF/IF11167 (accessed 3 October 2023).

Congressional Research Service (CRS). (2023), 'Russia's War Against Ukraine: European Union Responses and U.S.-EU Relations', Updated 15 May 2023. Available online: https://crsreports.congress.gov/product/pdf/IN/IN11897

Contiguglia, C. (2018), 'Trump: EU is One of United States' Biggest Foes', *Politico*, July 15th.

Conrad, J. (2022), 'The US and EU are Teaming Up to Contain Big Tech', *Wired*, 22 September. Available online: https://www.wired.com/story/the-us-and-eu-are-teaming-up-to-contain-big-tech/ (accessed 3 October 2023).

Cooper, R. (1968), *The Economics of Interdependence: Economic Policy in The Atlantic Community*, New York: McGraw-Hill for the Council on Foreign Relations.

Cooper, R. (2000), *The Postmodern State and the World Order*, London: Demos.

Copeland, P. and D. Papadimitriou (2012), *The EU's Lisbon Strategy: Evaluating Success, Understanding Failure*, London: Palgrave Macmillan.

Cornish, P. and G. Edwards (2001), 'Beyond the NATO/EU Dichotomy: The Beginnings of a European Strategic Culture', *International Affairs*, 77(3): 587–605.

Council of the European Union. (2003), *A Secure Europe in a Better World: European Security Strategy*, Brussels, 12 December.

Council of the European Union. (2019), 'Council Decision Authorising the Opening of Negotiations with the United States of America for an Agreement on the Elimination of Tariffs for Industrial Goods, 6052/19', 9 April. Available online: https://www.consilium.europa.eu/media/39180/st06052-en19.pdf (accessed 9 October 2023).

Council on Foreign Relations (CFR). (2022), *US Gun Policy: Global Comparisons.* https://www.cfr.org/backgrounder/us-gun-policy-global-comparisons (accessed 9 September 2022).

Cowles, M. G. (1996), 'The EU Committee of AmCham: The Powerful Voice of American Firms in Brussels', *Journal of European Public Policy*, 3(3): 339–58.

Cowles, M. G. (2001a), 'Private Firms and US-EU Policy-Making: The Transatlantic Business Dialogue', in E. Philippart and P. Winand (eds), *Ever-Closer Partnership: Policy-Making in US-EU Relations*, 229–66, Brussels: PI.E.-Peter Lang.

Cowles, M. G. (2001b), 'The Transatlantic Business Dialogue: Transforming The New Transatlantic Dialogue', in M. Pollack and G. Shaffer (eds), *Transatlantic Governance in the Global Economy*, 213–35, Lanham: Rowman & Littlefield.

Cox, M. (2003), 'Commentary: Martians and Venutians in the New World Order', *International Affairs*, 79(3): 523–32.

Cox, M. (2018), 'The Economic Rise of a Superpower: From Washington to Trump', in M. Cox and D. Stokes (eds), *US Foreign Policy*, 3rd edn, 56–75, Oxford: Oxford University Press.

Cox, M. and D. Stokes, eds (2018), *US Foreign Policy*, 3rd edn, Oxford: Oxford University Press.

Crawford, B. (1996), 'Explaining Defection from International Cooperation: Germany's Unilateral Recognition of Croatia', *World Politics*, 48(4): 482–521.

Crawford, N. (2023), 'The Energy Transition, Protectionism, and Transatlantic Relations', *Survival,* 65(2): 75–102.

Cromwell, W. (1969), *Political Problems of Atlantic Partnership: National Perspectives*, Bruges: College of Europe.

Crowe, B. (2003), 'A Common European Foreign Policy After Iraq?', *International Affairs*, 79(3): 533–46.

Curry, J. and F. Lee (2019), 'Non-Party Government: Bipartisan Lawmaking and Party Power in Congress', *Perspectives on Politics*, 17(1): 47–65.

Curry, J. and F. Lee (2020), *The Limits of Party: Congress and Lawmaking in a Polarized Era*, Chicago: University of Chicago Press.

Cushman, C. (2006), *An Introduction to the U.S. Congress*, London and New York: Taylor and Francis.

Czempiel, E.-O. and D. Rustow, eds (1976), *The Euro-American System*, Frankfurt: Campus.

Daalder, I. and J. Lindsay (2003), *America Unbound: The Bush Revolution in Foreign* Policy, Washington, DC: Brookings Institution Press.

Damro, C. (2001), 'Building an International Identity: The EU and Extraterritorial Competition Policy', *Journal of European Public Policy*, 8(2): 208–26.

Damro, C. (2004), 'Multilateral Competition Policy and Transatlantic Compromise', *European Foreign Affairs Review*, 9(2): 269–87.

Damro, C. (2006), 'The New Trade Politics and EU Competition Policy: Shopping for Convergence and Cooperation', *Journal of European Public Policy*, 13(6): 867–86.

Damro, C. (2012), 'Market Power Europe', *Journal of European Public Policy,* 19(5): 682–99.

Damro, C. and T. Guay (2012), 'Transatlantic Merger Relations: The Pursuit of Cooperation and Convergence', *Journal of European Integration*, 34(6): 643–61.

Damro, C. and T. R. Guay (2016), *European Competition Policy and Globalization*, Basingstoke: Palgrave.

Dannreuther, D., ed. (2003), *European Union Foreign and Security Policy: Towards a Neighbourhood Strategy*, London: Routledge.

Dannreuther, R. and J. Peterson, eds (2006), *Security Strategy and Transatlantic Relations*, London: Routledge.

De Bièvre, D. (2006), 'The EU Regulatory Trade Agenda and the Quest for WTO Enforcement', *Journal of European Public Policy*, 13(6): 851–66.

de Wilde, P. (2019), 'Media Logic and Grand Theories of European Integration', *Journal of European Public Policy*, 26(8): 1193–212.

Den Boer, M. and J. Monar (2002), '11 September and the Challenge of Global Terrorism to the EU as a Security Actor', in G. Edwards and G. Wiessala (eds), *The European Union: Annual Review of the EU 2001/2002*, Oxford: Blackwell.

DePorte, A. (1986), *Europe between the Superpowers: The Enduring Balance*, 2nd edn, New Haven: Yale University Press.

Deudney, D. and J. Meier (2018), 'American Exceptionalism', in M. Cox and D. Stokes (eds), *US Foreign Policy*, 3rd edn, 22–38, Oxford: Oxford University Press.

Deutsche Welle. (2017), 'Donald Trump and Jean-Claude Juncker Talk Trade Tariffs', 25 July 2017. Available online: https://www.dw.com/en/donald-trump-and-jean-claude-juncker-talk-trade-tariffs/a-44825737 (accessed 23 June 2021).

De Ville, F. and G. Siles-Brugge (2016), *TTIP: The Truth about the Transatlantic Trade and Investment Partnership.* Cambridge: Polity.

Devuyst, Y. (2001), 'Transatlantic Competition Relations', in M. Pollack and G. Shaffer (eds), *Transatlantic Governance in the Global Economy*, 127–52, Oxford: Rowman & Littlefield.

Diebold, W. (1959), *The Schuman Plan*, New York: Praeger.

Diebold, W. (1960), 'The Changed Economic Position of Western Europe: Some Implications for US Policy and International Organizations', *International Organization*,14(1): 1–19.

Diebold, W. (1972), *The United States and the Industrial World: American Foreign Economic Policy in the 1970s*, New York: Praeger for the Council on Foreign Relations.

Ding, Y., O. C. Hope, T. Jeanjean and H. Stolowy (2007), 'Differences Between Domestic Accounting Standards and IAS: Measurement, Determinants and Implications', *Journal of Accounting and Public Policy*, 26(1): 1–38.

Doctor, M. (2007), 'Why Bother with Inter-Regionalism? Negotiations for an EU-Mercosur Agreement', *Journal of Common Market Studies*, 45(2): 281–314.

Dominguez, R. (2021), 'The EU and Mexico: The Strategic Partnership in the Context of the Global Agreement', in L. Ferreira-Pereira, and M. Smith (eds), *The European Union's Strategic Partnerships: Global Diplomacy in a Contested World*, 269–88, Basingstoke: Palgrave Macmillan.

Drahos, P. (2007), 'Weaving Webs of Influence: The United States, Free Trade Agreements and Dispute Resolution', *Journal of World Trade*, 41(1): 191–207.

Duke, S. (2017), *Europe as a Stronger Global Actor; Challenges and Strategic Responses*, Basingstoke: Palgrave Macmillan.

Economist. (2023), 'Can the West Win Over the Rest of the World?', 16 May. Available online: https://www.economist.com/asia/2023/05/16/can-the-west-win-over-the-rest-of-the-world (accessed 10 December 2023).

Edwards, G. and E. Regelsberger, eds (1990), *Europe's Global Links: The European Community and Inter-Regional Cooperation*, London: Pinter.

Egan, M. and T. R. Guay (2023), 'Investment Screening, National Security, and Economic Development: Exploring Responses to Chinese Investment in Federal Political Systems', Paper presented at *The Politics and Regulation of Investment Screening Mechanisms Workshop*, Princeton University, Princeton.

Eichengreen, B. and R. Ghironi (1998), 'European Monetary Integration and International Monetary Cooperation', in B. Eichengreen (ed.), *Transatlantic Economic Relations in the Post-Cold War Era*, New York: Council on Foreign Relations.

Elgström, O. and M. Smith (2000), 'Introduction: Negotiation and Policy-Making in the European Union – Processes, System and Order', *Journal of European Public Policy,* 7(5): 673–83.

Eliasson, J., O. Costa and P. Garcia-Duran (2023), 'Is the EU's Trade Policy Aligning with America's Trade Policy?' *Journal of World Trade*, 57(2): 231–52.

Eliasson, J. and P. Garcia-Duran (2019), 'The Campaign Against the Transatlantic Trade and Investment Partnership', in J. Eliasson and P. Garcia-Duran (eds), *Civil Society, Rhetoric of Resistance, and Transatlantic Trade*, 51–79, Springer, New York: Palgrave Macmillan.

Ellwood, D. (1992), *Rebuilding Europe: Western Europe, America and Postwar Reconstruction*, London: Longman.

Erlanger, S. (2019a), 'Europe Holds Summit with China, more Skeptically this Time', *New York Times*, 10 April. Available online: https://www.nytimes.com/2019/04/09/world/europe/eu-china-summit.html (accessed 29 September 2023).

Erlanger, S. (2019b), 'Nuclear Deal Traps E.U. between Iran and U.S.', *New York Times,* 8 May. Available at https://www.nytimes.com/2019/05/08/world/europe/eu-iran-nuclear-sanctions.html (accessed 18 November 2019).

European Commission. (1994), *Towards a New Asia Strategy*, Communication from the Commission to the Council.

European Commission. (2004), *A Proactive Competition Policy for a Competitive Europe*, Communication from the Commission, 20 April, COM(2004) 293 final (accessed 15 August 2006).

European Commission. (2005), *Review of the Framework for Relations Between the European Union and the United States: An Independent Study*, report of an academic team led by Professor John Peterson, Brussels, 18 April.

European Commission. (2006), *External and intra-European Trade: Statistical Yearbook*. Available online: http://aei.pitt.edu/67458/1/1958%2D2005.pdf (accessed 1 November 2023).

European Commission. (2007), 'European Competition Policy in a Changing World and Globalised Economy: Fundamentals, New Objectives and Challenges Ahead', Speech by Commissioner Neelie Kroes at the GCLC/College of Europe conference, '50 Years of EC Competition Law', Brussels, 5 June.

European Commission. (2012), 'European Commission 2012: Infringements: Frequently Asked Questions'. Available online: https://ec.europa.eu/commission/presscorner/detail/en/MEMO_12_12 (accessed 15 June 2020).

European Commission. (2016), 'EU Negotiating Texts in TTIP', 14 July. Available online: https://policy.trade.ec.europa.eu/eu-trade-relationships-country-and-region/countries-and-regions/united-states/eu-negotiating-texts-ttip_en (accessed 9 October 2023).

European Commission. (2019), '2018 Commission Report on Monitoring the Application of EU Law'. Available online: https://ec.europa.eu/info/publications/2018-national-factsheets-monitoring-application-eu-law_en

European Commission. (2020a), 'Coronavirus: Commission Proposes to Activate Fiscal Framework's General Escape Clause to Respond to Pandemic', *Press Release*, 20 March. Available online: https://ec.europa.eu/commission/presscorner/detail/en/ip_20_499 (accessed 11 October 2023).

European Commission. (2020b), 'EU Foreign Investment Screening Mechanism Becomes Fully Operational', *Press Release*, 9 October. Available online: https://ec.europa.eu/commission/presscorner/detail/en/ip_20_1867 (accessed 29 September 2023).

European Commission. (2021a), 'The EU as a Borrower – Investor Relations'. Available online: https://commission.europa.eu/strategy-and-policy/eu-budget/eu-borrower-investor-relations_en (accessed 23 June 2021).

European Commission. (2021b), '2021-2027: Initial Cohesion Policy EU Budget Allocations'. Available online: https://cohesiondata.ec.europa.eu/stories/s/2021-2027-EU-allocations-available-for-programming/2w8s-ci3y/ (accessed 10 October 2023).

European Commission. (2023a). 'Overview of Top Trading Partners', 10 July. Available online: https://circabc.europa.eu/ui/group/50a0487d-086a-4a75-a1ff-92bdd2ec2c4b/library/09539941-7d09-4e97-84ae-a5cd21f53283/details (accessed 1 November 2023)

European Commission. (2023b), 'Statistics on Merger Cases'. Available online: https://competition-policy.ec.europa.eu/mergers/statistics_en (accessed 30 September 2023).

European Council. (2003), *A Secure Europe in a Better World: European Security Strategy*, Brussels. https://www.consilium.europa.eu/en/documents-publications/publications/european-security-strategy-secure-europe-better-world/ (26 April 2020).

European Council. (2022), 'COVID-19: The EU's Response to the Economic Fallout', 22 December. Available online: https://www.consilium.europa.eu/en/policies/coronavirus/covid-19-economy/ (accessed 15 December 2023).

European External Action Service. (2015), *The European Union in a Changing Global Environment: A more Connected, Contested and Complex World*. Brussels: EEAS.

European Union. (2016), *Shared Vision, Common Action: A Stronger Europe. A Global Strategy for the EU's Common Foreign and Security Policy,* Brussels: June.

European Union. (2022), *A Strategic Compass for Security and Defence: For a European Union that Protects its Citizens, Values and Interests and Contributes to International Peace and Security*, Brussels, 22 March.

Evenett, S., A. Lehmann and B. Steil (2000), 'Antitrust Policy in an Evolving Global Marketplace', in S. Evenett, A. Lehmann and B. Steil (eds), *Antitrust Goes Global*, 1–28, Washington and London: Brookings and RIIA.

Everts, S. (2004), *Engaging Iran: A Test Case for European Union Foreign Policy,* London: Centre for European Reform.

Fabbrini, S. (2005), *Democracy and Federalism in the European Union and the United States. Exploring Post-National Governance*, London: Routledge.

Fahey, E. and D. Curtin, eds (2014), *A Transatlantic Community of Law: Legal Perspectives on the Relationship between the EU and US Legal Orders*, Cambridge: Cambridge University Press.

Fahey, E. and F. Terpan (2021), 'Torn Between Institutionalisation & Judicialisation: The Demise of the EU-US Privacy Shield', *Indiana Journal of Global Legal Studies*, 28(2): 205–44. Available online: https://www.muse.jhu.edu/article/803960

Faini, R. and R. Portes, eds (1995), *European Union Trade with Eastern Europe: Adjustment and Opportunities,* London: Centre for Economic Policy Research.

Farrell, H. and A. Newman (2021), 'The New Age of Protectionism', *Foreign Affairs*, 5 April. Available online (with subscription): https://www.foreignaffairs.com/articles/europe/2021-04-05/new-age-protectionism

Faust, J. (2004), 'Blueprint for an Inter-Regional Future? The European Union and the Southern Cone', in V. Aggarwal and E. Fogarty (eds), *EU Trade Strategies: Between Regionalism and Globalism*, 41–63, Basingstoke: Palgrave Macmillan.

Featherstone, K. and R. Ginsberg (1996), *The United States and the European Union in the 1990s: Partners in Transition,* London: Macmillan.

Feinberg, R. (2003), 'The Political Economy of the United States' Free Trade Agreements', *World Economy*, 26(7): 1019–40.

Ferreira-Pereira, L. and M. Smith, eds (2021), *The European Union's Strategic Partnerships: Global Diplomacy in a Contested World*, Basingstoke: Palgrave Macmillan.

Foot, R., S. N. MacFarlane and M. Mastanduno, eds (2003), *US Hegemony and International Organizations,* Oxford: Oxford University Press.

Forelle, C. (2007), 'Microsoft Loss in Europe Raises American Fears', *Wall Street Journal*, 18 September. Available online: https://www.wsj.com/articles/SB119001194509829543 (accessed 3 October 2023).

Forsberg, T. and G. Herd (2006), *Divided West: European Security and the Transatlantic Relationship,* Oxford: Blackwell for the Royal institute of International Affairs.

Forster, A. (1999), 'EU and Southeast Asia Relations: A Balancing Act', *International Affairs*, 75(4): 743–58.

Forster, A. (2000), 'Evaluating the EU–ASEM Relationship: A Negotiated Order Approach', *Journal of European Public Policy*, 95: 787–805.

Forster, A. and W. Wallace (2000), 'Common Foreign and Security Policy: From Shadow to Substance?', in H. Wallace and W. Wallace (eds), *Policy-Making in the European Union*, 4th edn, 46–91, Oxford: Oxford University Press.

Fox, E. (2006a), 'The WTO's First Antitrust Case – Mexican Telecom: A Sleeping Victory for Trade and Competition', *Journal of International Economic Law*, 9(2): 271–92.

Fox, E. (2006b), 'Testimony before the Antitrust Modernisation Commission', *Hearing on International Issues*, 15 February. Available online: https://govinfo.library.unt.edu/amc/commission_hearings/pdf/Statement_Fox_final.pdf (accessed 2 October 2023).

Fox, E., R. J. R. Peritz and L. A. Sullivan (2004), *Cases and Materials on US Anti-Trust in a Global Context, Appendix A*, Rochester: Thomson West.

Freedman, L. (1982), 'The Atlantic Crisis', *International Affairs*, 58(3): 395–412.

Freedman, L., ed. (1983), *The Troubled Alliance,* London: Heinemann for the Royal Institute of International Affairs.

Freedom House. (2020), 'Nations in Transit 2020 Report: Dropping the Democratic Facade'. Available online: https://freedomhouse.org/sites/default/files/2020-04/05062020_FH_NIT2020_vfinal.pdf (accessed 25 January 2024).

Freedom House. (2023), 'Freedom in the World Country Report Hungary'. Available online: https://freedomhouse.org/country/hungary/freedom-world/2023 (accessed 10 October 2023).

Frelleson, T. (2001), 'Processes and Procedures in EU–US Foreign Policy Cooperation: From the Transatlantic Declaration to the New Transatlantic Agenda', in E. Philippart and P. Winand (eds), *Ever Closer Partnership: Policy-Making in US–EU Relations*, 313–47, Brussels: P.I.E.-Peter Lang.

Friis, L. and A. Murphy (2000), '"Turbo-Charged Negotiations": The EU and the Stability Pact for South Eastern Europe', *Journal of European Public Policy,* 7(5): 767–86.

Fursdon, E. (1980), *The European Defence Community: A History,* London: Macmillan.

Gagne, G. and J.-F. Morin (2006), 'The Evolving American Policy on Investment Protection: Evidence from Recent FTAs and the 2004 Model BIT', *Journal of International Economic Law*, 9(2): 357–82.

Gale, W.G. and C. Haldeman (2021), 'Searching for Supply-side Effects of the Tax Cuts and Jobs Act', *Brookings*, 6 July. Available online: https://www.brookings.edu/articles/searching-for-supply-side-effects-of-the-tax-cuts-and-jobs-act/ (accessed 11 October 2023).

Gallagher, P. (2007), *Inquit Database of SPS Notifications*. Available online: http://www.petergallagher.com.au/index.php/site/article/inquit-database-of-sps-notifications/ (accessed 7 August 2007).

Gamble, A. and A. Payne, eds (1996), *Regionalism and World Order*, Basingstoke: Macmillan.

Gann, L. and P. Duignan (1998), *Contemporary Europe and the Atlantic Alliance: A Political History,* Oxford: Blackwell.

Gardner, A. (2001), 'From the Transatlantic Declaration to the New Transatlantic Agenda: The Shaping of institutional Mechanisms and Policy Objectives by National and Supranational Actors', in E. Philippart and P. Winand (eds), *Ever Closer Partnership: Policy-Making in US-EU Relations*, 83–106, Brussels: P.I.E.-Peter Lang.

Genschel, P. and M. Jachtenfuchs, eds (2014), *Beyond the Regulatory Polity? The European Integration of Core State Powers,* Oxford: Oxford University Press.

Geranmayeh, E. (2017), *The Coming Clash; Why Iran will divide Europe from the United States*, ECFR Policy Brief, London: European Council on Foreign Relations.

Gilson, J. (2004), 'Weaving a New Silk Road: Europe Meets Asia', in V. Aggarwal and E. Fogarty (eds), *EU Trade Strategies: Between Regionalism and Globalism*, 64–92, Basingstoke: Palgrave Macmillan.

Ginsberg, R. (1989), *Foreign Policy Actions of the European Union,* Boulder: Rienner.

Ginsberg, R. (2001), *The European Union in International Politics: Baptism by Fire*, Lanham: Rowman & Littlefield.

Gnesotto, N., ed. (2004), *EU Security and Defence Policy: The First Five Years*, Paris: European Union Institute for Security Studies.

Goldstein, J. (2000), 'The United States and World Trade: Hegemony by Proxy?', in T. Lawton, J. Rosenau and A. Verdun (eds), *Strange Power: Shaping the Parameters of International Relations and International Political Economy,* Aldershot: Ashgate.

Gompert, D. and S. Larrabee, eds (1997), *America and Europe: A Partnership for a New Era,* Cambridge: Cambridge University Press.

Gordon, P. (2010), 'The Obama Administration's European Agenda', *Atlantic Council Transcript*, 17 November.

Gordon, P. and J. Shapiro (2004), *Allies at War: America, Europe, and the Crisis over Iraq,* New York: McGraw-Hill for the Brookings Institution.

Gordon, R. (2003), 'Exploding Productivity Growth: Context, Causes and Implications', *Brookings Papers on Economic Activity*, 34(2): 207–98.

Gourevitch, P. (1996), 'The Macro Politics of Micro-Institutional Differences in the Analysis of Comparative Capitalism', in S. Berger and R. Dore (eds), *Convergence or Diversity? National Models of Production and Distribution in a Global Economy,* Ithaca: Cornell University Press.

Gow, J. (1997), *Triumph of the Lack of Will: International Diplomacy and the Yugoslav War,* London: Hurst.

Grevi, G. and A. De Vasconcelos, eds (2008), *Partnerships for Effective Multilateralism: EU relationships with Brazil, China, India and Russia*, Chaillot Paper 109, Paris: EU Institute for Security Studies.

Gries, P. (2020), *The Politics of American Foreign Policy: How Ideology Divides Liberals and Conservatives on Foreign Policy*, Stanford: Stanford University Press.

Grosser, A. (1980), *The Western Alliance: European–American Relations since 1945,* London: Continuum.

Grugel, J. (2004), 'New Regionalism and Modes of Governance – Comparing US and EU Strategies in Latin America', *European Journal of International Relations*, 10(4): 603–26.

Guay, T. (1998), *At Arm's Length: The European Union and Europe's Defence Industry*, Basingstoke: Macmillan Press.

Guay, T. (1999), *The United States and the European Union: The Political Economy of a Relationship,* Sheffield: Sheffield Academic Press.

Guay, T. (2019), 'Free Trade Agreements and Regional Trade Agreements with Third Counties and European Business', in G. Suder, M. Riviere and J. Lindeque (eds), *The Routledge Companion to European Business*, 148–58, Abingdon: Routledge.

Guay, T. and M. Smith (2023), 'Divide and Conquer: Europe, China, and Policy Coherence', in Michelle Egan, Kolja Raube, Jan Wouters and Julien Chaisse (eds), *Contestation and Polarization in Global Governance: European Responses*, 160–78, Cheltenham: Edward Elgar.

Guzman, A. (1998), 'Is International Antitrust Possible?', *New York University Law Review*, 73(5): 1507.

Haftendorn, H. and C. Tuschhoff, eds (1993), *America and Europe in an Era of Change,* Boulder: Westview.

Hakim, P. (2006), 'Is Washington Losing Latin America?' *Foreign Affairs*, 85(1): 39–53.

Hall, S. and M. Heneghan (2023), 'Brexit and "Missing" Financial Services Jobs in the UK', *Contemporary Social Science*, 18(2): 235–49. Available online: https://www.tandfonline.com/doi/epdf/10.1080/21582041.2023.2189294?needAccess=true (accessed 10 October 2023).

Halper, S. and J. Clarke (2004), *America Alone: The Neo-Conservatives and the Global Order,* Cambridge: Cambridge University Press.

Hamilton, D. (2014), *The American Way of Partnership*, Working Paper 6, Madrid: FRIDE for the European Strategic Partnerships Observatory.

Hamilton, D. and J. Quinlan (2021), *The Transatlantic Economy 2021; Annual Survey of Jobs, Trade and Investment between the United States and Europe,* Washington DC: Foreign Policy Research Institute, SAIS, Johns Hopkins University/Woodrow Wilson Center.

Hamilton, D. and J. Quinlan (2023), *The Transatlantic Economy 2023: Annual Survey of Jobs, Trade and Investment between the United States and Europe*, Washington, DC: Foreign Policy Institute, Johns Hopkins University SAIS/Transatlantic Leadership.

Hanrieder, W., ed. (1974), *The United States and Western Europe: Political, Economic and Strategic Perspectives,* Cambridge: Winthrop.

Hanrieder, W., ed. (1982), *Economic Issues and the Atlantic Community,* New York: Praeger.

Harrison, M. (1982), *The Reluctant Ally: France and European Security,* Baltimore: Johns Hopkins University Press.

Haukkala, H. (2010), *The EU-Russia Strategic Partnership: The Limits of Post-Sovereignty in International Relations*, London and New York: Routledge.

Haukkala, H. (2016), 'The Perfect Storm: Or What Went Wrong and What Went Right for the EU in Ukraine', *Europe-Asia Studies,* 68(4): 653–64.

Haukkala, H. (2021), 'The End of Ambiguity: Excavating the Remains of the EU-Russia "Strategic Partnership"', in L. Ferreira-Pereira and M. Smith (eds), *The European Union's Strategic Partnerships: Global Diplomacy in a Contested World*, 177–98, Basingstoke: Palgrave Macmillan.

Held, D. and M. Koenig-Archibugi, eds (2004), *American Power in the 21st Century,* Cambridge: Polity.

Heldt, E. C. and T. Müller (2021), 'Bringing Independence and Accountability together: Mission Impossible for the European Central Bank?', *Journal of European Integration*, 44(6): 837–53.

Henderson, K., ed. (1999), *Back to Europe: Central and Eastern Europe and the European Union,* London: UCL Press.

Hettne, B., A. Inotai and O. Sunkel, eds (1999), *Globalism and the New Regionalism,* Basingstoke: Palgrave Macmillan.

Hill, C., ed. (1995), *The Actors in Europe's Foreign Policy,* London: Routledge.

Hill, C. (1998), 'Closing the Capability-Expectations Gap?', in J. Peterson and H. Sjursen (eds), *A Common Foreign Policy for Europe? Competing Visions of the CFSP*, 18–38, London: Routledge.

Hill, C. (2004), 'Renationalising or Regrouping? European Foreign Policy Since 11 September 2001', *Journal of Common Market Studies,* 42(1): 143–63.

Hill, C. and M. Smith, eds (2005), *International Relations and the European Union*, Oxford: Oxford University Press.

Hill, C., M. Smith and S. Vanhoonacker, eds (2023), *International Relations and the European Union,* 4th edn, Oxford: Oxford University Press.

Hix, S., A. Noury and G. Roland (2007), *Democratic Politics in the European Parliament,* Cambridge: Cambridge University Press.

Hix, S., A. Noury and G. Roland (2018), 'The Changing Battle Lines in the European Parliament', in N. Campos and J.-E. Sturm (eds), *Bretton Woods, Brussels, and Beyond: Redesigning the Institutions of Europe*, 51–60, CEPR Press.

Hocking, B. and M. Smith (1997), *Beyond Foreign Economic Policy: The United States, the Single European Market and the Changing World Economy,* London: Cassell/Pinter.

Hodson, D. and D. Mabbett (2009), 'UK Economic Policy and the Global Financial Crisis: Paradigm Lost?' *Journal of Common Market Studies*, 47(5): 1041–61.

Hodson, D. and L. Quaglia (2009), 'European Perspectives on the Global Financial Crisis: Introduction', *Journal of Common Market Studies*, 47(5): 939–53.

Hoffmann, S. (1968), *Gulliver's Troubles, or the Setting of American Foreign Policy,* New York: McGraw-Hill for the Council on Foreign Relations.

Hoffmann, S. (1978), *Primacy or World Order: American Foreign Policy since The Cold War,* New York: McGraw-Hill.

Hoffmann, S. (1996), 'Yugoslavia: Implications for Europe and for European Institutions', in R. Ullman (ed.), *The World and Yugoslavia's Wars*, 97–121, New York: Council on Foreign Relations Press.

Hoffmann, S. and C. Maier, eds (1984), *The Marshall Plan: A Retrospective,* Boulder: Westview.

Hogan, M. (1987), *The Marshall Plan: America, Britain, and the Reconstruction of Western Europe, 1947–1952,* Cambridge: Cambridge University Press.

Holland, M. (2000), 'Resisting Reform or Risking Revival? Renegotiating the Lomé Convention', in M. Green Cowles and M. Smith (eds), *The State of the European Union Volume 5: Risks, Reform, Resistance and Revival*, 390–410, Oxford: Oxford University Press.

Holland, M. (2002), *The European Union and the Third World,* Basingstoke: Palgrave Macmillan.

Holland, M. and M. Doidge (2012), *Development Policy of the European Union*, Basingstoke: Palgrave Macmillan.

Hooghe, L. and G. Marks (2001), *Multi-Level Governance and European Integration,* Oxford: Rowman and Littlefield.

Hopewell, K. (2021), 'When the Hegemon Goes Rogue: Leadership Amid the US Assault on the Liberal Trading Order', *International Affairs*, 97(4): 1025–43.

Hösli, M.O. (1997), 'Voting Strength in the European Parliament: The Influence of National and of Partisan Actors', *European Journal of Political Research*, 31: 351–66.

Howarth, D. and L. Quaglia (2021), 'Failing Forward in Economic and Monetary Union: Explaining Weak Eurozone Financial Support Mechanisms', *Journal of European Public Policy*, 28(10): 1555–72.

Howarth, D. and A. Verdun (2020), 'Economic and Monetary Union at Twenty: A Stocktaking of a Tumultuous Decade: Introduction', *Journal of European Integration*, 42(3): 287–93.

Howorth, J. (2003), 'Foreign and Defence Policy Cooperation', in J. Peterson and M. Pollack (eds), *Europe, America, Bush: Transatlantic Relations In the Twenty-First Century*, 13–28, London: Routledge.

Howorth, J. (2005), 'The Euro-Atlantic Security Dilemma: France, Britain and the ESDP', *Journal of Transatlantic Studies*, 3(1): 39–54.

Howorth, J. (2007), *Security and Defence Policy in the European Union,* Basingstoke: Palgrave Macmillan.

Howorth, J. (2014), *Security and Defence Policy in the European Unio,* 2nd edn, Basingstoke: Palgrave Macmillan.

Howorth, J. (2017), 'European Defence Policy Between Dependence and Autonomy: A Challenge of Sisyphean Dimensions', *British Journal of Politics and International Relations,* 19(1): 13–28.

Howorth, J. (2023), 'The EU's Security and Defence Policy: A New Leap Forward?', in C. Hill, M. Smith and S. Vanhoonecker (eds), *International Relations and the European Union,* 4th edn, 305–26, Oxford: Oxford University Press.

House of Commons Library. (2020), 'UK Policy Towards China', 2 May. Available online: https://researchbriefings.files.parliament.uk/documents/CDP-2019-0106/CDP-2019-0106.pdf (accessed 6 June 2024).

Huang, Y. (2016), 'Understanding China's Belt & Road Initiative: Motivation, Framework and Assessment', *China Economic Review*, 40: 314–21.

Hueglin, T. (2013), 'Treaty Federalism as a Model of Policy Making', *Canadian Public Administration*, 56(2): 185–202.

Hueglin, T. and A. Fenna (2015), *Comparative Federalism: A Systematic Inquiry*, Toronto: University of Toronto Press.

Hufbauer, G., ed. (1990), *Europe 1992: An American Perspective,* Washington, DC: Brookings Institution.

Hufbauer, G. (2014), 'A Good Deal Settles the Brazilian Cotton Dispute', *Peterson Institute for International Economics*, 2 October. Available online: https://www.piie.com

/blogs/trade-and-investment-policy-watch/good-deal-settles-brazil-cotton-dispute (accessed 28 January 2014).

Huntington, S. (1993), 'The Clash of Civilizations', *Foreign Affairs*, 72 (3): 2–49.

Ikenberry, G.J. (2018), 'The End of Liberal International Order?' *International Affairs*, 94(1): 7–23.

Ikenberry, J., ed. (2002), *America Unrivaled: The Future of the Balance of Power,* Ithaca: Cornell University Press.

Ikenberry, J., ed. (2006), *Liberal Order and Imperial Ambition,* Cambridge: Polity.

International Affairs (2013), Special Issue 'Negotiating the Rise of New Powers', edited by Amrita Narlikar, 89(3), May.

International Competition Network (ICN). (2007), 'Competition Authorities Agree to Develop Merger and Unilateral Conduct Guidance, Emphasize Co-operation, Outreach and Guidance', *News Release*, 1 June. Available online: https://www.ftc.gov/news-events/news/press-releases/2007/06/international-competition-network-presents-report-unilateral-conduct-announces-merger-convergence (accessed 2 October 2023).

International Competition Network (ICN). (2023), 'About the ICN', Available online: https://www.internationalcompetitionnetwork.org/about/ (accessed 2 October 2023).

International Monetary Fund (IMF). (2023), 'Currency Composition of Official Foreign Exchange Reserves (COFER)', 29 September. Available online: https://data.imf.org/?sk=e6a5f467-c14b-4aa8-9f6d-5a09ec4e62a4 (accessed 10 December 2023).

International Monetary Fund (IMF). (2024), 'GDP, Current Prices'. Available online: https://www.imf.org/external/datamapper/NGDPD@WEO/CHN/USA/EU (accessed 27 January 2024).

International Competition Network (ICN). (2007a), 'About the ICN'. Available online: http://www.internationalcompetitionnetwork.org/index.php/en/about-icn (accessed 15 June 2007).

Janow, M. (2000), 'Transatlantic Cooperation on Competition Policy', in S. Evenett, A. Lehmann and B. Steil (eds), *Antitrust Goes Global*, 29–56, Washington and London: Brookings and RIIA.

Jervis, R. (2005), *American Foreign Policy in a New Era,* London: Routledge.

Jervis, R. (2006), 'The Remaking of a Unipolar World', *Washington Quarterly*, 29(3): 7–19.

Jie, Y. and J. Wallace (2021), 'What is China's Belt and Road Initiative?', *Chatham House*. Available online: https://www.chathamhouse.org/2021/09/what-chinas-belt-and-road-initiative-bri (accessed 11 December 2023).

Jing Men and Wei Shen, eds (2014), *The EU, the US and China – Towards a New International order?* Cheltenham: Edward Elgar.

Joffe, J. (1987), *The Limited Partnership: Europe, the United States, and the Burdens of Alliance,* Cambridge: Ballinger.

Joint Communication. (2020), *A New EU-U.S. Agenda for Global Change*, JOIN (2020) 22 final, Brussels: European Commission/High Representative of the Union for Foreign Affairs and Security Policy, December.

Jokela, J. (2011), *The G-20: A Pathway to Effective Multilateralism?* Chaillot Papers, Paris: EU Institute for Security Studies.

Jones, E. (2006), 'Europe's Market Liberalisation is a Bad Model for a Global Trade Agenda', *Journal of European Public Policy*, 13(6): 943–57.

Jørgensen, K. E. and K. Laatikainen, eds (2013), *Routledge Handbook on the European Union and International Institutions: Performance, Policy, Power*, London: Routledge.

Jurkovic, P. (2023), 'What is in the Inflation Reduction Act?' *UK in a Changing Europe Explainer*. Available online: https://ukandeu.ac.uk/explainers/what-is-the-inflation-reduction-act/ (accessed 11 October 2023).

Kagan, R. (2003), *Of Paradise and Power: America and Europe in the New World Order,* New York: Knopf.

Kaiser, K. (1973), *Europe and America: The Future of the Relationship*, Washington, DC: Columbia Books.

Kaiser, K. (1974), 'Europe and America: A Critical Phase', *Foreign Affairs*, 52(4): 725–41.

Kaiser, K. and H.-P. Schwartz, eds (1977), *America and Western Europe: Problems and Prospects,* Lexington: Heath.

Kaldor, M. (2004), 'American Power: From "Compellance" to Cosmopolitanism?', in D. Held and M. Koenig-Archibugi (eds), *American Power in the 21st Century*, 181–213, Cambridge: Polity.

Kaldor, M., M. Martin and S. Selchow (2007), 'Human Security: A New Strategic Narrative for Europe', *International Affairs*, 83(2): 273–88.

Kamin, D. and R. Kysar (2023), 'The Perils of the New Industrial Policy', *Foreign Affairs*, May/June: 92–103.

Kelemen, D. (2004), *The Rules of Federalism. Institutions and Regulatory Politics in the EU and Beyond*. Cambridge, MA: Harvard University Press.

Kelemen, D. (2011), *Eurolegalism. The Transformation of Law and Regulation in the European Union*, Cambridge, MA: Harvard University Press.

Keleman, D. (2020), 'The European Union's Authoritarian Equilibrium', *Journal of European Public Policy*, 27(3): 481–99.

Kelemen, D.I. and S. Schmidt (2011), 'Introduction– the European Court of Justice and Legal Integration: Perpetual Momentum?' *Journal of European Public Policy*, 19(1): 1–7.

Keohane, R. (1979), 'American Policy Toward Advanced Industrial Countries: The Struggle to Make Others Adjust', in K. Oye, R. Rothchild and R. Lieber (eds), *Eagle Entangled: U.S. Foreign Policy in a Complex World*, 91–122, New York: Longman.

Keohane, R. (2003a), 'Ironies of Sovereignty: The EU and the US', in J. Weiler, I. Begg and J. Peterson (eds), *Integration in an Expanding European Union: Reassessing the Fundamentals*, 307–30, Oxford: Blackwell.

Keohane, R. (2003b), 'Global Governance and Democratic Accountability', in D. Held and M. Koenig-Archibugi (eds), *Taming Globalization: Frontiers of Governance*, 130–59, Cambridge: Polity.

Keohane, R. and S. Hoffmann, eds (1993), *After the Cold War: International Institutions and State Strategies in Europe, 1989–92,* Cambridge, MA: Harvard University Press.

Keukeleire, S. (2003), 'The European Union as a Diplomatic Actor: Internal, Traditional and Structural Diplomacy', *Diplomacy and Statecraft*, 14(3): 31–56.

Keukeleire, S. and T. Delreux (2014), *Foreign and Security Policy of the European Union*, Basingstoke: Palgrave Macmillan.

Keukeleire, S. and T. Delreux (2022), *The Foreign Policy of the European Union*, London: Bloomsbury.

Khanna, R. (2023), 'The New Industrial Age', *Foreign Affairs*, January/February: 141–54.

Kirby, J. (2020), 'USMCA, Trumps' New NAFTA Deal, Explained in 600 Words', *Vox*, 1 July. Available online: https://www.vox.com/2018/10/3/17930092/usmca-mexico-nafta-trump-trade-deal-explained (accessed 9 October 2023).

Kissack, R. (2010), *Pursuing Effective Multilateralism: The European Union, International Organizations and the Politics of Decision-Making*, Basingstoke: Palgrave Macmillan.

Kissack, R. (2015), 'The EU and Human Rights Promotion', in K.E. Jørgensen, E. Aarstad, K. Drieskens, K. Laatikainen and B. Tonra (eds), *The SAGE Handbook of European Foreign Policy Volume 2*, 822–36, London: SAGE.

Knodt, M. (2004), 'International Embeddedness of European Multi-Level Governance', *Journal of European Public Policy*, 11(4): 701–19.

Kolodziej, E. (1980–81), 'Europe: The Partial Partner', *International Security*, 5(3): 104–31.

Konisky, D. and P. Nolette (2022), 'The State of American Federalism 2021-22: Federal Courts, State Legislatures, and the Conservative Turn in the Law', *Publius: The Journal of Federalism*, 52(3): 353–81.

Koops, J. and G. Macaj, eds (2015), *The European Union as a Diplomatic Actor*, Basingstoke: Palgrave Macmillan.

Kothari, S.P., K. Ramanna and D. J. Skinner (2010), 'Implications for GAAP from an Analysis of Positive Research in Accounting', *Journal of Accounting and Economics*, 50(2–3): 246–86. Available online: https://www.sciencedirect.com/science/article/pii/S0165410110000352 (accessed 12 December 2023).

Krampf, A. (2014), 'From the Maastricht Treaty to Post-crisis EMU: The ECB and Germany as Drivers of Change', *Journal of Contemporary European Studies*, 22(3): 303–17.

Krasner, S. (1982), 'Structural Causes and Regime Consequences: Regimes as Intervening Variables', *International Organization,* 36(2): 185–205.

Krause, L. (1968), *European Economic Integration and the United States,* Washington, DC: Brookings Institution.

Krauthammer, C. (2002), 'The Unipolar Moment Revisited', *The National Interest*, 70: 5–18.

Kreppel, A. (2012). 'The normalization of the European Union', *Journal of European Public Policy*, 19(5), 635–45.

Kundnani, H. (2016), 'TTIP must Die so the West can Live', *Foreign Policy*, 13 May. Available online: https://foreignpolicy.com/2016/05/13/ttip-tpp-eu-trade-obama-asia/ (accessed 9 October 2023).

Kupchan, C. (2002), *The End of the American Era: US Foreign Policy and the Geopolitics of the Twenty-First Century,* New York: Vintage.

Laatikainen, K. and K. Smith, eds (2006), *The European Union at the United Nations: Intersecting Multilateralisms,* Basingstoke: Palgrave Macmillan.

Laffan, B., R. O'Donnell and M. Smith (2000), *Europe's Experimental Union: Rethinking Integration,* London: Routledge.

Lardy, N. (2005), 'China: The Great New Economic Challenge?', in F. Bergsten (ed.), *The United States and the World Economy: Foreign Economic Policy for the Next Decade*, 121–41, Washington, DC: Institute for International Finance.

Larrabee, S. (1997), 'Security Challenges on Europe's Eastern Periphery', in D. Gompert and S. Larrabee (eds), *America and Europe: A Partnership for a New Era*, 166–90, Cambridge: Cambridge University Press.

Larres, K. (2020), 'Trump's Trade Wars: America, China, Europe, and Global Disorder', *Journal of Transatlantic Studies,* 18(1): 103–29.

Larres, K. (2022), *Uncertain Allies: Nixon, Kissinger, and the Threat of a United Europe*, New Haven: Yale University Press.

Lawton, T. and S. McGuire. (2005), 'Adjusting to Liberalization: Tracing the Impact of the WTO on European Textiles and Chemicals Industries', *Business and Politics*, 7(3): 1–23.

Leffler, M. and J. Legro, eds (2008), *To Lead the World: American Foreign Policy after the Bush Doctrine,* New York: Oxford University Press.

Leiserson, G. and J. Rohaly (2006), 'The Distribution of the 2001–2006 Tax Cuts: Updated Projections, November', *Tax Policy Centre*, Washington. Available online: http://www.urban.org//UploadedPDF/411378_tax_cuts.pdf (accessed 10 January 2007).

Lieber, R. (1979), 'Europe and America in the World Energy Crisis', *International Affairs*, 55(4): 552–7.

Lieber, R. (2007), *The American Era: Power and Strategy for the 21st Century,* Cambridge: Cambridge University Press.

Lieven, A. (2002), 'The End of the West?' *Prospect*, September: 20–5.

Lieven, A. (2004), *America Right or Wrong: An Anatomy of American Nationalism,* Oxford and New York: Oxford University Press.

Light, M. (2003), 'US and European Perspectives on Russia', in J. Peterson and M. Pollack (eds), *Europe, America, Bush: Transatlantic Relations in the Twenty-First Century*, 69–84, London: Routledge.

Light, M., S. White and J. Lowenhardt (2000), 'A Wider Europe: The View From Moscow and Kyiv', *International Affairs*, 76(1): 77–88.

Lijphart, A. (2012) *Patterns of Democracy: Government Forms and Performance in Thirty-Six Countries,* 2nd edn, New Haven: Yale University Press.

Lindberg, T., ed. (2005), *Beyond Paradise and Power: Europe, America, and the Future of a Troubled Partnership,* London: Routledge.

Lindeque, J. and S. McGuire (2007), 'The United States and the WTO: Hegemony Constrained or Confirmed?', *Management International Review*, 47(5): 725–44.

Lindstrom, G., ed. (2003), *Shift or Rift? Assessing EU-US Relations After Iraq,* Paris: EU Institute for Security Studies.

Lindstrom, G. (2005), *EU-US Burdensharing: Who Does What?* Chaillot Paper 82, Paris: European Union Institute for Security Studies.

Lindstrom, G. and B. Schmitt, eds (2004), *One Year On: Lessons from Iraq,* Chaillot Paper 68, Paris: European Union Institute for Security Studies.

Lister, M., ed. (1999), *New Perspectives on European Union Development Cooperation,* Boulder: Westview.

Litan, R. E. (2000), 'The First Microsoft Case', in S. J. Evenett, A. Lehmann and B. Steil (eds), *Antitrust Goes Global: What Future for Transatlantic Cooperation?* 174–6, Washington, DC and London: Brookings and RIIA.

Litwak, R. (2019), *Nuclear Crises with North Korea and Iran: From Transformational to Transactional Diplomacy*, Washington, DC: Woodrow Wilson Center.

Ludlow, P. (1982), *The Making of the European Monetary System: A Case Study of the Politics of the European Community,* London: Butterworth.

Lundestad, G. (1998), *'Empire' By Integration: The United States and European Integration, 1945–1997,* Oxford: Oxford University Press.

Lundestad, G. (2005), *The United States and Western Europe Since 1945: From 'Empire' by Integration to Transatlantic Drift,* Oxford: Oxford University Press.

Lundestad, G., ed. (2008), *Just Another Major Crisis? The United States and Europe since 2000*, Oxford: Oxford University Press.

Maas, H. (2020). *Time for a New Beginning in the Transatlantic Partnership*. Available online: https://www.auswaertiges-amt.de/en/newsroom/news/-/2409524 (accessed 25 January 2024).

Macrotrends. (2023), 'Euro Dollar Exchange Rate (EUR USD) Historical Chart'. Available online: https://www.macrotrends.net/2548/euro-dollar-exchange-rate-historical-chart (accessed 10 December 2023).

Mahnke, D., W. Rees and W. Thompson (2004), *Redefining Transatlantic Security Relations: The Challenge of Change,* Manchester: Manchester University Press.

Mak, E. (2014), 'The US Supreme Court and the Court of Justice of the European Union: Emergence, Nature and Impact of Transatlantic Judicial Communication', in E. Fahey and D. Curtin (eds), *A Transatlantic Community of Law: Legal Perspectives on the Relationship between the EU and US Legal Orders*, 9–34, Cambridge: Cambridge University Press.

Mazzocco, I. and A. L. Palazzi (2023), 'Italy Withdraws from China's Belt and Road Initiative', *Center for Strategic and International Studies*, 14 December. Available online: https://www.csis.org/analysis/italy-withdraws-chinas-belt-and-road-initiative (accessed 29 January 2024).

Mandelbaum, M. (2005), *The Case for Goliath: How America Acts as the World's Government in the 21st Century*, New York: Public Affairs.

Mandelbaum, M. (2022), *The Four Ages of American Foreign Policy: Weak Power, Great Power, Superpower, Hyperpower*, New York: Oxford University Press.

Manger, M. (2005), 'Competition and Bilateralism in Trade Policy: The Case of Japan's Free Trade Agreements', *Review of International Political Economy*, 12(5): 804–28.

Mann, M. (2003), *Incoherent Empire,* London and New York: Verso.

Manners, I. (2006), 'Normative Power Europe Reconsidered: Beyond the Crossroads', *Journal of European Public Policy*, 13(2): 182–99.

Manners, I. and R. Whitman (2003), 'The "Difference Engine": Constructing and Representing the International Identity of the European Union', *Journal of European Public Policy*, 10(3): 380–404.

Mao, F. (2020), 'How Reliant is Australia on China?' *BBC*, 17 June. Available online: https://www.bbc.com/news/world-australia-52915879 (accessed 9 October 2023).

Mardell, J. (2022), 'Can China Achieve its BRICS Ambitions?' *The Diplomat*, 2 July. Available online: https://thediplomat.com/2022/07/can-china-achieve-its-brics-ambitions/ (accessed 14 December 2023).

Matthijs, M. and C. Parsons (2022), 'Single-Market Power: How Europe Surpassed America in the Quest for Economic Integration', *Foreign Affairs*, May/June: 165–76.

McBride, J., N. Berman and A. Chatzky (2023), 'China's Massive Belt and Road Initiative', *Council on Foreign Relations*, 2 February. Available online: https://www.cfr.org/backgrounder/chinas-massive-belt-and-road-initiative (accessed 11 December, 2023).

McBride, J. and A. Chatzky (2019), 'What is the Trans-Pacific Partnership (TPP)', *Council on Foreign Relations*, 4 January. Available online: https://www.cfr.org/backgrounder/what-trans-pacific-partnership-tpp (accessed 9 October 2023).

McBride, J., A. Siripurapu and N. Berman (2023), 'What does the G20 Do?' *Council on Foreign Relations*, 11 October. Available online: https://www.cfr.org/backgrounder/what-does-g20-do (accessed 11 December 2023).

McCormick, J. (2007), *The European Superpower,* Basingstoke: Palgrave Macmillan.

McElwee, L. (2023), *The Rise and Demise of the EU-China Investment Agreement: Takeaways for the Future of German Debate on China*, Washington, DC: Center for Strategic & International Studies, 20 March. Available online: https://www.csis.org/analysis/rise-and-demise-eu-china-investment-agreement-takeaways-future-german-debate-china (accessed 29 September 2023).

McGowan, L. and M. Cini (1999), 'Discretion and Politicization in EU Competition Policy: The Case of Merger Control', *Governance*, 12(2): 175–200.

McGuire, S. (1997), *Airbus Industrie: Cooperation and Conflict in US-EC Trade Relations,* Basingstoke: Macmillan.

McGuire, S. (2004), 'Firms and Governments in International Trade', in B. Hocking and S. McGuire (eds), *Trade Politics*, 2nd edn, 276–88, London: Routledge.

McGuire, S. and M. Smith (2008), *The European Union and the United States: Competition and Convergence in the Global Arena*, Basingstoke: Palgrave Macmillan.

McKinsey. (2022), 'The CHIPS and Science Act: Here's What's in it', 4 October. Available online: https://www.mckinsey.com/industries/public-sector/our-insights/the-chips-and-science-act-heres-whats-in-it (accessed 3 October 2023).

McMahon, J. (1998), 'ASEAN and the Asia-Europe Meeting: Strengthening the European Union's Relationship with Southeast Asia', *European Foreign Affairs Review*, 3(2): 233–51.

Mee, C. (1984), *The Marshall Plan: The Launching of the Pax Americana,* New York: Simon & Schuster.

Meixier, E. and J. Creery (2022), 'EU Targets Myanmar's Lucrative Energy Sector in Latest Sanctions', *FT Online*, 22 February. Available online: https://www.ft.com/content/9a772d31-9cbd-4bbd-a8a6-ff73388304ea (accessed 27 August 2022).

Melamed, D. (1998), 'Antitrust Enforcement in the Global Economy', speech at the Fordham Corporate Law Institute, New York, 22 October. Available online: http://www.usdoj.gov/atr/public/speeches/2043.htm (accessed 21 August 2006).

Menon, A. and M. A. Schain, eds (2006), *Comparative Federalism: the European Union and the United States in Comparative Perspective*, Oxford: Oxford University Press.

Meunier, S. (2005), *Trading Voices: The European Union in International Commercial Negotiations,* Princeton: Princeton University Press.

Meunier, S. (2014), 'Divide and Conquer? China and the Cacophony of Foreign Investment Rules in the EU', *Journal of European Public Policy*, 21(7): 996–1016.

Meunier, S. and Z. Chan (2022), 'Behind the Screen: Understanding National Support for a Foreign Investment Screening Mechanism in the European Union', *Review of International Organizations*, 17: 513–41.

Meunier, S. and K. Nicolaïdis (2006), 'The European Union as a Conflicted Trade Power', *Journal of European Public Policy,* 13(6): 906–25.

Meunier, S. and K. Nicolaïdis (2018), 'The European Union as a Conflicted Trade Power', in J. Peterson and A. Young (eds), *The European Union and the New Trade Politics*, 112–31, London: Routledge.

Meunier, S. and K. Nicolaidis (2019), 'The Geopoliticization of European Trade and Investment Policy', *Journal of Common Market Studies*, 57(S1): 103–13.

Meunier, S. and K. Nicolaidis (2023), 'The European Union as a Trade Power', in C. Hill, M. Smith and S. Vanhoonacker (eds), *International Relations and the European Union*, 4th Edition, 155–80, Oxford: Oxford University Press.

Millar, P. (2023), 'How the BRICS Nations Failed to Rebuild the Global Financial Order', *Reuters*, 24 August. Available online: https://www.france24.com/en/economy/20230824-how-the-brics-nations-failed-to-rebuild-the-global-financial-order (accessed 14 December 2023).

Milward, A. (1984), *The Reconstruction of Western Europe, 1945–1951,* London: Methuen.

Ministry of National Defence (Republic of Poland). (2018), 'The Foundation of Fort Trump is an Investment in Our Security'. Available online: https://www.gov.pl/web/national

-defence/the-foundation-of-fort-trump-is-an-investment-in-our-security (accessed 23 June 2021).

Monar, J. (2004), 'The European Union as an International Actor in the Domain of Justice and Home Affairs', *European Foreign Affairs Review*, 9(3): 395–416.

Morgan, E. and S. McGuire (2004), 'Transatlantic Divergence: GE-Honeywell and the EU's Merger Policy', *Journal of European Public Policy*, 11(1): 39–56.

Morgenstern-Pomorski, Jost-Henrik (2018), *The Contested Diplomacy of the European External Action Service: Inception, Establishment and Consolidation*, Abingdon: Routledge.

Morin, J.-F., T. Novotná, F. Ponjaert and M. Telò, eds (2015), *The Politics of Transatlantic Trade Negotiations: TTIP in a Globalized World,* Farnham: Ashgate.

Mowery, D. and N. Rosenberg (1998), 'Introduction', in D. Mowery and N. Rosenberg (eds), *Paths of Innovation*, 1–10,Cambridge: Cambridge University Press.

Mühlböck, M. (2019), *Voting in European Union Politics*. Oxford Research Encyclopedia of Politics. Available online: https://oxfordre.com/politics/view/10.1093/acrefore/9780190228637.001.0001/acrefore-9780190228637-e-1073 (accessed 2 June 2020).

Müller-Brandeck-Bocquet, G. (2000), 'Perspectives for a New Regionalism: Relations Between the EU and the MERCOSUR', *European Foreign Affairs Review*, 5(4): 561–79.

Munyati, C. (2023), 'The African Union has been made a Permanent Member of the G20 – What does it mean for the Continent?' *World Economic Forum*, 14 September. Available online: https://www.weforum.org/agenda/2023/09/african-union-g20-world-leaders/ (accessed 11 December 2023).

Musu, C. and W. Wallace (2003), 'The Middle East: Focus of Discord?', in J. Peterson and M. Pollack (eds), *Europe, America, Bush: Transatlantic Relations in the Twenty-First Century*, 99–114, London: Routledge.

Nau, H. (1990), *The Myth of American Decline: Leading the World Economy into the 1990s*, New York: Oxford University Press.

Nau, H. (2002), *At Home Abroad: Identity and Power in American Foreign Policy,* Ithaca: Cornell University Press.

Nello, S. and K. Smith (1998), *The European Union and Central and Eastern Europe,* Aldershot: Ashgate.

Niblett, R. and W. Wallace, eds (2001), *Rethinking European Order: West European Perspectives, 1989–1997*, Basingstoke: Palgrave Macmillan.

Nicolaidis, K. (2001), 'Conclusion: The Federal Vision beyond the Federal State', in K. Nicolaidis and R. Howse (eds), *The Federal Vision: Legitimacy and Levels of Governance in the United States and the European Union*, 439–81, Oxford: Oxford University Press.

Nugent, N., ed. (2004), *European Union Enlargement,* Basingstoke: Palgrave Macmillan.

Nugent, N. (2017), *The Government and Politics of the European Union*, 8th edn, London: Red Globe Press.

Nuttall, S. (1994), 'The EC and Yugoslavia: *Deus ex Machina* or *Machina Sine Deo*?', in N. Nugent (ed.), *The European Union 1993: Annual Review of Activities*, 104–20, Oxford: Blackwell.

Nye, J. (2002), *The Paradox of American Power: Why the World's Only Superpower Can't Go It Alone,* New York: Oxford University Press.

Nye, J. (2004a), *Soft Power: The Means to Succeed in World Politics,* New York: Public Affairs Press.

Nye, J. (2004b), 'Hard Power, Soft Power, and "The War on Terrorism"', in D. Held and M. Koenig-Archibugi (eds), *American Power in the 21st Century*, 114–33, Cambridge: Polity.

Nye, J. (2012), 'Obama and Smart Power', in M. Cox and D. Stokes (eds), *US Foreign Policy*, 2nd edn, 97–107, Oxford: Oxford University Press.

Nye, J. (2018), 'The Twenty-first Century and Smart Power', in M. Cox and D. Stokes (eds), *US Foreign Policy*, 3rd edn, 111–22, Oxford: Oxford University Press.

Oestergaard, K. (2023), 'Airbus and Boeing Report December and Full-Year 2022 Commercial Aircraft Orders and Deliveries', *Flightplan*, 16 January. Available online: https://flightplan.forecastinternational.com/2023/01/16/airbus-and-boeing-report-december-and-full-year-2022-commercial-aircraft-orders-and-deliveries/ (accessed 9 October 2023).

Olienyk, J. and R. J. Carbaugh (2011), 'Boeing and Airbus: Duopoly in Jeopardy?' *Global Economy Journal*, 11 (1): 1–9.

Olsen, G. (2002), 'Promoting Democracy, Preventing Conflict: The European Union and Africa', *International Politics*, 39 (3): 311–28.

Olsen, G.R. (2022), '"America is Back" or "America First" and the Transatlantic Relationship', *Politics and Governance*, 10(2): 154–64.

Organization for Economic Cooperation and Development (OECD). (2020a), 'Foreign Direct Investment Regulatory Restrictiveness Index'. Available online: https://goingdigital.oecd.org/en/indicator/74 (accessed 29 September 2023).

Organization for Economic Cooperation and Development (OECD). (2020b), *Focus On: Public Funding of Health Care*. Paris: OECD. Available online https://www.oecd.org/health/Public-funding-of-health-care-Brief-2020.pdf (accessed 5 January 2021).

Organization for Economic Cooperation and Development (OECD) Tax Policy Centre. (2018), 'Special Feature: Convergence of Tax Levels and Tax Structures in OECD Countries', in *Revenue Statistics 2018*, Paris: OECD Tax Policy Center.

Orsini, A. (2014), *The European Union with(in) International Organizations: Commitment, Consistency and Effects Across Time*, Aldershot: Ashgate.

Ortega, M., ed. (2003), *The European Union and the Crisis in the Middle East,* Chaillot Paper 62, Paris: European Union Institute for Security Studies.

Ortega, M., ed. (2007), *Building the Future: The EU's Contribution to Global Governance*, Chaillot Paper 100, Paris: EU Institute for Security Studies.

Owen, D. (1995), *Balkan Odyssey*, New York: Harcourt Brace.

Oye, K., R. Lieber and R. Rothchild, eds (1983), *Eagle Defiant: US Foreign Policy in the 80s*,Boston: Little, Brown.

Oye, K., R. Lieber and R. Rothchild, eds (1987), *Eagle Resurgent? The Reagan Era in American Foreign Policy*, Boston: Little, Brown.

Papa, M., Z. Han and F. O'Donnell (2023), 'The Dynamics of Informal Institutions and Counter-hegemony: Introducing a BRICS Convergence Index', *European Journal of International Relations*, 29(4): 960–89. Available online: https://journals.sagepub.com/doi/10.1177/13540661231183352 (accessed 14 December 2023).

Pape, R. (2005), 'Soft Balancing Against the United States', *International Security*, 30(1): 7–45.

Patel, K. and K. Weisbrode, eds (2013), *European Integration and the Atlantic Community in the 1980s,* Cambridge: Cambridge University Press.

Patrick, S. (2017), 'Trump and World Order: The Return of Self-help', *Foreign Affairs*, 96(2): 52–7.

Payne, A., ed. (2004), *The New Regional Politics of Development,* Basingstoke: Palgrave Macmillan.

Pelkmans, J. and A. Winters (1988), *Europe's Domestic Market,* London: Routledge & Kegan Paul for the Royal Institute of International Affairs.

Petersmann, E.-U. (2003), 'Prevention and Settlement of Transatlantic Economic Disputes: Legal Strategies for EU/US Leadership', in E.-U. Petersmann and M. Pollack (eds), *Transatlantic Economic Disputes: The EU, the US and the WTO*, 3–64, Oxford: Oxford University Press.

Petersmann, E.-U. and M. Pollack, eds (2003), *Transatlantic Economic Disputes: The EU, the US and the WTO*, Oxford: Oxford University Press.

Peterson, J. (1996a), 'Research and Development Policy', in H. Kassim and A. Menon (eds), *The European Union and National Industrial Policy*, 226–46, London: Routledge.

Peterson, J. (1996b), *Europe and America in the 1990s: The Prospects for Partnership*, 2nd edn, London: Routledge.

Peterson, J. (2003), 'The US and Europe in the Balkans', in J. Peterson and M. Pollack (eds), *Europe, America, Bush: Transatlantic Relations in the Twenty-First Century*, 85–98, London: Routledge.

Peterson, J. (2004), 'Europe, America, Iraq: Worst Ever, Ever Worsening', in L. Miles (ed.), *The European Union: Annual Review 2003–2004*, 9–26, Oxford: Blackwell.

Peterson, J. (2018), 'Present at the Destruction? The Liberal Order in the Trump Era', *The International Spectator*, 53(1): 28–44.

Peterson, J., R. Alcaro and N. Tocci (2016), 'Multipolarity, Multilateralism and Leadership: The Retreat of the West?' in R. Alcaro, J. Peterson and E. Greco (eds), *The West and the Global Power Shift: Transatlantic Relations and Global Governance*, 43–74, Basingstoke: Palgrave Macmillan.

Peterson, J. and M. Pollack, eds (2003), *Europe, America, Bush: Transatlantic Relations in the Twenty-First Century,* London: Routledge.

Pew Research Center. (2012), *Partisan Polarisation Surges in Bush, Obama Years*, Washington, DC: Pew Research Center. Available online: https://www.pewresearch.org/politics/2012/06/04/partisan-polarization-surges-in-bush-obama-years/02x_pp_12-05-25_values_slideshow/ (accessed 24 November 2020).

Pew Research Center. (2017), *The Shift in American Public's Political Values 1994-2017*, Washington, DC: Pew Research Center. Available online: https://www.pewresearch.org/politics/interactives/political-polarization-1994-2017/ (accessed 24 November 2020).

Pew Research Center. (2018), *Conflicting Partisan Priorities for U.S. Foreign Policy: Terrorism, Protecting U.S. Jobs Top the Public's Agenda*, Washington, DC: Pew Research Center. Available online: https://www.pewresearch.org/politics/2018/11/29/conflicting-partisan-priorities-for-u-s-foreign-policy/ (accessed 25 January 2024).

Pew Research Centre. (2020), *Americans' Views of Government: Low Trust, but Some Positive Performance Ratings.* Washington, DC: Pew Research Center. Available online: https://www.pewresearch.org/politics/2020/09/14/americans-views-of-government-low-trust-but-some-positive-performance-ratings/ (accessed 24 November 2020).

Pew Research Center. (2021), *Key Facts about Americans and Guns*. Washington, DC: Pew Research Center. Available online: https://www.pewresearch.org/short-reads/2023/09/13/key-facts-about-americans-and-guns/ (accessed 08 September 2022).

Pfaltzgraff, R. (1969), *The Atlantic Community: A Complex Imbalance,* New York: Van Nostrand Reinhold.

Philippart, E. and P. Winand, eds (2001), *Ever Closer Partnership: Policy-Making in US–EU Relations,* Brussels: P.I.E./Peter Lang.

Philippon, T. (2019), *The Great Reversal: How America Gave Up on Free Markets*, Cambridge, MA: Belknap Press of Harvard University Press.

Pigman, G. (2004), 'Continuity and Change in US Trade Policy, 1993–2003', in B. Hocking and S. McGuire (eds), *Trade Politics*, 2nd edn, 306–16, London: Routledge.

Pinder, J. (1983), 'Interdependence: Problem or Solution?', in L. Freedman (ed.), *The Troubled Alliance*, 67–87, London: Heinemann for the Royal Institute of International Affairs.

Pollack, M. (1997), 'Delegation, Agency, and Agenda Setting in the European Community', *International Organization*, 51(1): 99–134.

Pollack, M. (2003a), 'Unilateral America, Multilateral Europe?', in J. Peterson and M. Pollack (eds), *Europe, America, Bush: Transatlantic Relations in the Twenty-First Century*, 115–27, London: Routledge.

Pollack, M. (2003b), 'Managing System Friction: Regulatory Conflicts and Transatlantic Relations in the WTO', in E.-U. Petersmann and M. Pollack (eds), *Transatlantic Economic Disputes: The EU, the US and the WTO*, 595–602, Oxford: Oxford University Press.

Pollack, M. (2005), 'The New Transatlantic Agenda at Ten: Reflections on an Experiment in International Governance', *Journal of Common Market Studies*, 43(5): 899–919.

Pollack, M. and G. Shaffer, eds (2001), *Transatlantic Governance in the Global Economy,* Lanham: Rowman & Littlefield.

Pond, E. (2004), *Friendly Fire: The Near-Death of the Transatlantic Alliance,* Washington, DC: Brookings Institution Press for the European Union Studies Association.

Porter, T. (2005), 'The United States in International Trade Politics: Liberal Leader or Heavy-Handed Hegemon?', in D. Kelly and W. Grant (eds), *The Politics of International Trade in the 21st Century: Actors, Issues and Regional Dynamics,* Basingstoke: Palgrave Macmillan.

Posch, W., ed. (2006), *Iranian Challenges*, Chaillot Paper 89, Paris: European Union Institute for Security Studies.

Posen, A. (2005), *The Euro at Five: Ready for a Global Role?,* Washington, DC: Institute for International Economics.

Posen, B. (2006), 'European Security and Defense Policy: Response to Unipolarity?' *Security Studies*, 15(2): 149–86.

Poushter, J. and S. Schumacher (2020), 'Amid Coronavirus Crisis, Americans and Germans see Changing World in Different Ways', *Pew Research Center*, 18 May. Available online: https://www.pewresearch.org/fact-tank/2020/05/18/amid-coronavirus-crisis-americans-and-germans-see-changing-world-in-different-ways/ (accessed 9 October 2023).

Prime Minister's Office. (2017), 'Prime Minister's Letter to Donald Tusk Triggering Article 50', Published 29 March 2017. Available online: https://www.gov.uk/government/publications/prime-ministers-letter-to-donald-tusk-triggering-article-50.

Puetter, U. (2012), 'Europe's Deliberative Intergovernmentalism: The Role of the Council and European Council in EU Economic Governance', *Journal of European Public Policy*, 19(2): 161–78.

Puetter, U. (2014), *The European Council and the Council: New Intergovernmentalism and Institutional Change*, New York: Oxford University Press.

Putnam, R. (1988), 'Diplomacy and Domestic Politics: The Logic of Two-Level Games', *International Organization*, 42(3): 427–60.

Quaglia, L., R. Eastwood and P. Holmes (2009), 'The Financial Turmoil and EU Policy Co-operation in 2008', *Journal of Common Market Studies*, 47: 63–87.

Rachman, G. (2019), 'Europe Rightly Aspires to be a Power Project', *Financial Times*, 8 October.

Rappeport, A. and L. Alderman (2021), 'Global Deal to End Tax Havens Moves Ahead as Nations Back 15% Rate', *New York Times*, 8 October. Available online: https://www.nytimes.com/2021/10/08/business/oecd-global-minimum-tax.html?searchResultPosition=10 (accessed 30 September 2023).

Rappeport, A. and K. Bradsher (2020), 'Trump Says He will Raise Existing Tariffs on Chinese Goods to 30%', *New York Times*, 23 August. Available online: https://www.nytimes.com/2019/08/23/business/china-tariffs-trump.html (accessed 29 September 2023).

Ravenhill, J. (2004), 'Back to the Nest? Europe's Relations with the African, Caribbean and Pacific Group of Countries', in V. Aggarwal and E. Fogarty (eds), *EU Trade*

Strategies: Between Regionalism and Globalism, Basingstoke: Palgrave Macmillan: 118-47.

Rees, W. (2006), *Transatlantic Counter-Terrorism Cooperation: The New Imperative,* London: Routledge.

Rees, W. (2009), *The US-EU Security Relationship,* Basingstoke: Palgrave Macmillan.

Rees, W. and R. Aldrich (2005), 'Contending Cultures of Counterterrorism: Transatlantic Divergence or Convergence?', *International Affairs*, 81, no. 5 (October): 905–24.

Reich, R. (2020), *The European Union and Emerging Powers in the 21st Century*, Aldershot: Ashgate.

Renard, T. and S. Biscop (2012), *The System: Who Rigged it, How to Fix it*, New York: Knopf.

Reuters. (2016), 'Trump Warns He could End NATO Guarantee, Scrap NAFTA'. Available online: https://www.reuters.com/article/us-usa-election-nato-idUSKCN1010MC (accessed 23 June 2021).

Reuters. (2019), 'With Eyes on China, EU Lawmakers Back Investment Screening', 14 February. Available online: https://www.reuters.com/article/us-eu-china-investment/with-eyes-on-china-eu-lawmakers-back-investment-screening-idUSKCN1Q31JU (accessed 29 September 2023).

Reuters. (2023), 'What is BRICS, which Countries want to Join and Why?', 21 August. Available online: https://www.reuters.com/world/what-is-brics-who-are-its-members-2023-08-21/ (accessed 13 December 2023).

Riddervold, M. and A. Newsome (2018), 'Transatlantic Relations in Times of Uncertainty: Crises and EU-US Relations', *Journal of European Integration*, 40(5): 505–21.

Ripoll Servent, A. (2017), *The European Parliament*, London: Red Globe Press.

Rose, M. and J. Mason (2022), 'U.S. Inflation Reduction Act "Super Aggressive," Macron Tells Lawmakers', *Reuters*, 30 November. Available online: https://www.reuters.com/world/europe/macron-visits-nasa-talks-space-cooperation-us-visit-begins-2022-11-30/ (accessed 3 October 2023).

Rosecrance, R., ed. (1976), *America as an Ordinary Country: US Foreign Policy and the Future,* Ithaca: Cornell University Press.

Rosecrance, R. (1986), *The Rise of the Trading State: Commerce and Conquest in the Modern World*, New York: Basic Books.

Rosecrance, R. (1993), 'Trading States in a New Concert of Europe', in H. Haftendorn and C. Tuschhoff (eds), *America and Europe in an Era of Change*, 127–46, Boulder: Westview.

Ross, R., Ø. Tunsjø and T. Zhang, eds (2010), *US-China-EU Relations: Managing the New World Order*, London: Routledge.

Roth, F., E. Baake, L. Jonung and D. Nowak-Lehmann (2019), 'Revisiting Public Support for the Euro, 1999-2017: Accounting for the Crisis and the Recovery', *Journal of Common Market Studies*, 57(6): 1262–73.

Ryner, M. and A. Cafruny (2017), *The European Union and Global Capitalism: Origins, Development, Crisis,* Basingstoke: Palgrave Macmillan.

Sally, R. (2004), 'The WTO in Perspective', in B. Hocking and S. McGuire (eds), *Trade Politics*, 2nd edn, 105–19, London: Routledge.

Sandholtz, W. and J. Zysman (1989), '1992: Recasting the European Bargain', *World Politics*, 42(1): 95–128.

Sanger, D. (2019), 'In Confronting Iran, President may Find the World is Wary', *New York Times,* 18 September.

Santiso, J. (2007), 'The Emergence of Latin Multinationals', *Deutsche Bank Research*, March.

Satariano, A. (2022), 'E.U. Takes Aim at Big Tech's Power with Landmark Digital Act', *New York Times*, 24 March. Available online: https://www.nytimes.com/2022/03/24/technology/eu-regulation-apple-meta-google.html (accessed 3 October 2023).

Sauer, T. (2015), 'The EU as a Coercive Diplomatic Actor? The EU-3 Initiative towards Iran', in J. Koops and G. Macaj (eds), *The European Union as a Diplomatic Actor*, 103–19, Basingstoke: Palgrave Macmillan.

Sbragia, A. (1998), 'Institution-Building from Above and Below: The European Community in Global Environmental Politics', in W. Sandholtz and A. Stone Sweet (eds), *European Integration and Supranational Governance*, 283–303, Oxford: Oxford University Press.

Sbragia, A. (2010), 'The EU, the US, and Trade Policy: Competitive Interdependence in the Management of Globalization', *Journal of European Public Policy,* 17(2): 368–82.

Scazzieri, L. (2020), 'Trump's COVID-19 Response is Deepening the Transatlantic Rift', Centre for European Reform *CER Bulletin*, Issue 132, June/July.

Schade, D. (2023), 'A Strained Partnership? A Typology of Tensions in the EU-US Transatlantic Relationship', in M. Roos and D. Schade (eds), *The EU under Strain? Current Crises Shaping European Union Politics*, 191–209, The Hague: De Gruyter.

Scheinert, C. (2023), 'Financial Services Policy', Fact Sheets on the European Union–European Parliament, October. Available online: https://www.europarl.europa.eu/factsheets/en/sheet/83/financial-services-policy (accessed 15 December 2023).

Schimmelfennig, F. (2018), 'European Integration (Theory) in Times of Crisis: A Comparison of the Euro and Schengen Crises', *Journal of European Public Policy*, 25(7): 969–89.

Schirm, S. (2002), *Globalization and the New Regionalism,* Cambridge: Polity.

Schröder, M. (2019), 'Varieties of Capitalism and Welfare Regime Theories: Assumptions, Accomplishments, and the Need for Different Methods.' *Kölner Zeitschrift für Soziologie und Sozialpsychologie*, 71: 53-73.

Schwok, R. (1991), *U.S.–EC Relations in the Post-Cold War Era: Conflict or Partnership?* Boulder: Westview.

Scott, R. E. and Z. Mokhiber (2020), 'Growing China Trade Deficit Cost 3.7 Million American Jobs between 2001 and 2018', *Economic Policy Institute*, 30 January. Available online: https://www.epi.org/publication/growing-china-trade-deficits-costs-us-jobs/ (accessed 9 October 2023).

Sedelmeier, U. (2004), 'Eastern Enlargement', in H. Wallace, W. Wallace and M. Pollack (eds), *Policy-Making in the European Union*, 5th edn, 401–28, Oxford: Oxford University Press.

Sell, S. (2003), *Private Power, Public Law: The Globalization of Intellectual Property Rights,* Cambridge: Cambridge University Press.

Sen, G. (2003), 'The United States and the GATT/WTO System', in R. Foot, S. N. McFarlane and M. Mastanduno (eds), *US Hegemony and International Organizations*, 115–38, Oxford: Oxford University Press.

Senate.gov. (2021), 'Institution – Origins and Development'. Available online: https://www.senate.gov/history/instdev.htm (accessed 23 June 2021).

Shaffer, G. (2003), *Defending Interests: Public–Private Partnerships in WTO Litigation,* Washington, DC: Brookings Institution.

Shiroyama, H. (2007), 'The Harmonisation of Automobile Environmental Standards Between Japan, the United States and Europe: The "De-Politicising Strategy" by Industry and the Dynamics Between Firms and Governments in a Transnational Context', *Pacific Review*, 20(3): 351–70.

Shonfield, A. and H. Oliver, eds (1976), *International Economic Relations of the Western World, 1959–1971,* London: Oxford University Press for the Royal Institute of International Affairs.

Skogstad, G. (2002), 'Ideas, Paradigms and Institutions: Agricultural Exceptionalism in the European Union and the United States', *Governance,* 11(4): 463–90.

Sloan, S. (2005), *NATO, the European Union and the Atlantic Community: The Transatlantic Bargain Challenged*, 2nd edn, Lanham: Rowman & Littlefield.

Sloan, S. (2016), *Defense of the West: NATO, the European Union and the Transatlantic Bargain*, Manchester: Manchester University Press.

Smeltz, D., I. Daalder, K. Friedhoff and C. Kafura (2015), *America Divided: Political Partisanship and US Foreign Policy.* Results of the 2015 Chicago Council Survey of American Public Opinion and US Foreign Policy, Chicago: Chicago Council on Global Affairs.

Smith, A. (2000), *The Return to Europe: The Reintegration of Eastern Europe into the European Economy,* Basingstoke: Macmillan.

Smith, H. (1995), *European Union Foreign Policy and Central America,* Basingstoke: Macmillan.

Smith, H. (1998), 'Actually Existing Foreign Policy – Or Not? The EU in Latin and Central America', in J. Peterson and H. Sjursen (eds), *A Common Foreign Policy for Europe? Competing Visions of the CFSP*, 152–68, London: Routledge.

Smith, K. (1999), *The Making of European Union Foreign Policy: The Case of Eastern Europe,* London: Macmillan.

Smith, K. (2000), 'The End of Civilian Power EU: A Welcome Demise or Cause for Concern?' *International Spectator*, 35(2): 11–28.

Smith, K. (2003), *European Union Foreign Policy in a Changing World,* Cambridge: Polity.

Smith, K. (2005a), 'Enlargement and European Order', in C. Hill and M. Smith (eds), *International Relations and the European Union*, 270–91, Oxford: Oxford University Press.

Smith, K.(2005b), 'The Outsiders: The Neighbourhood Strategy', *International Affairs*, 81(4): 757–74.

Smith, K. (2005c), 'Beyond the Civilian Power EU Debate', in B. Irondelle (ed.), *A la Recherché de la politique étrangère européenne,* Paris: L'Harmattan.

Smith, K. (2006a), 'The European Union, Human Rights and the United Nations', in K. Laatikainen and K. Smith (eds), *The European Union at the United Nations: Intersecting Multilateralisms*, 157–74, Basingstoke: Palgrave Macmillan.

Smith, K. (2006b), 'The Limits of Proactive Cosmopolitanism: The EU and Burma, Cuba and Zimbabwe', in O. Elgström and M. Smith (eds), *The European Union's Roles in International Politics: Concepts and Analysis*, 155–71, London: Routledge.

Smith, K. (2015), 'The EU as a Diplomatic Actor in the Field of Human Rights', in J. Koops and G. Maciaj (eds), *The European Union as a Diplomatic Actor*, 155–77, Basingstoke: Palgrave Macmillan.

Smith, K. (2023), 'An End to Enlargement: The EU, its Neighbourhood and European Order', in C. Hill, M. Smith and S. Vanhoonacker (eds), *International Relations and the European Union*, 4th edn, 281–304, Oxford: Oxford University Press.

Smith, M. (1978), 'From the "Year of Europe" to a Year of Carter: Continuing Patterns and Problems in Euro-American Relations', *Journal of Common Market Studies*, 17(1): 26–44.

Smith, M. (1992), '"The Devil You Know": The United States and a Changing European Community', *International Affairs*, 68(1): 103–20.

Smith, M. (1998), 'Competitive Cooperation and EU-US Relations: Can the EU be a Strategic Partner for the US in the Global Political Economy?', *Journal of European Public Policy*, 5(4): 561–77.

Smith, M. (2000), 'Negotiating New Europes: The Roles of the European Union', *Journal of European Public Policy*, 7(5): 806–22.

Smith, M. (2001a), 'The United States, the European Union and the New Transatlantic Market-place: Public Strategy and Private Interests', in P. Winand and E. Philippart (eds), *Ever Closer Partnership: Policy-making in US-EU Relations*, 267–82, Brussels: P.I.E. /Peter Lang.

Smith, M. (2001b), 'European Foreign and Security Policy', in S. Bromley (ed.), *Governing the European Union*, 255–86, London: Sage.

Smith, M. (2004), 'Between Two Worlds? The European Union, the United States and World Order', *International Politics*, 41(1): 96–117.

Smith, M. (2005a), 'Taming the Elephant? The European Union and the Management of American Power', *Perspectives on European Politics and Society*, 6(1): 129–54.

Smith, M. (2005b), 'The European Union and the United States of America: The Politics of "Bi-Multilateral" Negotiations', in O. Elgström and C. Jönsson (eds), *European Union Negotiations: Processes, Networks and Institutions*, 164–82, London: Routledge.

Smith, M. (2005c), 'European Union Enlargement and the United States: 2004 in Perspective', Paper presented *to the Annual and Research Conference of the*

University Association for Contemporary European Studies, Zagreb, Croatia, September.

Smith, M. (2005d), 'Crises and Crisis Management in the Euro-American System: Past, Present and Future', Paper presented at *the Biennial Conference of the European Union Studies Association,* Austin, April.

Smith, M. (2006a), 'European Foreign Policy in Crisis? EU Responses to the George W. Bush Administration', *European Political Science*, 5(1): 41–51.

Smith, M. (2006b), 'The Shock of the Real? Trends in European Foreign and Security Policy Since September 2001', *Studia Diplomatica*, 59(1): 27–44.

Smith, M. (2008), 'The European Union and International Order: European and Global Dimensions', *European Foreign Affairs Review*, 12(4): 437–56..

Smith, M. (2009), 'Perceptions, Misperceptions and Transatlantic Relations: Past, Present and Future', in N. Fernández Sola and M. Smith (eds), *Perceptions and Policy in Transatlantic Relations: Prospective Visions from the US and Europe*, 59–76, London: Routledge.

Smith, M. (2010), 'The EU, the US and Global Governance', in U. Wunderlich and D. Bailey (eds), *The European Union and Global Governance: A Handbook*, 264–73, London: Routledge.

Smith, M. (2011a), 'European Responses to US Diplomacy: "Special Relationships", Transatlantic Governance and World Order', *The Hague Journal of Diplomacy*, 6: 65–83.

Smith, M. (2011b), 'The European Union, the United States and Global Public Goods: Competing Models or Two Sides of the Same Coin?' in R. Whitman (ed.), *Normative Power Europe: Empirical and Theoretical Perspectives*, 127–40, Basingstoke: Palgrave Macmillan.

Smith, M. (2012), 'Still Rooted in Maastricht: EU External Relations as a "Third-generation Hybrid"', *Journal of European Integration*, 34(7): 699–715.

Smith, M. (2014) 'The EU, the US and China: Strategic Engagement, Political Commitment and Diplomatic Interaction in Multilateral Arenas', in Jing Men and Wei Shen (eds), *The EU, the US and China – Towards a New International Order*, 8–25, Cheltenham: Edward Elgar.

Smith, M. (2018a), 'The USA and the EU', in M. Cox and D. Stokes (eds), *US Foreign Policy,* 3rd edn, 196–218, Oxford: Oxford University Press.

Smith, M. (2018b), 'The European Union, the United States and the Crisis of Contemporary Multilateralism', *Journal of European Integration*, 40(5): 539–53.

Smith, M. (2021), 'European Union Diplomacy and the Trump Administration: Multilateral Diplomacy in a Transactional World?', in R. Haar, T. Christiansen, S. Lange and S. Vanhoonacker (eds), *The Making of European Security Policy*, 179–97, London: Routledge.

Smith, M. (2023a), 'The External Challenge: Crises and the EU's Quest for Strategic Autonomy', in N. Nugent, W. Paterson and M. Rhinard (eds), *Crises and Challenges for the European Union*, 317–35, London: Bloomsbury.

Smith, M. (2023b), 'After the Deluge: Europe, the European Union and Crisis in the World Arena', in D. Schade and M. Roos (eds), *The EU under Strain: Current Crises Shaping European Union Politics*, 135–54, The Hague: De Gruyter.

Smith, M. and O. Elgström (2013), 'The European Union and International Regimes', in K. E. Jørgensen and K. Laatikainen (eds), *Routledge Handbook on the European Union and International Institutions: Performance, Policy, Power*, 297–310, London: Routledge.

Smith, M. and R. Steffenson (2005), 'The European Union and the USA', in C. Hill, and M. Smith (eds), *International Relations and the European Union*, 343–63, Oxford: Oxford University Press.

Smith, M. and R. Steffenson (2023), 'The European Union and the USA', in C. Hill, M. Smith and S. Vanhoonacker (eds), *International Relations and the European Union*, 4th edn, 372–99, Oxford: Oxford University Press.

Smith, M. and S. Woolcock (1993), *The United States and the European Community in a Transformed World,* London: Pinter for the Royal Institute of International Affairs.

Smith, M. and S. Woolcock (1994), 'Learning to Cooperate: The Clinton Administration and the European Union', *International Affairs*, 70(3): 459–76.

Smolenska, A. (2021), 'EU Bank Regulation after the Great Financial Crisis: Swinging the Regulatory Pendulum into a New Paradigm', in A. Drach and C. Youssef (eds), *Financial Deregulation: A Historical Perspective*, 163–81, Oxford: Oxford University Press. Available online: https://academic.oup.com/book/39320/chapter/338930548 (accessed 15 December 2023).

Soderbaum, F., P. Stalgren and L. van Langenhove (2005), 'The EU as a Global Actor and the Dynamics of Inter-Regionalism: A Comparative Analysis', *Journal of European Integration*, 27(3): 365–80.

Spence, D. (1991), *Enlargement Without Accession: The EC's Response to German Unification*, Discussion Paper 36, London: Royal Institute for International Affairs.

Statham, P. (2010), 'What Kind of Europeanized Public Politics?', In R. Koopmans and P. Statham (eds), *The Making of a European Public Sphere: Media Discourse and Political Contention, Communication, Society and Politics*, 277–306, Cambridge: Cambridge University Press. https://doi.org/10.1017/CBO9780511761010.017

Statista. (2023), 'Number of Merger and Acquisition (M&A) Transactions Worldwide from 1985 to April 2023'. Available online: https://www.statista.com/statistics/267368/number-of-mergers-and-acquisitions-worldwide-since-2005/ (accessed 30 September 2023).

Steffenson, R. (2005), *Managing EU–US Relations: Actors, Institutions and the New Transatlantic Agenda,* Manchester: Manchester University Press.

Stiglitz, J. (2016), *The Euro: How a Common Currency Threatens the Future of Europe*, New York: W.W. Norton.

Stokes, B. (2016), 'Republicans, Especially Trump Supporters, see Free Trade Deals as Bad for U.S.', *Pew Research Center*, 31 March. Available online: https://www

.pewresearch.org/fact-tank/2016/03/31/republicans-especially-trump-supporters-see-free-trade-deals-as-bad-for-u-s/ (accessed 9 October 2023).

Story, J., ed. (1993), *The New Europe,* Oxford: Blackwell.

Streeck, W. (2022), 'The EU after Ukraine', *American Affairs,* VI, no. 2 (Summer): 107–24.

Sunder, S. (2011), 'IFRS Monopoly: The Pied Piper of Financial Reporting', *Accounting and Business Research*, 41(3): 291–306.

Tan, S.L. (2020), 'Why has the China-Australia Relationship Deteriorated into What Some are Calling "Trade War 2.0"', *South China Morning Post*, 1 July. Available online: https://www.scmp.com/economy/china-economy/article/3091182/why-has-china-australia-relationship-deteriorated-what-some (accessed 9 October 2023).

Taylor, S., M. Shugart, A. Lijphart and B. Grofman (2014), *A Different Democracy. American Government in Thirty-One-Country Perspective,* New Haven: Yale University Press.

Teló, M., ed. (2001), *European Union and New Regionalism,* Aldershot: Ashgate.

Telò, M., ed. (2013), *European Union and New Regionalism: Regional Actors and Global Governance in a Post-hegemonic Era*, Aldershot: Ashgate.

TheCityUK. (2023), 'Key Facts about the UK as an International Financial Centre 2022', January. Available online: https://www.thecityuk.com/media/wympuijs/key-facts-about-the-uk-as-an-international-financial-centre-2022.pdf (accessed 10 October 2023).

Thomas, P. (2023), 'Smithfield Foods CEO Defends Pork Producer's Chinese Ownership', *Wall Street Journal*, 14 March. Available online: https://www.wsj.com/articles/smithfield-foods-ceo-defends-pork-producers-chinese-ownership-a78827da (accessed 29 September 2023).

Thurbon, E. and L. Weiss (2006), 'From Player to Pawn: Howard's Trade Legacy', *Australian Review of Public Affairs*, 26 February. Available online: http://www. australianreview.net/digest/2006/02/thurbon_weiss.html (accessed 14 March 2007).

Tocci, N. (2017), *Framing the EU Global Strategy: A Stronger Europe in a Fragile World,* Basingstoke: Palgrave Macmillan.

Todd, E. (2003), *After the Empire: The Breakdown of the American Order,* New York: Columbia University Press.

Todorov, F. and A. Valke (2006), 'Judicial Review of Merger Control Decisions in the European Union', *The Anti-Trust Bulletin*, 51(2): 339–81.

Tortola, P. D. (2014), 'The Limits of Normalization: Taking Stock of the EU-US Comparative Literature.' *Journal of Common Market Studies*, 52(6): 1342–57.

Toygür, I. (2022), *A New Way Forward for EU-Turkey Relations*, Brussels: Carnegie Europe.

Treib. (2020), 'Euroscepticism is here to Stay: What Cleavage Theory can Teach us about the 2019 European Parliament Elections', *Journal of European Public Policy*. https://doi.org/10.1080/13501763.2020.1737881

Trenz, H.J. (2008), 'In Search of the European Public Sphere: Between Normative Overstretch and Empirical Disenchantment', in *Arena Online Working Paper*, No. 12, Oslo: ARENA Centre for European Studies.

Treverton, G. (1985), *Making the Alliance Work: The United States and Western Europe,* London: Macmillan.

Treverton, G., ed. (1991), *The Shape of the New Europe,* New York: Council on Foreign Relations.

Tsebelis, G. (2000), 'Veto Players and Institutional Analysis', *Governance*, 13(4): 441–74.

Tsoukalis, L., ed. (1986), *Europe, America and the World Economy*, Oxford: Blackwell.

Tsoukalis, L. (2000), 'Economic and Monetary Union: Political Conviction and Economic Uncertainty', in H. Wallace and W. Wallace (eds), *Policy Making in the European Union*, 149–78, Oxford: Oxford University Press.

United Nations Conference on Trade and Development (UNCTAD). (2006), *World Investment Report: FDI from Developing and Transition Economies: Implications for Development,* Geneva: UNCTAD.

United Nations Conference on Trade and Development (UNCTAD). (2023), 'World Investment Report, Annex Table 01. FDI Inflows, by Region and Economy, 1990-2022', 5 July. Available online: https://unctad.org/en/Pages/DIAE/World%20Investment%20Report/Annex-Tables.aspx (accessed 29 September 2023).

United States Bureau of Economic Analysis. (2023), 'Direct Investment by Country and Industry, 2022', 20 July. Available online: https://www.bea.gov/sites/default/files/2023-07/dici0723.pdf (accessed 6 June 2024).

United States Census Bureau. (2021), 'Foreign Trade: Top Trading Partners'. Available online: https://www.census.gov/foreign-trade/statistics/highlights/top/index.html (accessed 9 October 2023).

United States Census Bureau. (2024a), 'Foreign Trade: Top Trading Partners '. December 2023. https://www.census.gov/foreign-trade/statistics/highlights/top/top2312yr.html#total (accessed 5 July 2024).

United States Census Bureau. (2024b), 'Trade in Goods with European Union'. Available online: https://www.census.gov/foreign-trade/balance/c0003.html (accessed 5 July 2024).

United States Department of Commerce Bureau of Economic Analysis (BEA).(2023), 'Direct Investment by Country and Industry, 2022', 20 July. Available online: https://www.bea.gov/sites/default/files/2023-07/dici0723.pdf (accessed 10 December 2023).

United State Department of State. (2024), 'United States Bilateral Investment Treaties'. Available online: https://www.state.gov/investment-affairs/bilateral-investment-treaties-and-related-agreements/united-states-bilateral-investment-treaties/ (accessed 6 June 2024).

United States Department of State. (2006), 'US Bilateral Investment Treaty Program', *Fact Sheet*. Available online: https://ustr.gov/archive/Trade_Agreements/BIT/Summary_of_US_Bilateral_Investment_Treaty_(BIT)_Program.html (accessed 2 October 2023).

United States Securities and Exchange Commission. (2007), 'SEC Announces Next Steps Relating to International Financial Reporting Standards'. Available online: https://www.sec.gov/news/press/2007/2007-72.htm (accessed 6 June 2024).

United States Trade Representative (USTR), Office of the. (2004), 'United States and Morocco Sign Historic Free Trade Agreement', *Press Release*, 18 June. Available online: https://ustr.gov/about-us/policy-offices/press-office/press-releases/archives/2004/june/united-states-and-morocco-sign-historic-free (accessed 2 October 2023).

United States Trade Representative (USTR), Office of the. (2014), 'Overview of TPP'. Available online: (https://ustr.gov/tpp/overview-of-the-TPP (accessed 9 October 2023).

US Census. (2023), 'U.S. Trade in Goods and Services – Balance of Payments (BoP) Basis'. Available online: https://www.census.gov/foreign-trade/statistics/historical/gands.pdf (accessed 9 December 2023).

Van Bohemen, S., W. de Koster and J. van der Waal (2019), 'Euroscepticism among Dutch Leftist and Rightist Populist Constituencies: How can the U-Curve be Understood?' *JCMS: Journal of Common Market Studies*, 57: 371–87.

Van Esch, F. (2012), 'Why Germany Wanted EMU: The Role of Helmut Kohl's Belief System and the Fall of the Berlin Wall', *German Politics*, 21(1): 34–52.

Vanhoonacker, S. (2001), *The Bush Administration (1989–1993) and the Development of a European Security Identity,* Aldershot: Ashgate.

Vanhoonacker, S. (2005), 'The Institutional Framework', in C. Hill and M. Smith (eds), *International Relations and the European Union*, 67–90, Oxford: Oxford University Press.

Veljanovski, V. (2004), 'EC Merger Policy After GE/Honeywell and Airtours', *The Anti-Trust Bulletin*, 49(2): 153–93.

Verdun, A. (2020), 'The European Central Bank', in *Oxford Research Encyclopedia Politics*, New York: Oxford University Press.

Vernon, R. (1973), 'Rogue Elephant in the Forest: An Appraisal of Transatlantic Relations', *Foreign Affairs*, 52(2): 163–79.

Verola, N. (2019), 'The Āge of Assertive Bilateralism', *Aspenia* Special Issue 'History Is Back: Europe, China, the United States and the Vicissitudes of Power' Nos. 82/83/84: 169–79.

Vogler, J. (2016), *Climate Change in World Politics*, Basingstoke: Palgrave Macmillan.

Vogler, J. (2023), 'The Challenge of Environment, Energy and Climate Change', in C. Hill, M. Smith and S. Vanhoonacker (eds), *International Relations and the European Union*, 4th edn, 207–35, Oxford: Oxford University Press.

Vogler, J. and C. Bretherton (2006), 'The European Union as a Protagonist to the United States on Climate Change', *International Studies Perspectives,* 7: 1–22.

Walla, K. (2021), 'Emmanuel Macrons Plan to Rebuild US-Europe Relations'. Available online: https://www.atlanticcouncil.org/blogs/new-atlanticist/emmanuel-macrons-plan-to-rebuild-us-europe-relations/ (accessed 25 January 2024).

Wallace, W. (2000), 'From the Atlantic to the Bug, from the Arctic to the Tigris? The Transformation of the EU', *International Affairs*, 76(3): 475–94.

Warnecke, S., ed. (1972), *The European Community in the 1970s,* New York: Praeger.

Wasserfallen, F. (2013), 'Political and Economic Integration in the EU: The Case of Failed Tax Harmonization', *Journal of Common Market Studies*, 52(2): 420–35.

Webber, M. (1996), *The International Politics of Russia and the Successor States,* Manchester: Manchester University Press.

Webber, M., ed. (2000), *Russia and Europe: Conflict or Cooperation?* Basingstoke: Macmillan.

Webber, M. (2001), 'Third Party Inclusion in European Security and Defence Policy: A Case Study of Russia', *European Foreign Affairs Review*, 6(4): 407–26.

Webber, M. (2007), *Inclusion, Exclusion and the Governance of European Security,* Manchester: Manchester University Press.

Weissert, C. (2011), 'Beyond Marble Cake and Picket Fences: What US Federalism Scholars can Learn from Comparative Work', *The Journal of Politics*, 73(4): 965–79.

Weller, M. (1999), 'The Rambouillet Conference on Kosovo', *International Affairs*, 75(2): 211–52.

Whalley, J. and C. Leith (2003), 'Competitive Liberalisation and a US-SACU FTA', *National Bureau of Economic Research, Working Paper 10168*, December.

White, S., I. McAllister and M. Light (2002), 'Enlargement and the New Outsiders', *Journal of Common Market Studies*, 40(1): 135–54.

The White House. (2021), 'Background Press Call by Senior Administration Official on President Biden's Engagement at NATO Summit', 14 June 2021. Available online: https://www.whitehouse.gov/briefing-room/press-briefings/2021/06/14/background-press-call-by-a-senior-administration-official-on-president-bidens-engagements-at-nato-summit (accessed 23 June 2021).

The White House. (2023a), 'Historical Tables'. Available online: https://www.whitehouse.gov/omb/budget/historical-tables/ (accessed 9 December 2023).

Wan, M. (2007) 'The United States, Japan and the European Union: Comparing Political Economy Approaches to China', *Pacific Review*, 20(3): 397–421.

Weber, K., M. E. Smith and M. Baun, eds (2007), *Governing Europe's Neighbourhood: Partners or Periphery?* Manchester: Manchester University Press.

The White House. (2023b), 'Factsheet: The Biden-Harris Administration's Abiding Commitment to Democratic Renewal at Home and Abroad', *The White House*, 29 March 2023 (accessed 15 October 23).

Whitman, R. (1998), *From Civilian Power to Superpower? The International Identity of the European Union,* Basingstoke: Macmillan.

Wilkinson, R. (2005), 'The World Trade Organization and the Regulation of International Trade', in D. Kelly and W. Grant (eds), *The Politics of International Trade in the 21st Century: Actors, Issues and Regional Dynamics,* London: Palgrave Macmillan.

Wilks, S. (2005), 'Agency Escape: Decentralisation or Dominance of the European Commission in the Modernisation of Competition Policy?', *Governance*, 18(3): 431–52.

Winand, P. (1993), *Eisenhower, Kennedy and the United States of Europe,* London: Macmillan.

Wonka, A. (2007), 'Technocratic and Independent? The Appointment of European Commissioners and its Policy Implications', *Journal of European Public Policy*, 14(2): 169–89.

Woodward, B. (2006), *State of Denial: Bush at War, Part III,* New York: Simon & Schuster.

Woodward, B. (2010), *Obama's Wars: The Inside Story*, New York: Simon & Schuster.

Woolcock, S. and H. van der Ven, eds (1986), *International Trade in the Post-Multilateral Era,* Cambridge, MA: Harvard University Press.

Workman, S. (2015), *The Dynamics of Bureaucracy in the US Government: How Congress and Federal Agencies Process Information and Solve Problems*, Cambridge: Cambridge University Press.

World Trade Organization (WTO). (2001a), 'International Trade Statistics 2001', Tables I.5, I.6. Available online: https://www.wto.org/english/res_e/statis_e/its2001_e/stats2001_e.pdf (accessed 9 October 2023).

World Trade Organization (WTO). (2001b), 'Ministerial Declaration', 14 November. Available online: http://www.wto.org/english/thewto_e/minist_e/min01_e/mindecl_e.htm#relationship (accessed 2 October 2023).

World Trade Organization (WTO). (2004), 'WT/DS265/R, European Communities – Export Subsidies on Sugar', 15 October.

World Trade Organization (WTO). (2006), *World Trade Report 2006*, Geneva: WTO, Appendix Table 1, p.11.

World Trade Organization (WTO). (2011), 'International Trade Statistics 2011', Tables I.8, I.9. Available online: https://www.wto.org/english/res_e/statis_e/its2011_e/its2011_e.pdf (accessed 9 October 2023).

World Trade Organization (WTO). (2023), *World Statistical Review 2023*, Geneva: WTO, Tables A6, A7, A8, A9. Available online: https://www.wto.org/english/res_e/booksp_e/wtsr_2023_e.pdf (accessed 9 October 2023).

Wurzel, R. and C. Connelly, eds (2010), *The European Union as a Leader in International Climate Change Politics,* London: Routledge.

Young, A. (2004), 'The Incidental Fortress: The Single European Market and World Trade', *Journal of Common Market Studies*, 42(2): 393–414.

Young, A. and J. Peterson (2006), 'The EU and the New Trade Politics', *Journal of European Public Policy*, 13(6): 795–814.

Young, A. and J. Peterson (2014), *Parochial Global Europe: 21st Century Trade Politics*, Oxford: Oxford University Press.

Young, O. (1972), 'The Actors in World Politics', in J. Rosenau, V. Davis and M. East (eds), *The Analysis of International Politics*, 125–44, New York: Free Press.

Youngs, R. (2006), *Europe and the Middle East: In the Shadow of September 11,* Boulder: Rienner.

Youngs, R. (2011), *The EU's Role in World Politics: A Retreat from Liberal Internationalism*, London: Routledge.

Youngs, R. and M. Smith (2018), 'The EU and the Global Order: Contingent Liberalism', *The International Spectator*, 53(1): 45–56.

Zabarowski, M., ed. (2006a), *Friends Again? EU-US Relations After the Crisis,* Paris: EU Institute for Security Studies.

Zabarowski, M., ed. (2006b), *Facing China's Rise: Guidelines for an EU Strategy*, Chaillot Paper 94, December, Paris: EU Institute for Security Studies.

Zelikow, P. and C. Rice (1995), *Germany Unified and Europe Transformed: A Study in Statecraft,* Cambridge, MA: Harvard University Press.

Zhang, D. (2018), 'Exit the Dragon? Chinese Investment in Germany', *Deutsche Welle*, 2 May. Available online: https://www.dw.com/en/exit-the-dragon-chinese-investment-in-germany/a-42457712 (accessed 29 September 2023).

Zucconi, M. (1996), 'The EU in the Former Yugoslavia', in A. Chayes and A. Chayes (eds), *Preventing Conflict in the Post-Communist World: Mobilizing International and Regional Organizations*, 237–80, Washington, DC: Brookings Institution.

Index

www.ingramcontent.com/pod-product-compliance
Ingram Content Group UK Ltd.
Pitfield, Milton Keynes, MK11 3LW, UK
UKHW020233290926
15470UKWH00002B/512

9 781350 414273